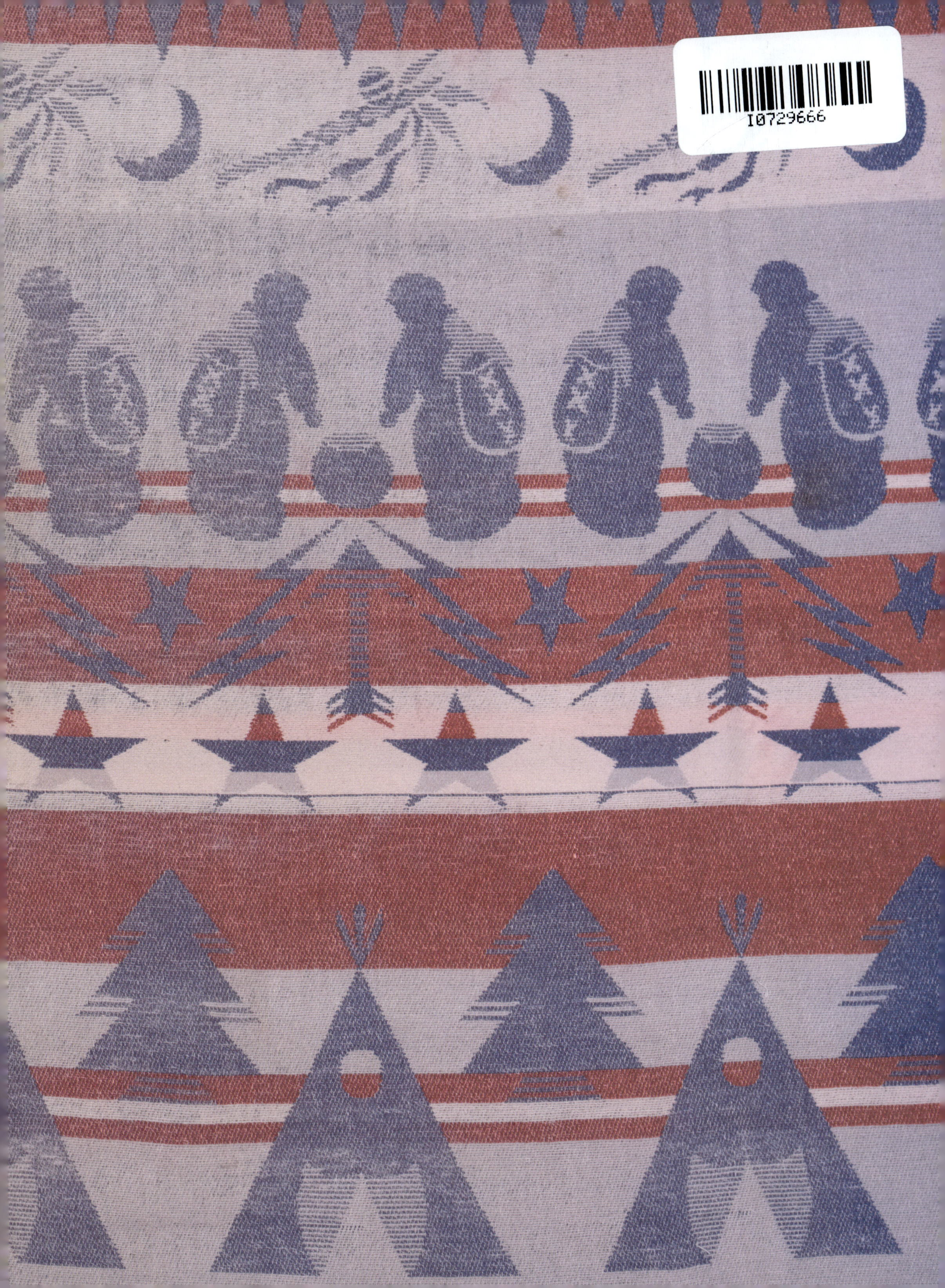

THE SQUARZI ARCHIVE:

THE VINTAGE COLLECTION OF
AN ITALIAN STYLE ICON

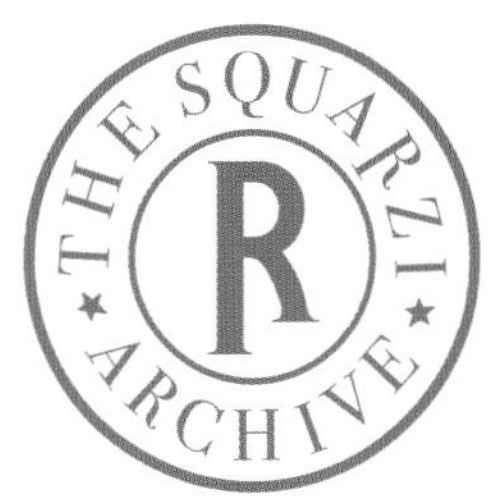

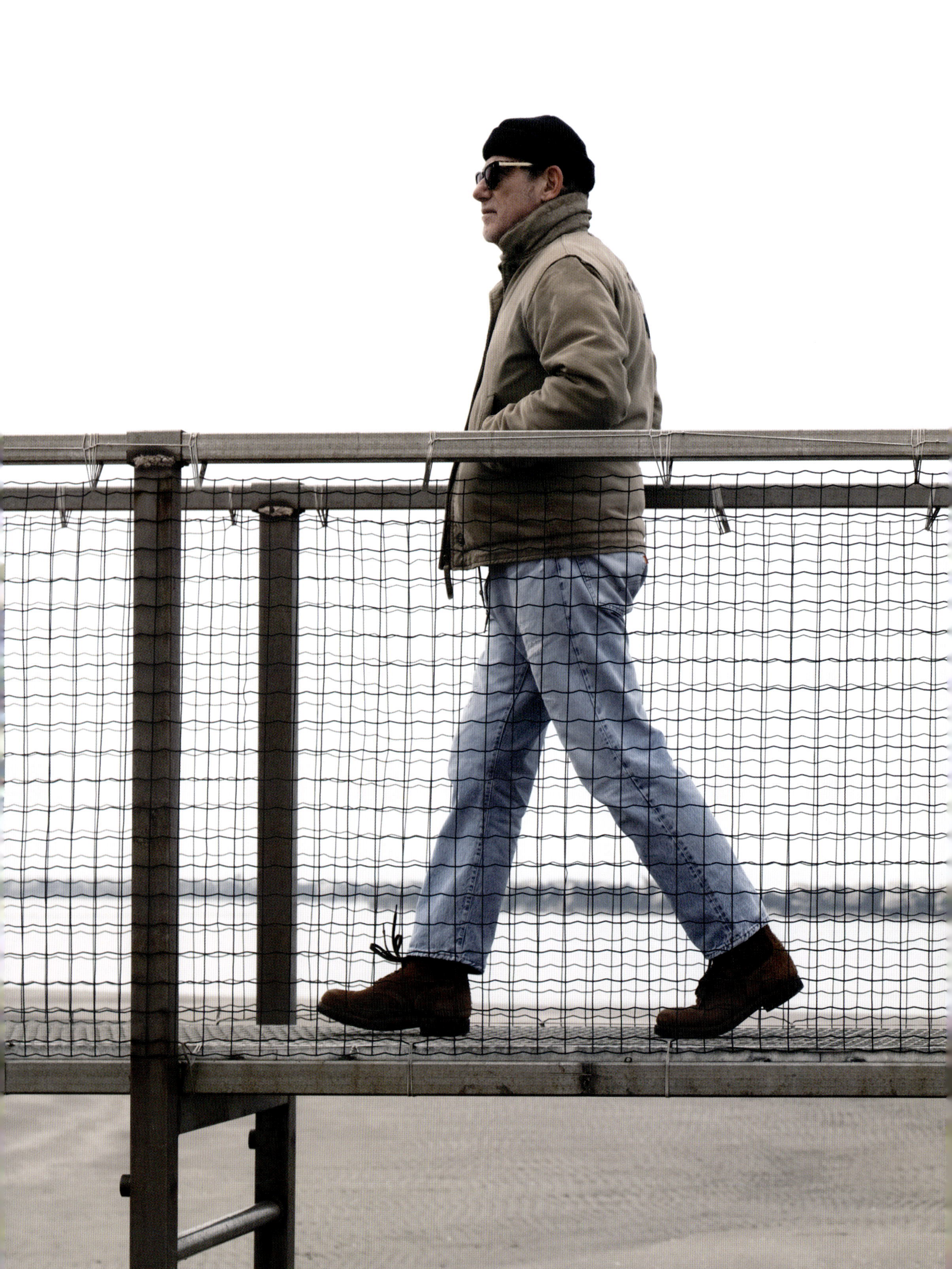

Andrea Ventura, Mirko Di Giovanni
Photography by David Petrini

THE SQUARZI ARCHIVE:

THE VINTAGE COLLECTION OF AN ITALIAN STYLE ICON

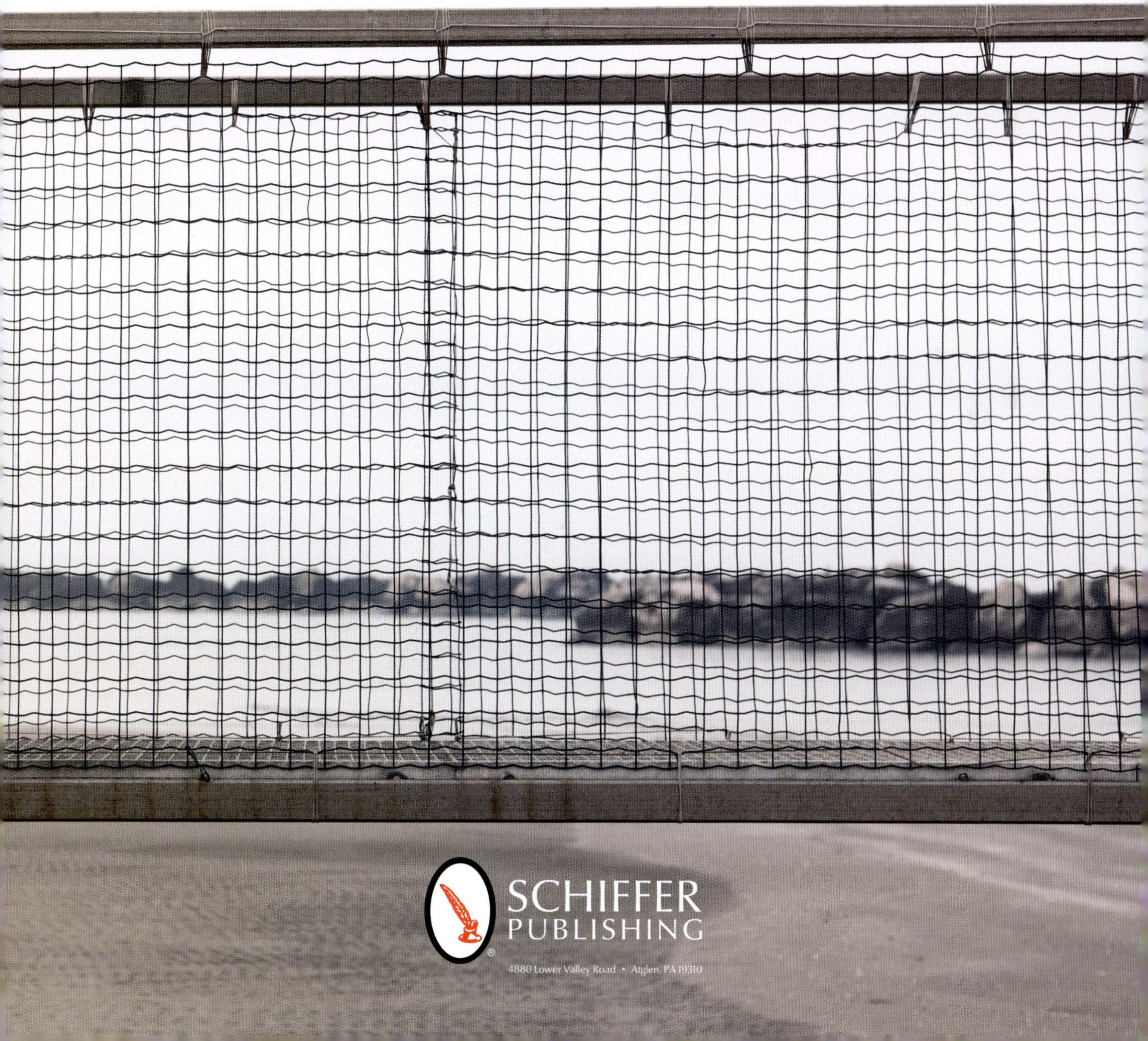

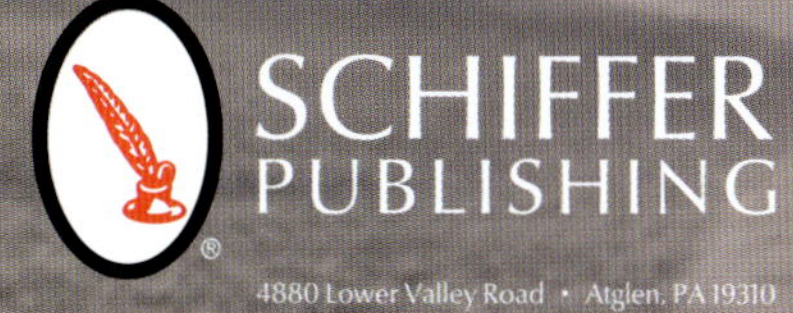

FOREWORD

"One of the most important traits of a stylish man is curiosity.

Alessandro Squarzi is one of the most stylish men I know, and also one of the most curious.

He loves learning about clothing of the past: its design details, its purpose, and what type of people wore it.

His strength is in then understanding how to update and share those qualities with a modern audience so they can share in the beauty he sees."

Scott Schuman

AKNOWLEDGMENTS

We would like to thank Mr. Scott Schuman for the charming words of the foreword, Matteo Zuretti for helping us in the translation of the text, Carlotta Comelli for coordinating our work with the other thousand commitments of Alessandro, the gentlemen from Forli's Maneggio Cortesi for hosting us, and, finally, Cassano, Alessandro's thoroughbred, for his majesty.

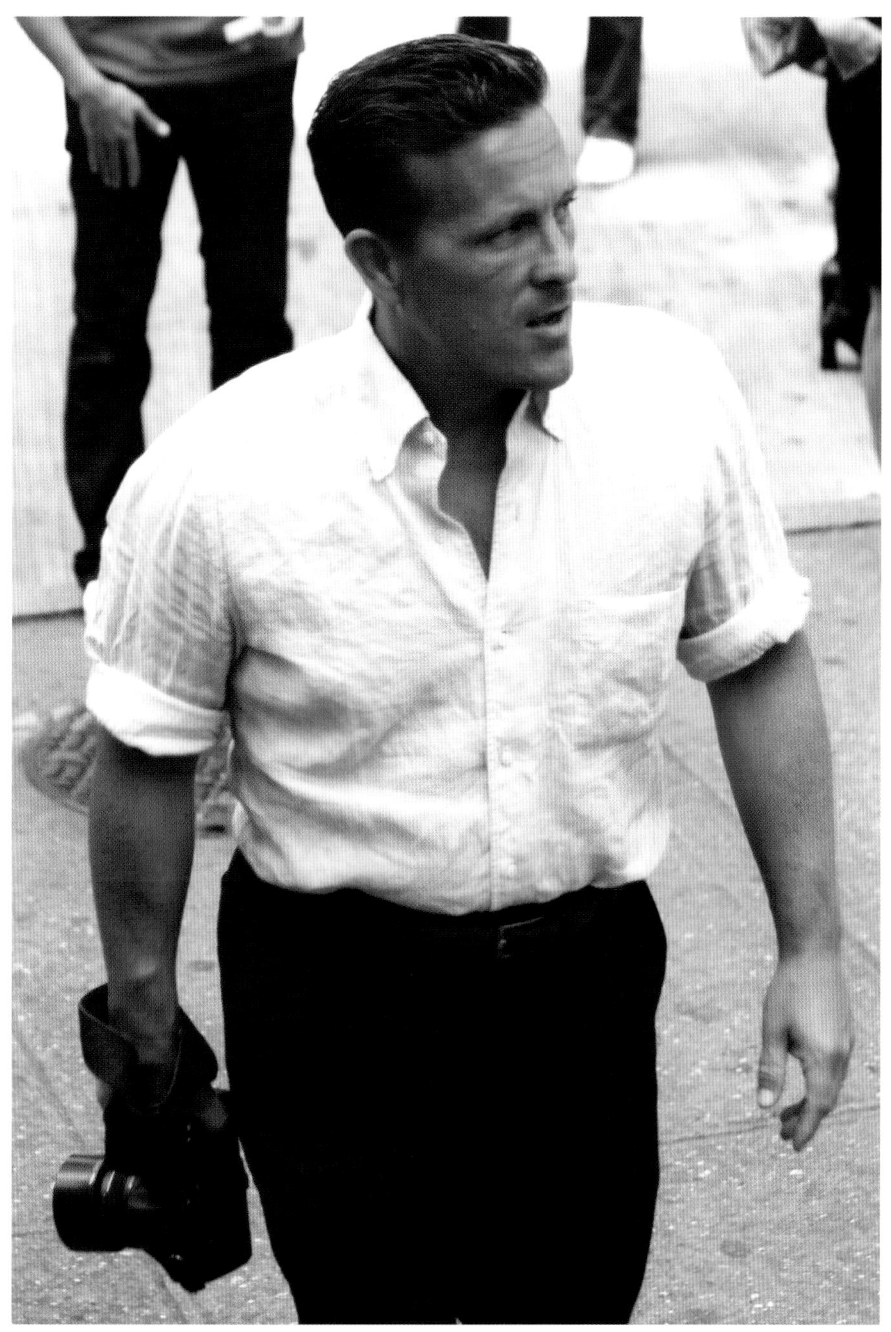

Mr. Scott Schuman
Photographer/Blogger "The Sartorialist"

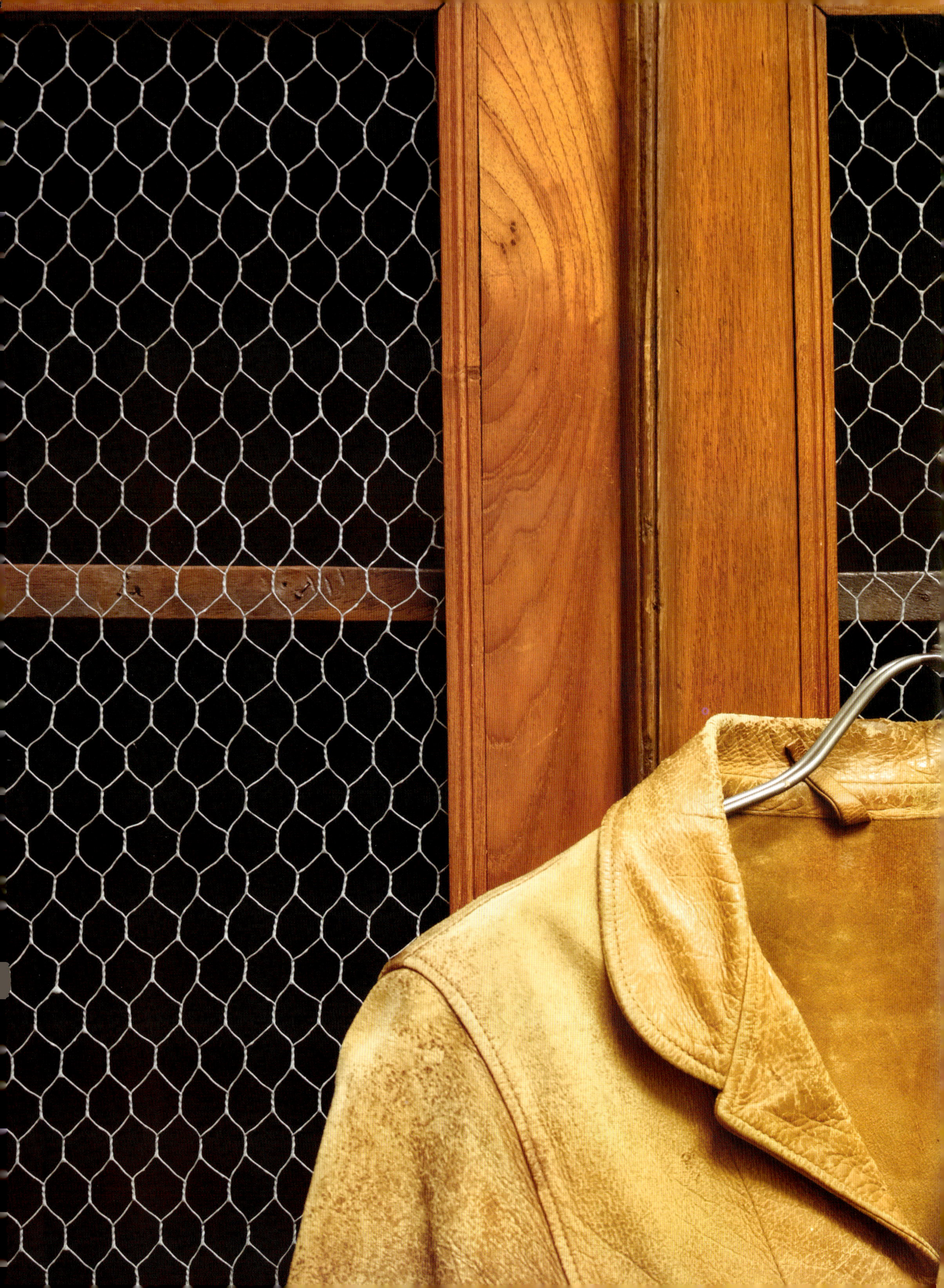

Contents

"The Squarzi Archive"

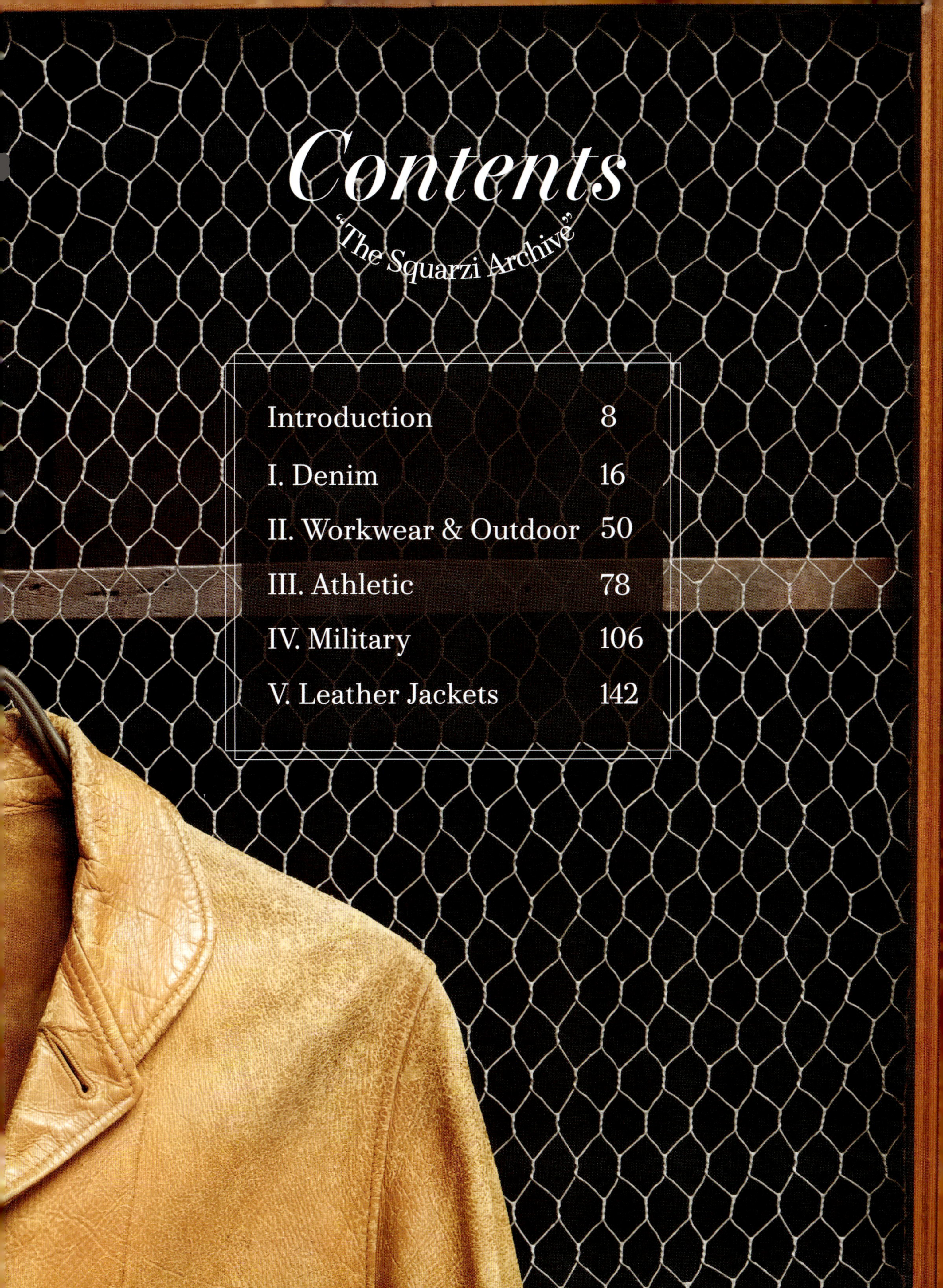

INTRODUCTION

Six thousand pieces, including jackets, shirts, pants, sweatshirts, shoes, and more. A collection that traces the history of American clothing from the 1930s onward: material after material, design after design, and purpose after purpose. A heritage not only of the American tradition but one that embraces its English and Italian influences. Six thousand items concentrated in a single industrial warehouse, above which floats an iron sign with "S Q U A R Z I." On day one of the project, on a cold Saturday morning in December 2021, we met Alessandro in his personal and inaccessible "Area 51."

Mr. Squarzi, with his genuine, persuasive, and cheeky demeanor straight from Romagna, had proposed a month earlier that we create a photographic book of his archive. As high-profile vintage collectors, we were at first skeptical and unaware of the actual value, quality, and quantity of the garments.

Fortunately, thanks to the enthusiasm of our publisher, we agreed to embark on this editorial project. For the first time, we had exclusive access to the Squarzi Archive.

Anyone who runs in fashion and vintage-clothing circles knows Alessandro Squarzi: entrepreneur, designer, and, for a time, influencer. Alessandro is a globally recognized style icon with distinctive features that make him original and a category unto himself.

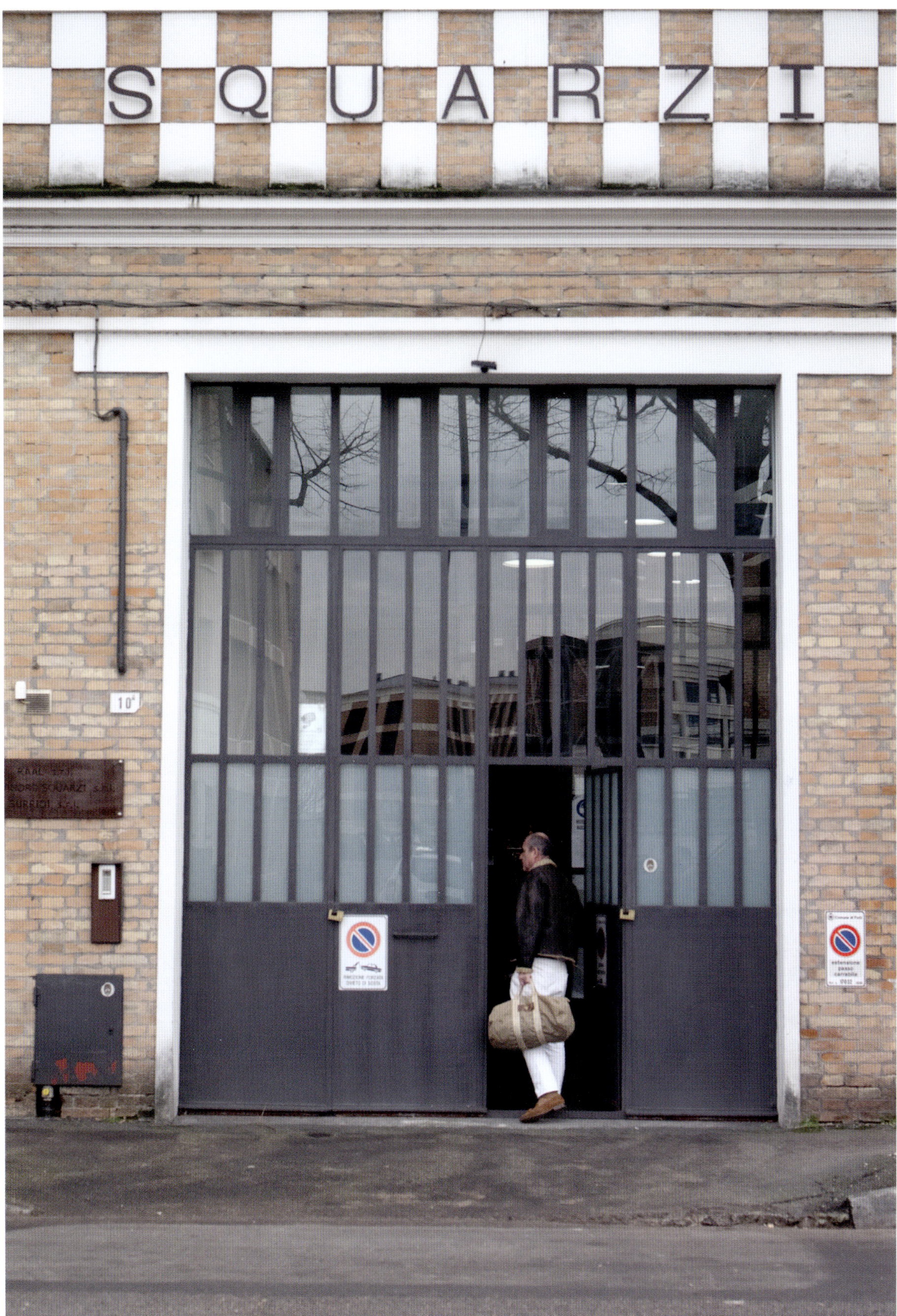
SQUARZI
10ª

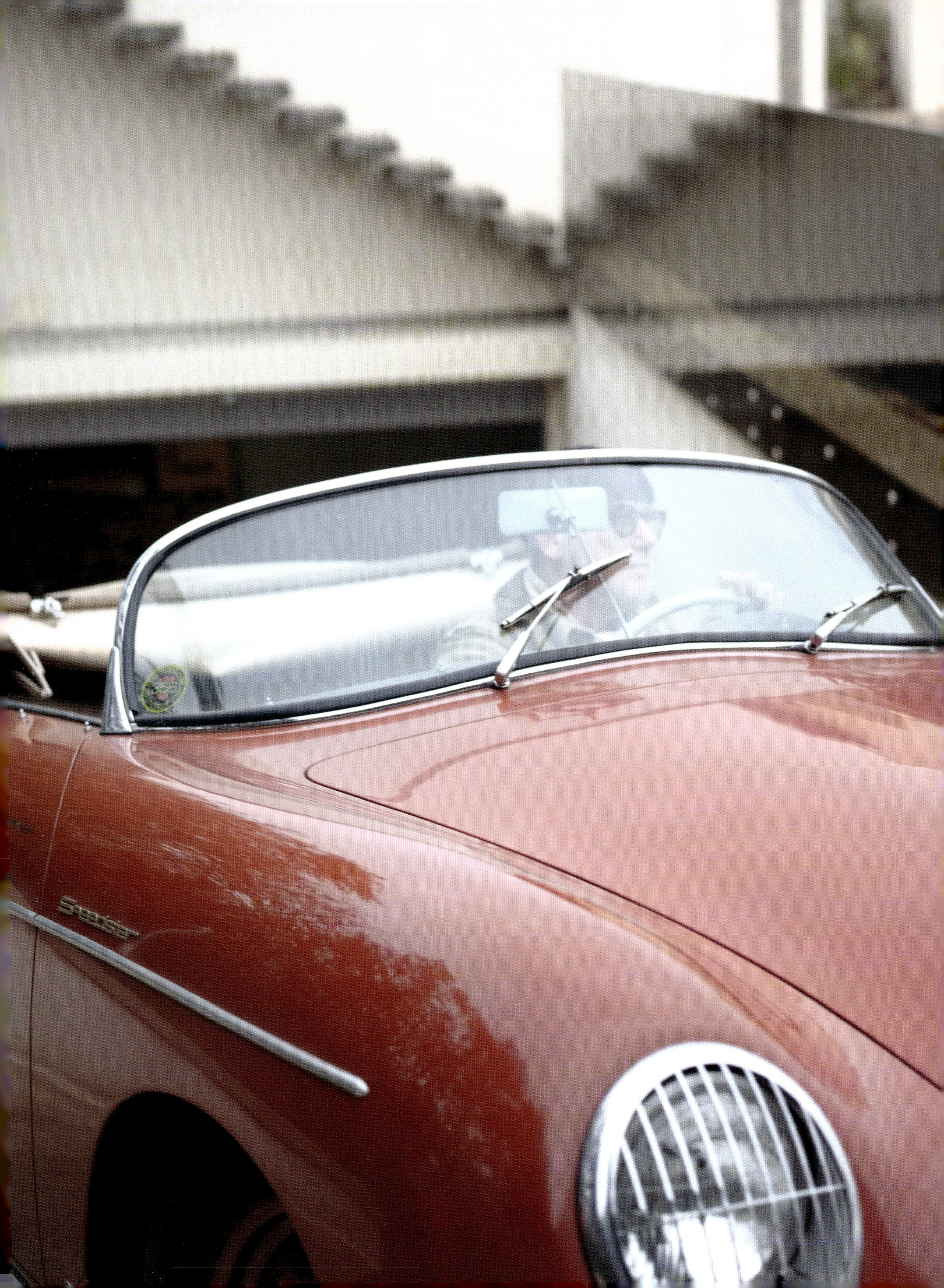

Italian to the core in sensibility, he is inspired by historic America. He is almost revered in Japan and Korea. Alessandro Squarzi was born in 1965 in Italy, in Romagna Forlì (an ancient city founded in the second century BCE by the ancient Romans, originally designated by the Latin name Forum Livii). He is the son of a butcher and a housewife.

As a teenager, he showed a great passion for clothing and always sported impeccable outfits. After he spent a brief period as a representative for Messegue products, his passion for clothing became his job. From his origins as a young local representative of a casual clothing company, his evolution to world fame became unstoppable. Over the past thirty years, between strokes of genius, perfectly timed marketing operations, and collaborations with famous fashion houses, his archive has been built piece by piece.

He brings the same passion to many other style projects: his own retro-inspired brand Fortela, his multibrand showrooms located in Milan and Bologna, and collaborations with high-end brands such as Fay and their stylish capsule collection, the "Fay Archive." He has even more projects, for now shrouded by secrecy.

During long conversations over Romagna piadina (a Romagnan-style flatbread) and fettuccine, Alessandro, with the passion of a twenty-year-old, recalled almost piece by piece where he found the thousands of garments that make up his treasure trove: flea markets in the United States (such as RoseBowl in Pasadena), highly sought-after shops in Harajuku (Tokyo's vintage district), Italian and French markets, and online stock sites. A six-thousand-piece puzzle that took him thirty years to assemble.

The vast amount of items present, which combined would have filled a twenty-volume encyclopedia, made the sorting and organizing of his collection an almost bloody task. At times, we struggled to find an orderly and rational way to share its contents. Ultimately, drawing inspiration from the traditional Japanese book and magazine standard for cataloging vintage items, we opted to divide the chapters by applying a hybrid formula factoring in the materials, the typology, and the style of each piece. The end result is a selection of 230 garments, selected in agreement with Alessandro.

The story of this archive is enriched with some shots of Alessandro himself, sharing moments of his work and his free time with us. Throughout, these moments are tied together by a "fil rouge" of his love for things from the past.

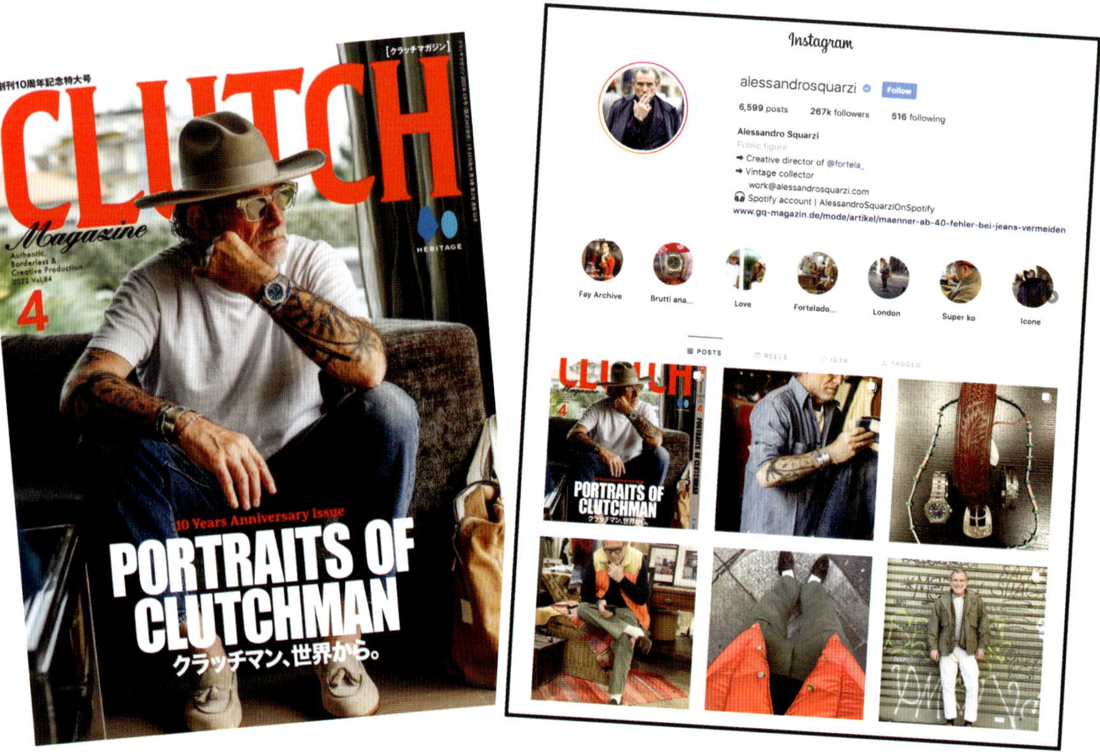

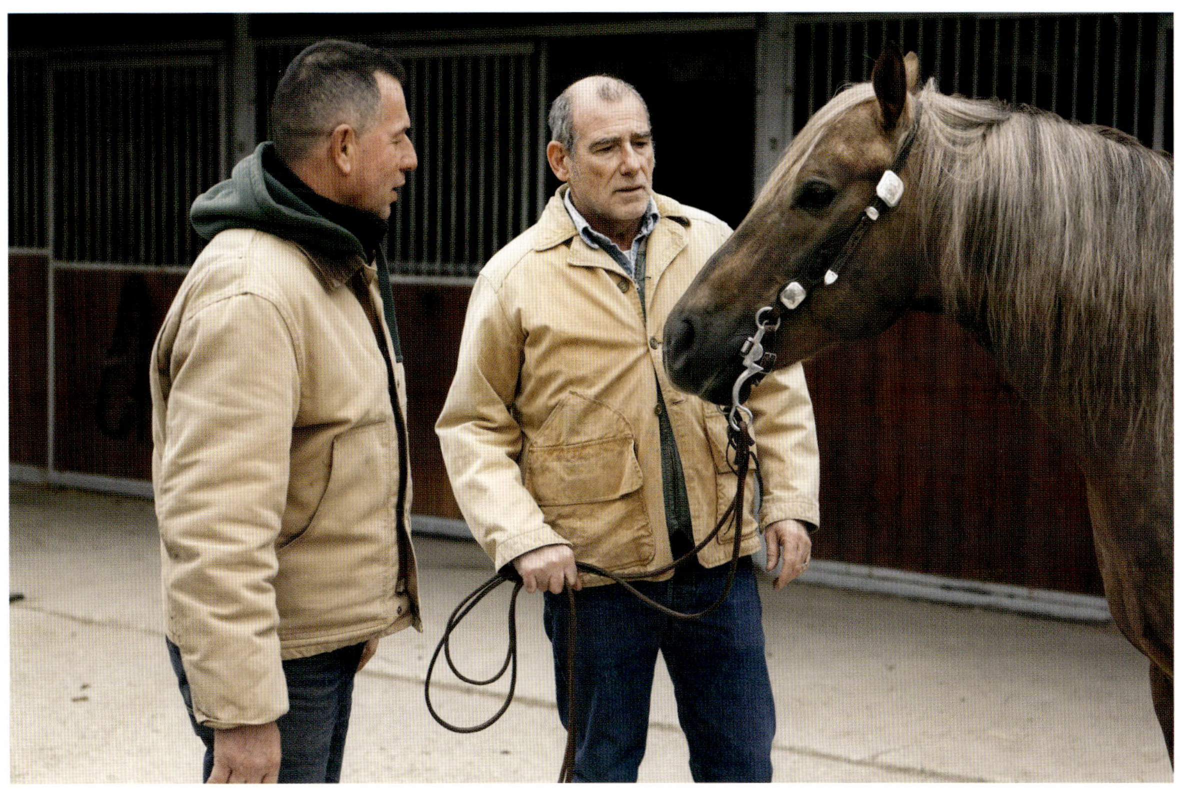

at Maneggio Cortesi
Forli

In a rollercoaster of emotions, he allowed us to enter his house. He showed us a part of his vintage military watch collection, we admired him whizzing away on his thundering 1955 Porsche 356 at the Rimini seafront, and we admired him riding his thoroughbred, "Cassano," like a perfect ranchero by the stables in Forli.

We were also privileged to witness moments of his daily work life in Milan, in his showroom, and in the shops of his Fortela brand.

Always with his effortless coolness, always sporting an impeccable outfit.

10 QUESTIONS TO ALESSANDRO

1. What garment do you consider the first in your archive?
My first Levi's garment was bought at Montagnola in Bologna. I think that is the root of my archive.

2. When did you decide to create a vintage archive?
It was never really decided; it was born as a result of the passion I developed for these garments.

3. What are your favorite garments?
The Levi's Big Es and my deck jackets.

4. Which would you consider the most valuable?
All my pieces are like children to me; I have a love for every one, and I don't value them.

5. Which is the most difficult to find?
The blue deck jacket.

6. What's missing from your collection?
Many things; it would take a book to list them all (*smiles*, editor's note).

7. Which one do you wear most often?
The Levi's Big E.

8. Which typology inspired you the most in your work as a designer?
My Fortela brand is nothing more than the fruit of everything I have collected over the years.

9. Which garment do you think is impossible to replicate?
Sweatshirts with waffle fabric inside.

10. What direction will the "vintage movement" take in the years to come?
There is so much noise around; there are many new generations who are becoming passionate about the subject. The thing that makes me very happy is that in recent years I have probably been an advocate for, or at least I think I have contributed to bringing many young people closer to, the vintage movement.

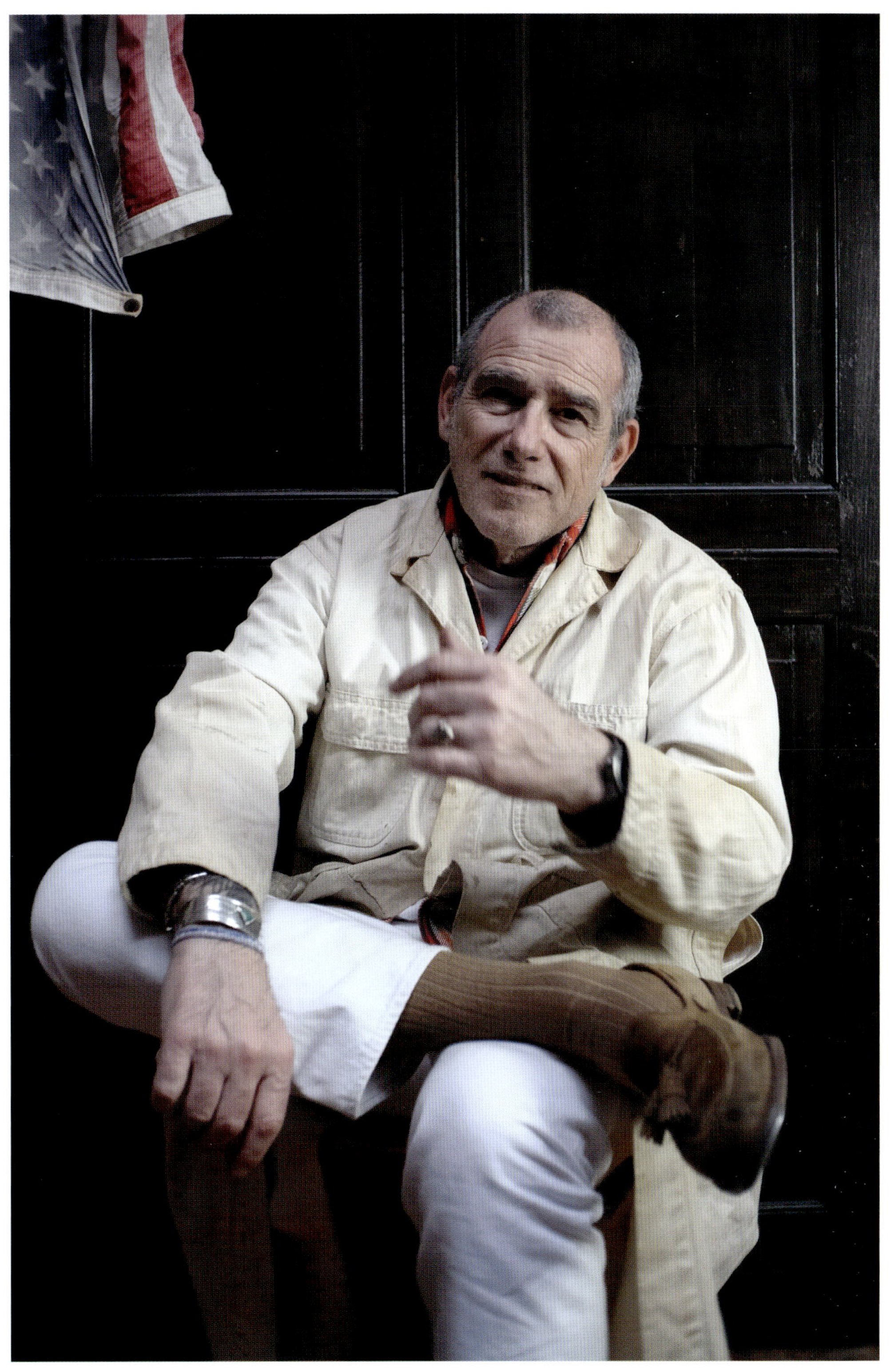

at Alessandro Squarzi archive
Forlì

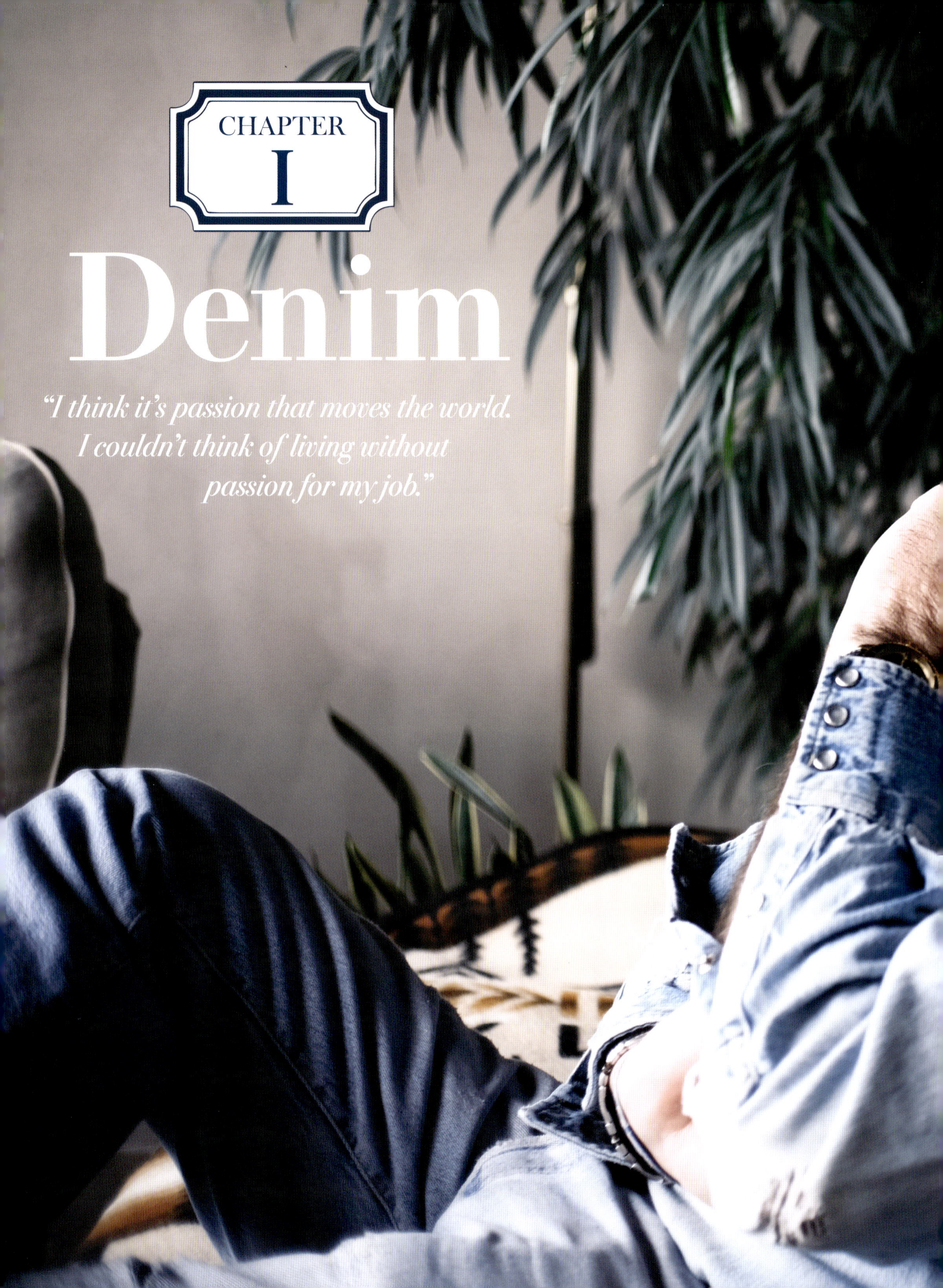
CHAPTER
I

Denim

"I think it's passion that moves the world.
I couldn't think of living without
passion for my job."

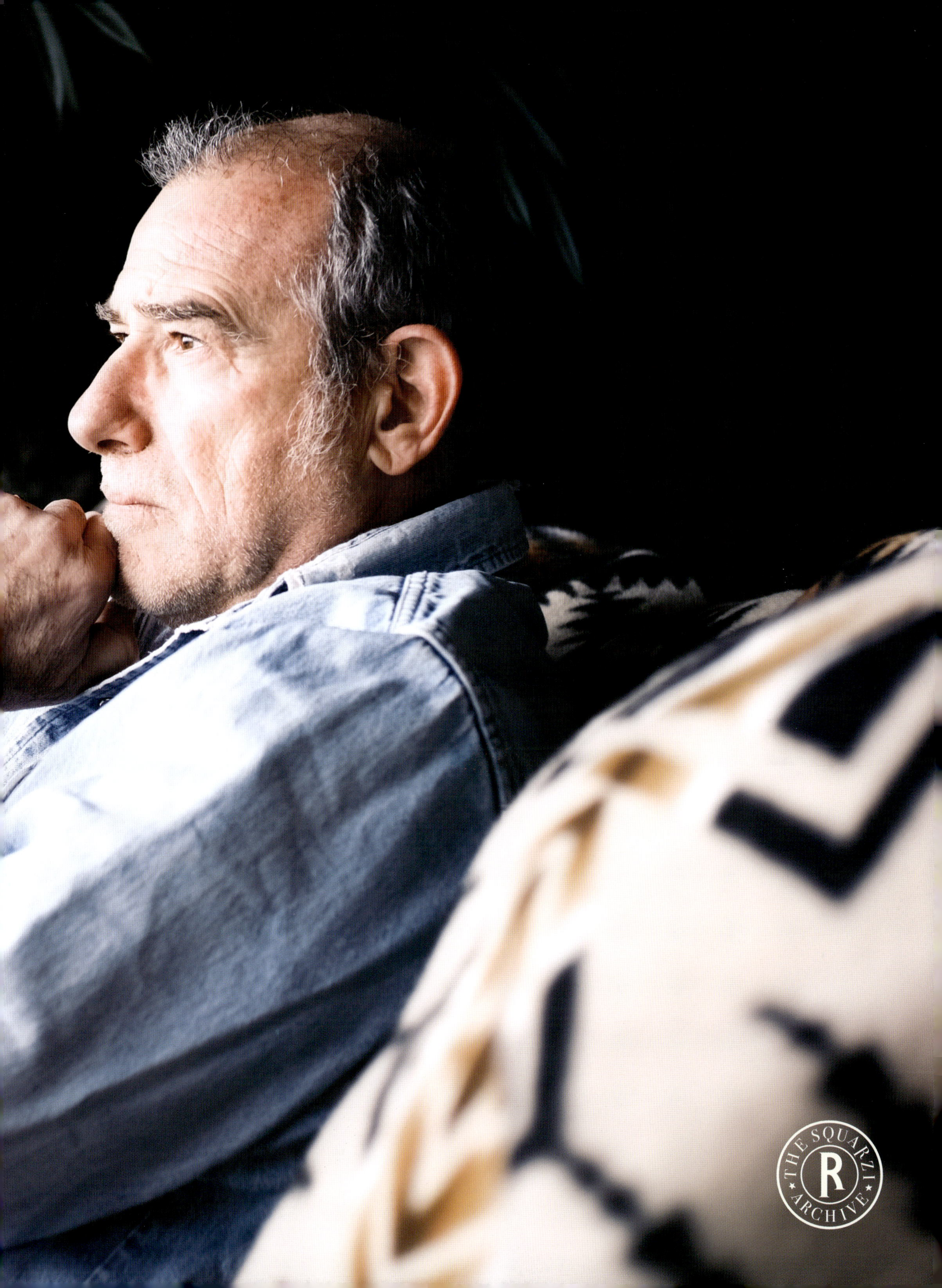

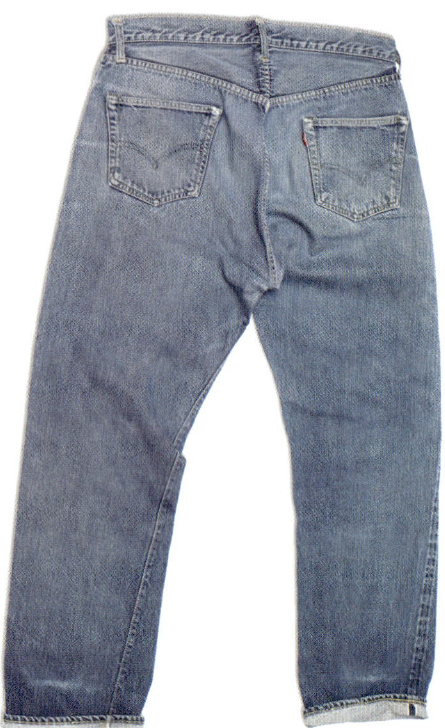

1960's
LEVI'S 501XX
"hidden rivets"

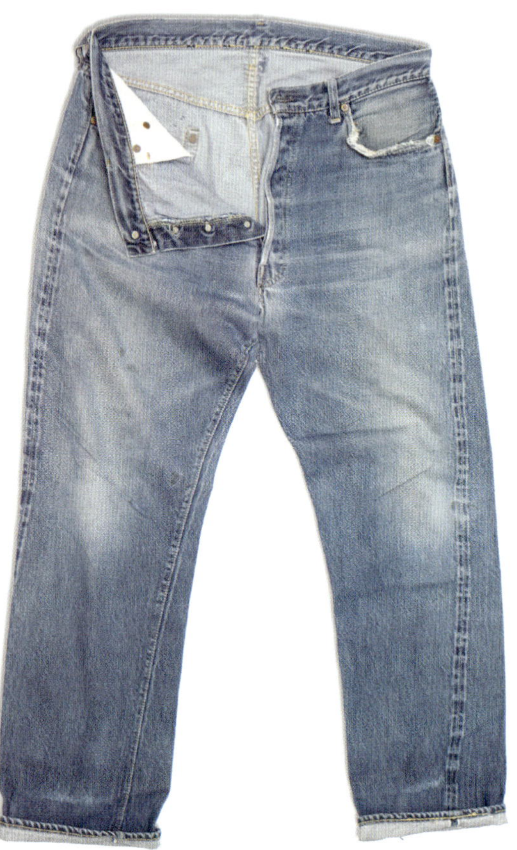

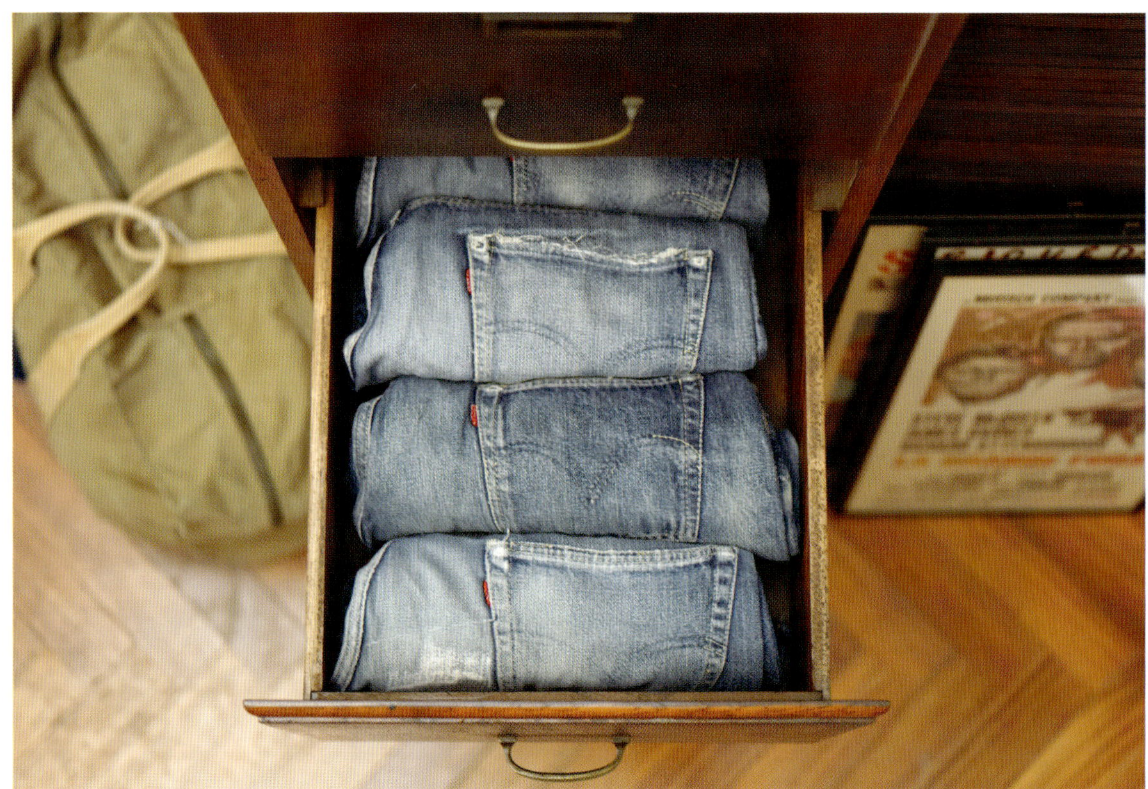

at Alessandro Squarzi archive
Forlì

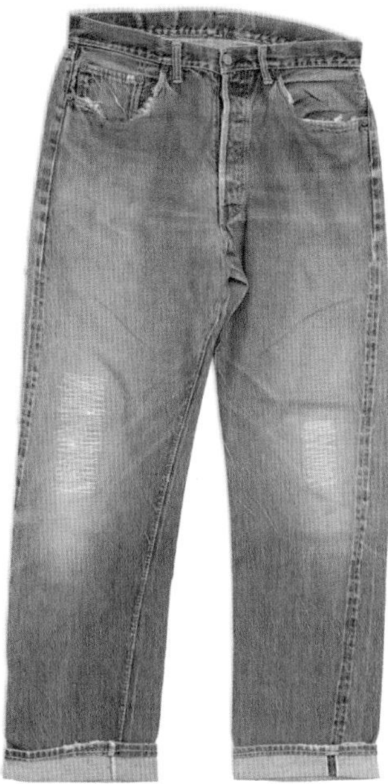
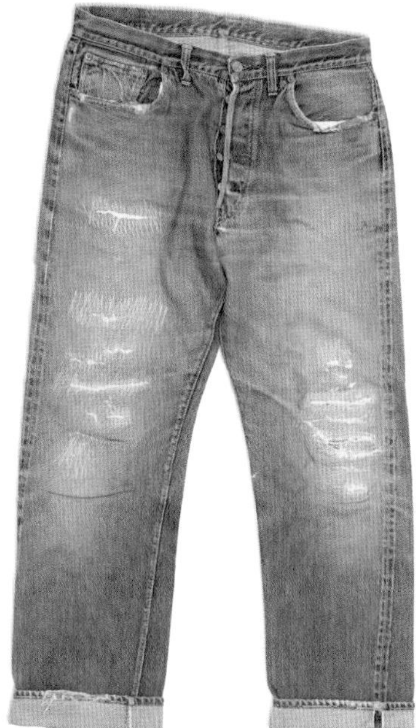
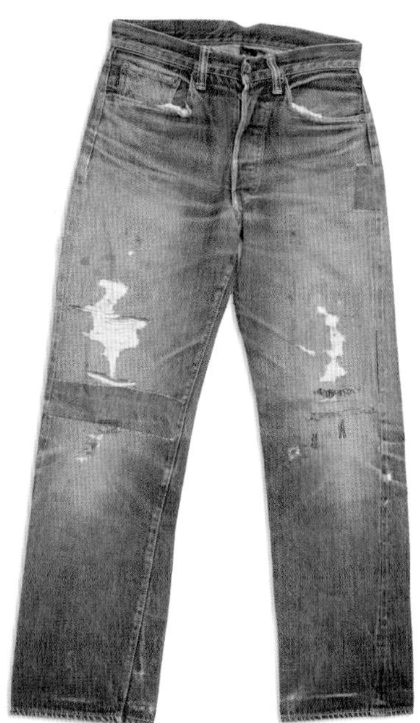

1960's
LEVI'S selvedge denim pants
"Big E"

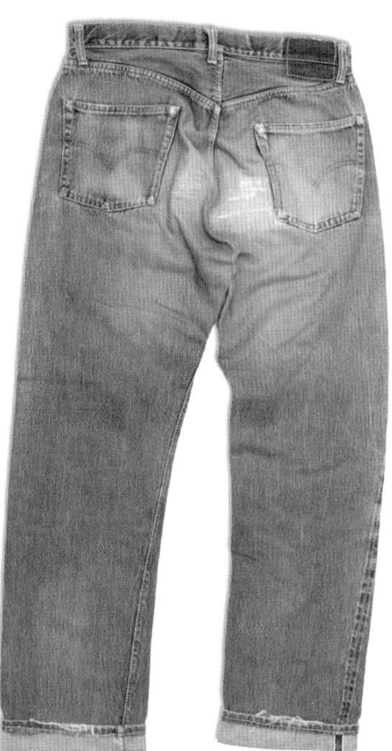
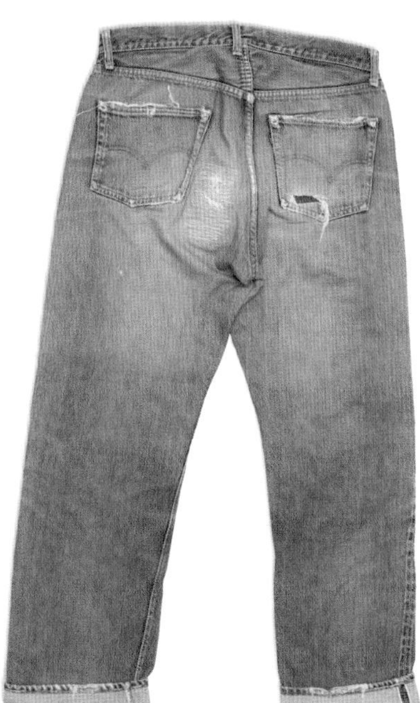
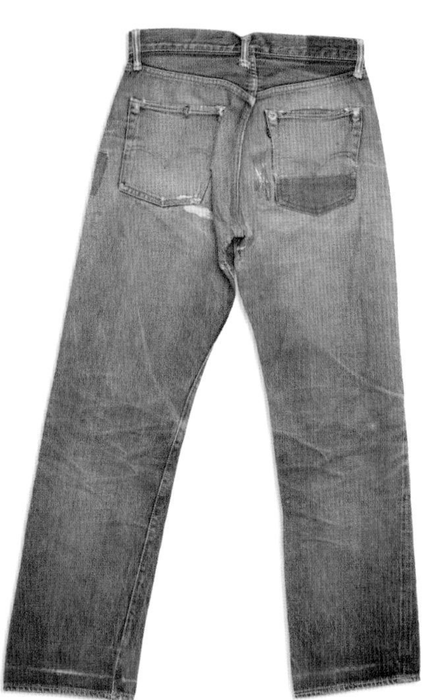

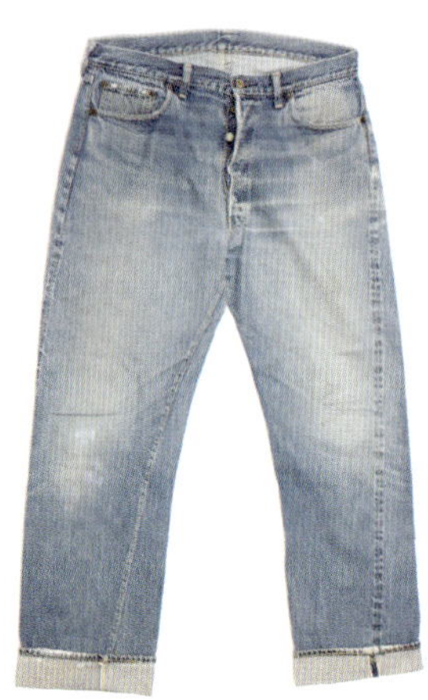

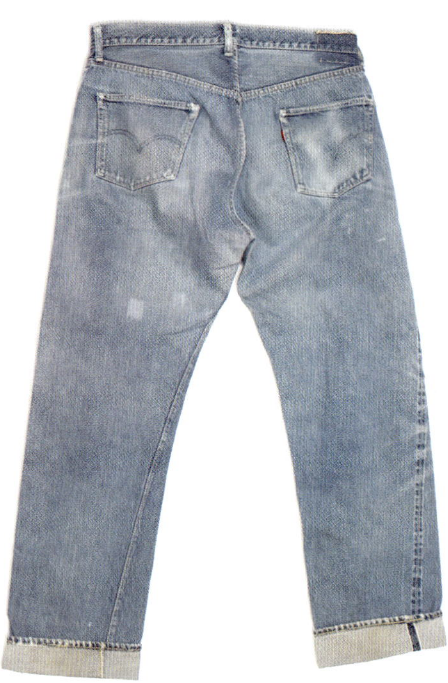

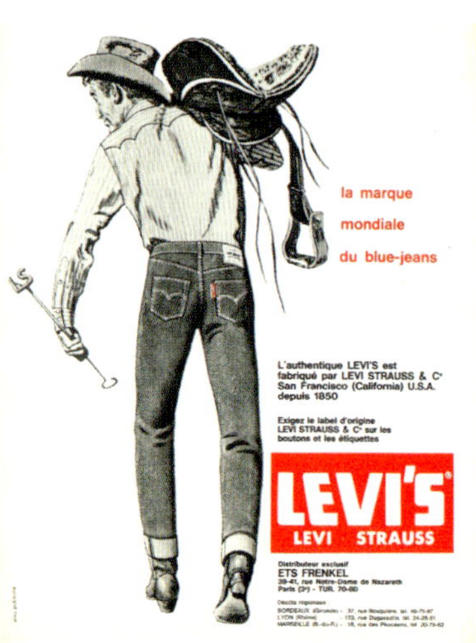

1950's advertising

1960's
LEVI'S selvedge denim pants
"Big E"

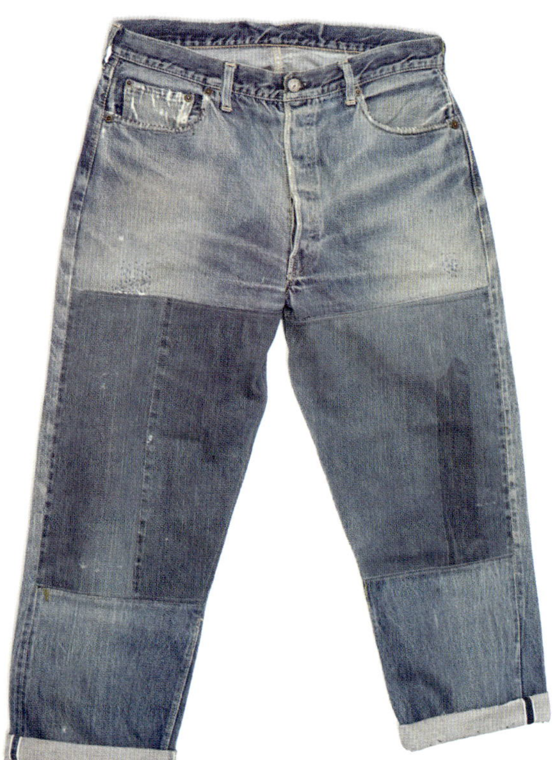

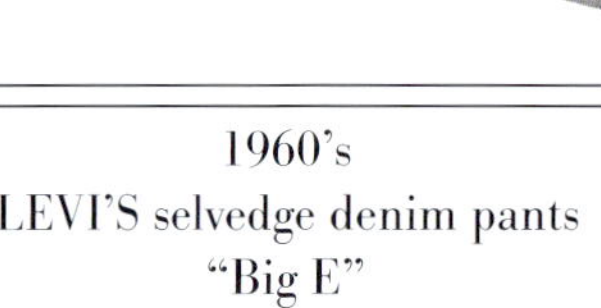

1960's
LEVI'S selvedge denim pants
"Big E"

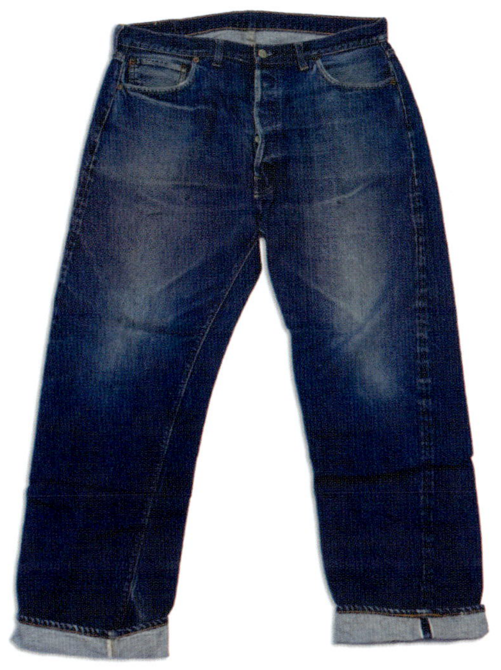

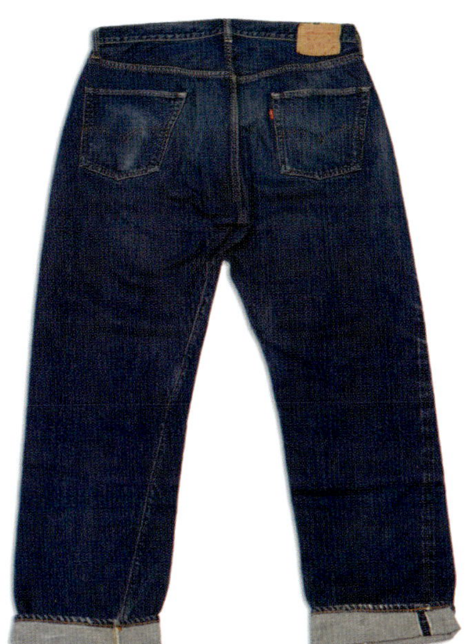

1960's
LEVI'S selvedge denim pants
"Big E"

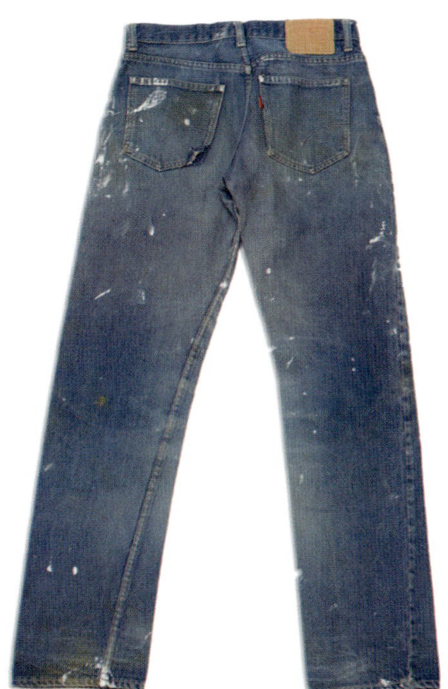

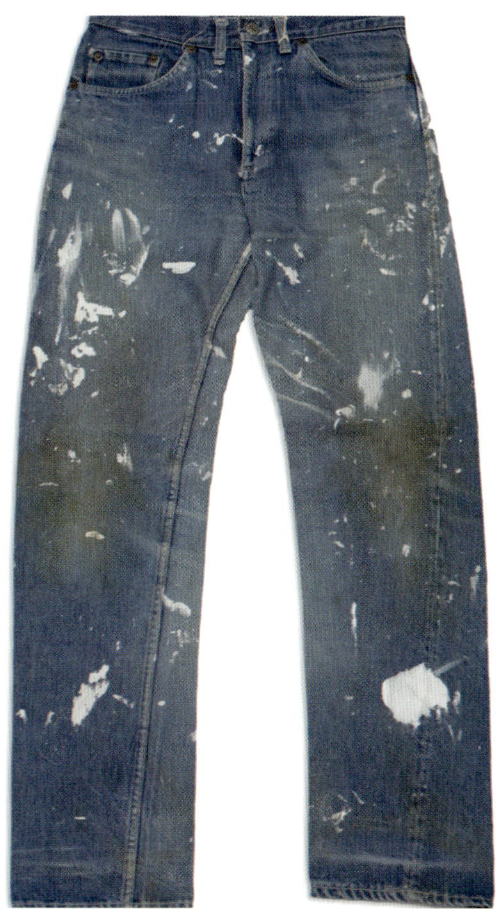

1960's
LEVI'S selvedge denim pants
"Big E"

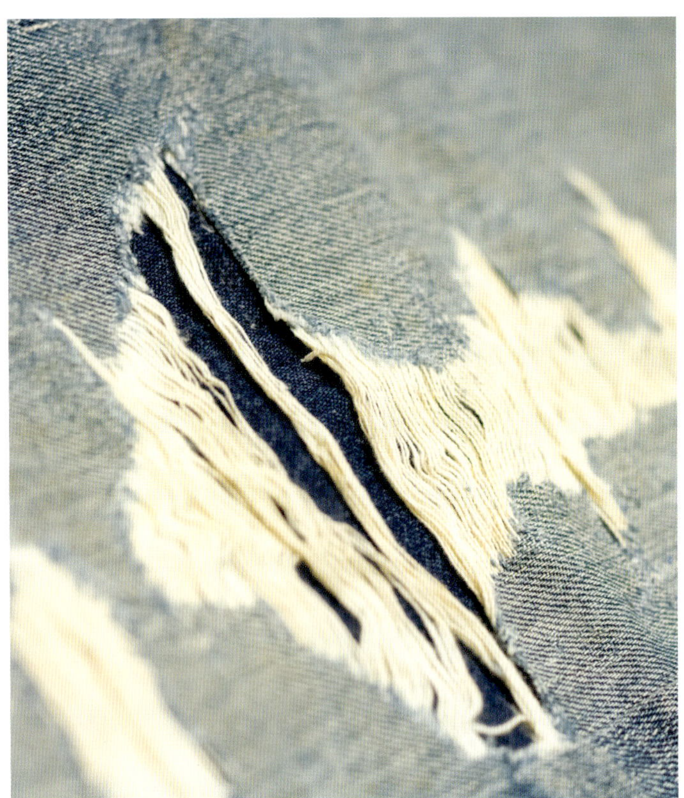

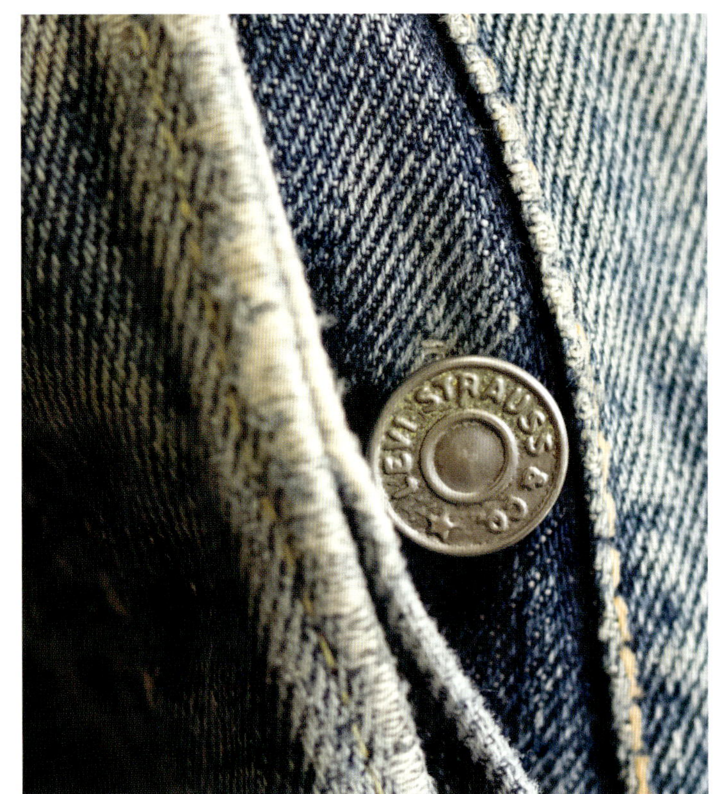

"Long R" metal button

1960's
LEVI'S selvedge denim pants
"Big E"

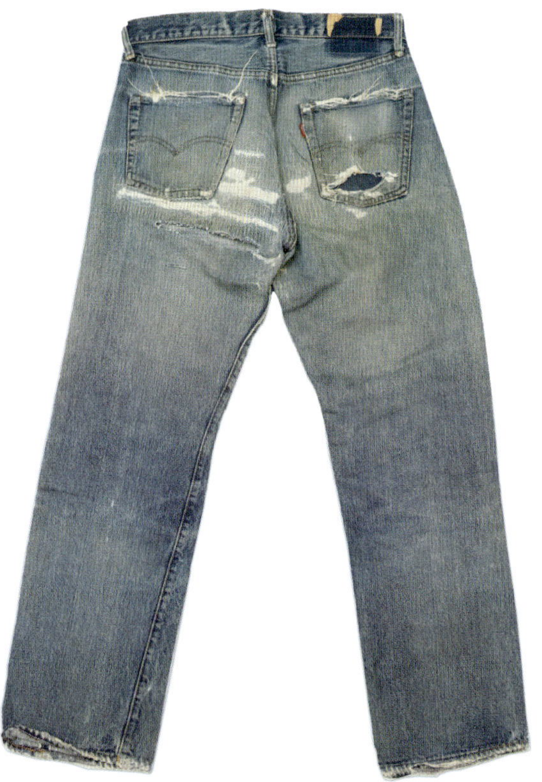

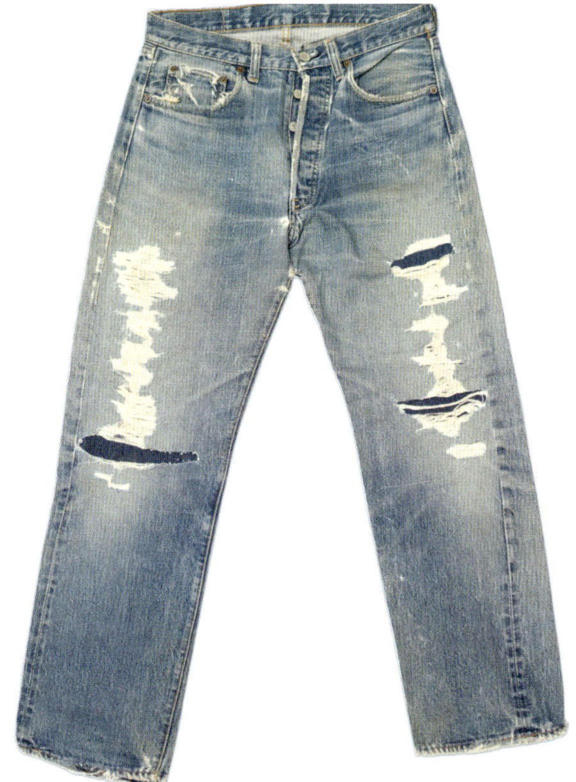

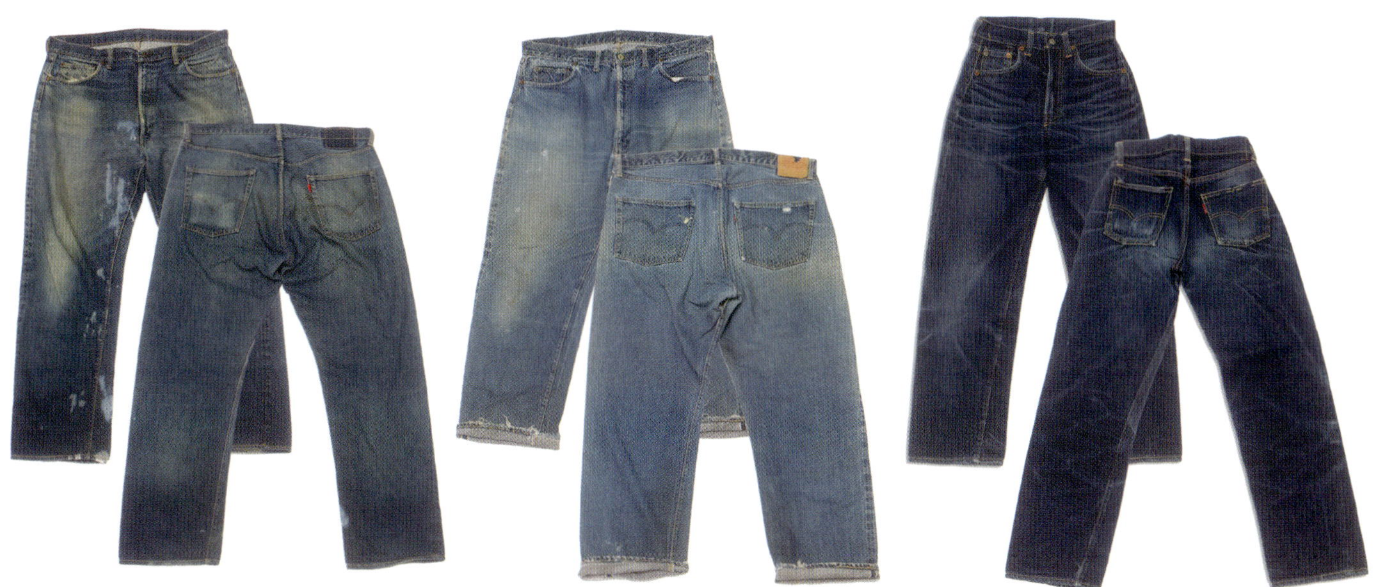

1960's
LEVI'S selvedge denim pants
"Big E"

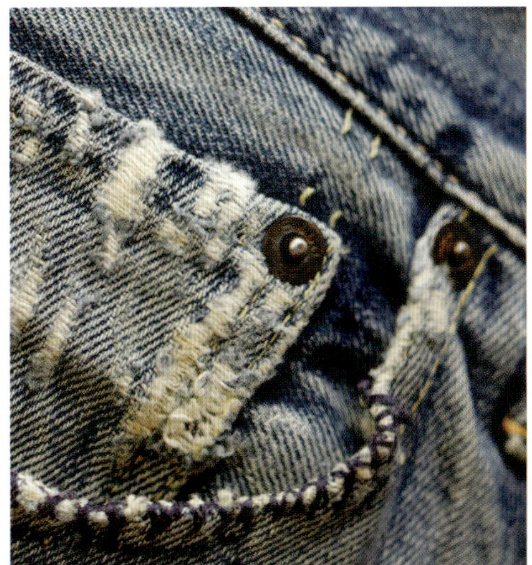

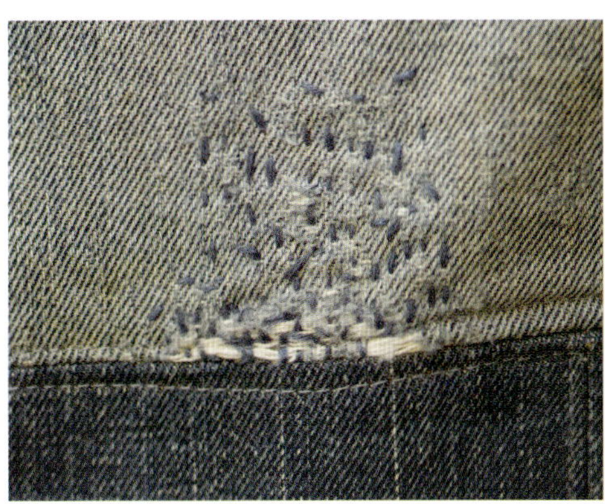

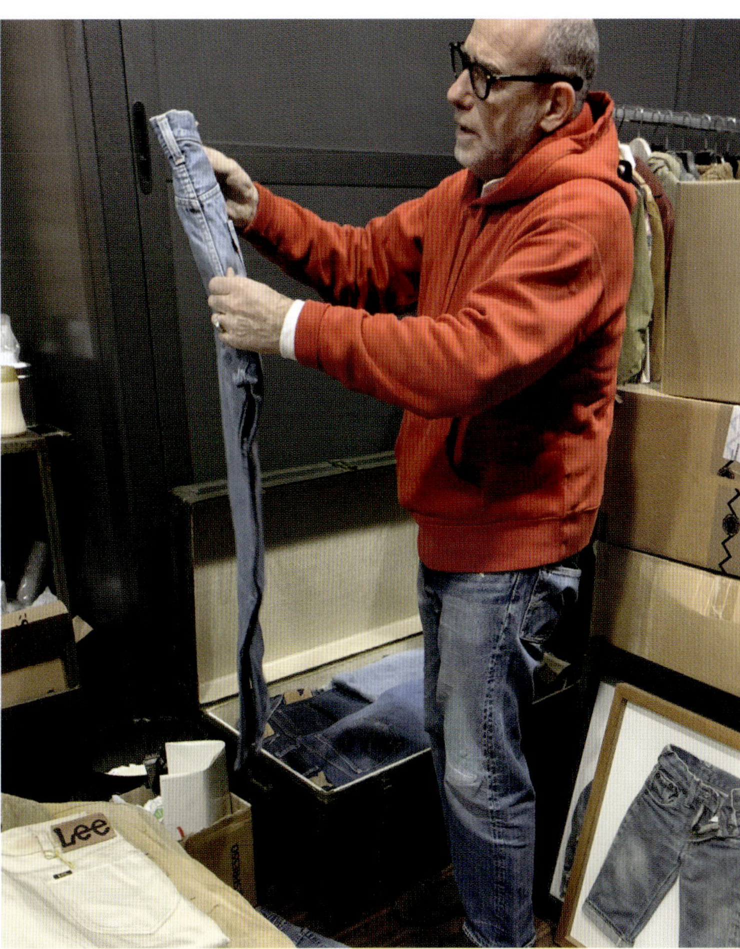

at Alessandro Squarzi archive
Forli

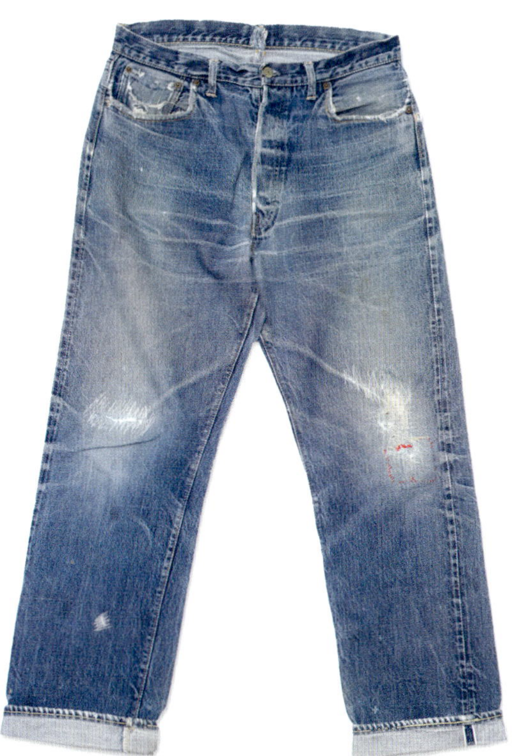 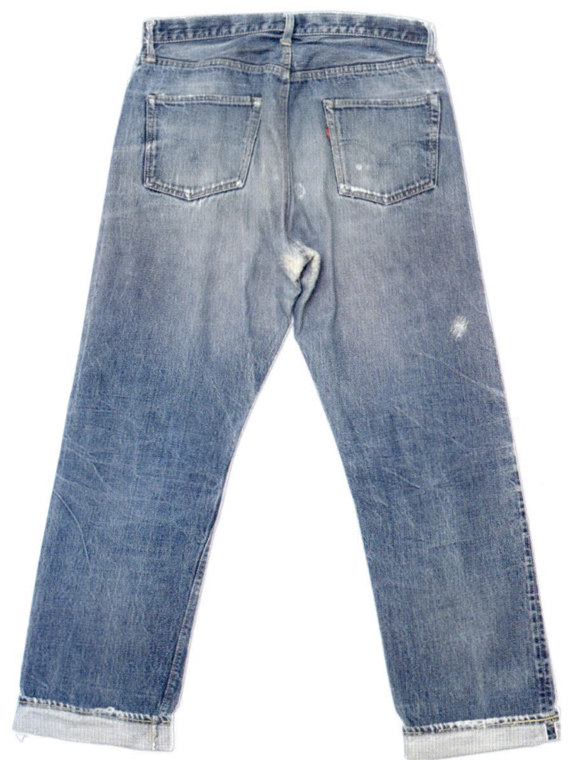

1960's
LEVI'S selvedge denim pants
"Big E"

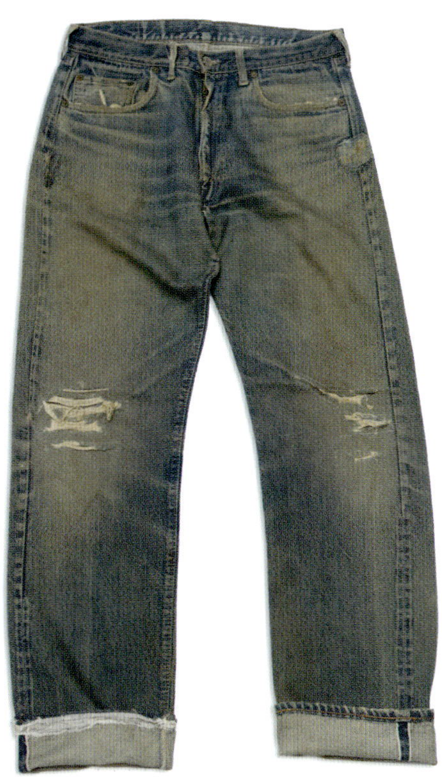 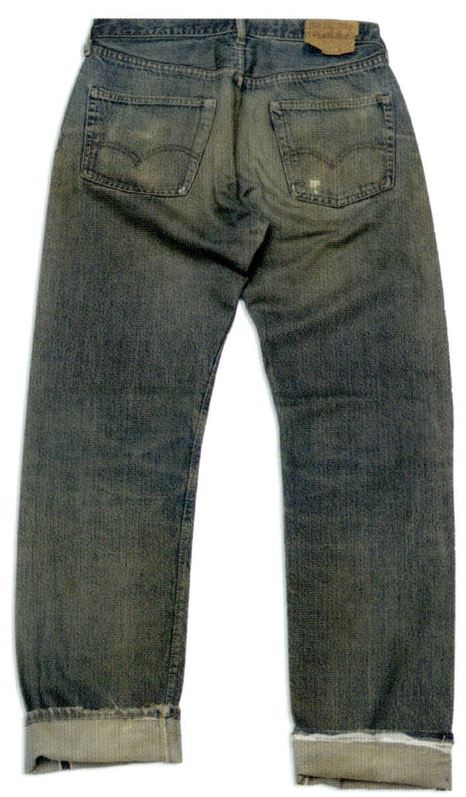

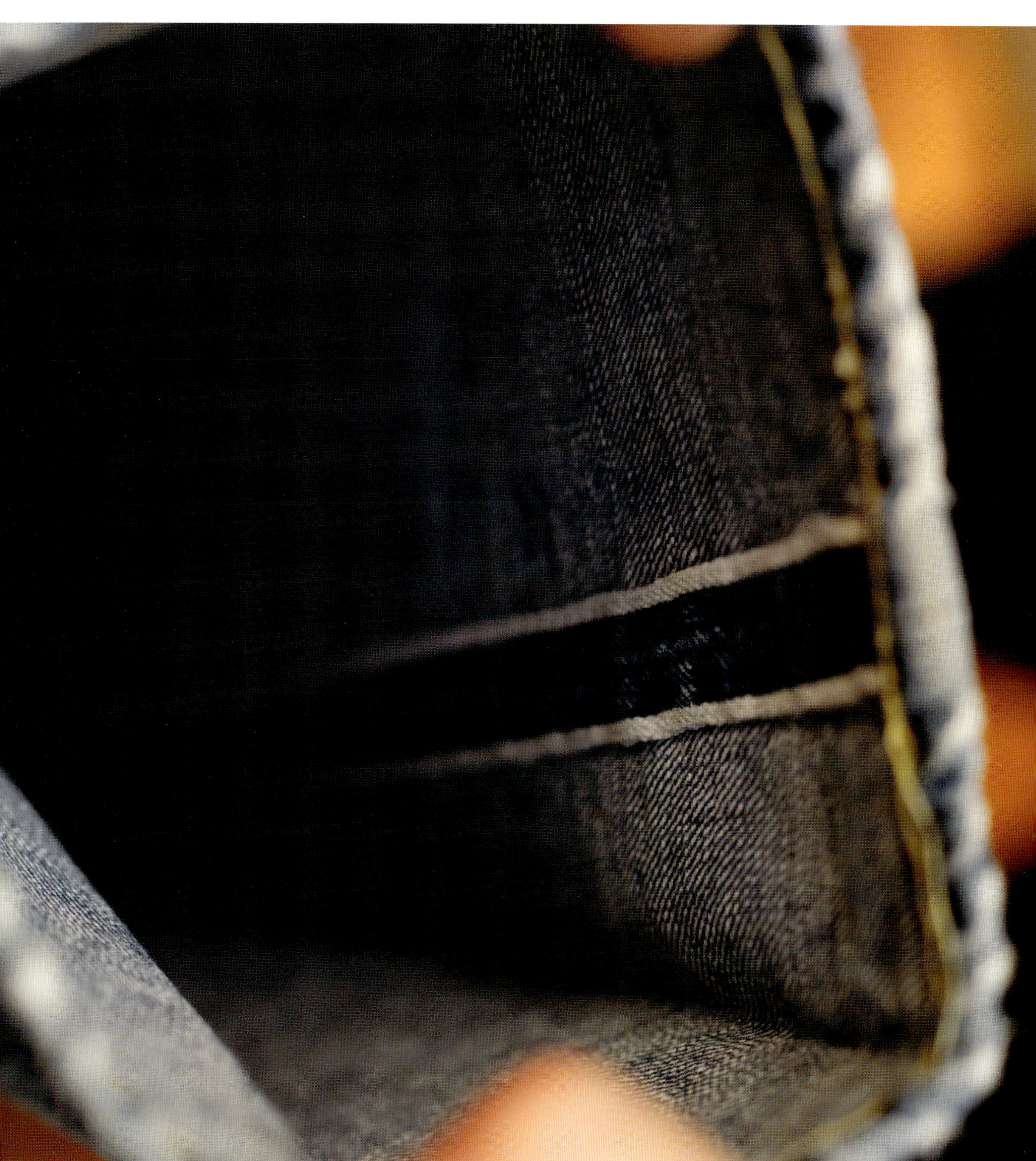

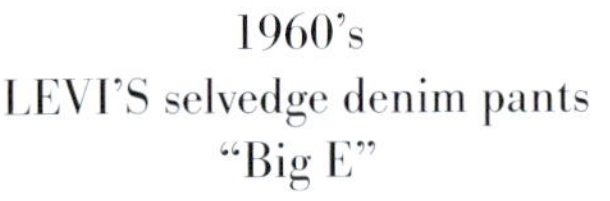

1960's
LEVI'S selvedge denim pants
"Big E"

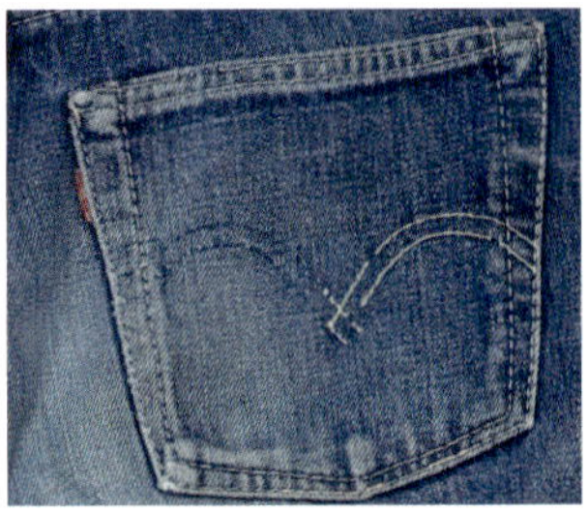

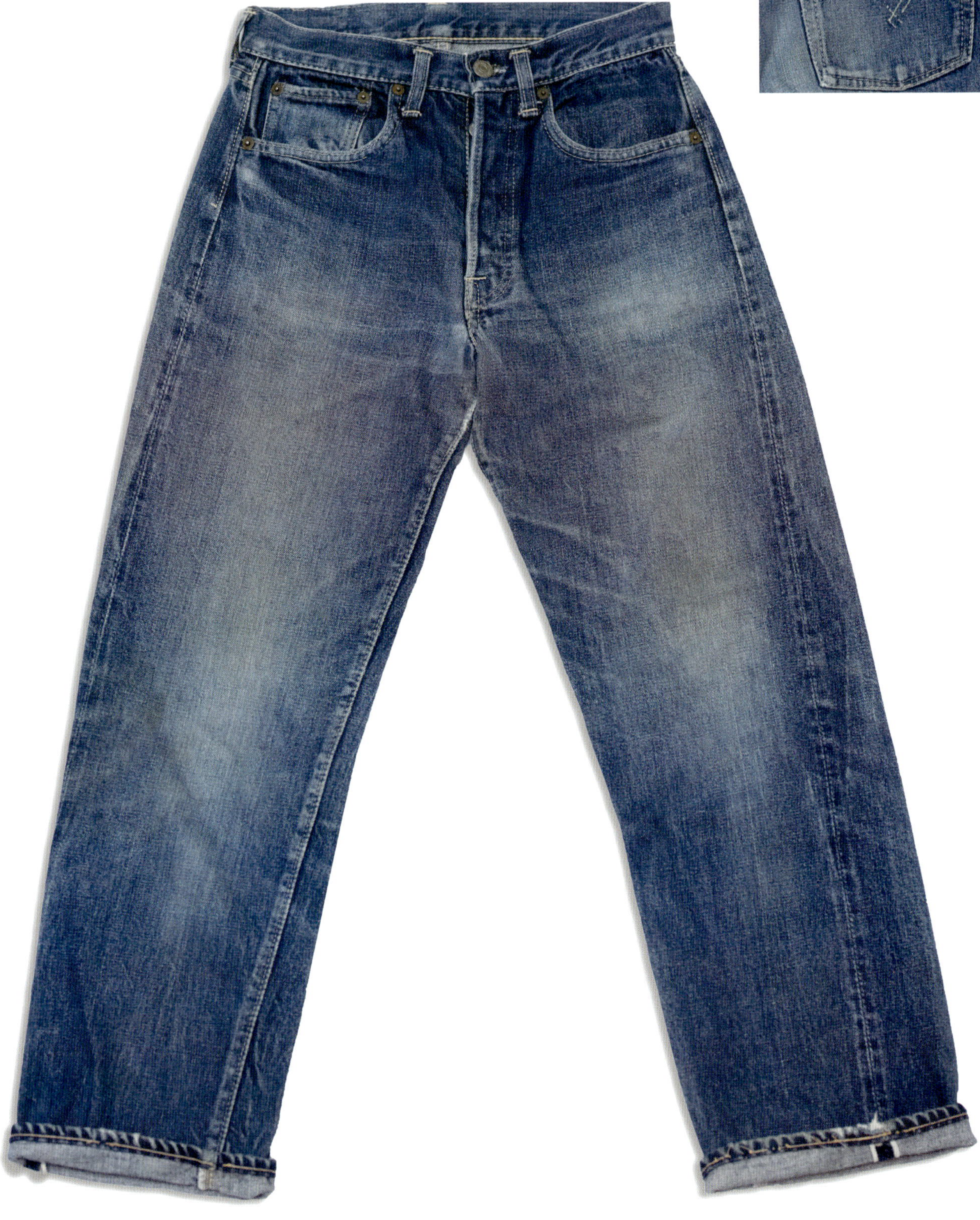

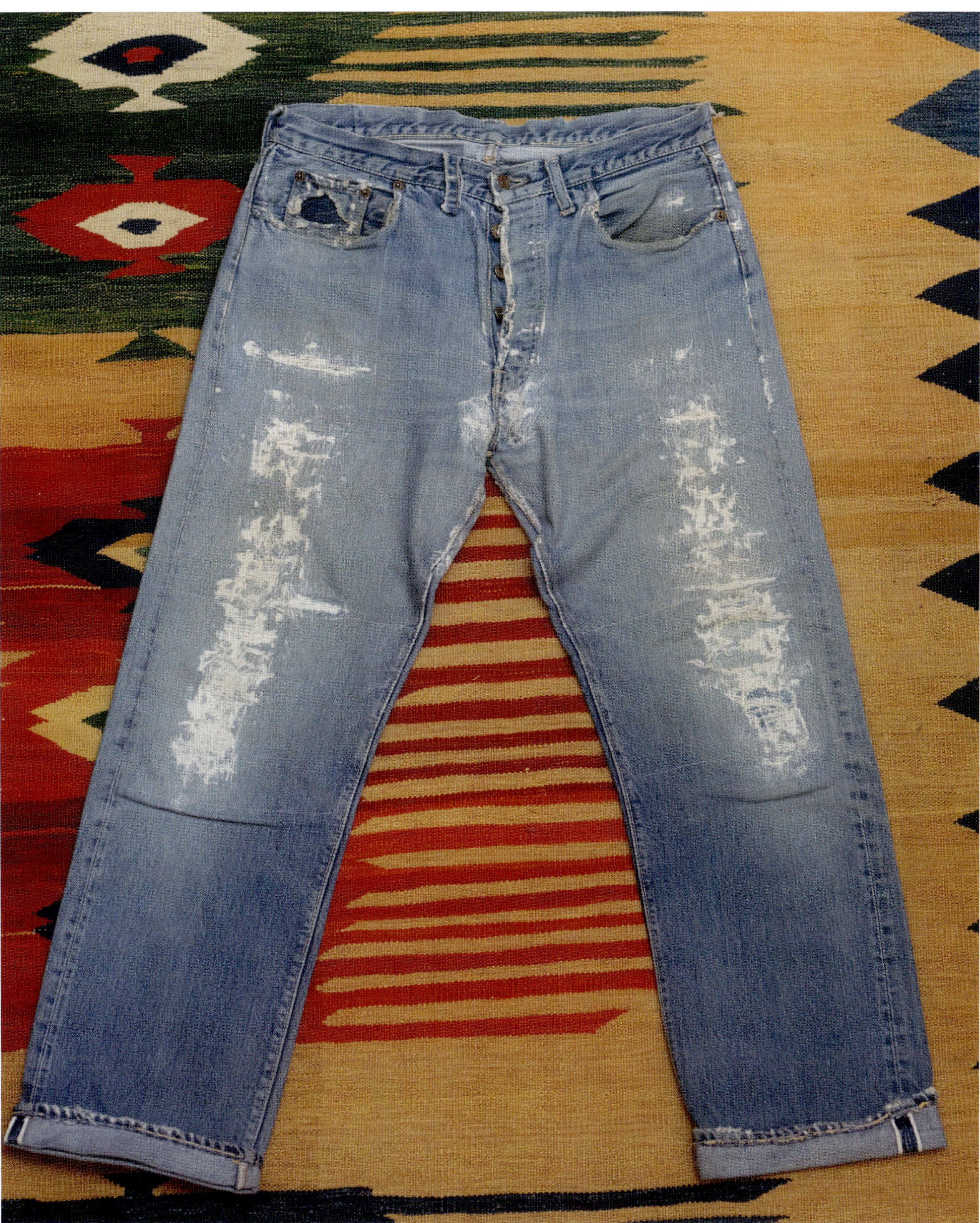

First piece of the archive

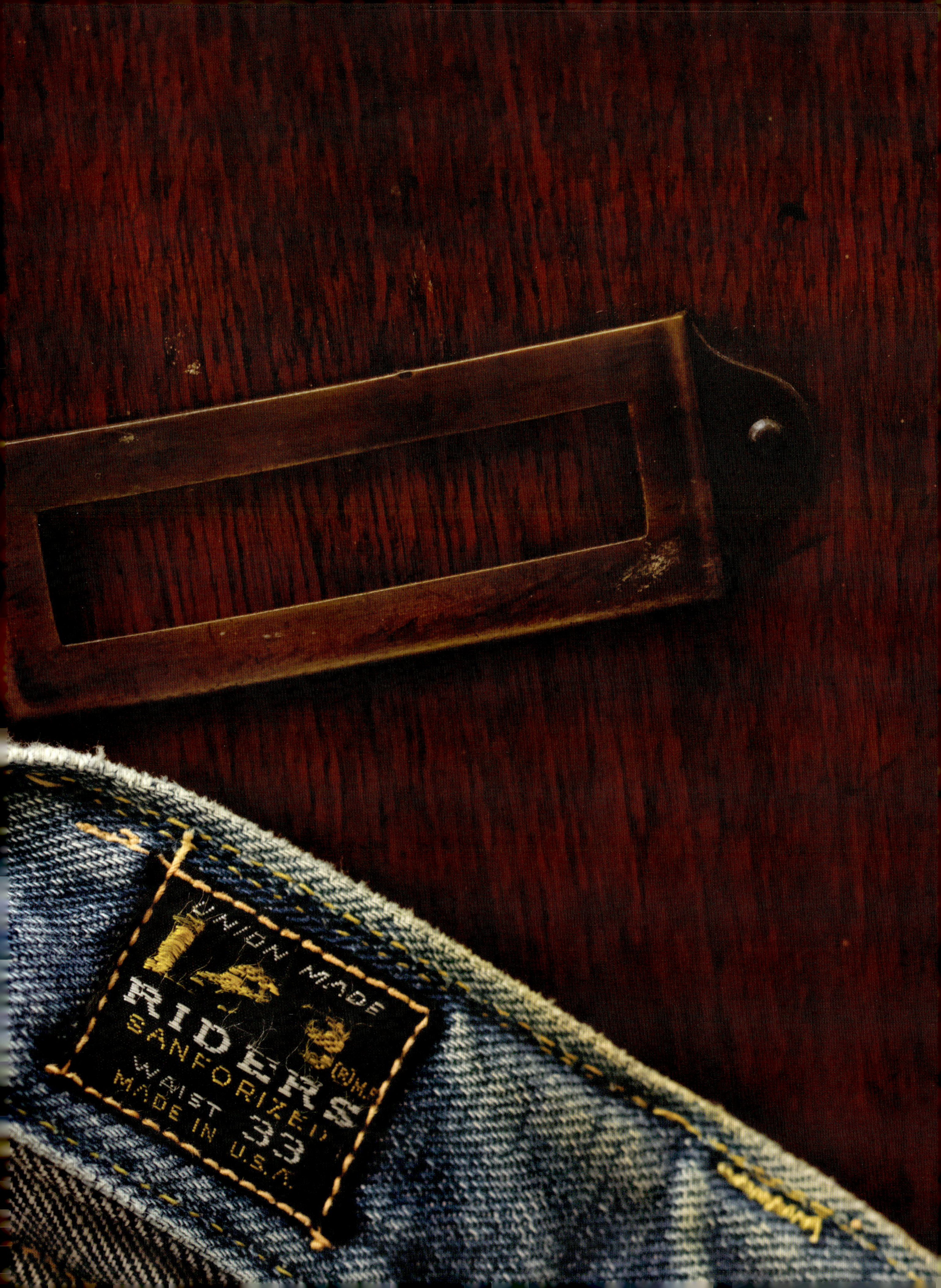

UNION MADE
RIDERS
(R) M.F.
SANFORIZED
WAIST 33
MADE IN U.S.A.

1960's
LEE denim pants
"half selvedge"

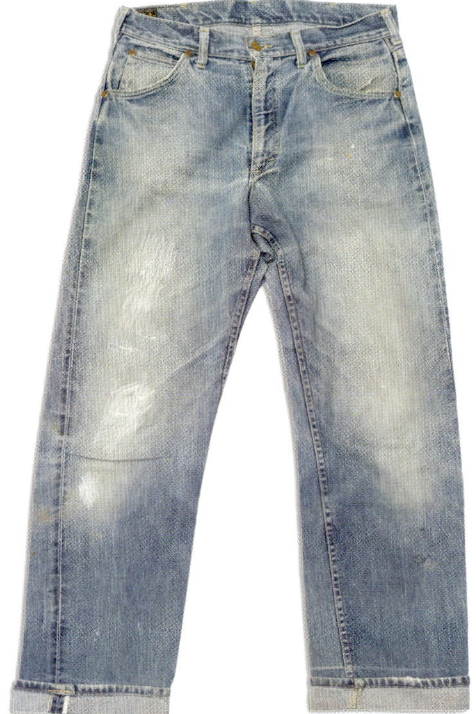

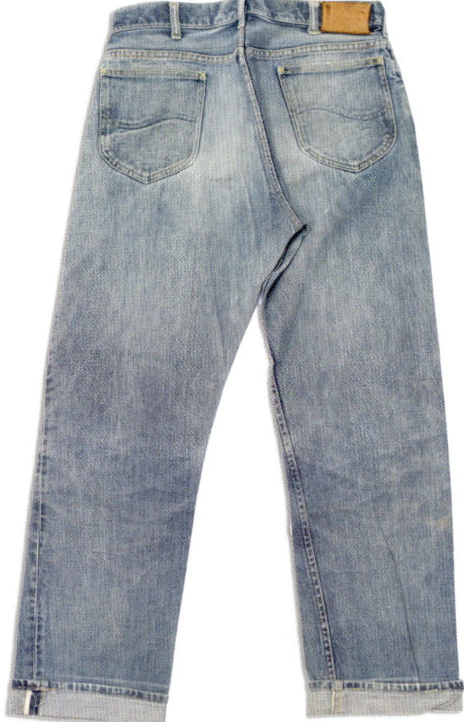

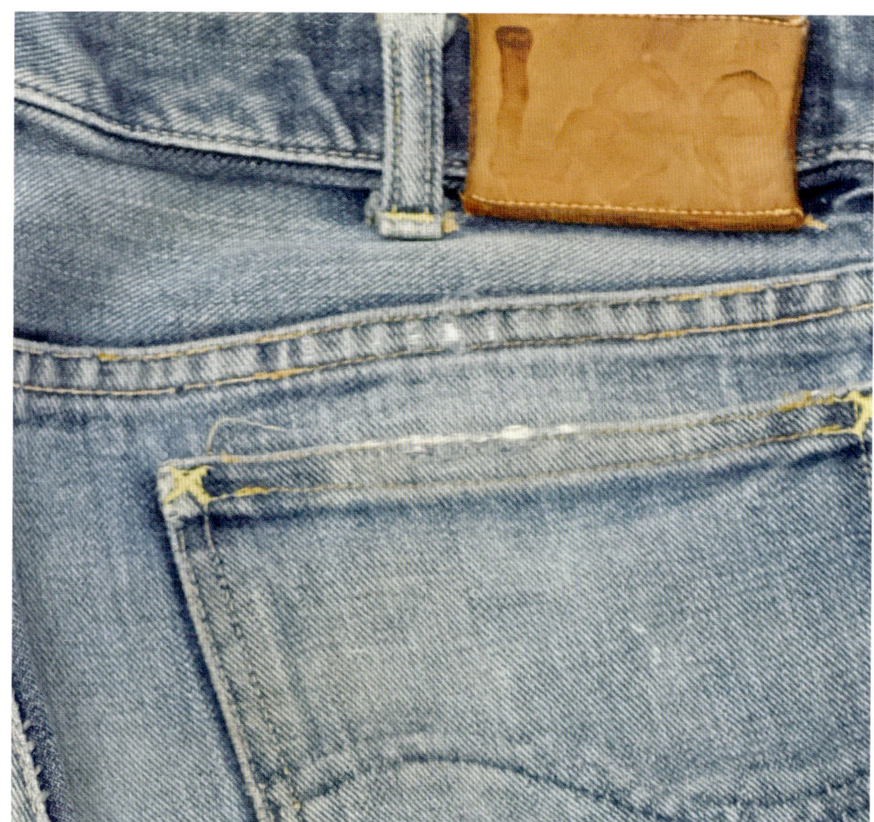

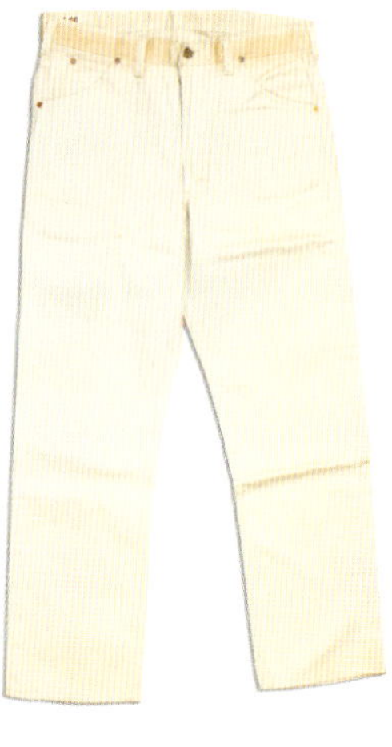

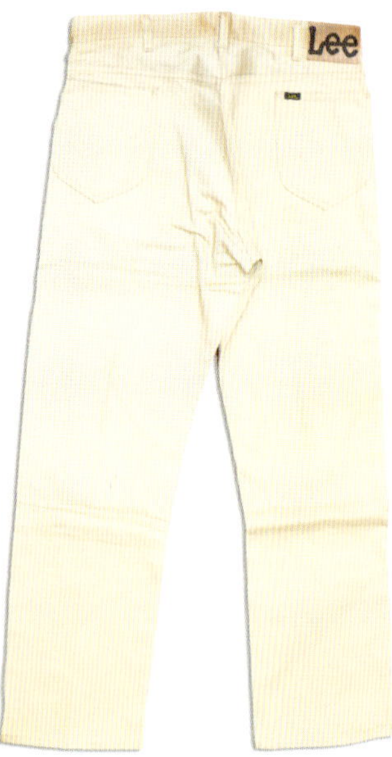

1960's
LEE denim pants
"Riders"

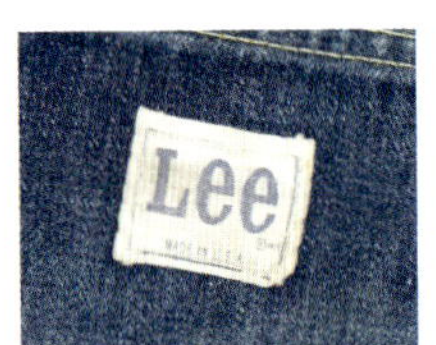

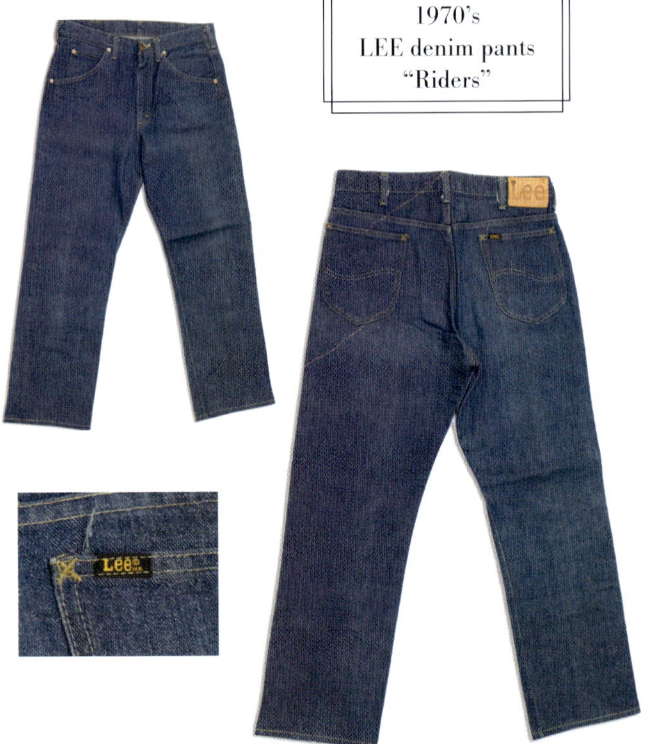

1970's
LEE denim pants
"Riders"

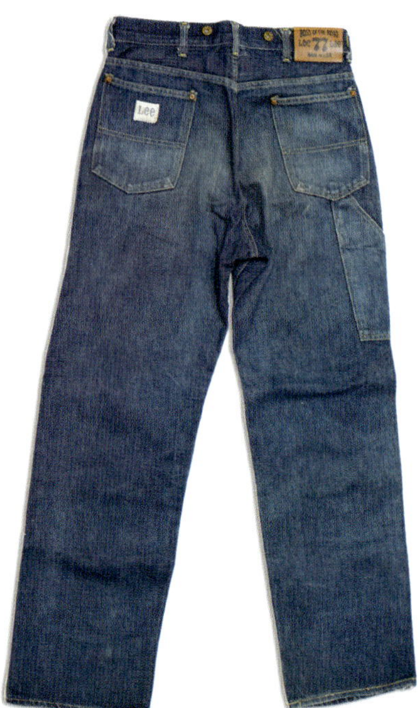

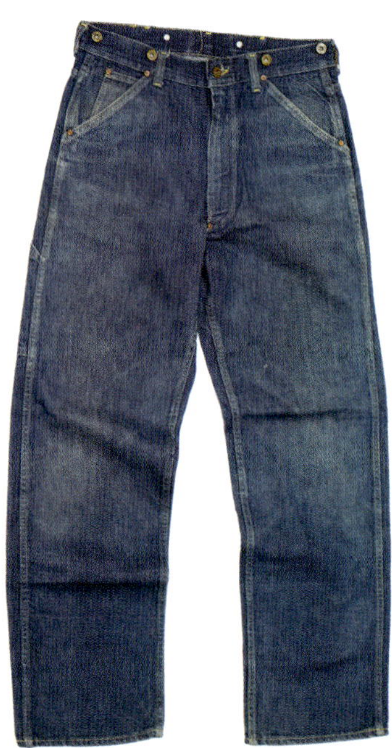

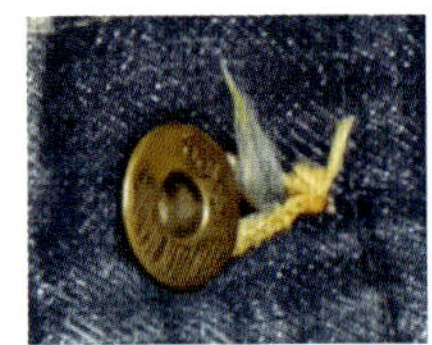

1970's
LEE denim pants
"Boss of the Road"

1960's
Wrangler denim pants
"Blue Bell"

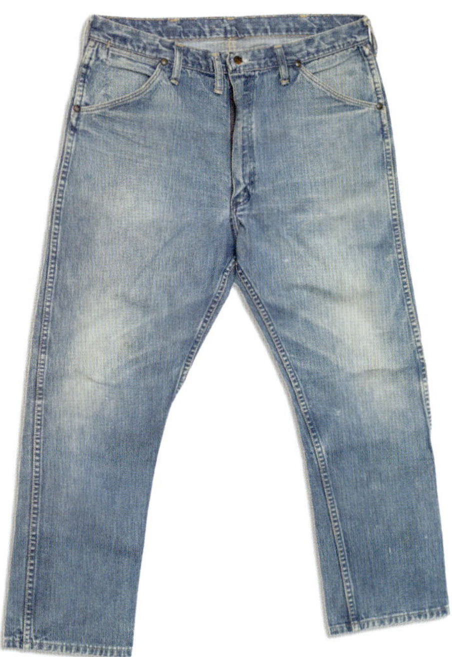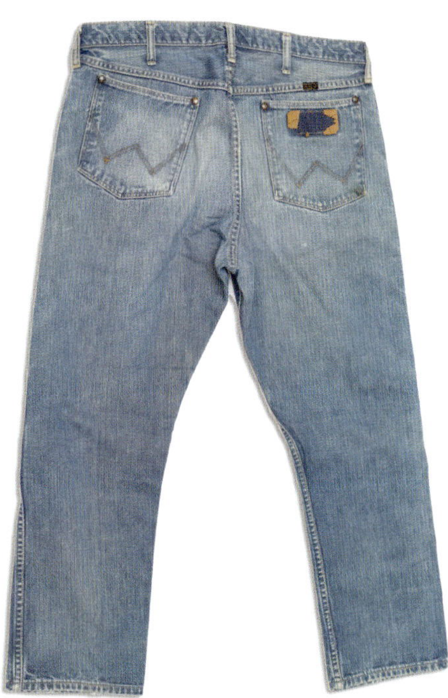

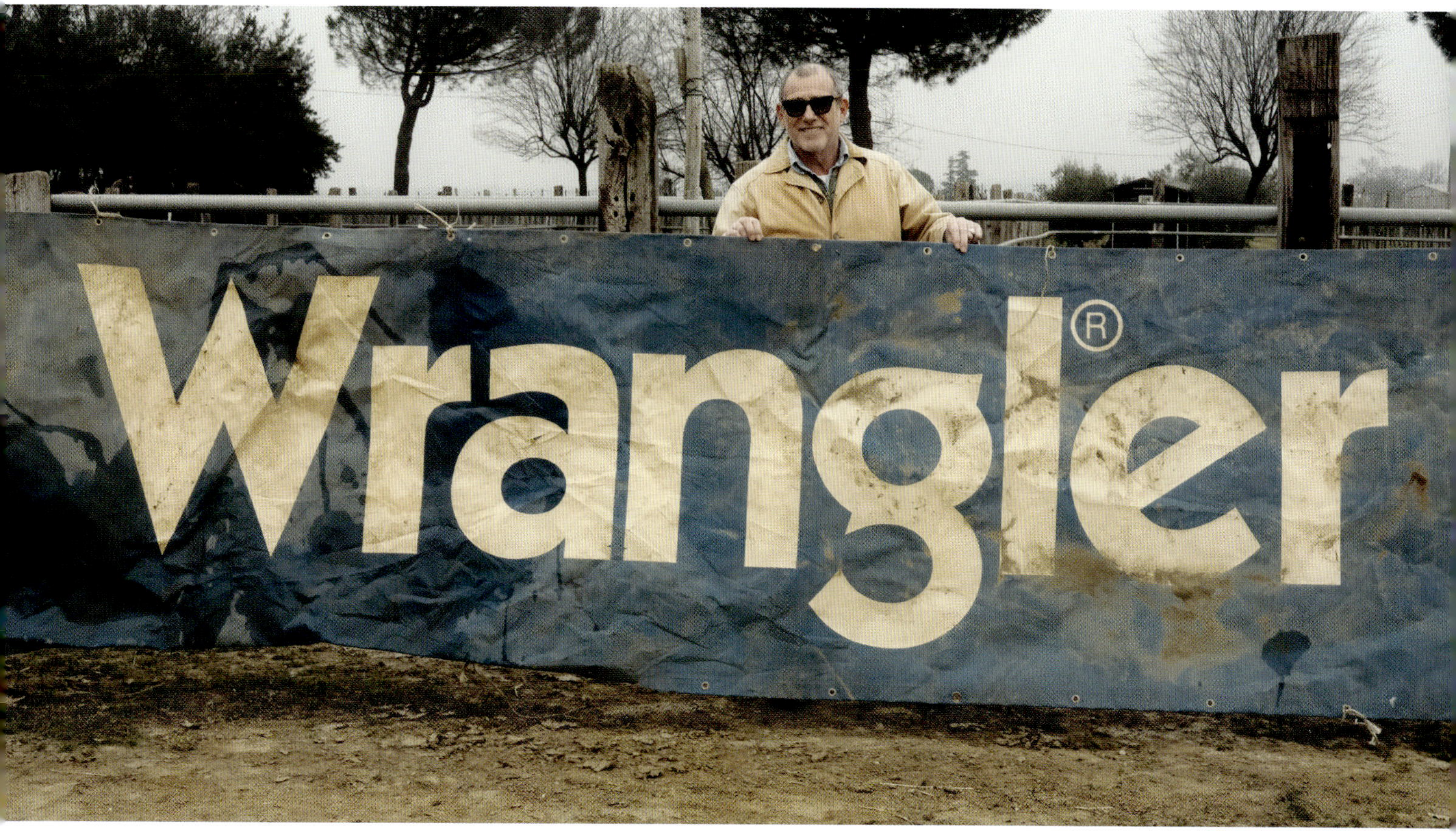

at Maneggio Cortesi, Forli

1940's
U.S.N.
denim dungarees

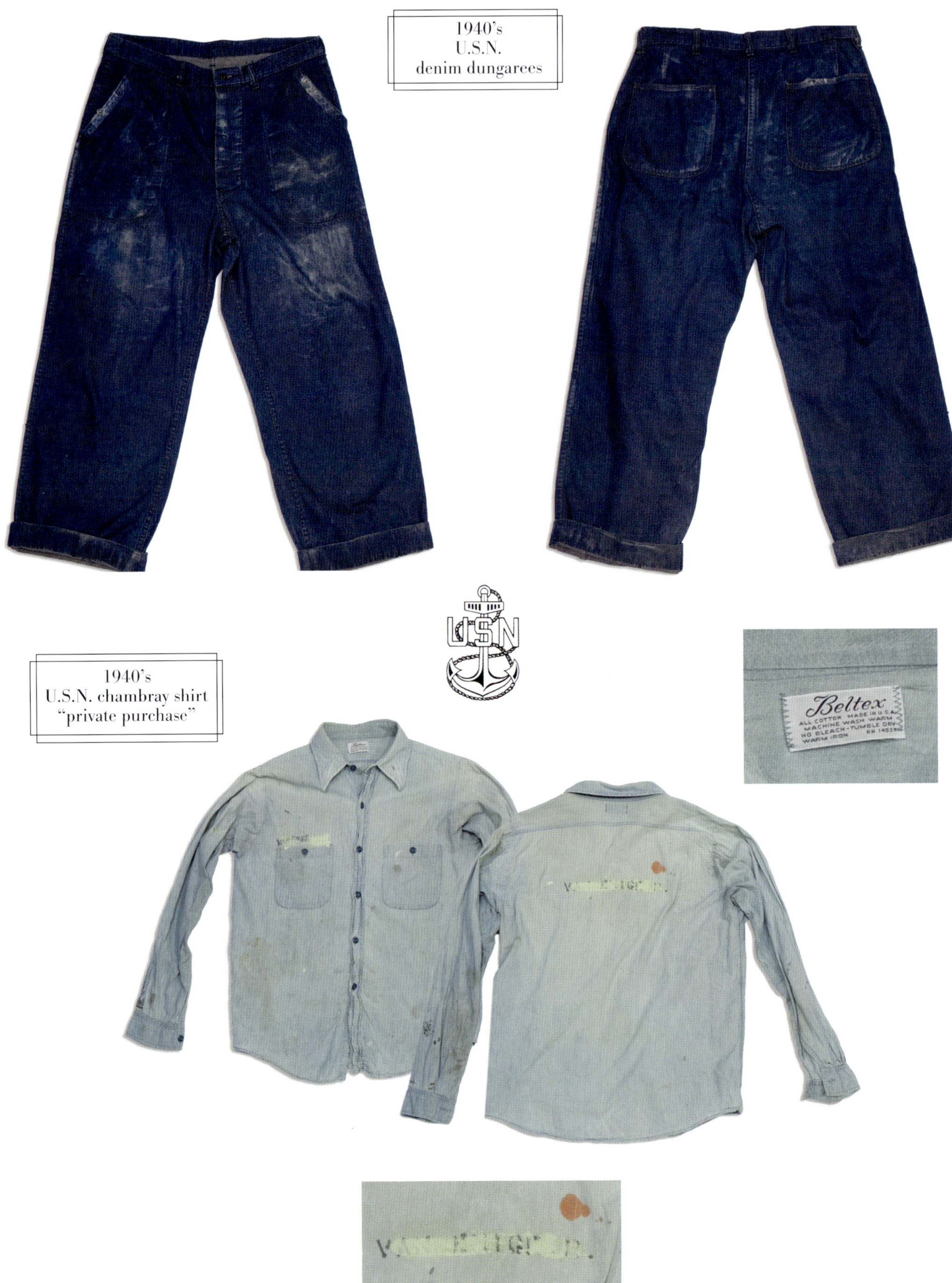

1940's
U.S.N. chambray shirt
"private purchase"

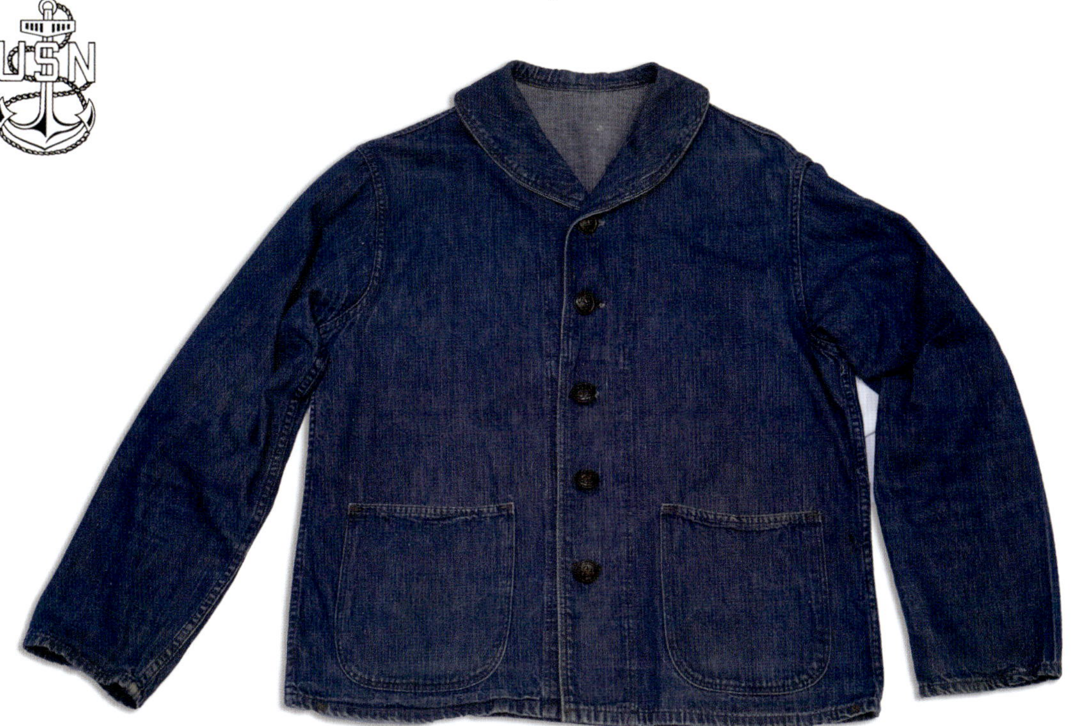

1940's
U.S.N.
denim deck jacket

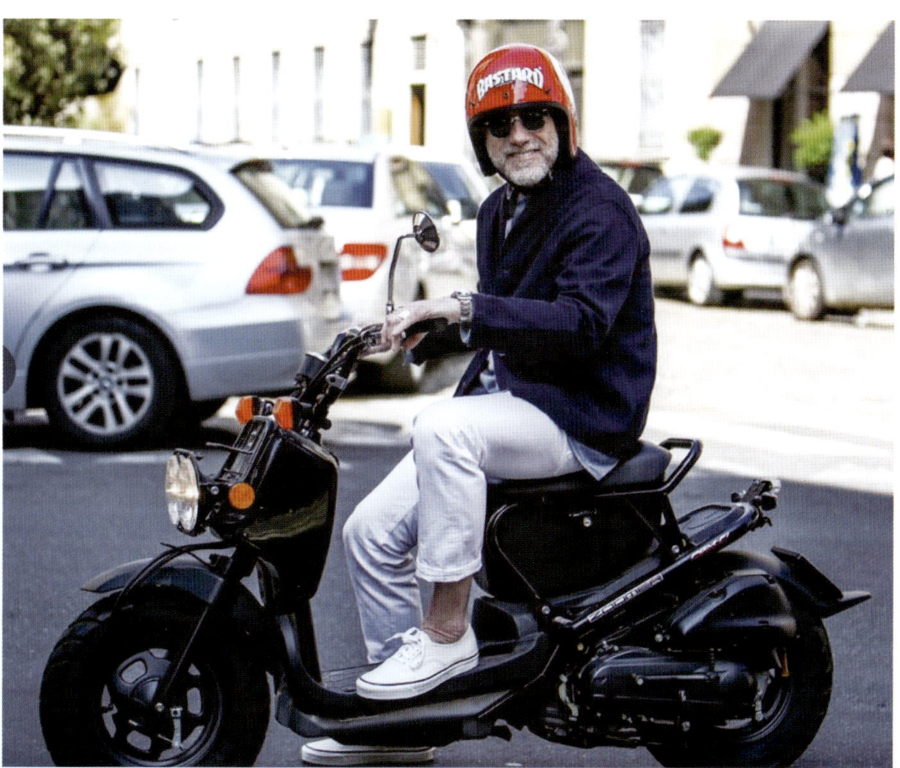

Downtown, Milano
Alessandro Squarzi photo archive

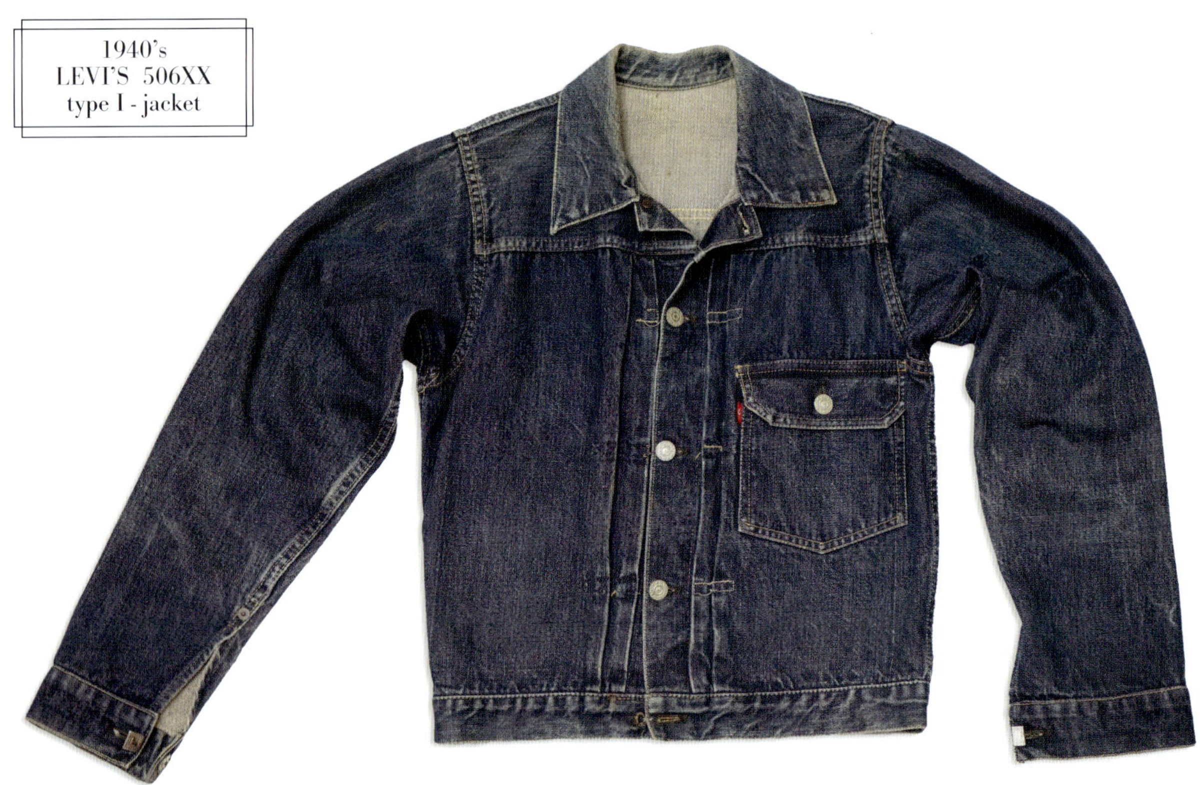

1940's
LEVI'S 506XX
type I - jacket

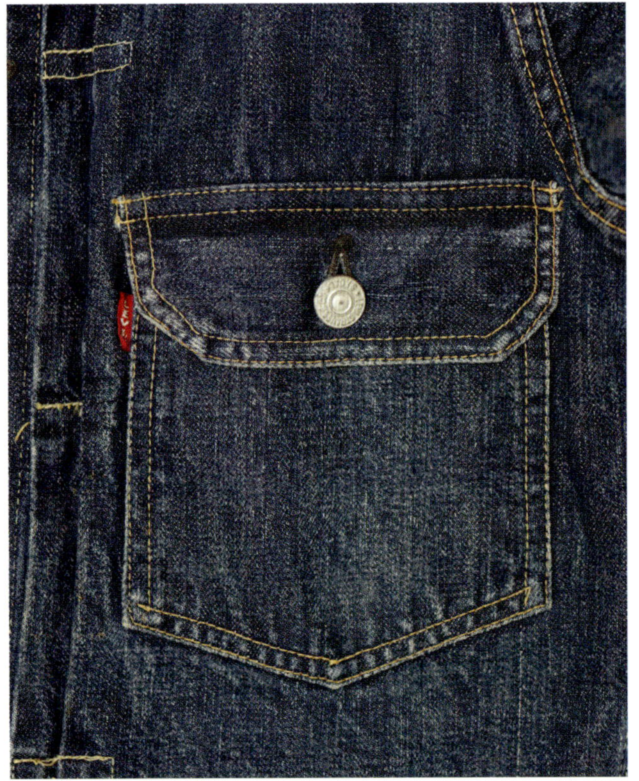

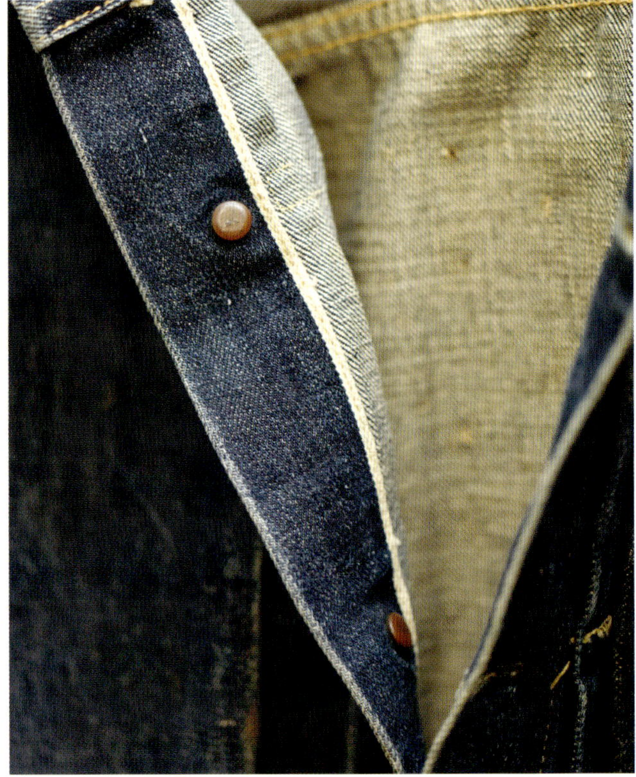

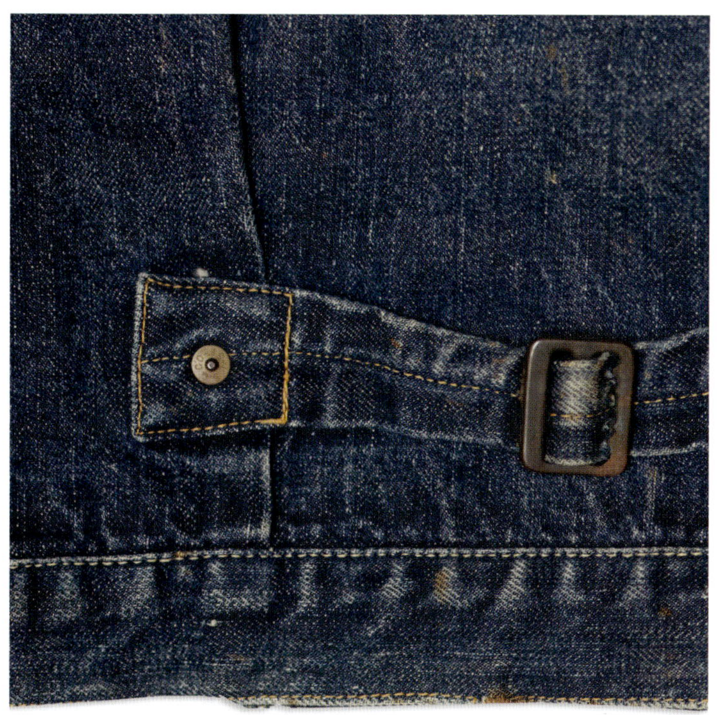

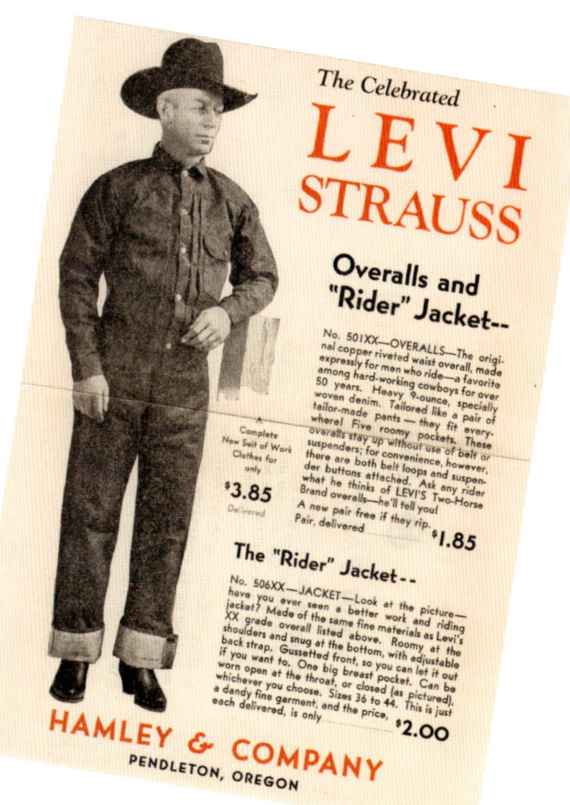

1940's advertising

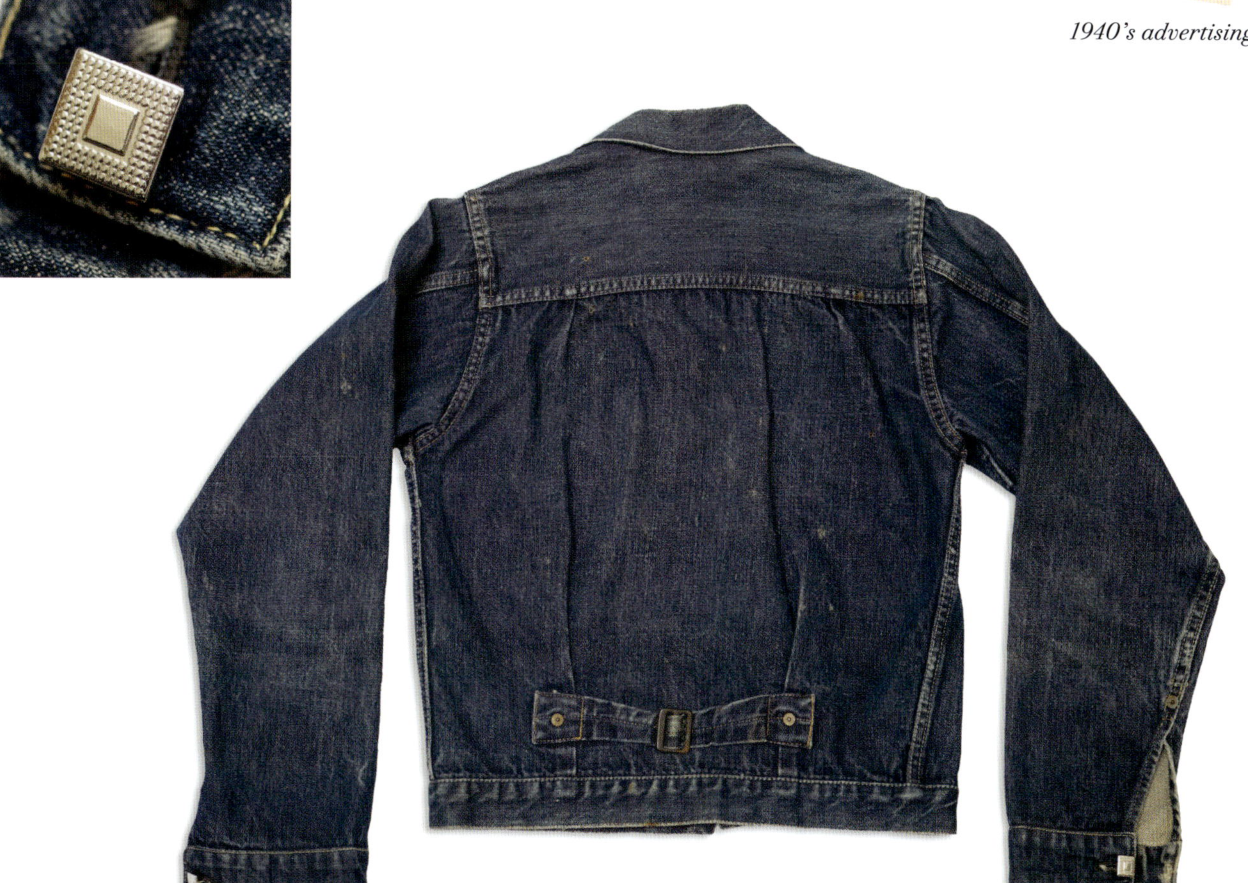

1950's
LEVI'S 507 XX
type II - jacket

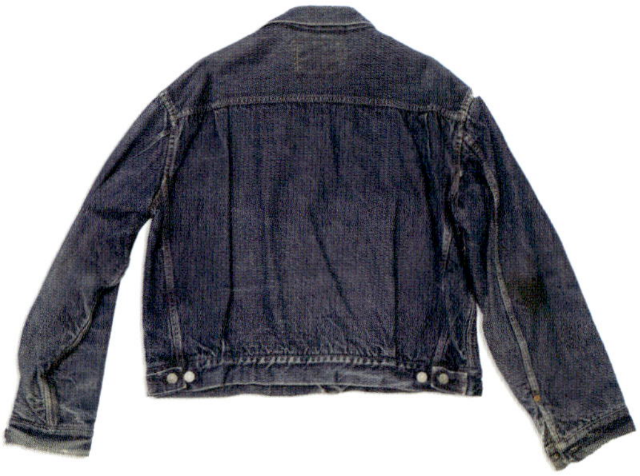

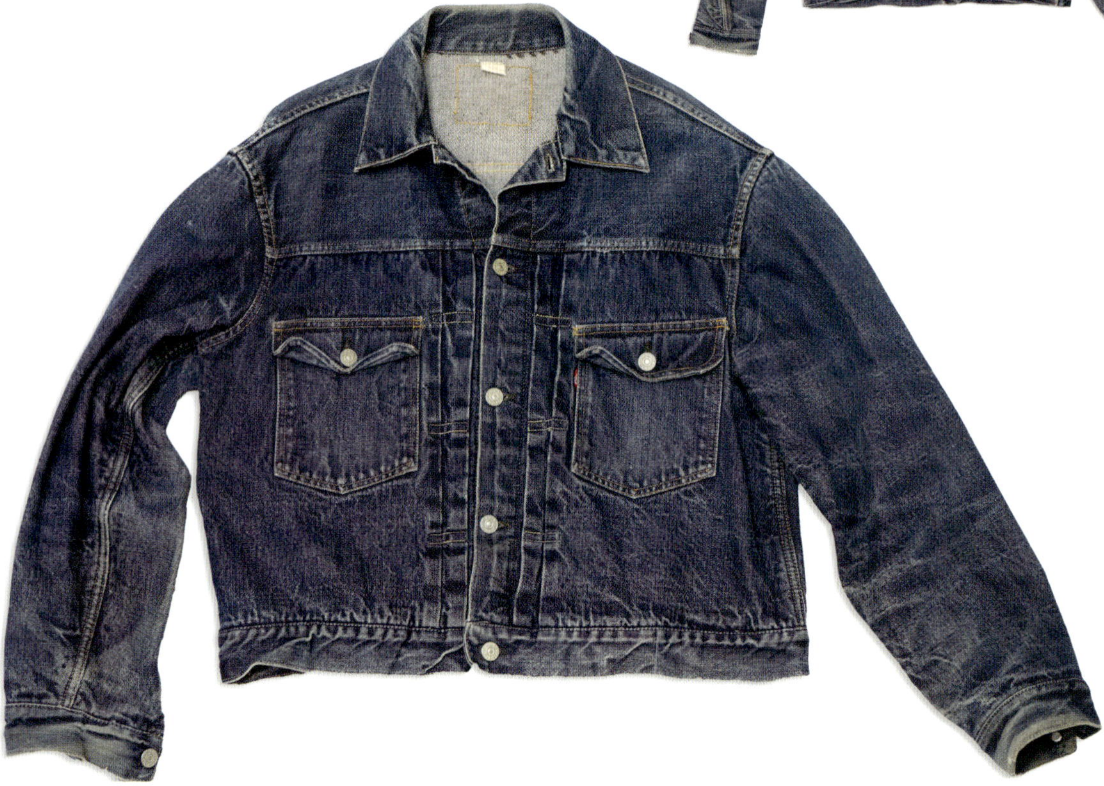

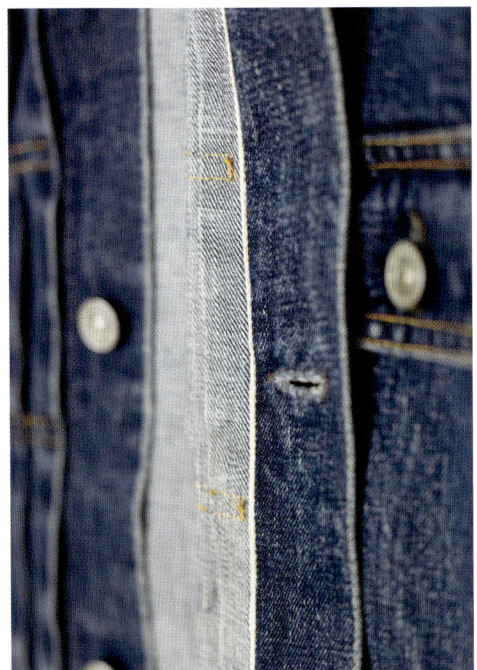

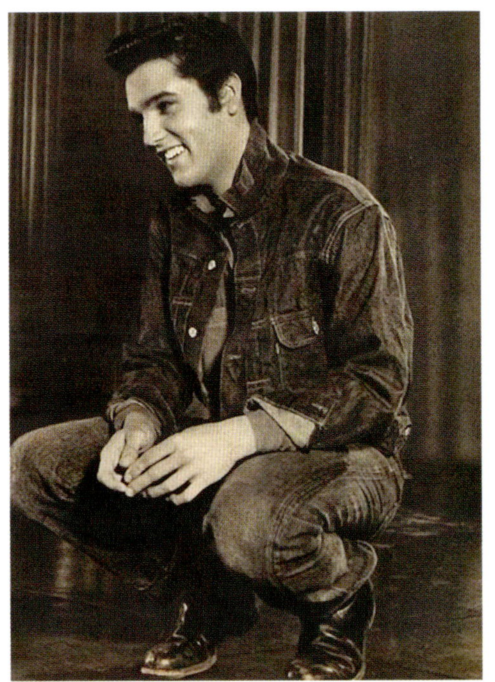

Elvis in denim "total look" - 1950's

1950's
LEVI'S 507 XX
type II - jacket

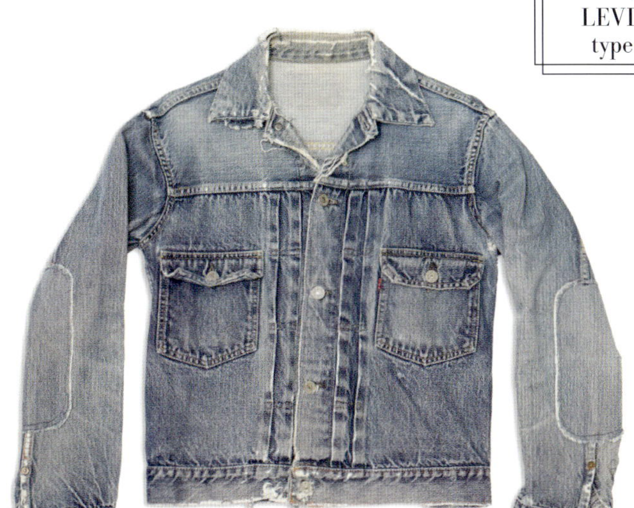
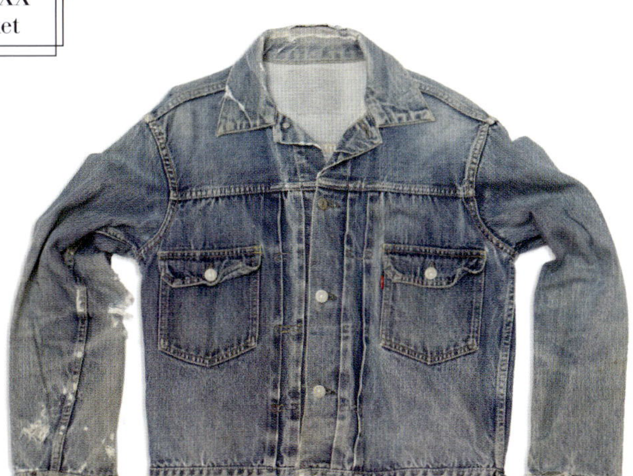

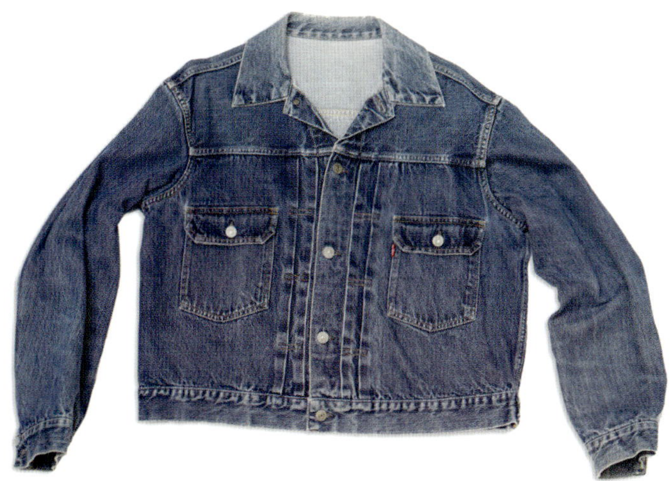
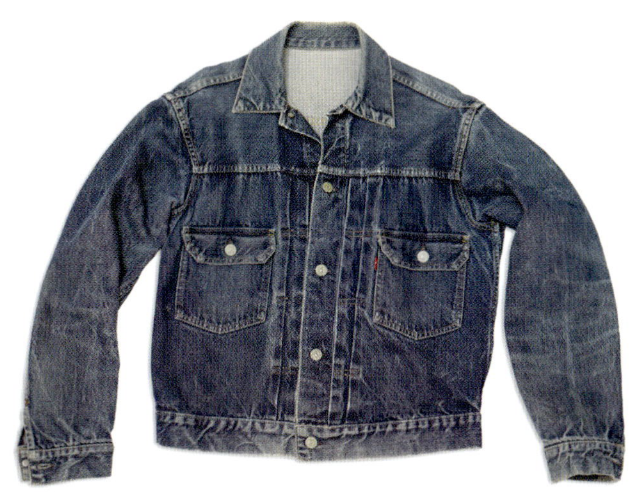

1950's
LEVI'S 517 XX
type II - jacket

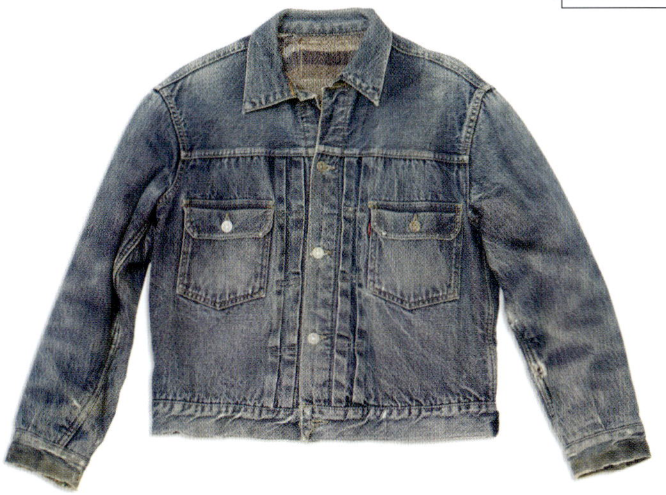
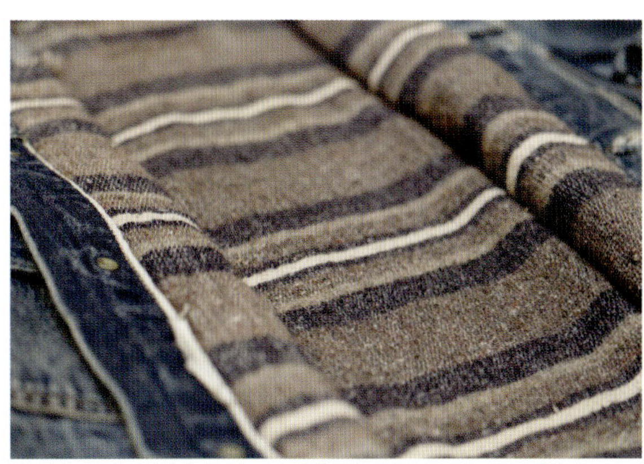

1960's
LEVI'S type III - jacket
"BIG E"

1960's
LEVI'S type III - jacket
"BIG E"

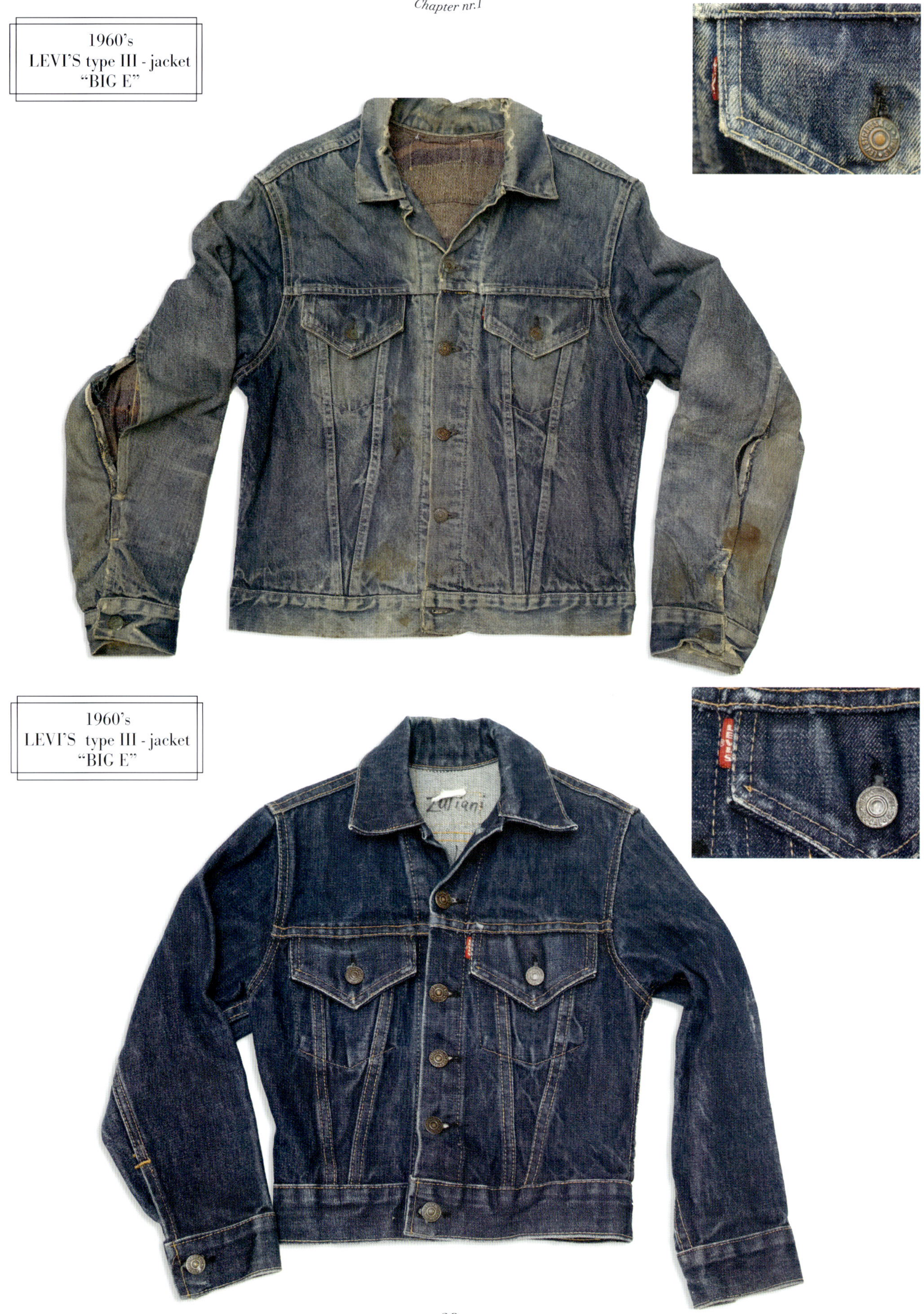

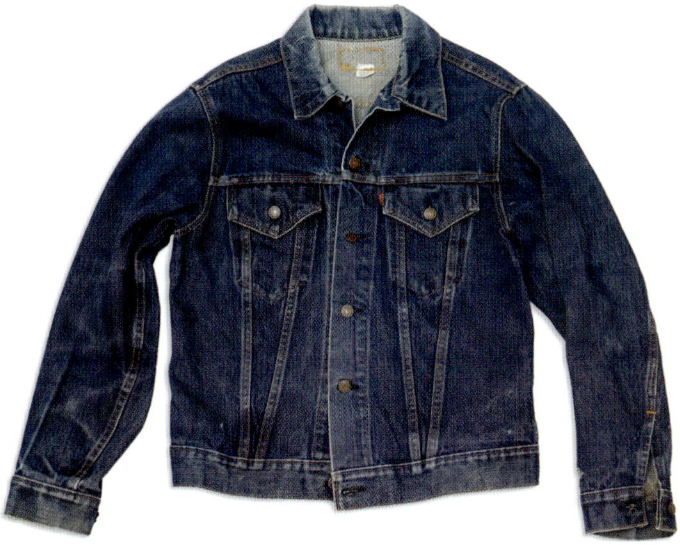

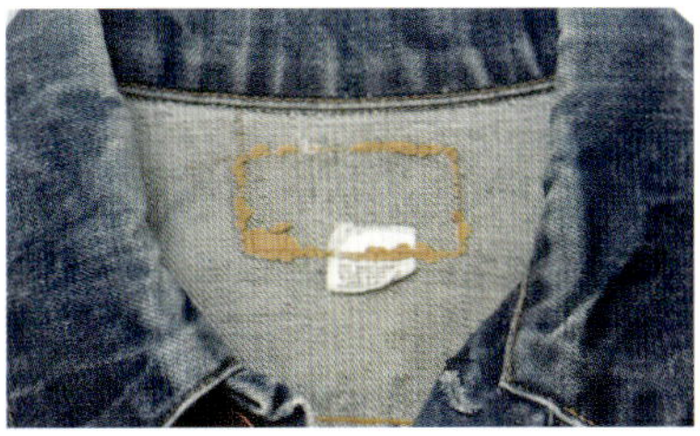

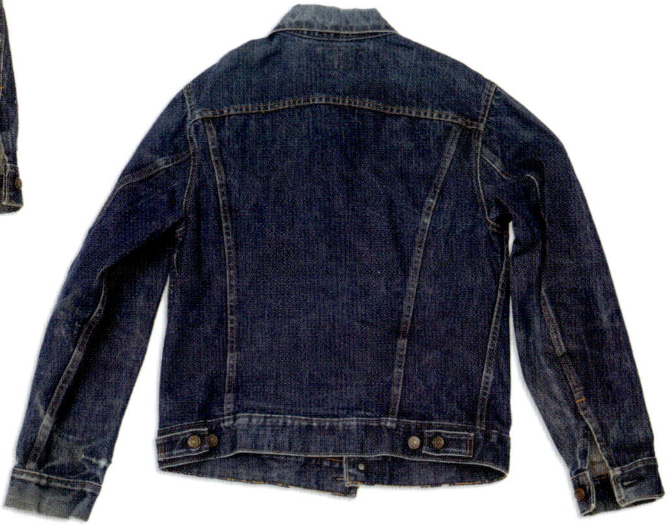

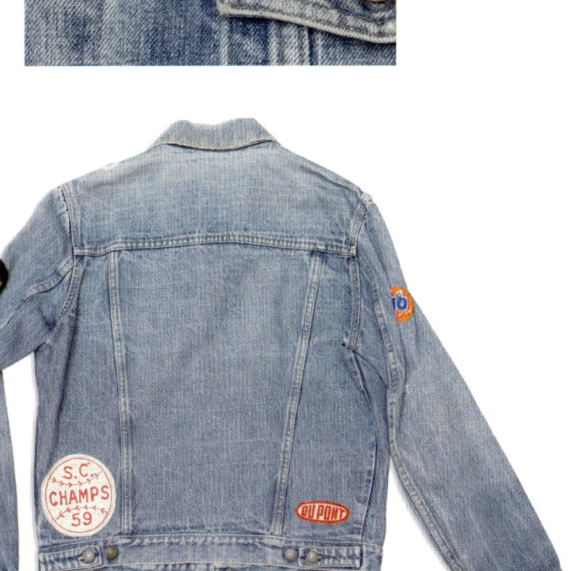

1960's
LEVI'S type III - jacket
"BIG E"

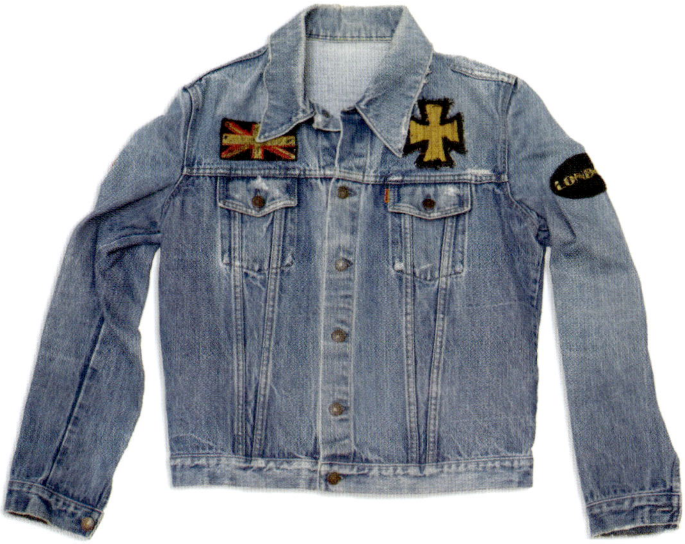

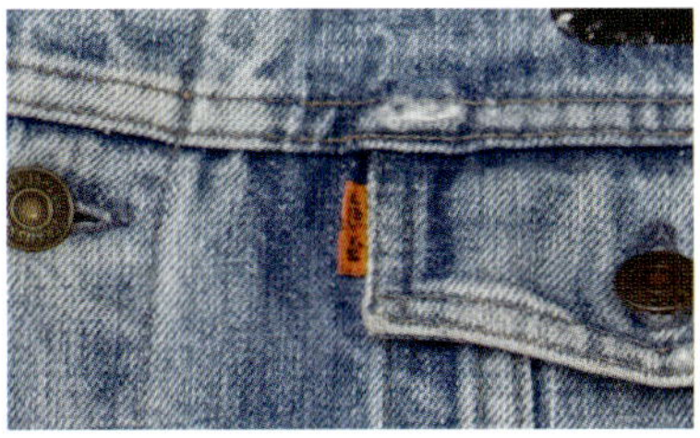

1970's
LEVI'S type III - jacket
"Orange Tab"

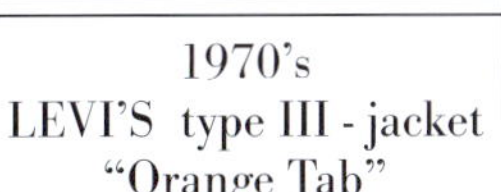

1950's
LEE denim jacket
101-J

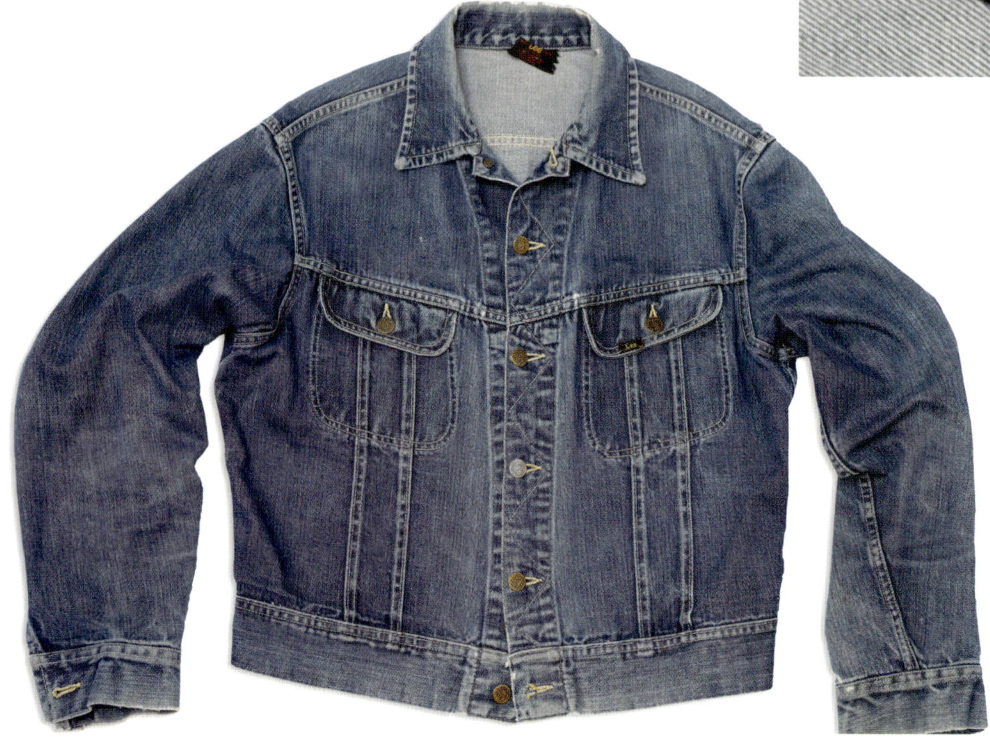

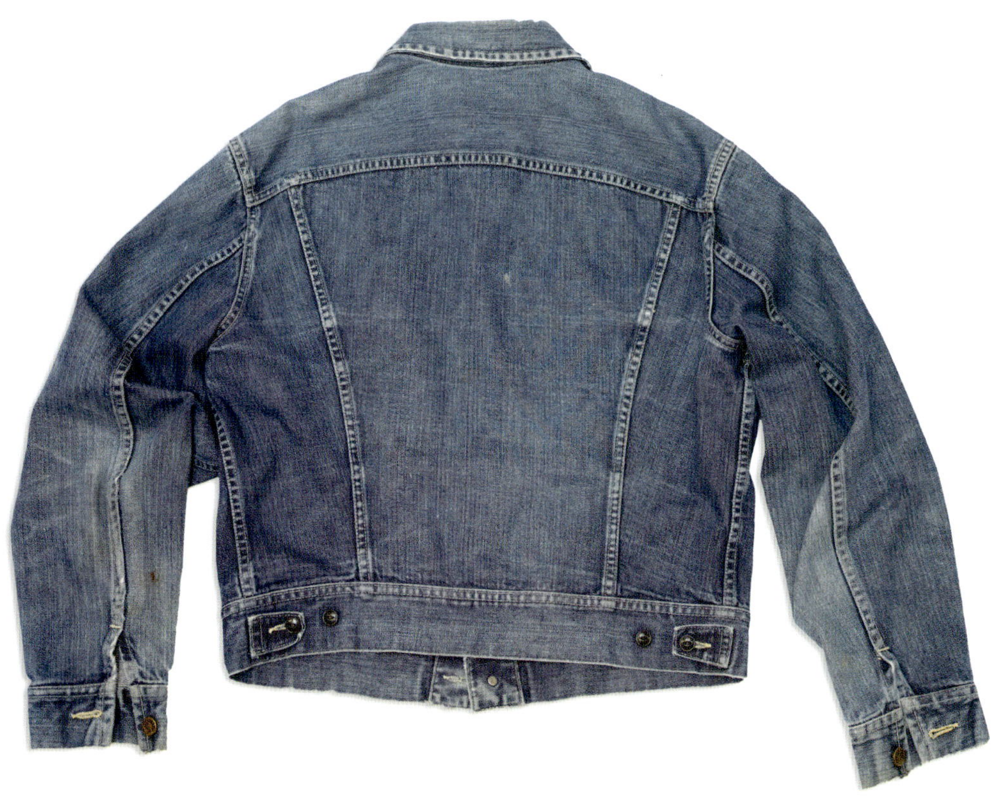

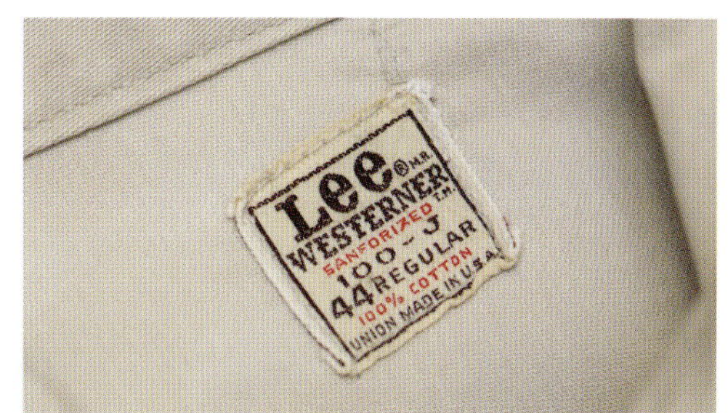

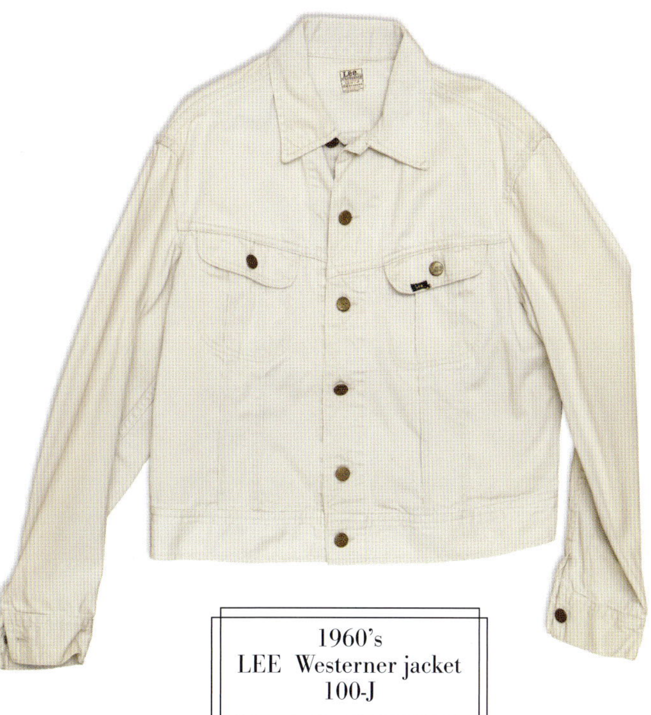

1960's
LEE Westerner jacket
100-J

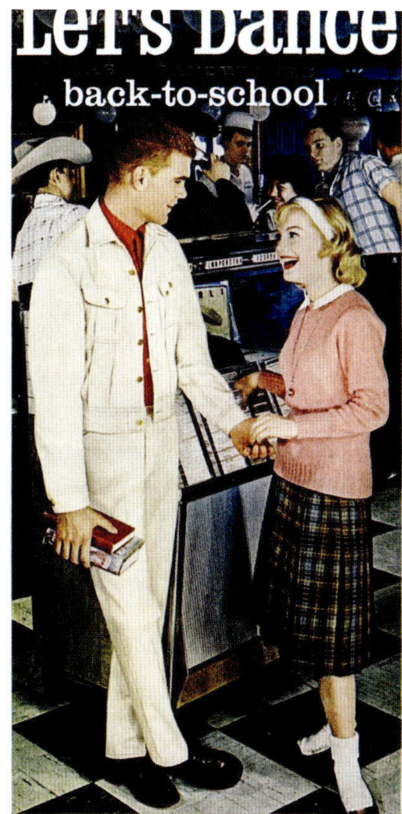

1960's advertising

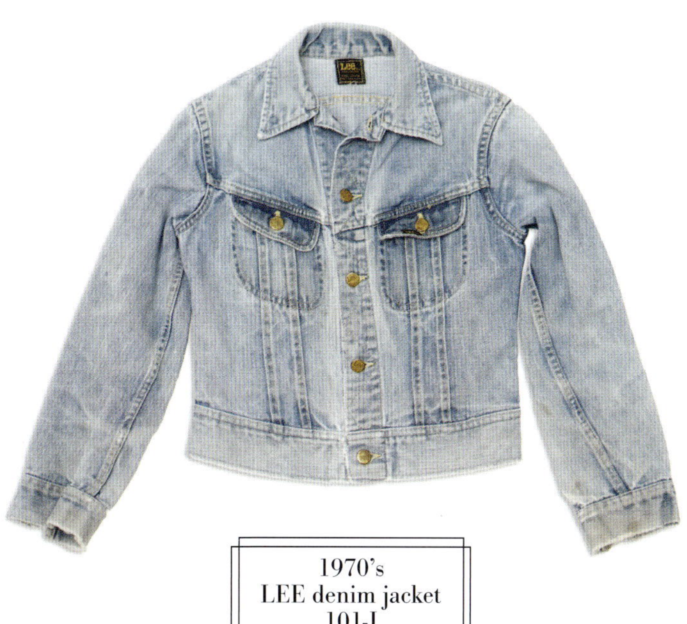

1970's
LEE denim jacket
101-J

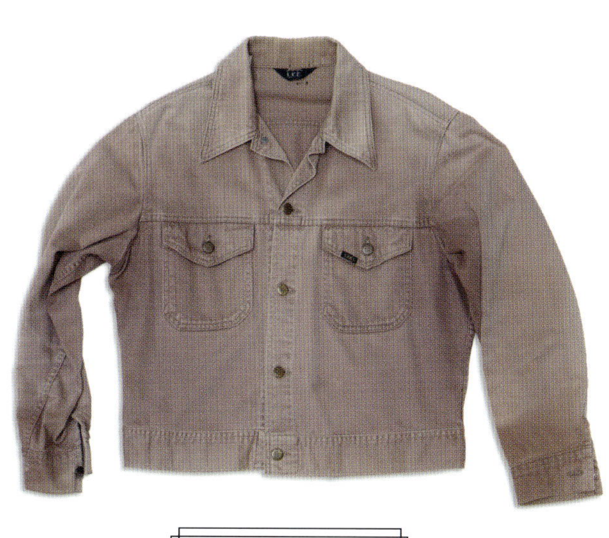

1970's
LEE jacket

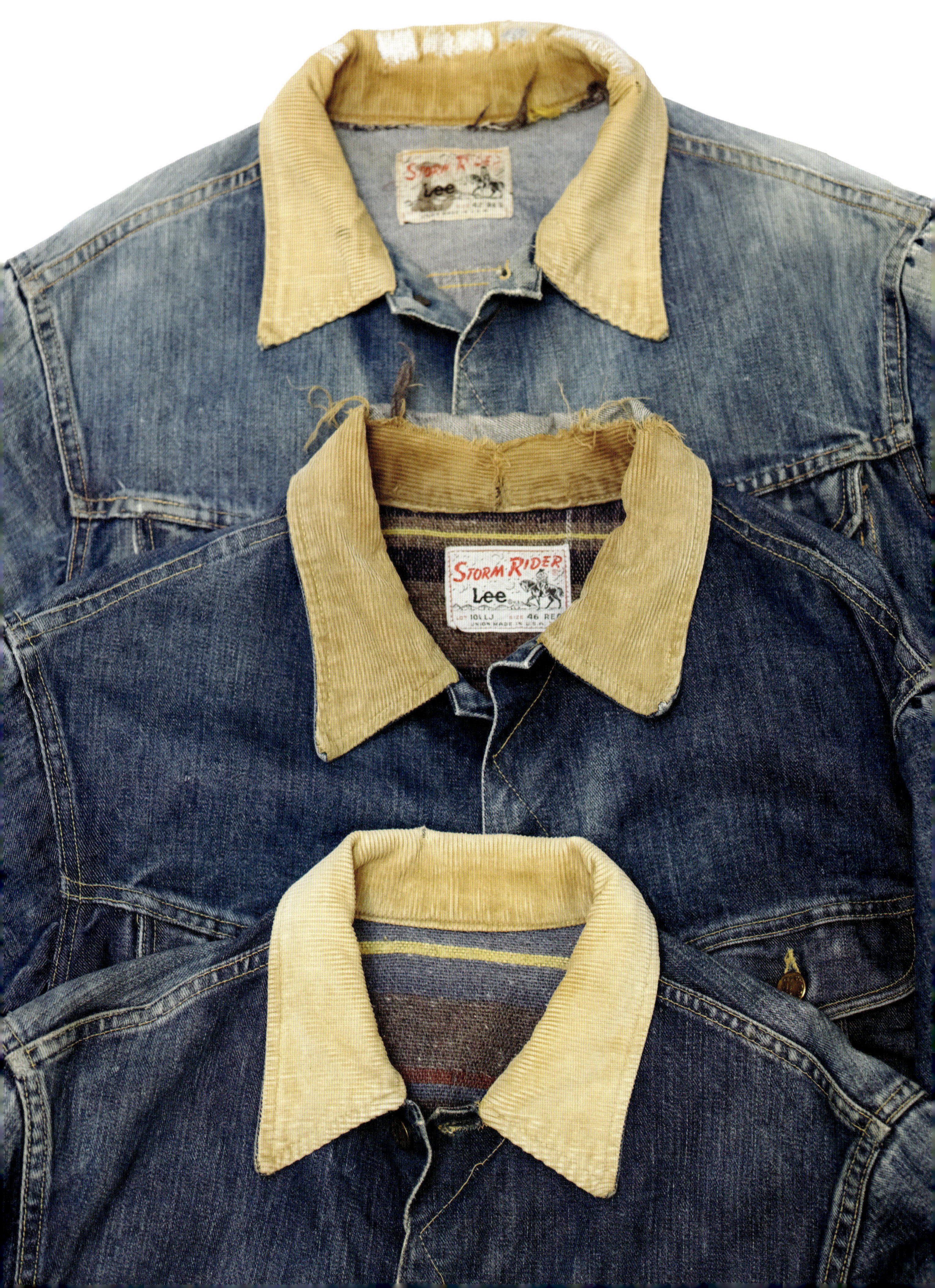

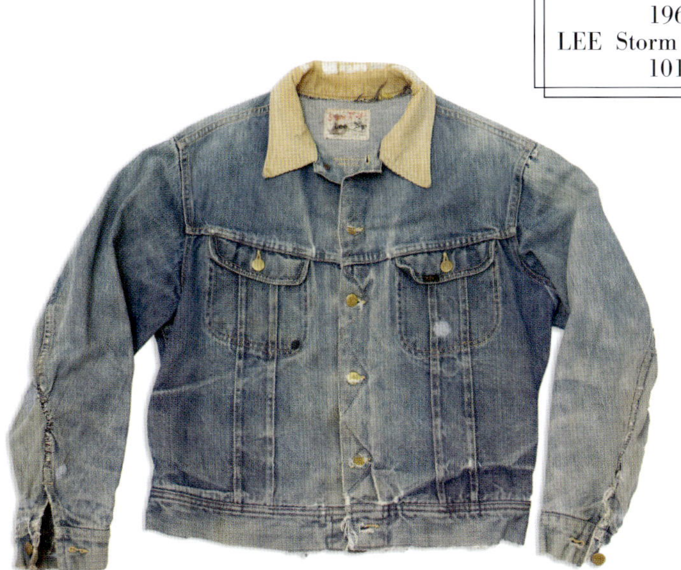

1960's
LEE Storm Rider jacket
101-LJ

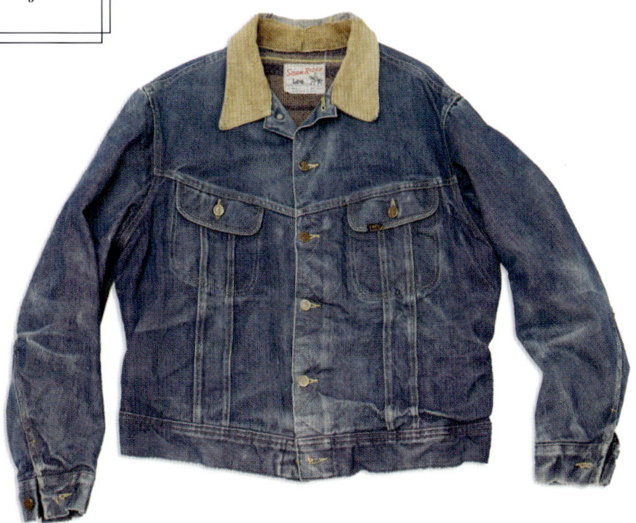

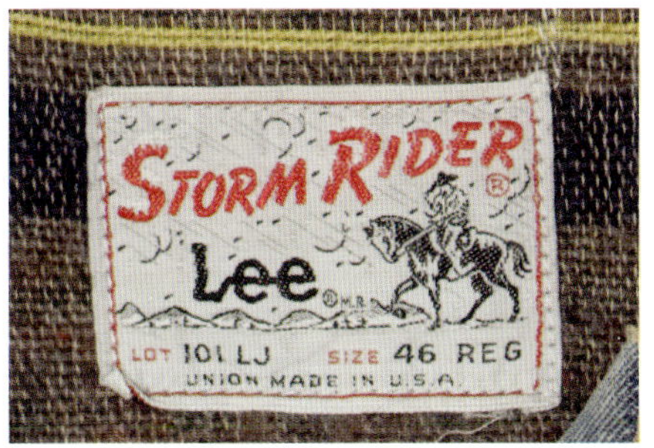

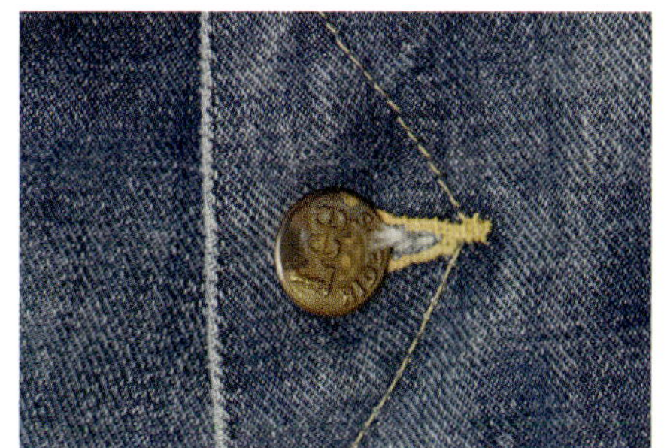

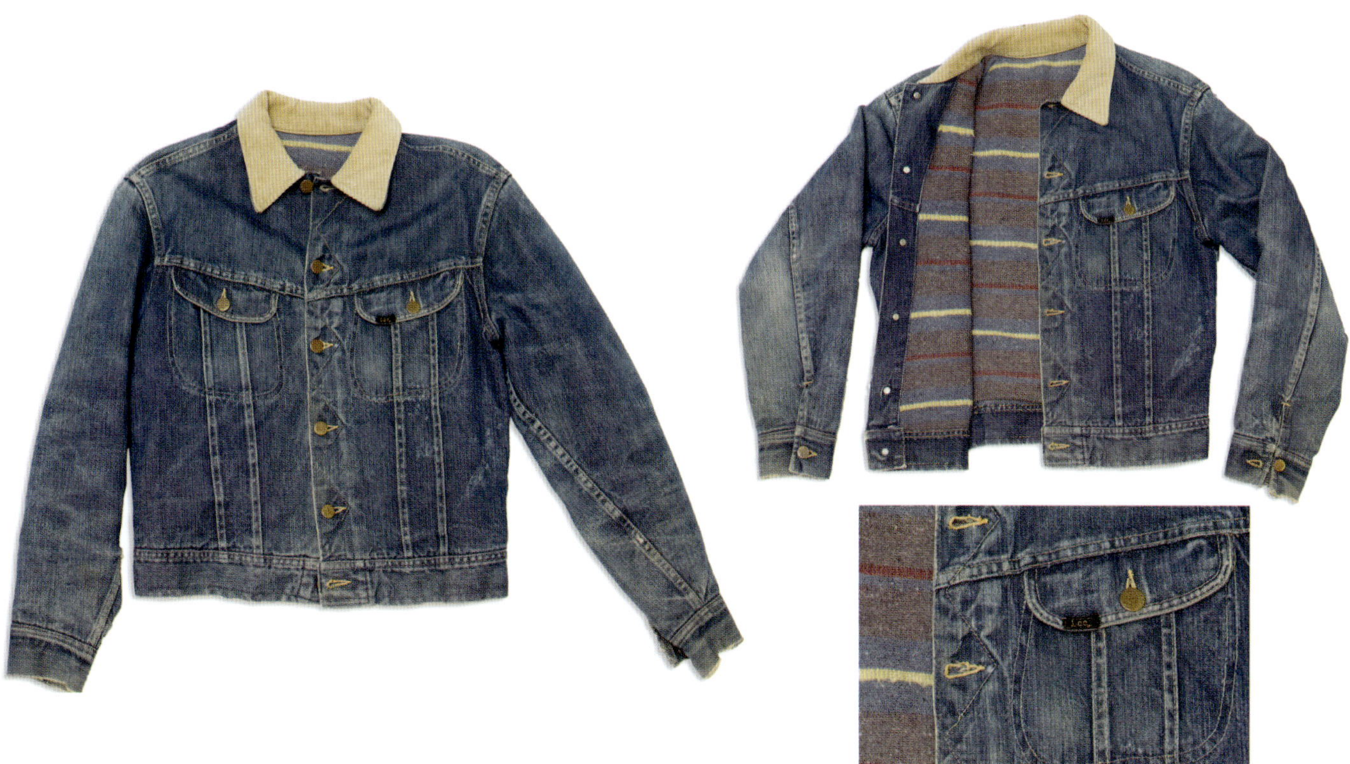

1960's
Wrangler jacket
"Blue Bell"

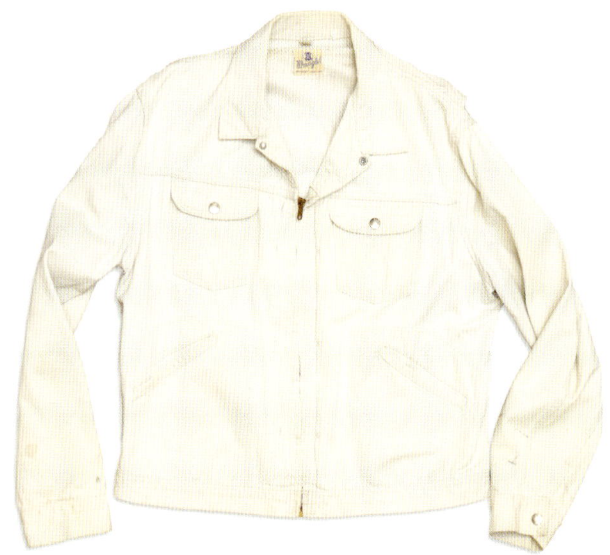

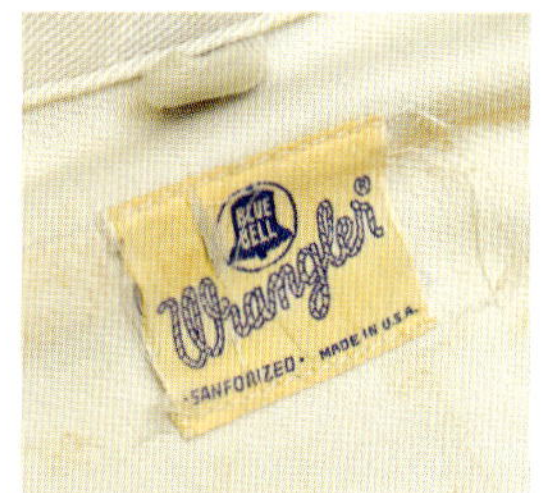

1960's
Wrangler denim jacket
"Blue Bell"

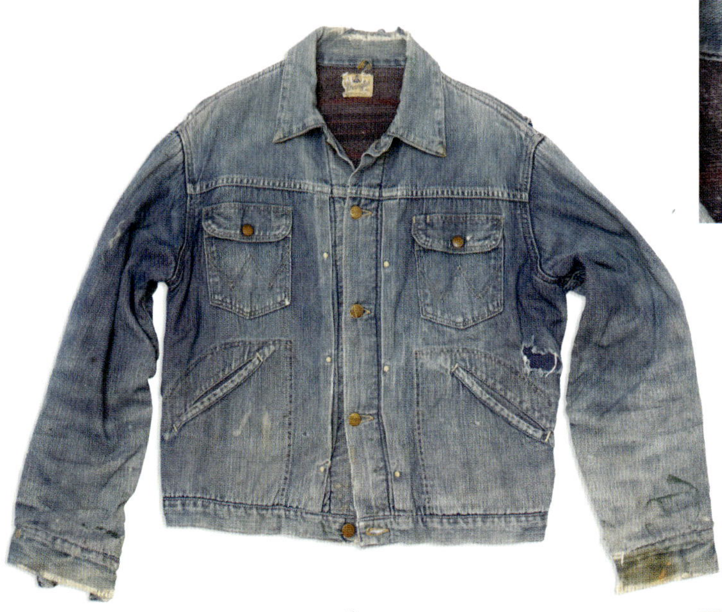

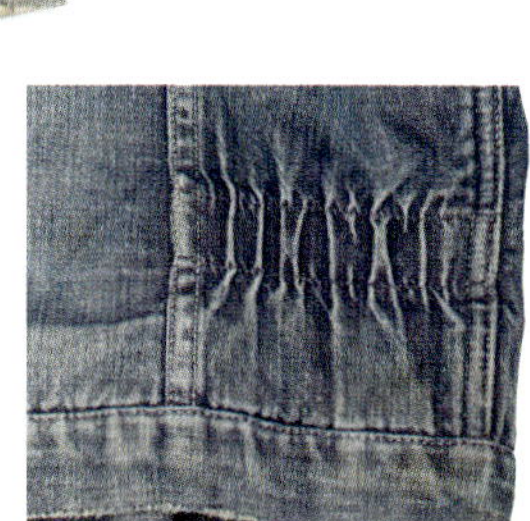

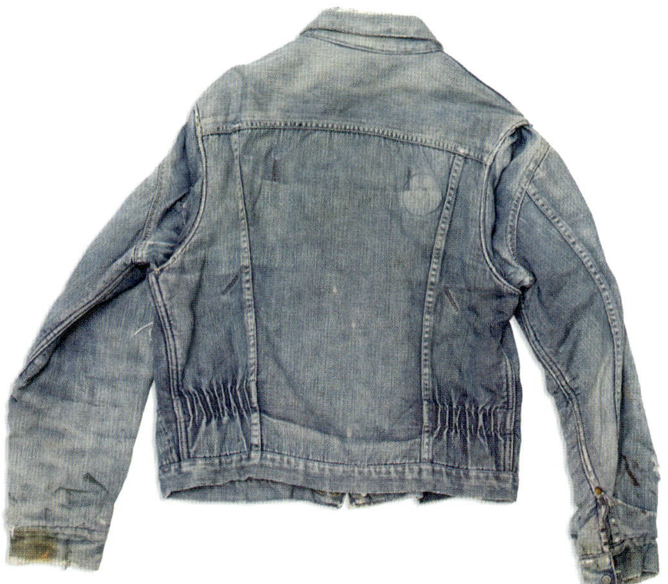

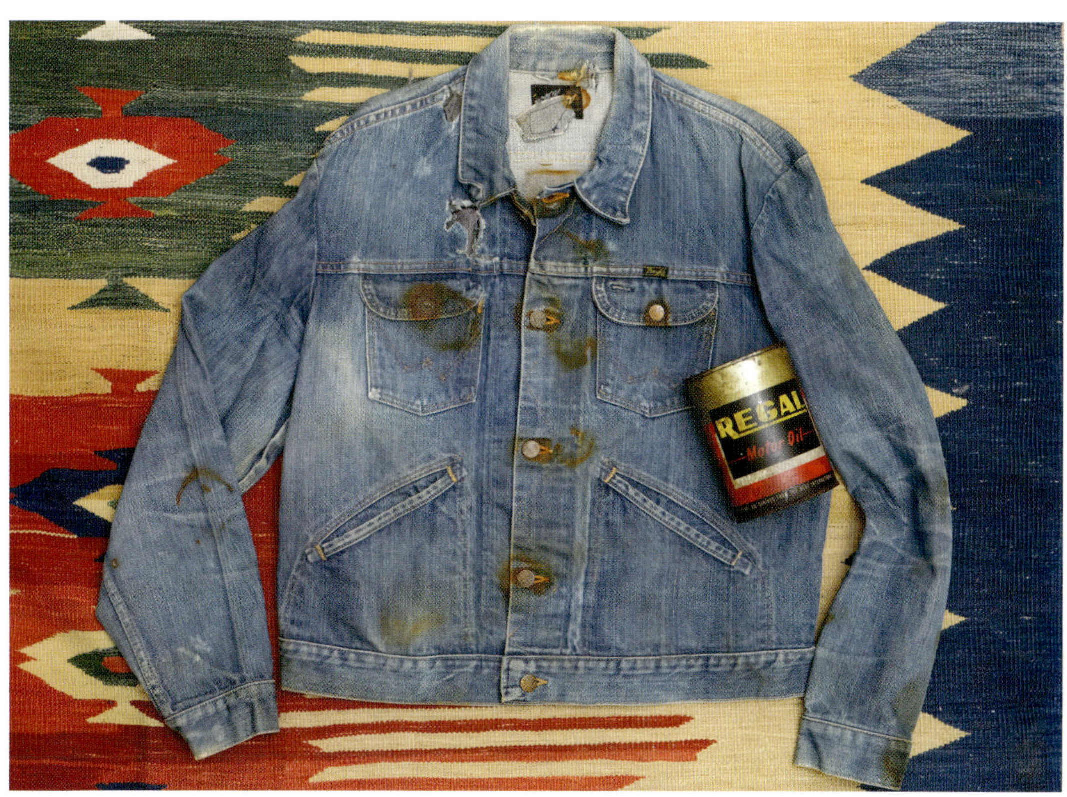

1970's
Wrangler denim jacket
"Black label"

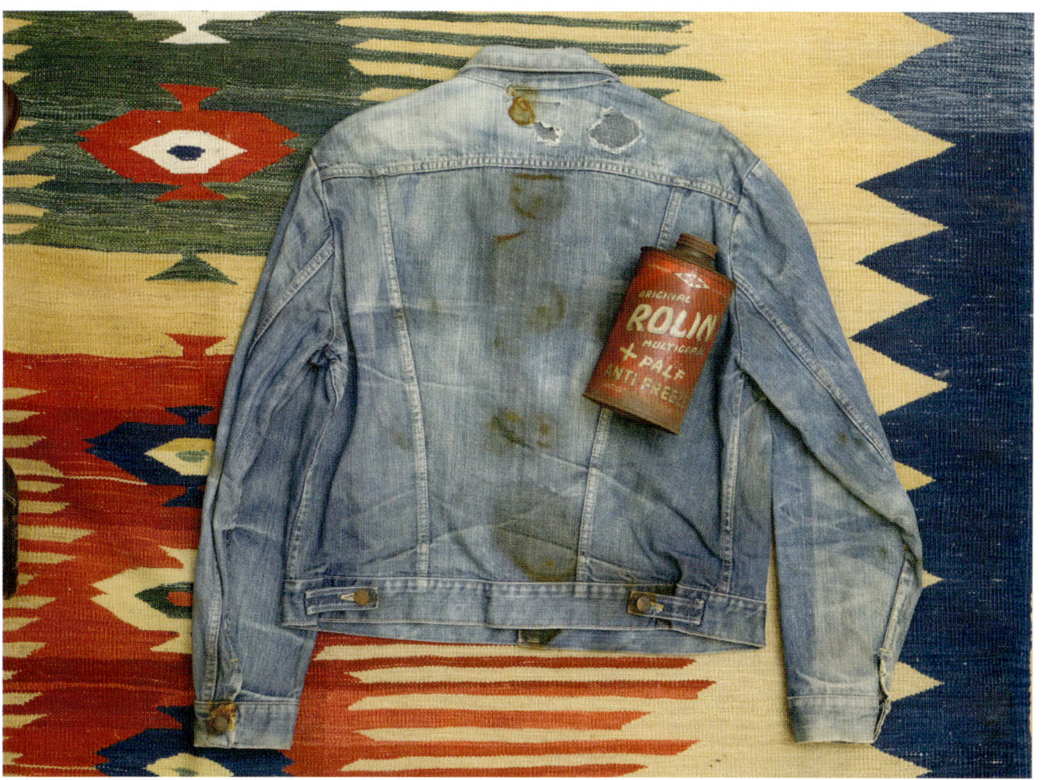

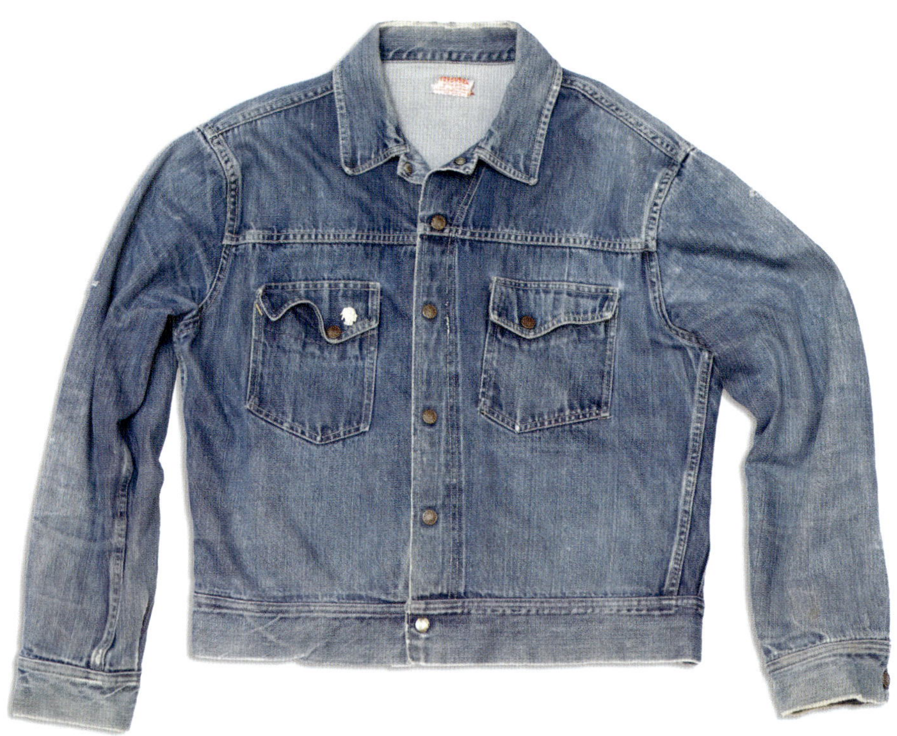

1950's
Longhorn of Texas
denim jacket

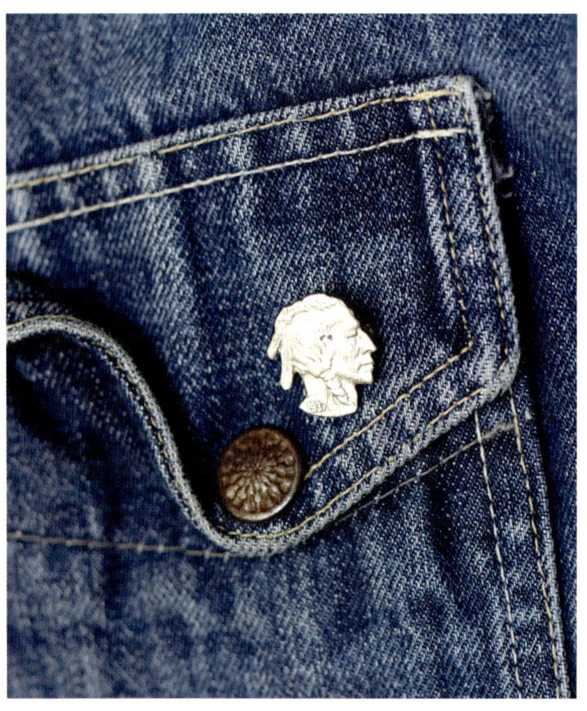

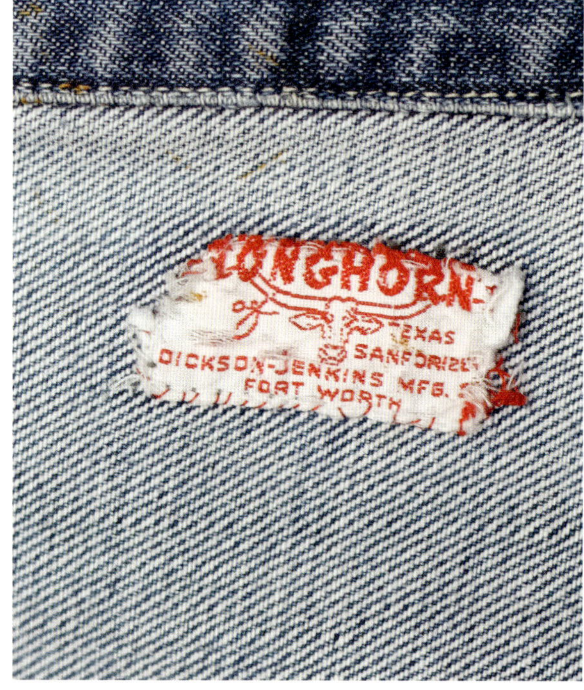

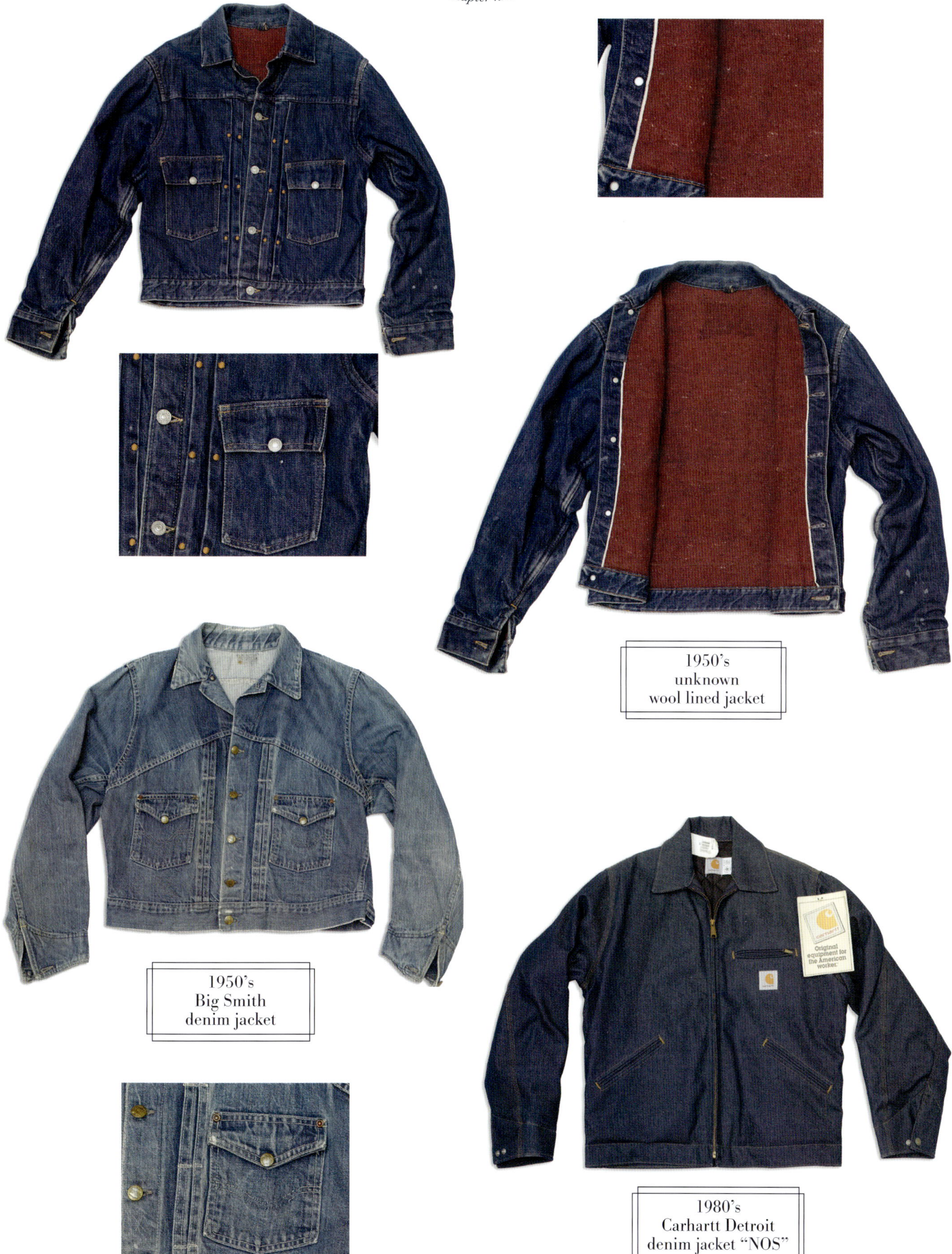

1950's
unknown
wool lined jacket

1950's
Big Smith
denim jacket

1980's
Carhartt Detroit
denim jacket "NOS"

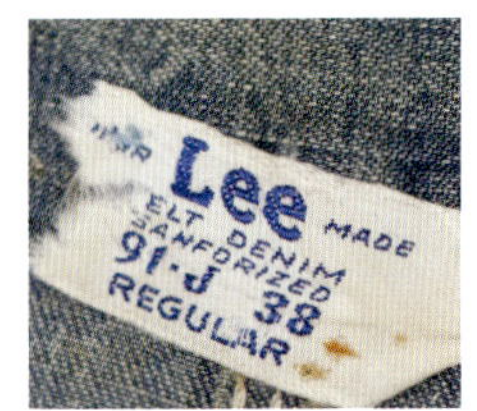

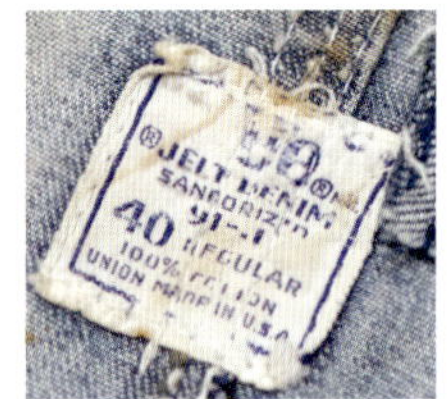

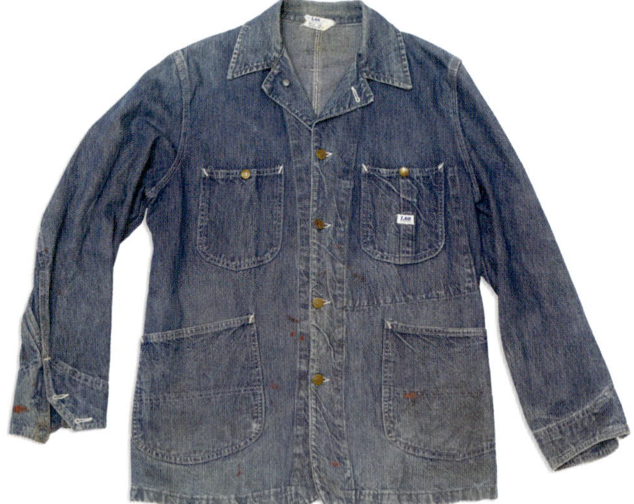

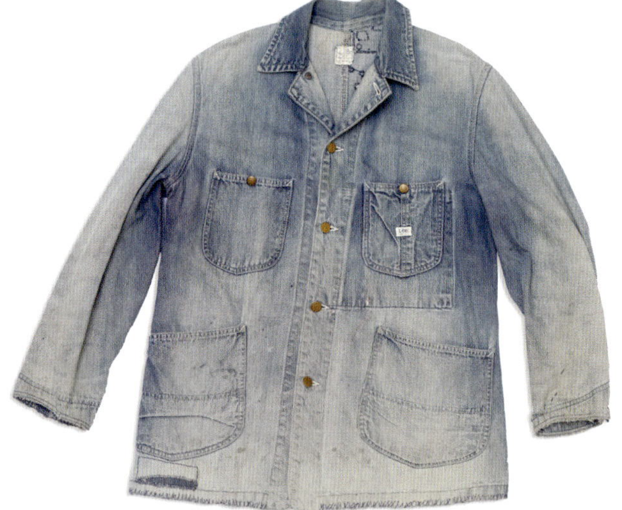

1950's
LEE chore coat
91-J

1950's
LEE chore coat
91-J

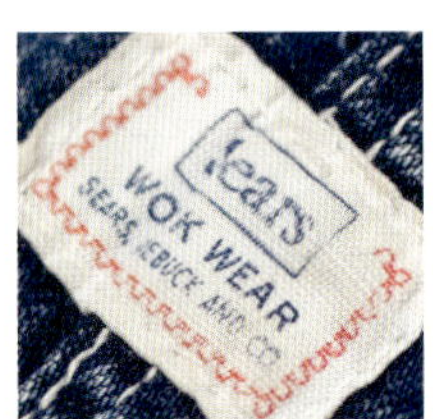

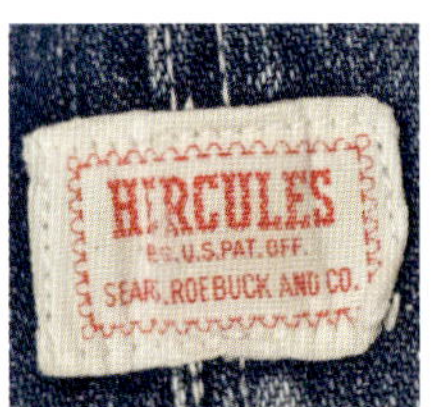

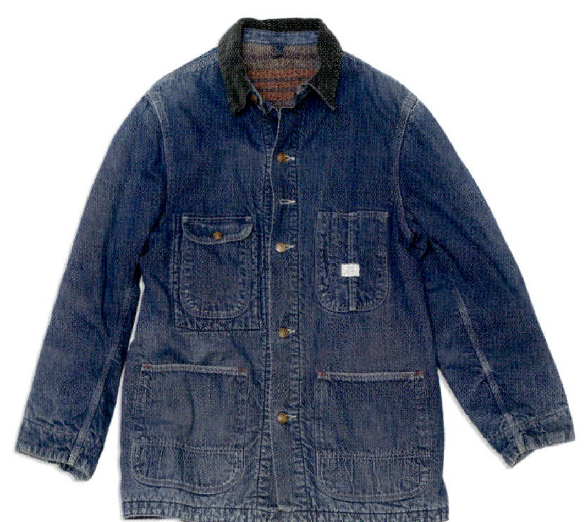

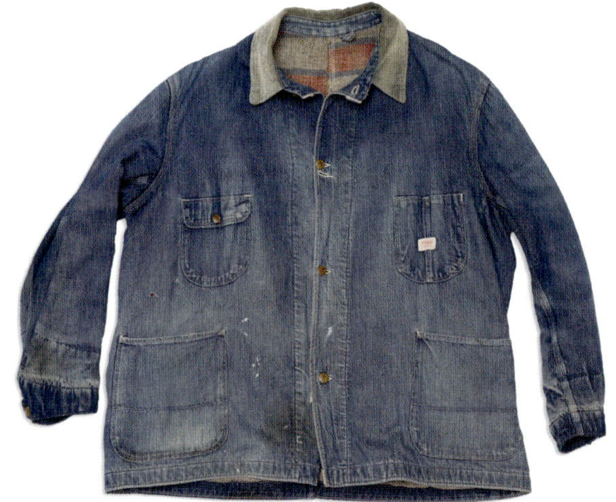

1960's
Sears
chore coat

1950's
Hercules
chore coat

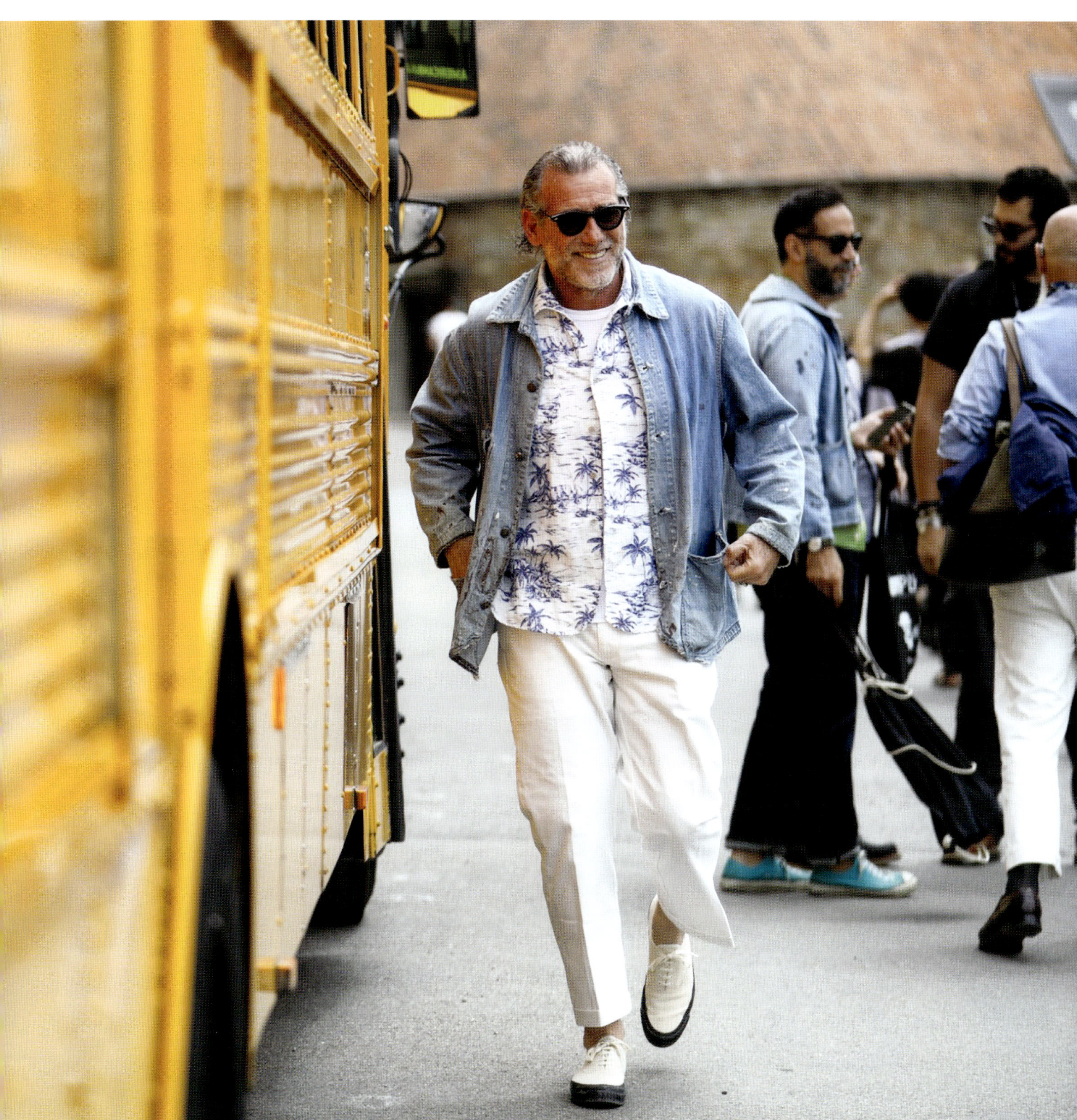

at Pitti Immagine Uomo trade show, Firenze
Alessandro Squarzi photo archive
Courtesy of Gentleman's Journal

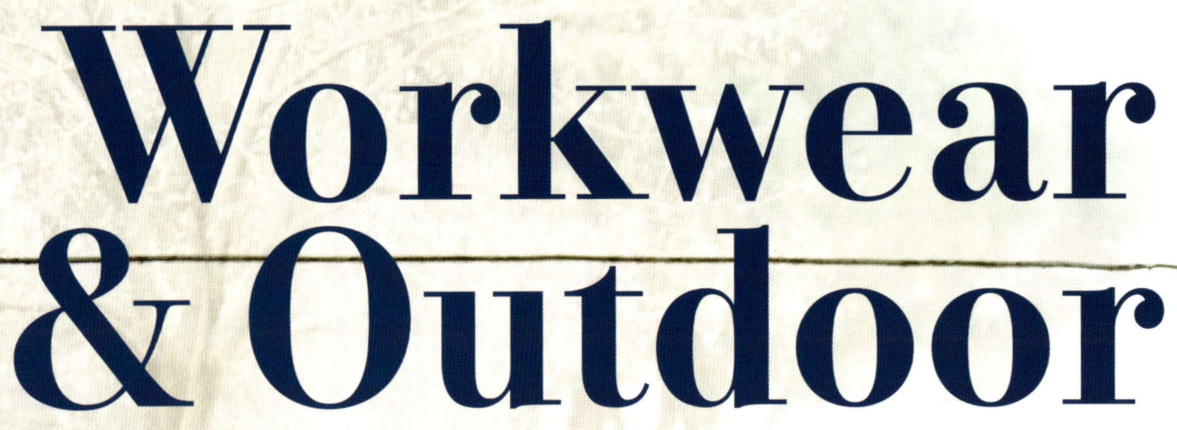

Workwear & Outdoor

CHAPTER
2

*"Cultivating one's projects with passion
is equivalent to the work of a farmer
who cultivates his land and, in due course,
can enjoy the fruits of his labor."*

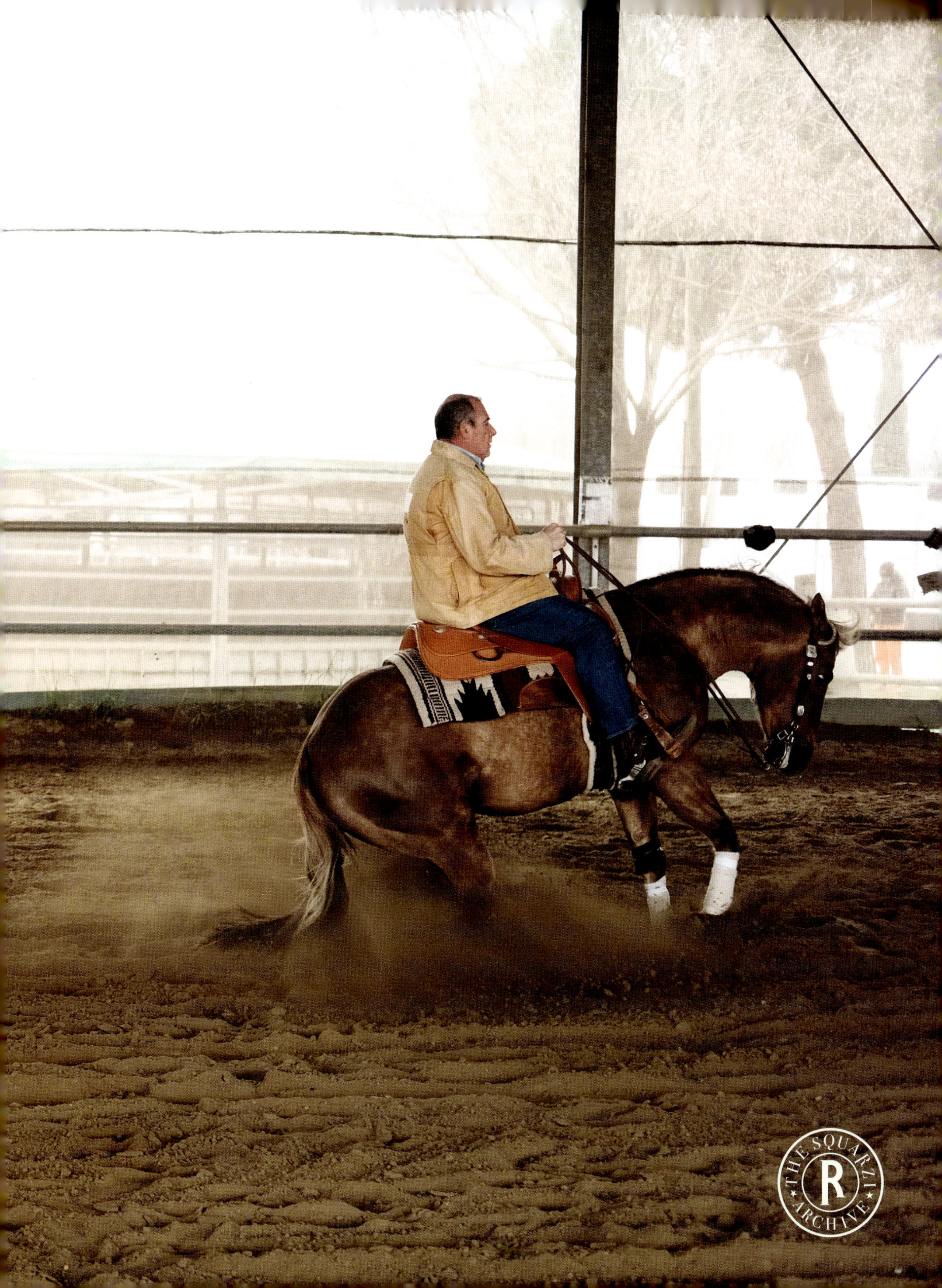
THE SQUARZI
R
ARCHIVE

1950's
Big Mac by Penney's
"shop coat"

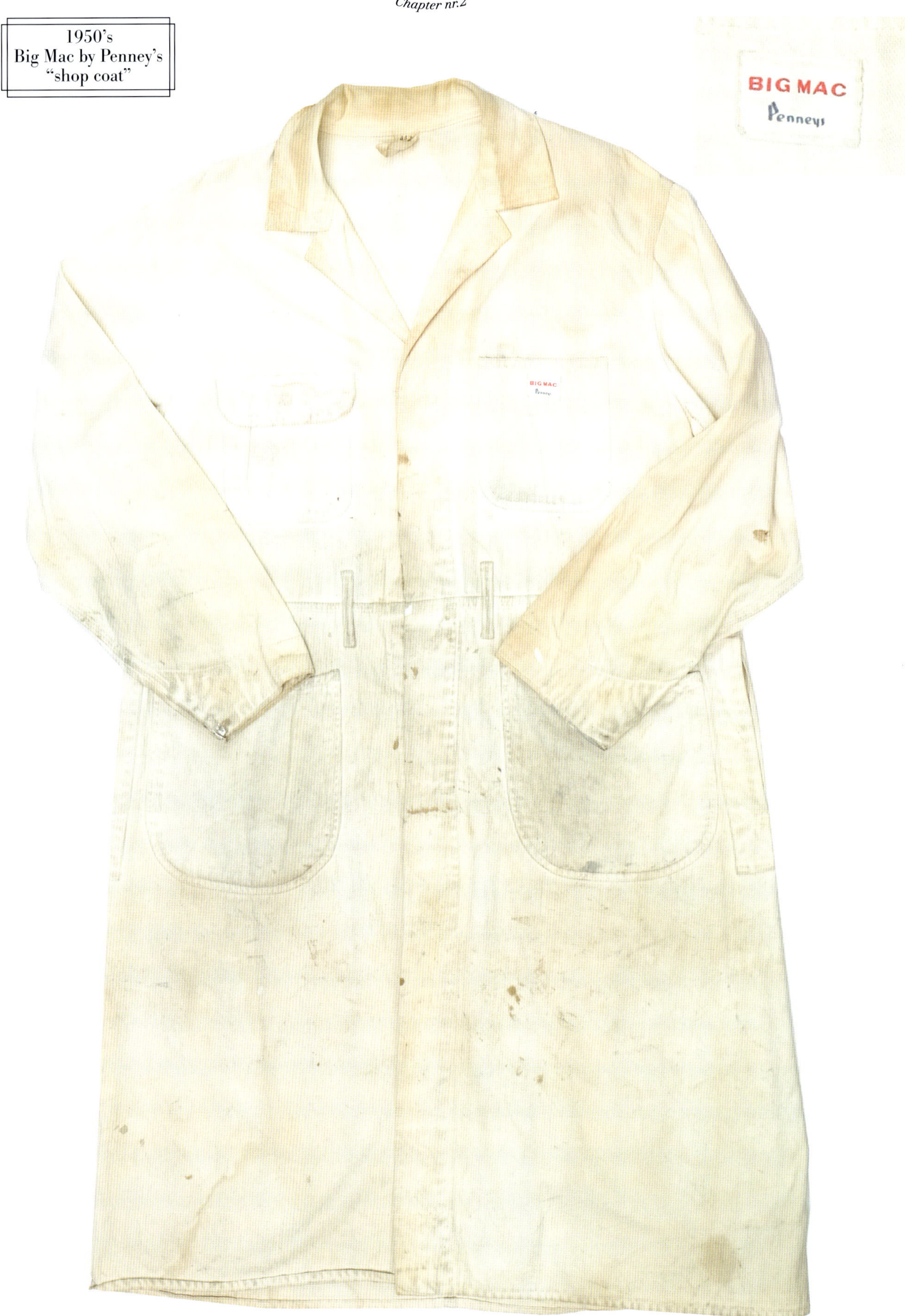

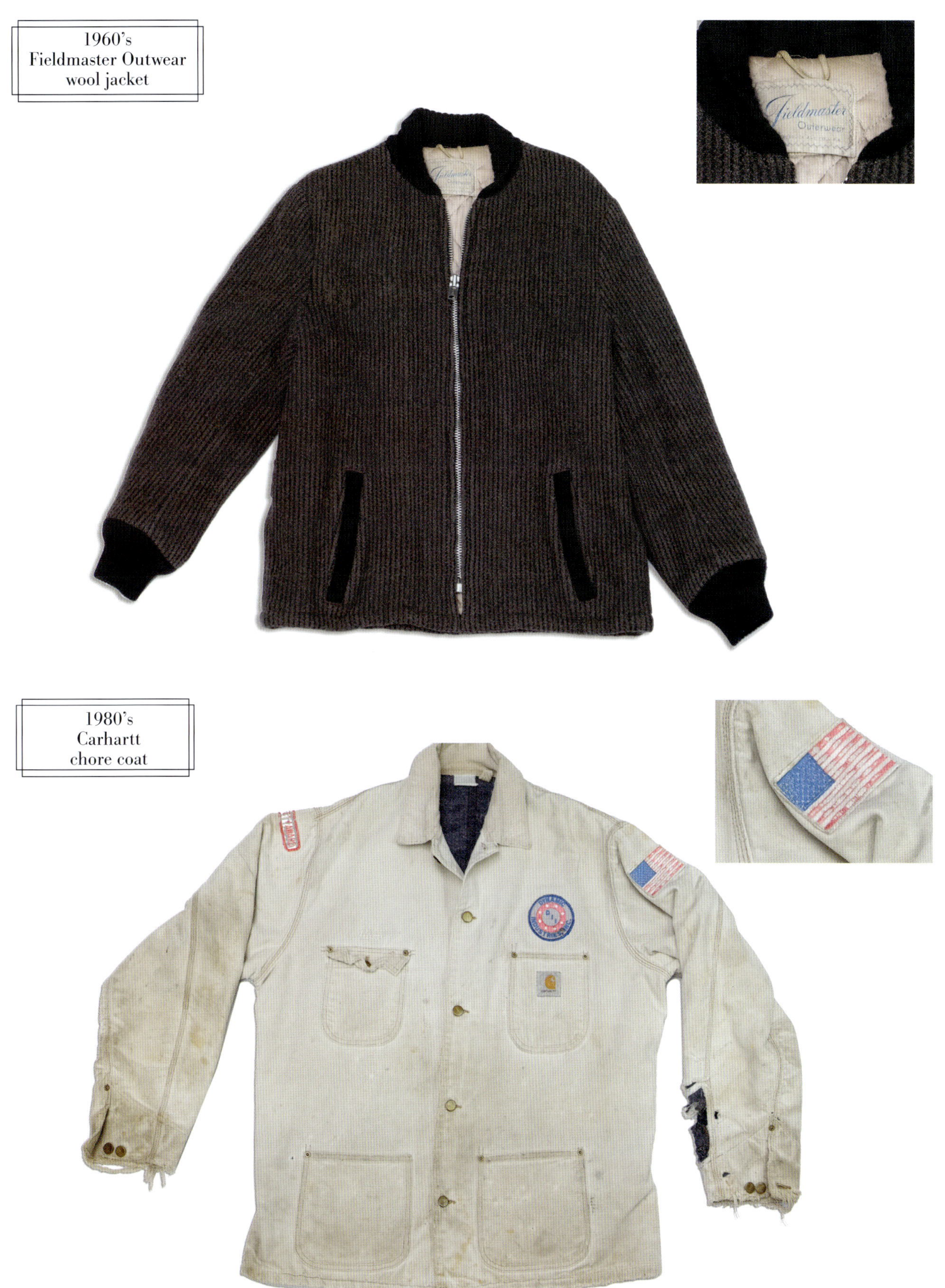

1960's
Fieldmaster Outwear
wool jacket

1980's
Carhartt
chore coat

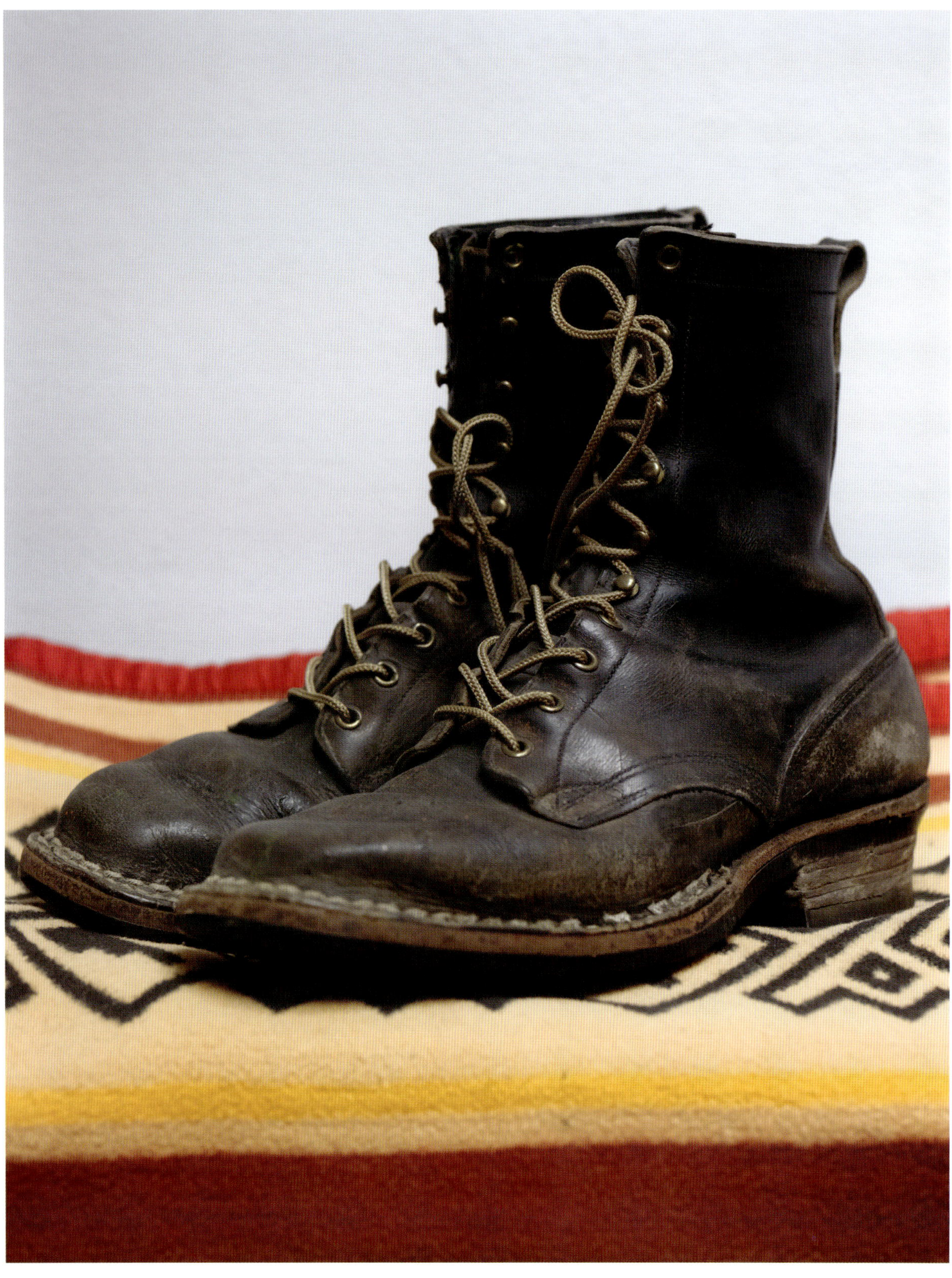

Vintage
unknown
"logger Boots"

1980's
Carhartt Detroit jacket

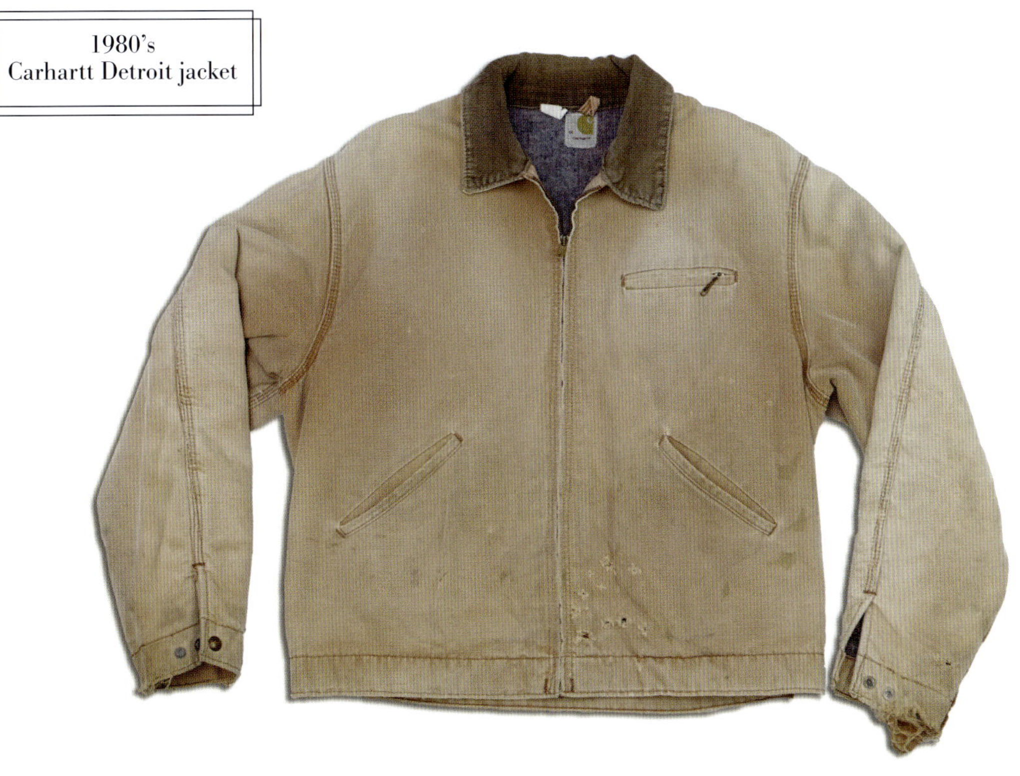

1990's
Dickies pants
"painter"

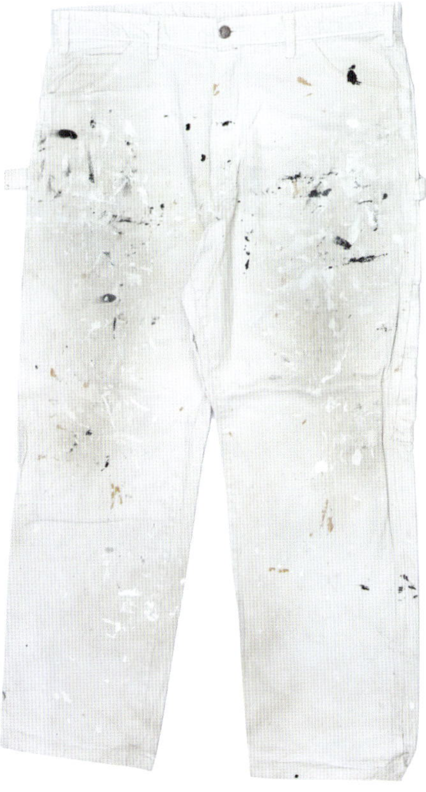

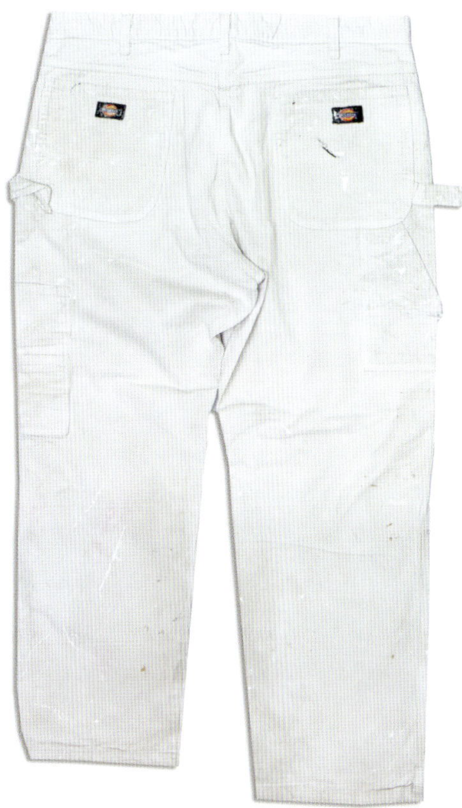

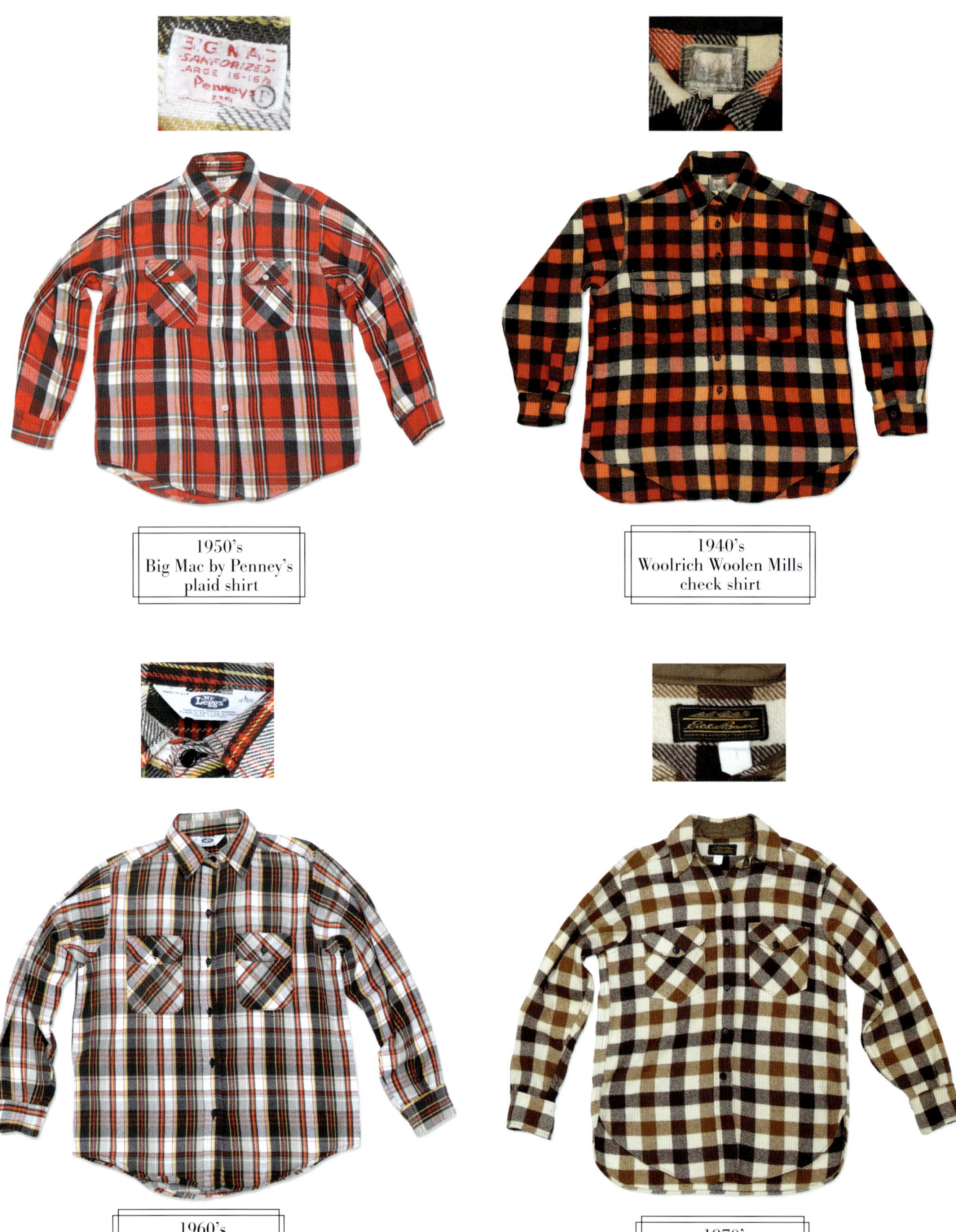

1950's
Big Mac by Penney's
plaid shirt

1940's
Woolrich Woolen Mills
check shirt

1960's
Mr. Leggs
plaid shirt

1970's
Eddie Bauer
check shirt

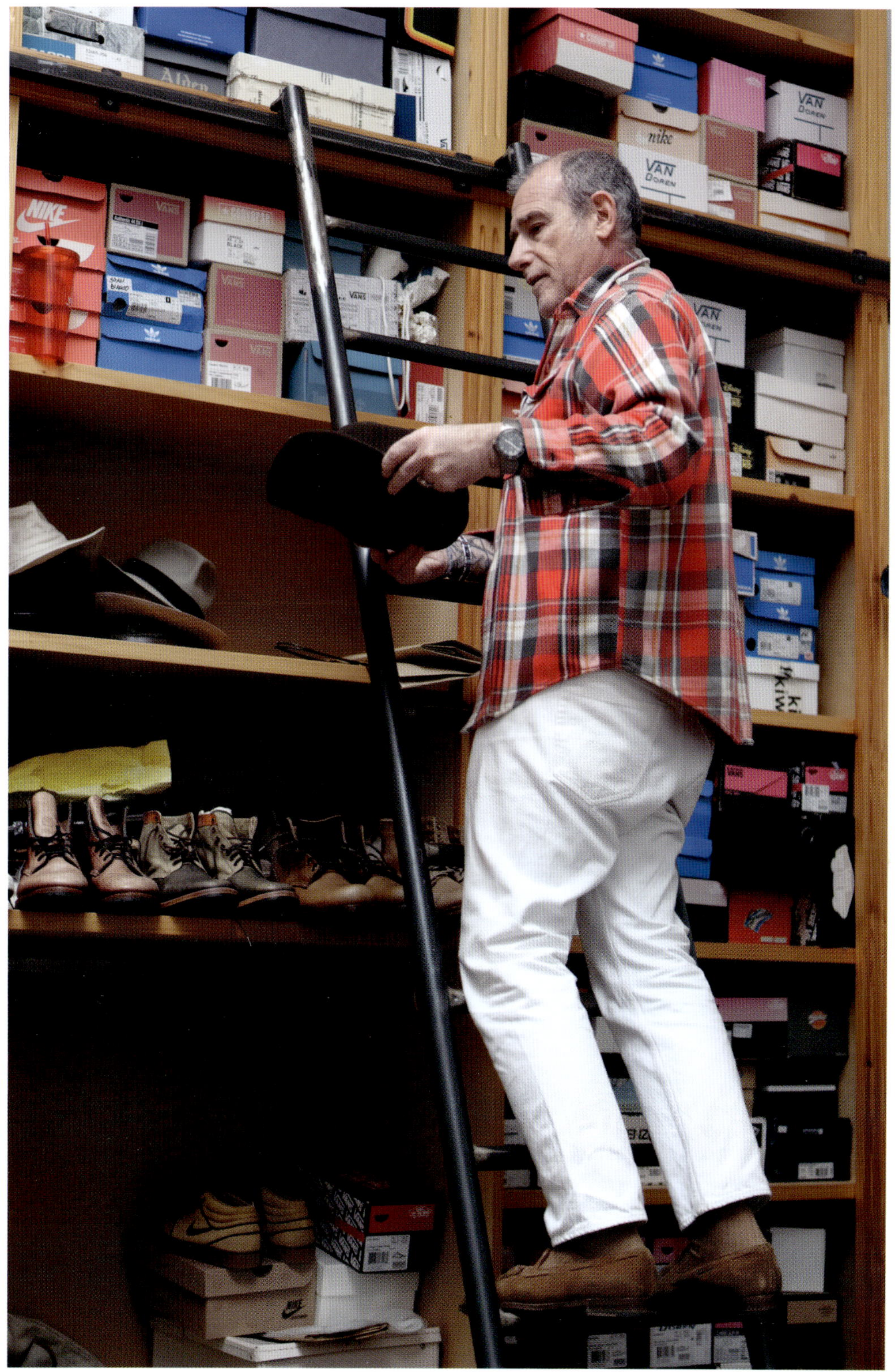

at Alessandro Squarzi archive
Forli

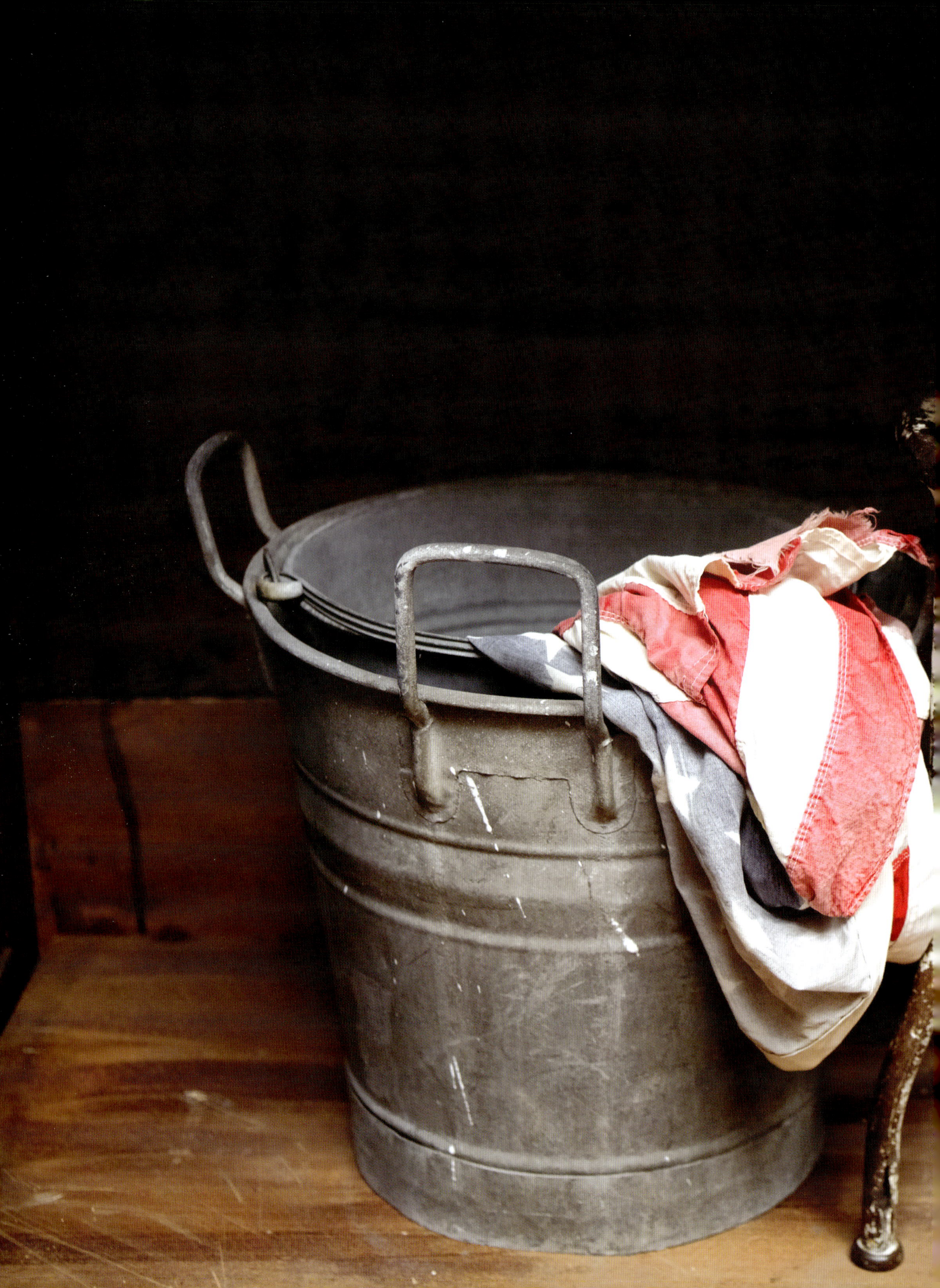

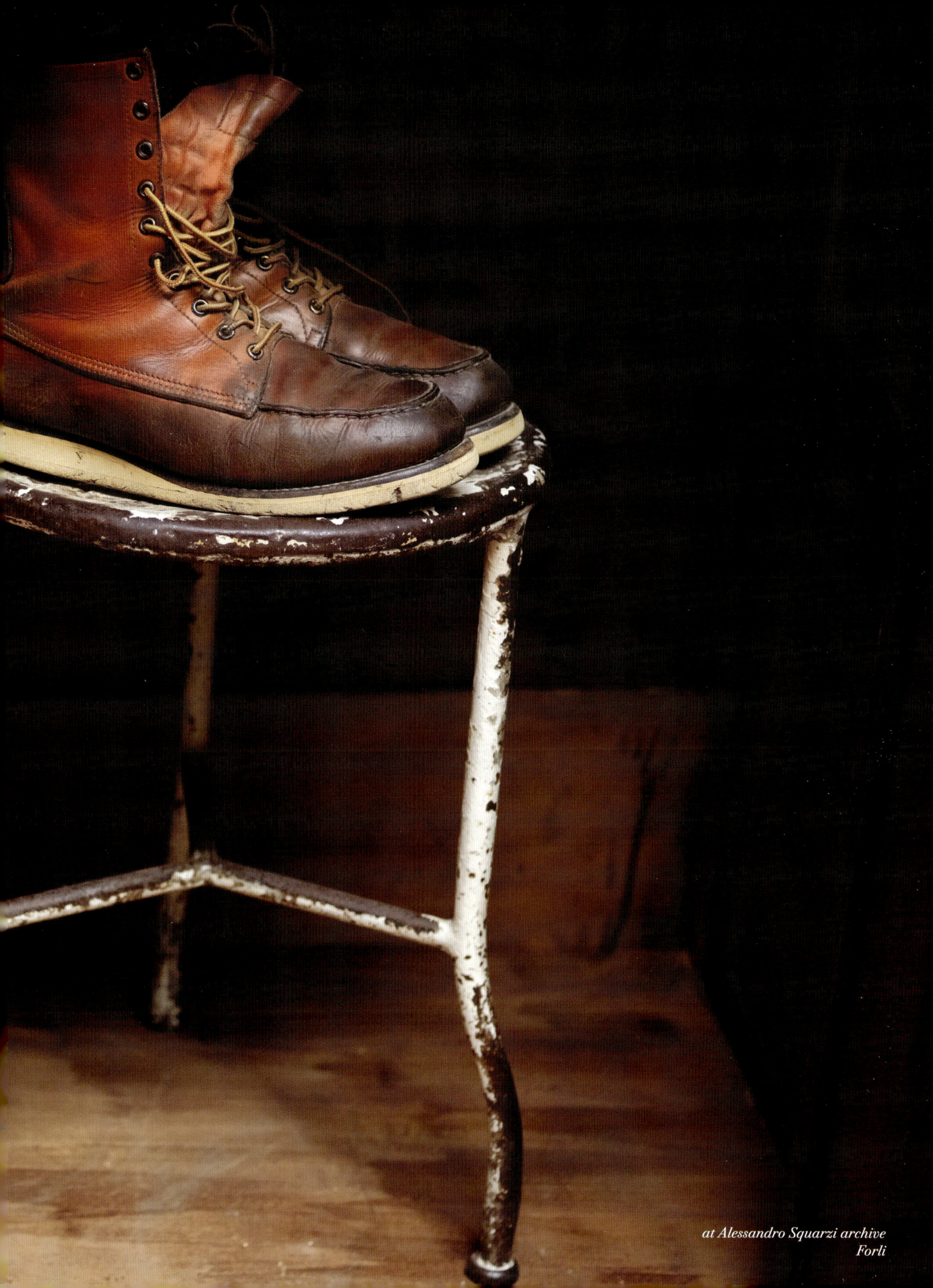

at Alessandro Squarzi archive
Forlì

1940's
Duxbak hunting jacket
buffalo check

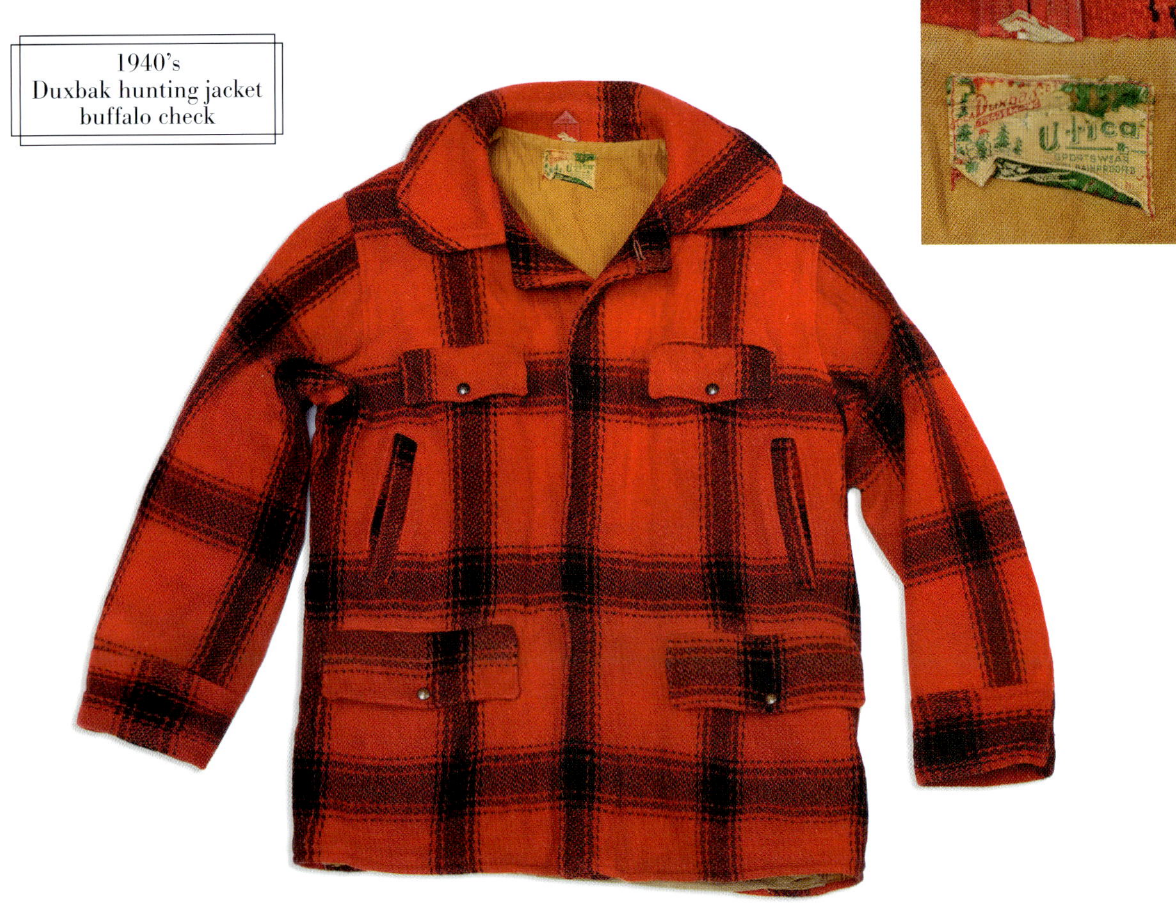

1940's
unknown hunting jacket
buffalo check

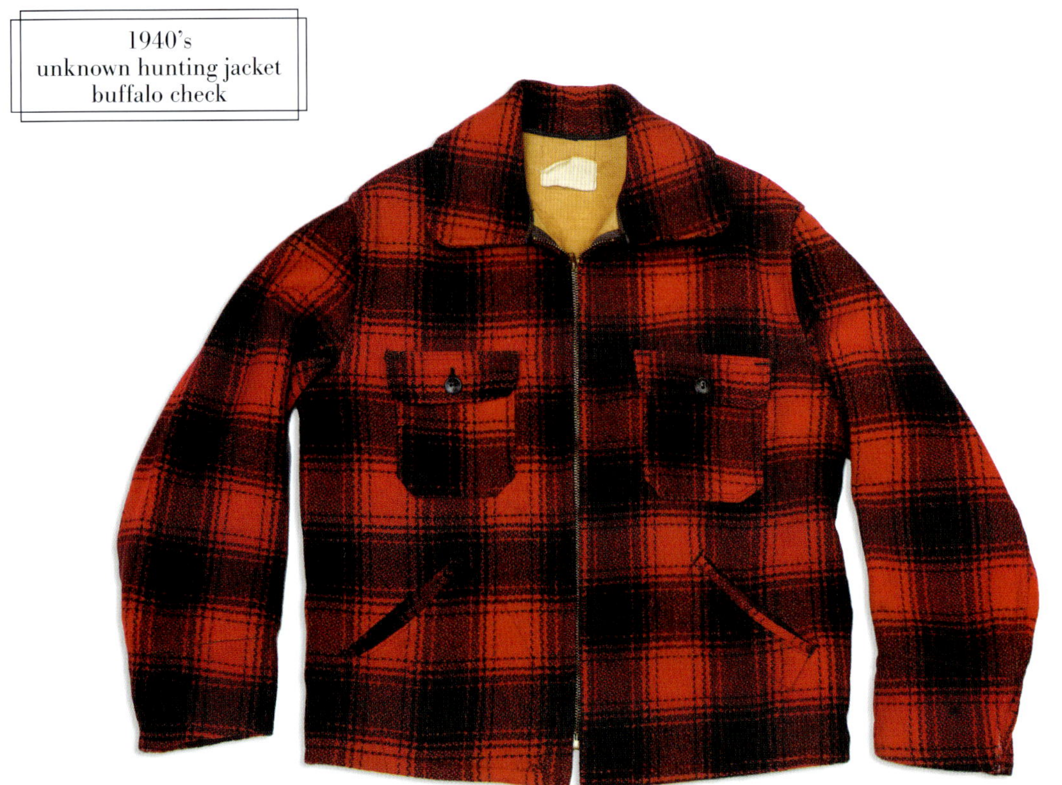

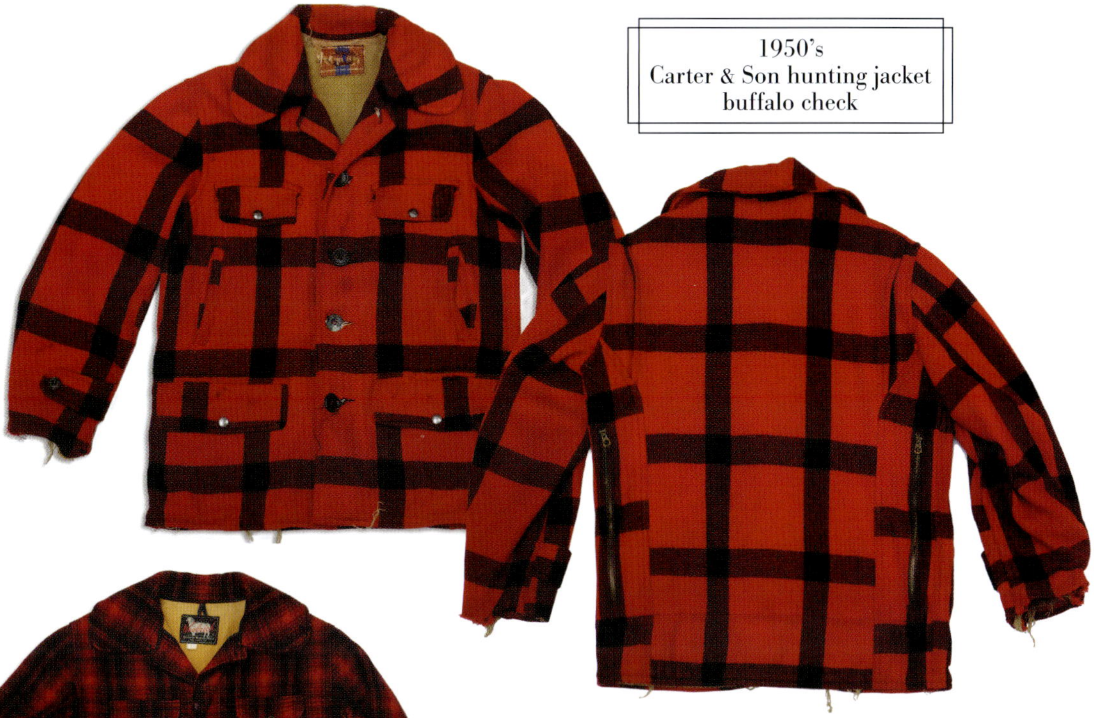

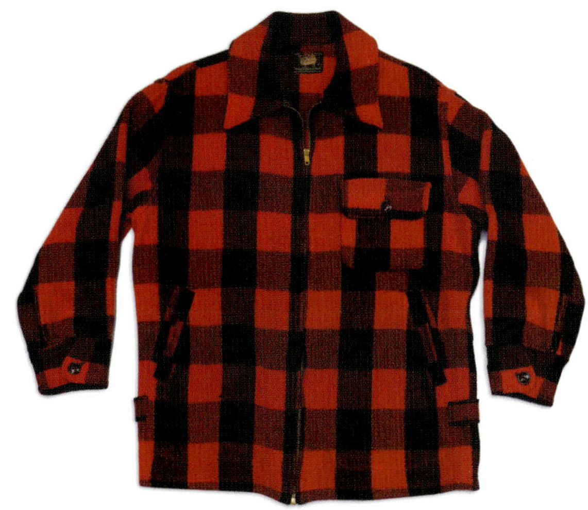

1940's
Woolrich Woolen Mills
hunting jacket, buffalo check

1950's
Carter & Son hunting jacket
buffalo check

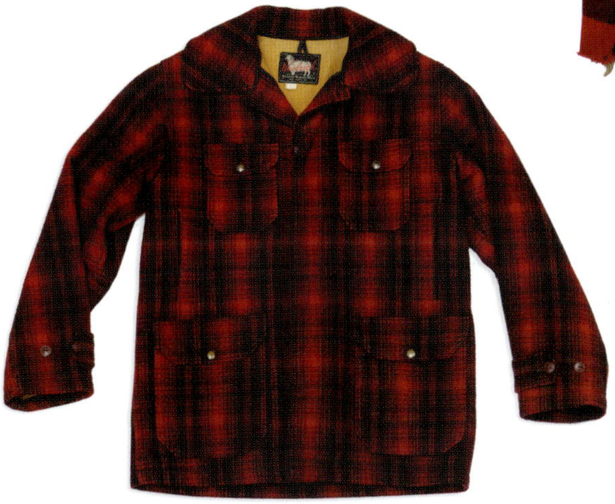

1940's
Woolrich Woolen Mills
hunting jacket, buffalo check

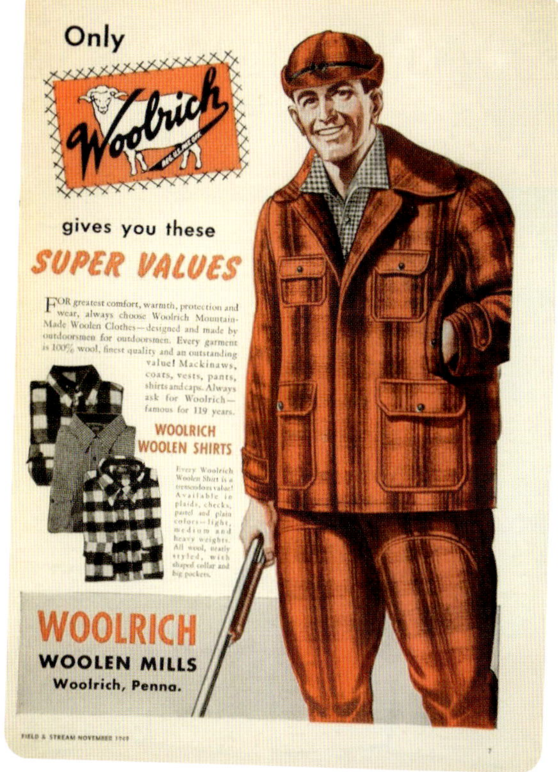

1940's advertising

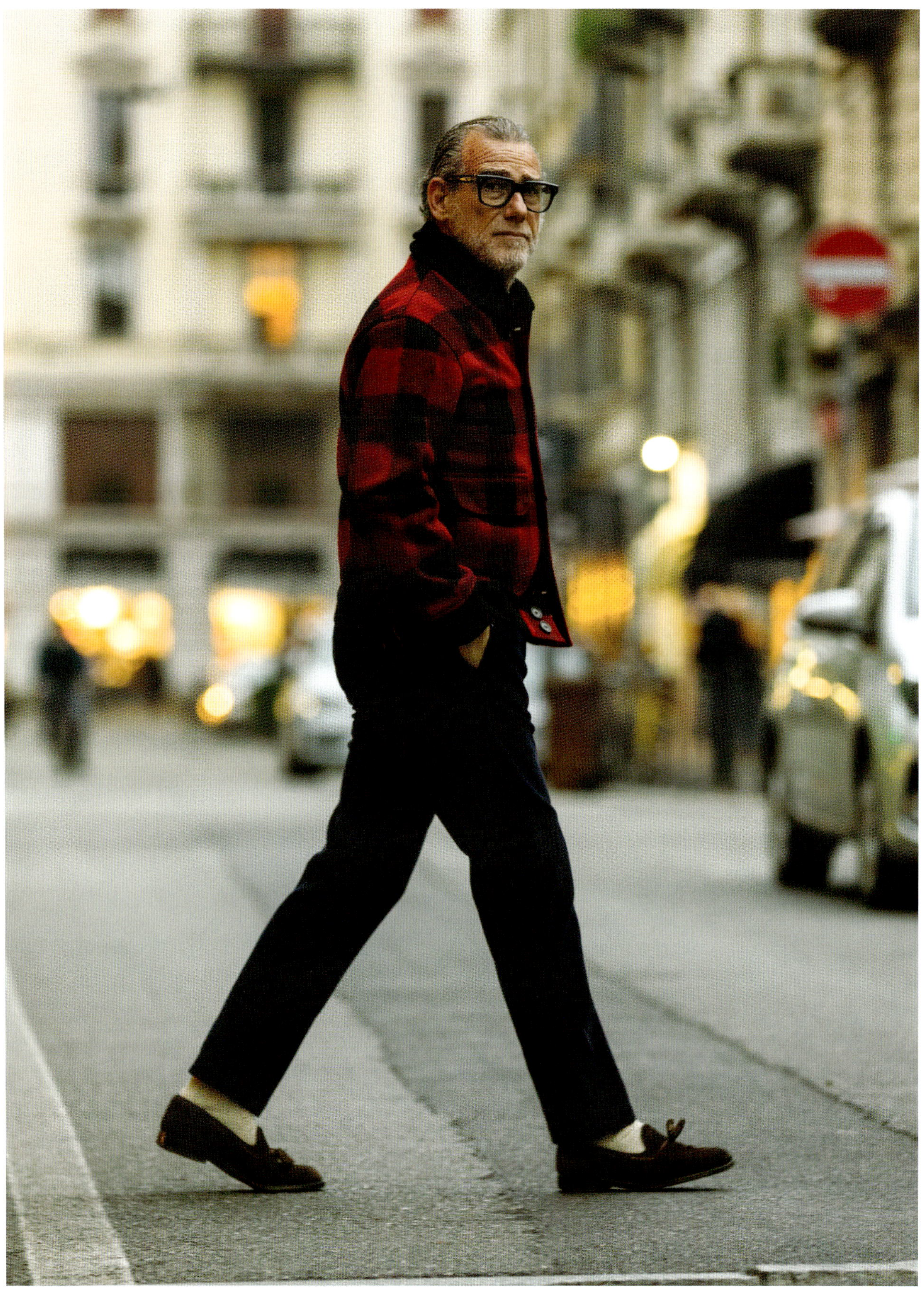

Downtown, Milano
Alessandro Squarzi photo archive
Courtesy of Matteo Bianchessi

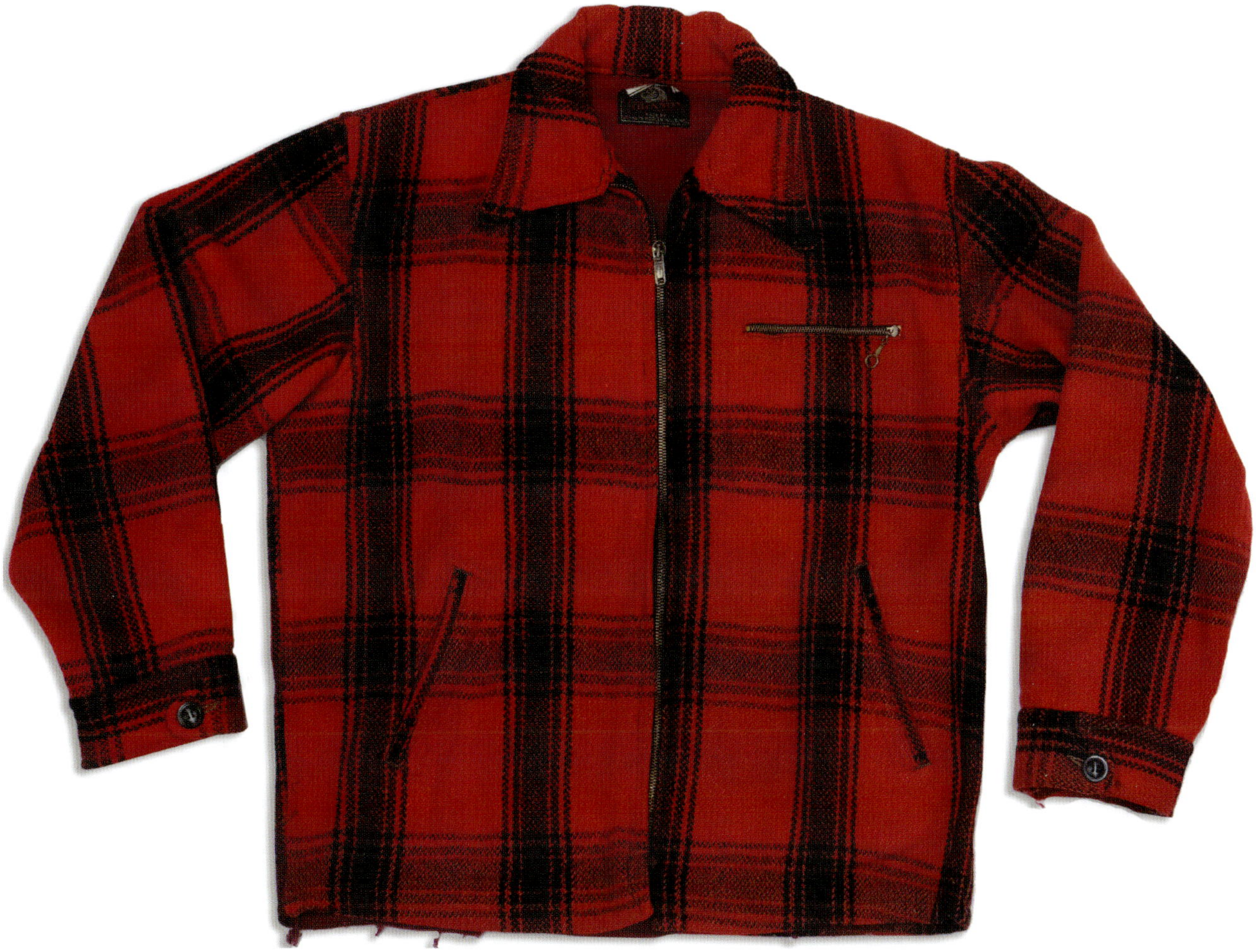

1950's
Johnson hunting jacket
buffalo check

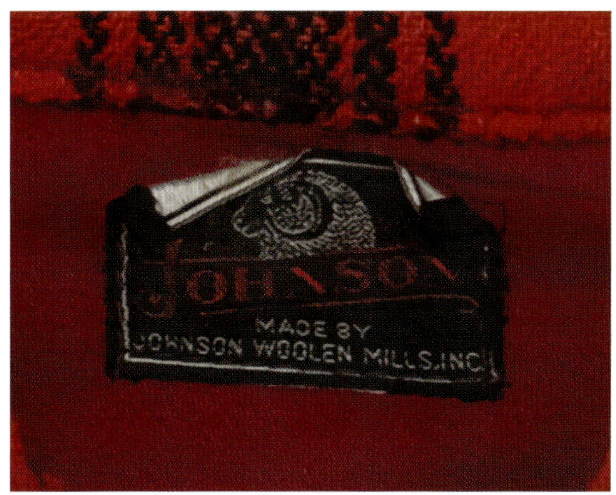

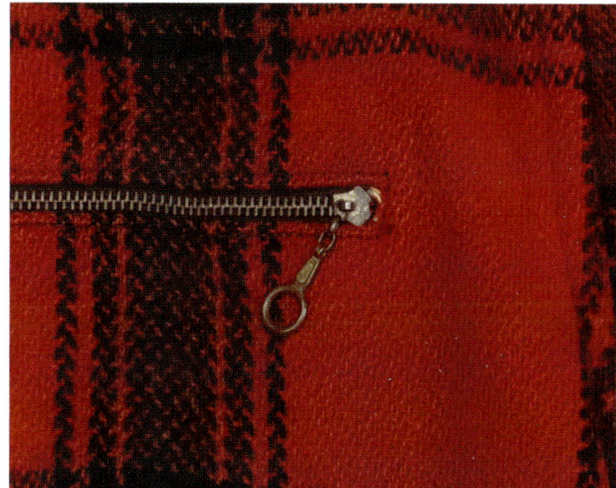

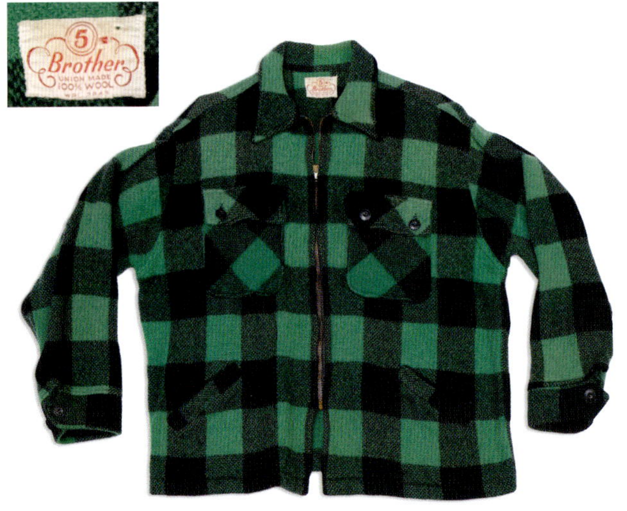

1960's
5 Brother wool jacket
buffalo check

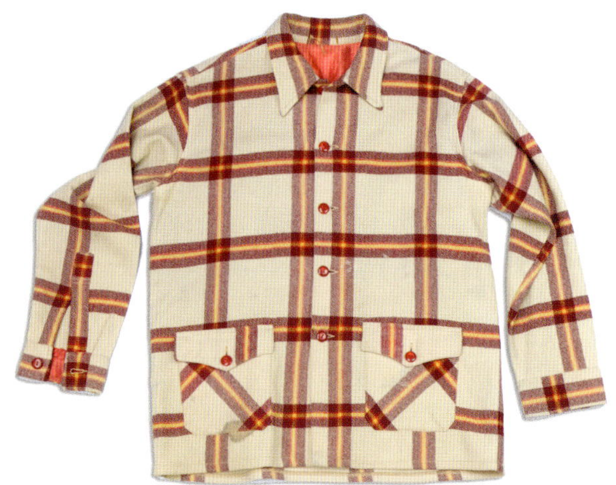

1940's
unknown wool jacket
plaid

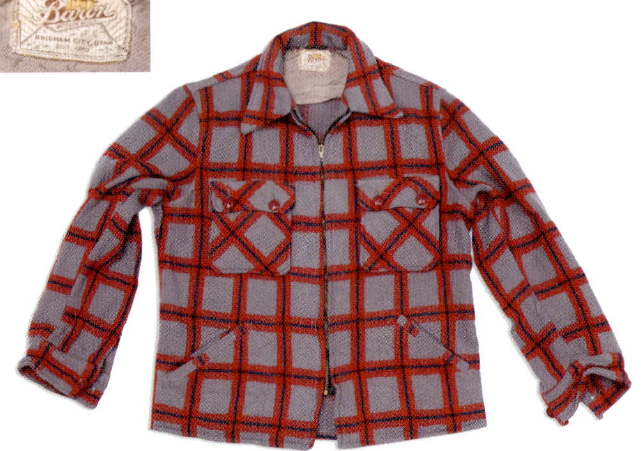

1950's
Baron wool jacket
plaid

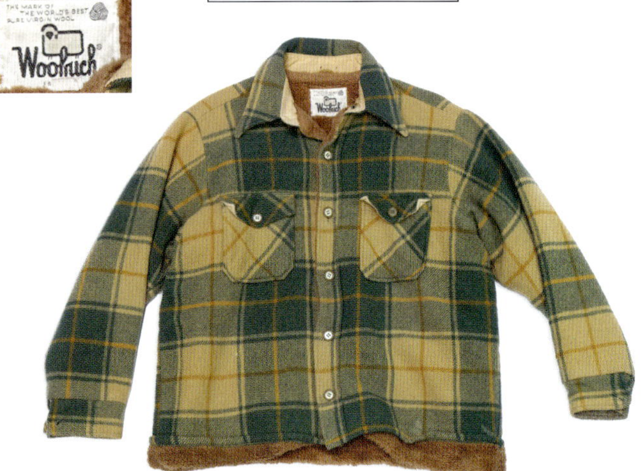

1970's
Woolrich overshirt
plaid, fur lined

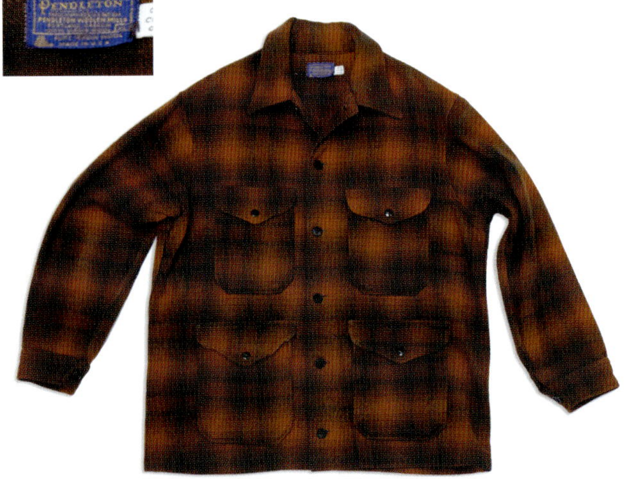

1960's
Pendleton wool jacket
plaid

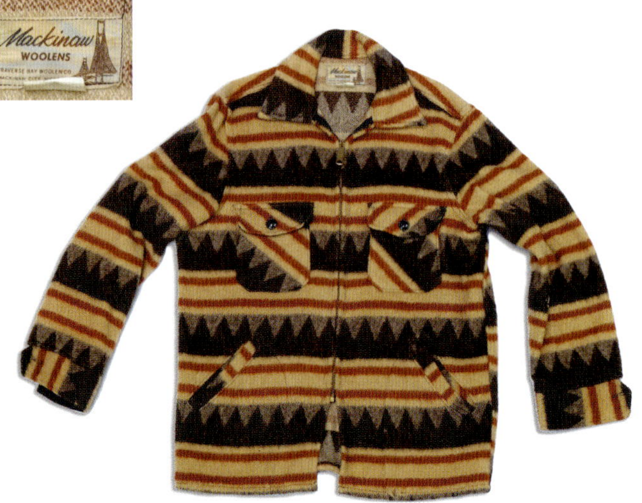

1970's
Mackinaw Woolens jacket
native pattern

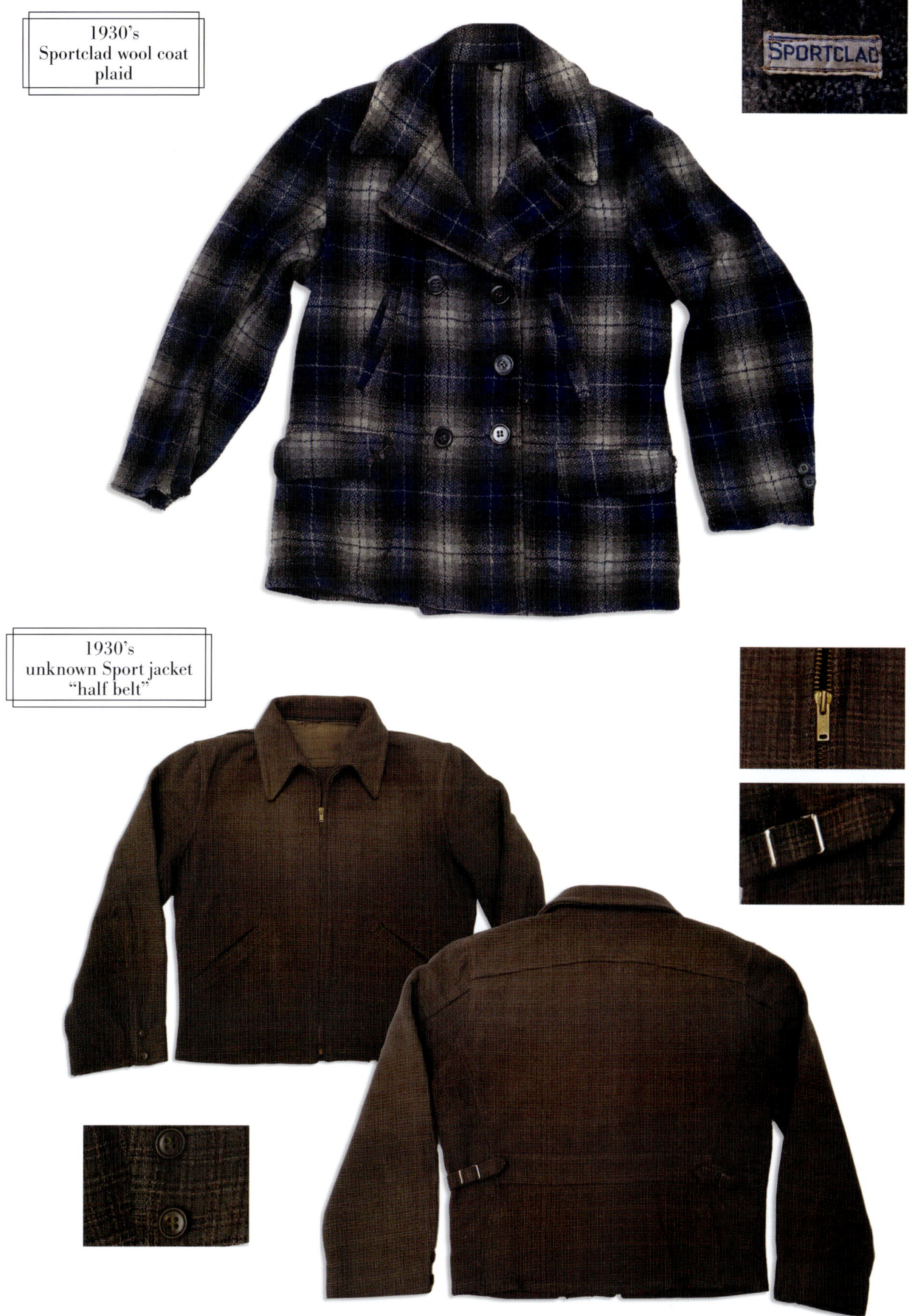

1930's
Sportclad wool coat
plaid

1930's
unknown Sport jacket
"half belt"

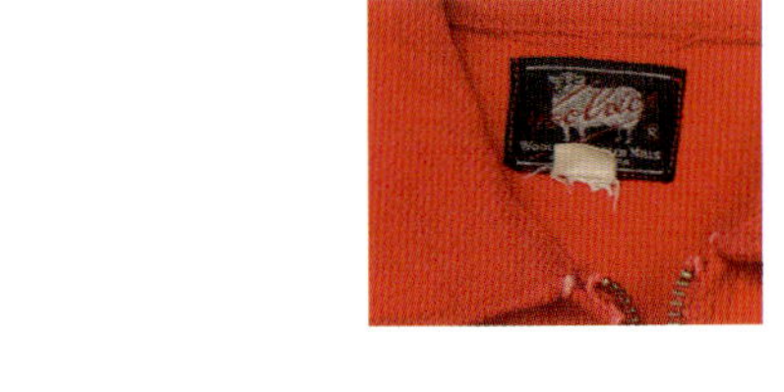

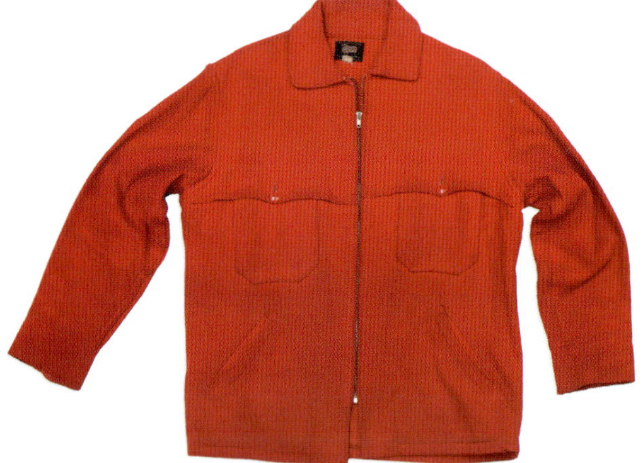

1940's
Woolrich Woolen Mills
wool jacket

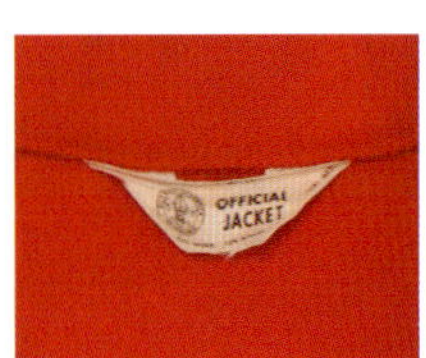

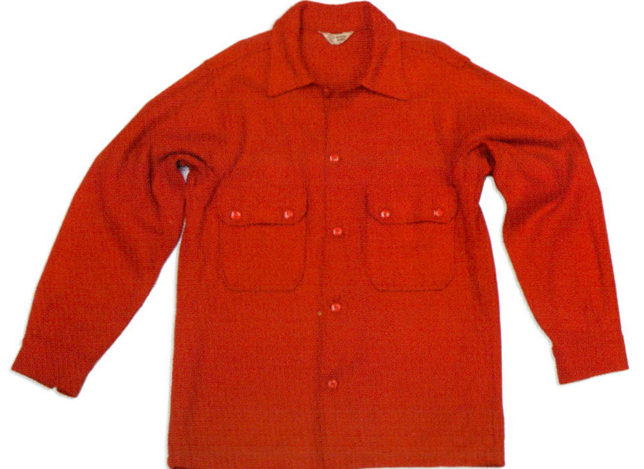

1950's
Boys Scout of America
wool shirt

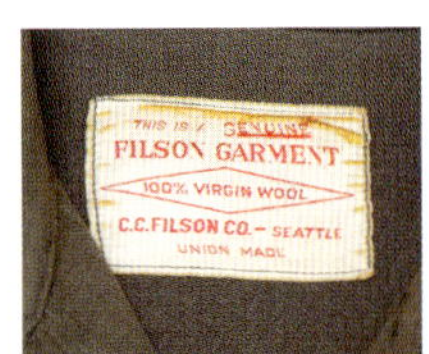

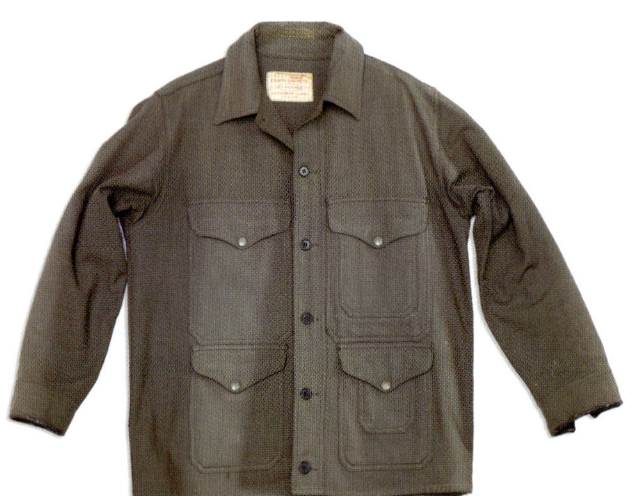

1950's
Filson Garment
wool jacket

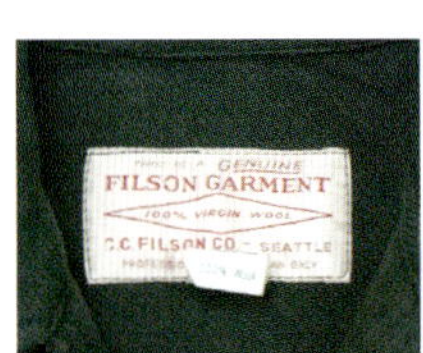

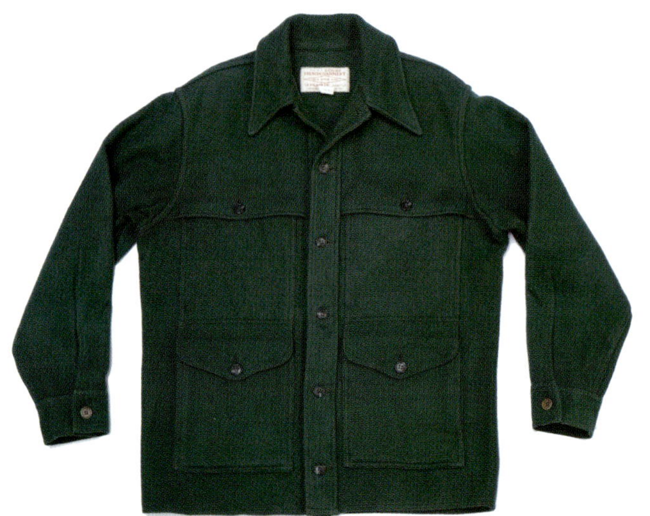

1970's
Filson Garment
wool jacket

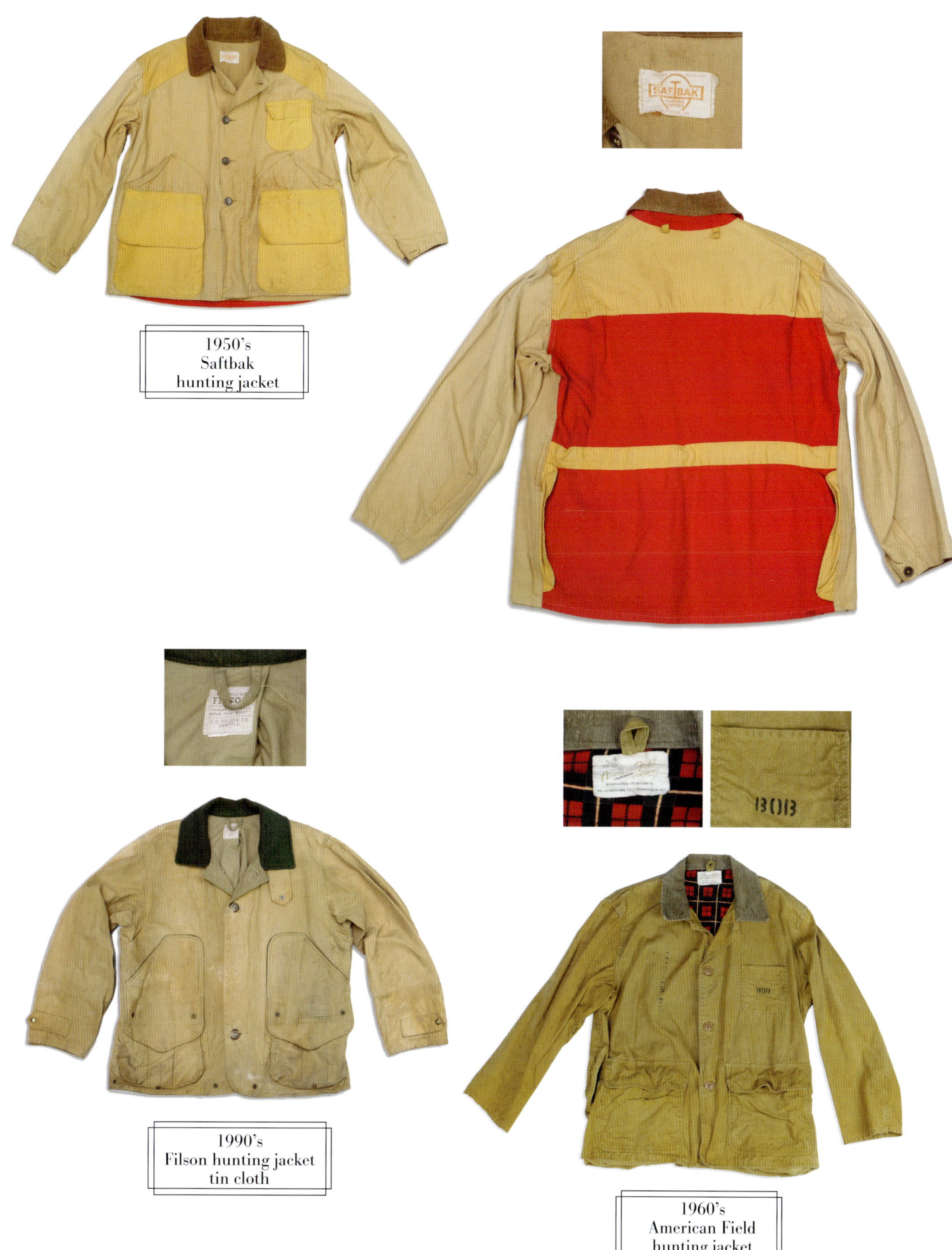

1950's
Saftbak
hunting jacket

1990's
Filson hunting jacket
tin cloth

1960's
American Field
hunting jacket

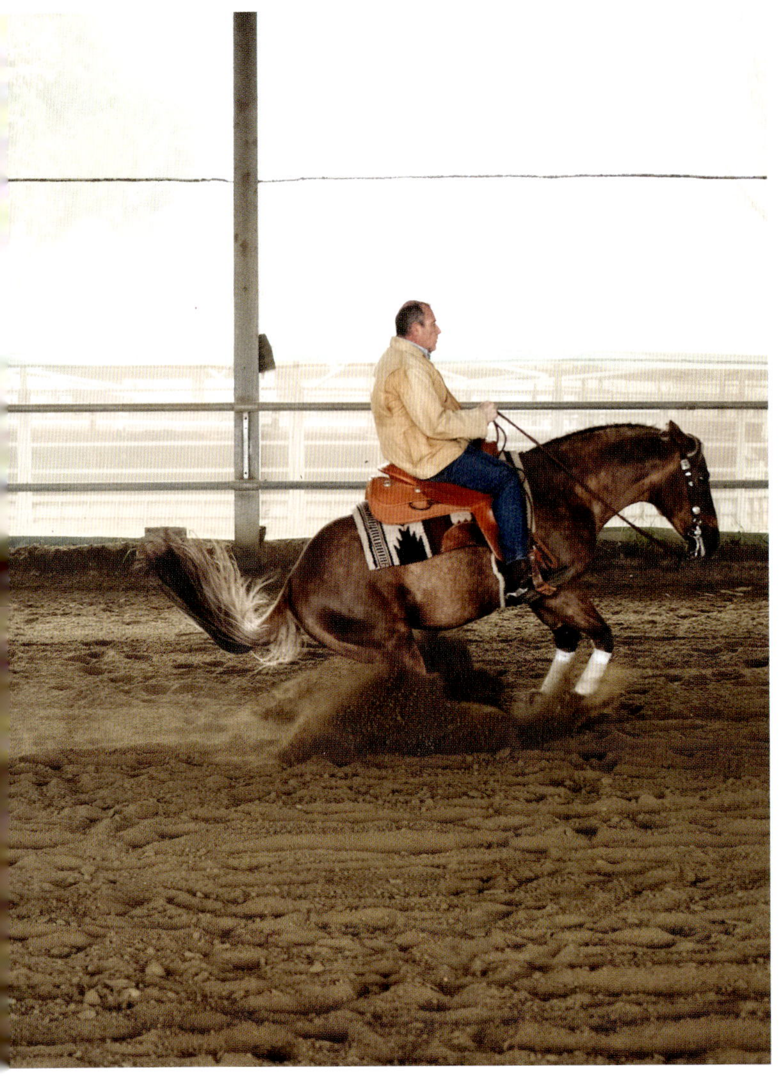

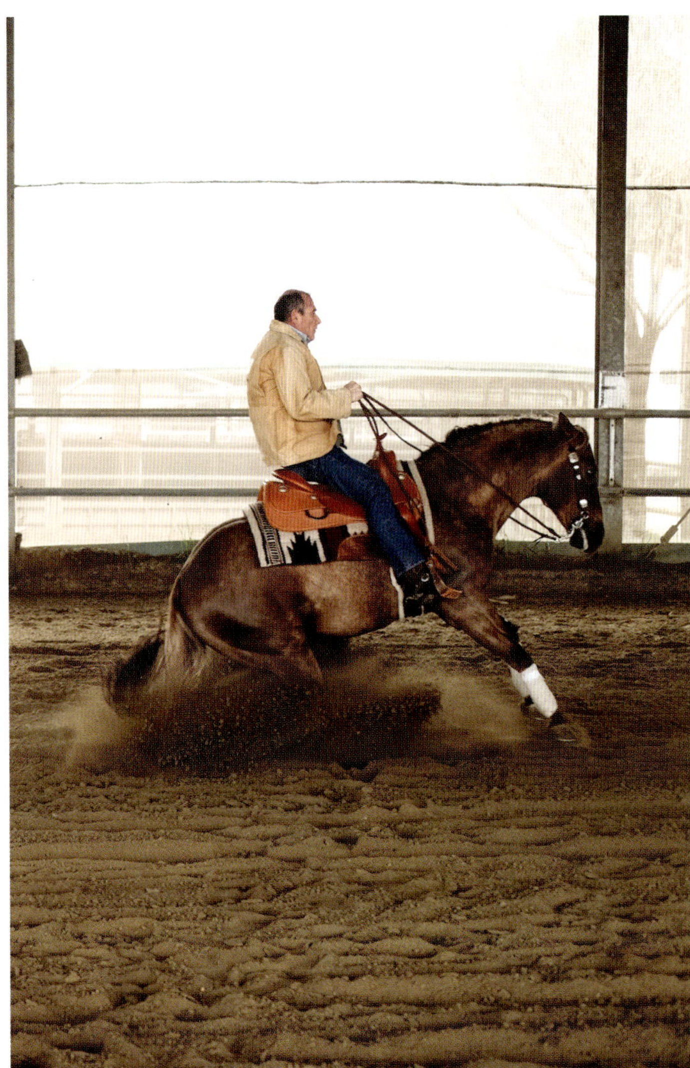

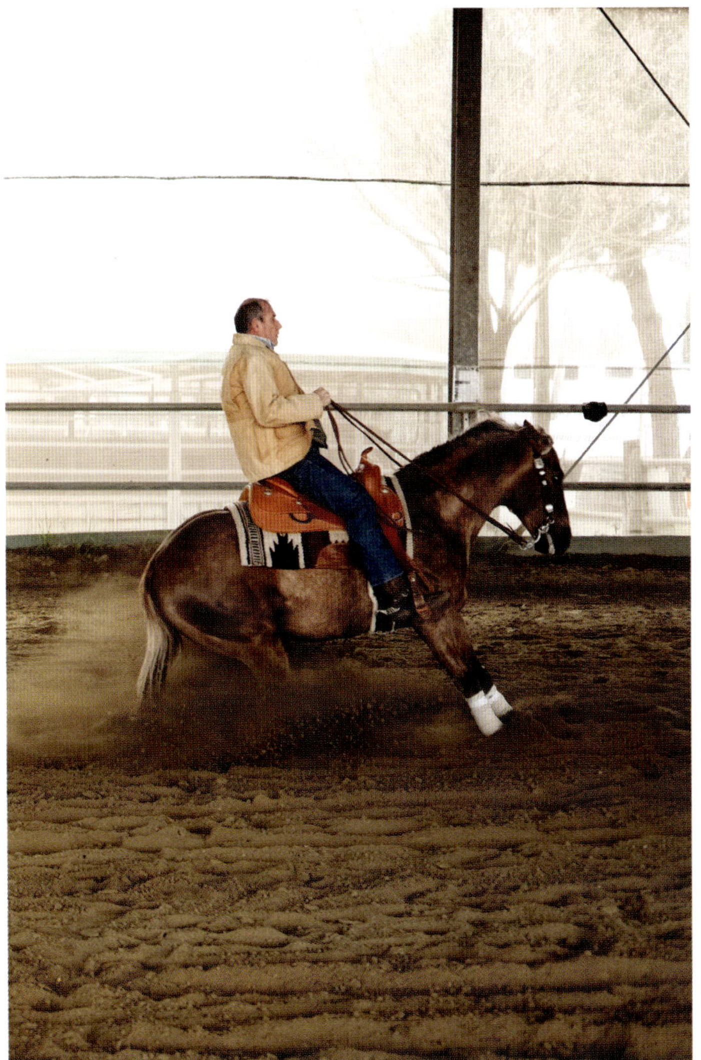

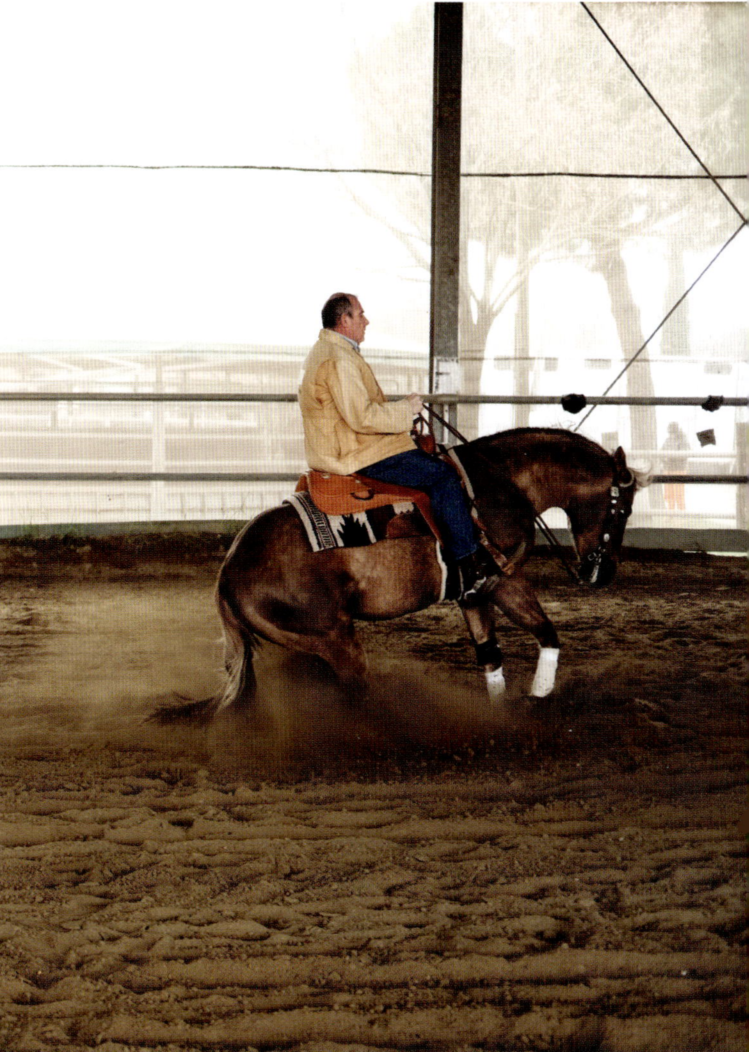

at Maneggio Cortesi
Forlì

1950's
Duxbak
hunting jacket

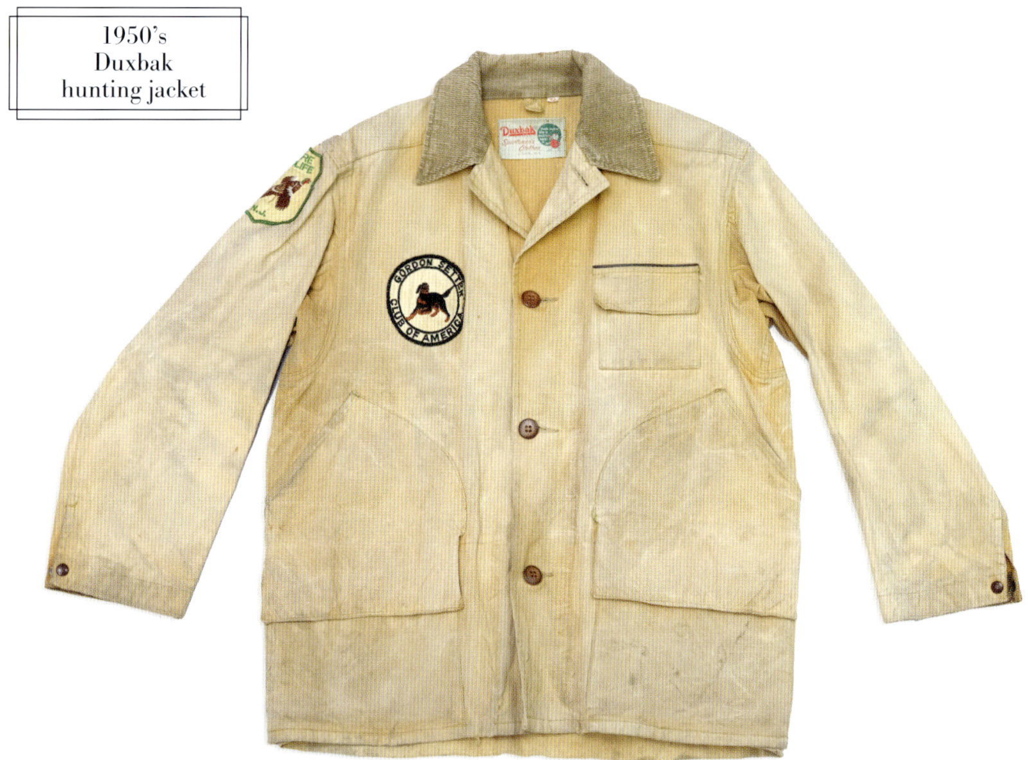

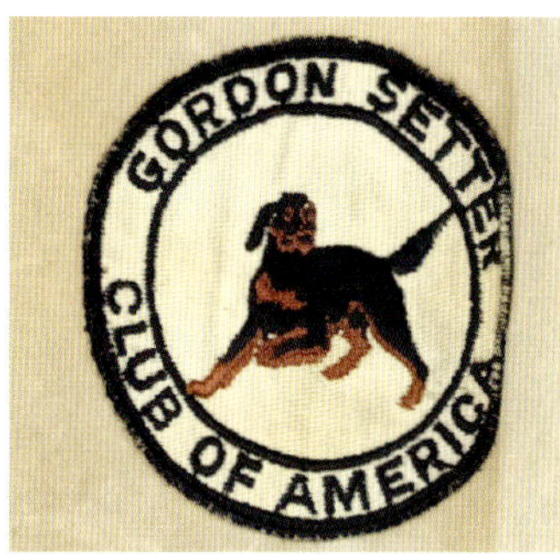

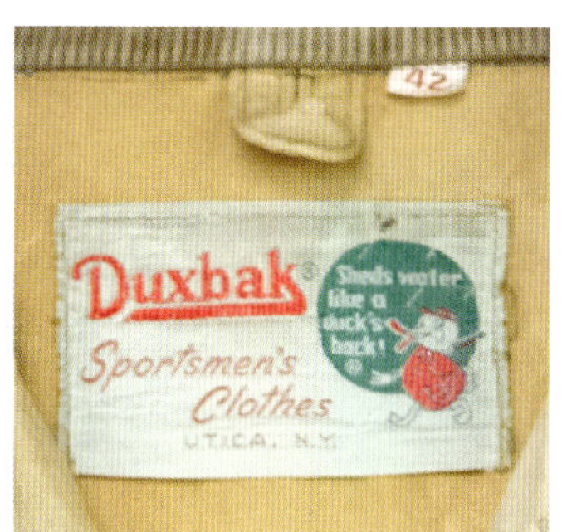

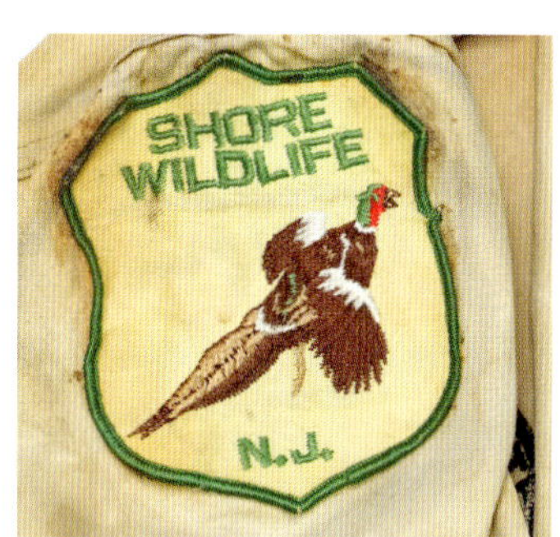

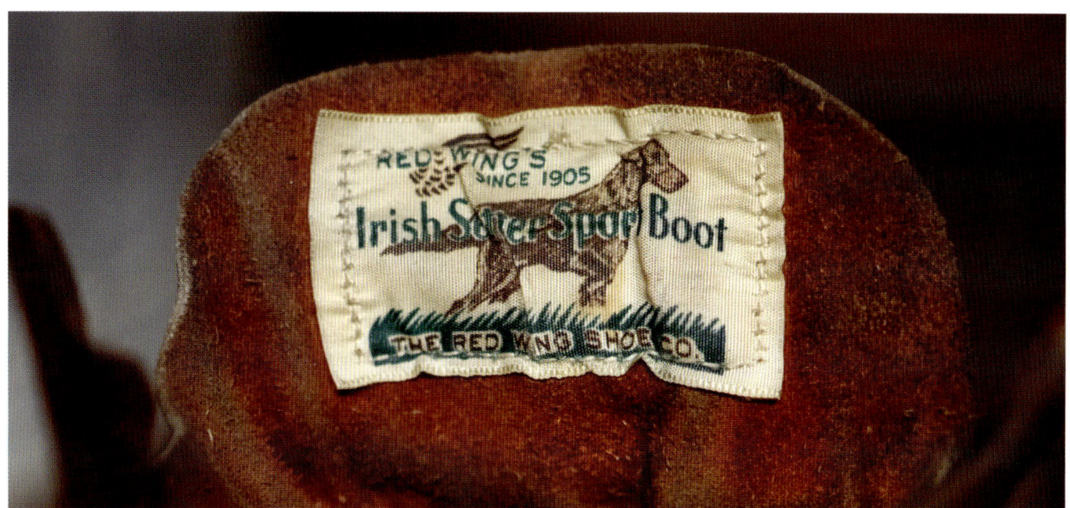

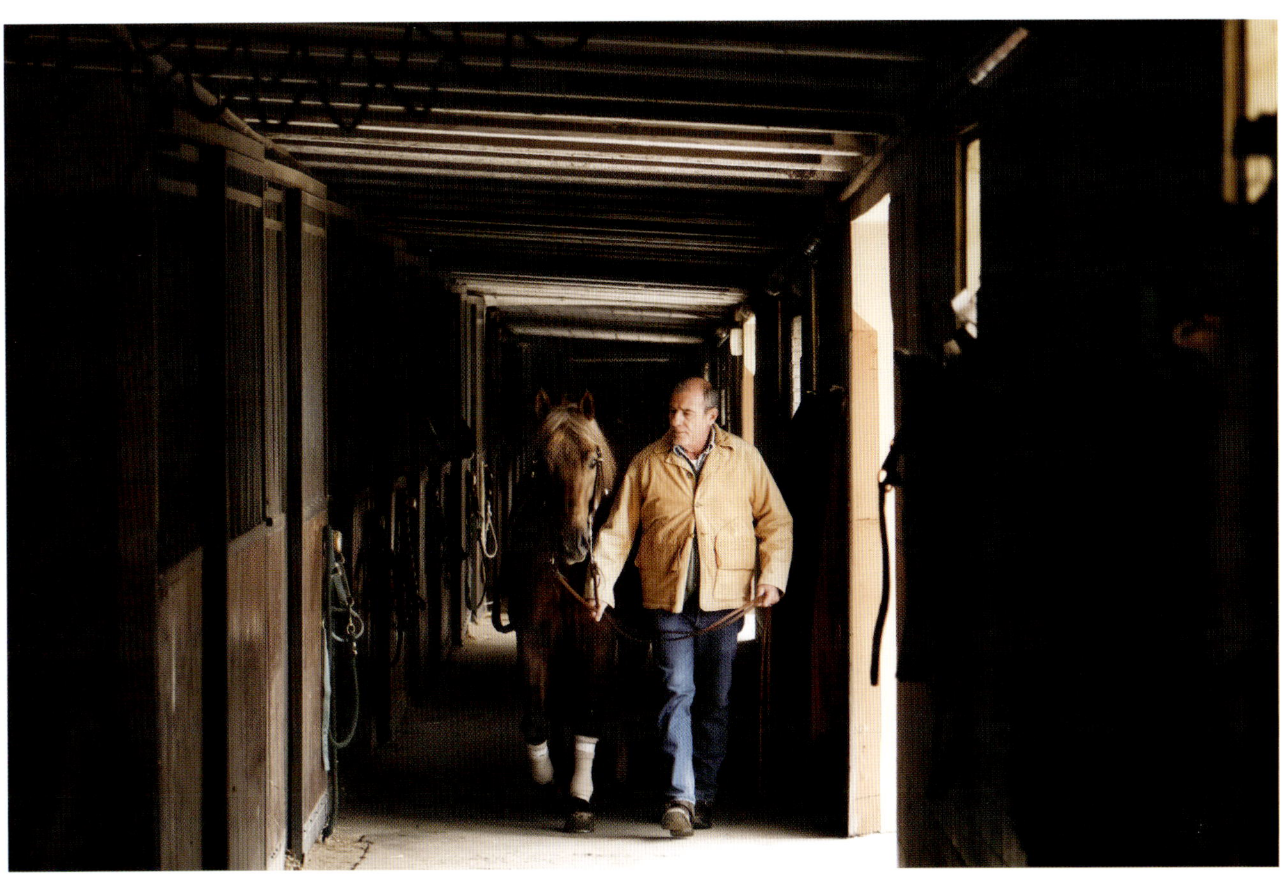

at Maneggio Cortesi
Forlì

1940's
Hinson
hunting jacket

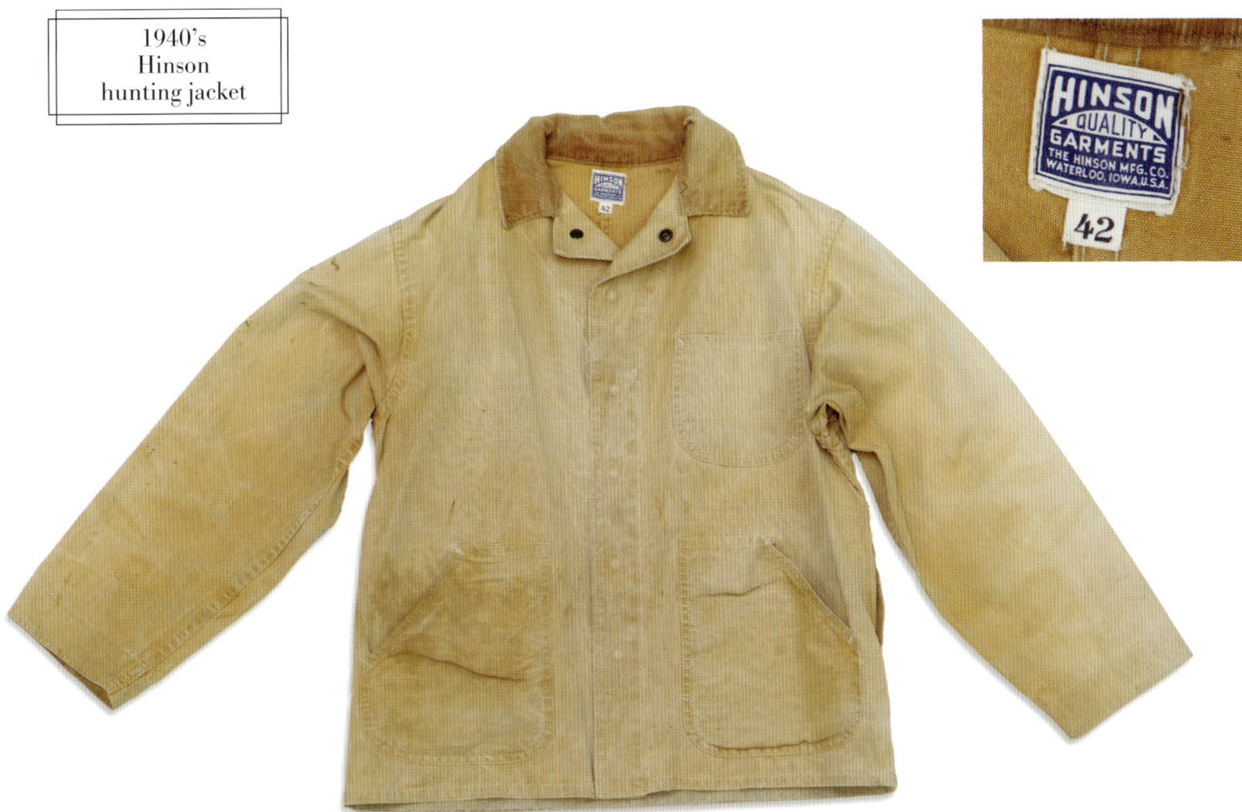

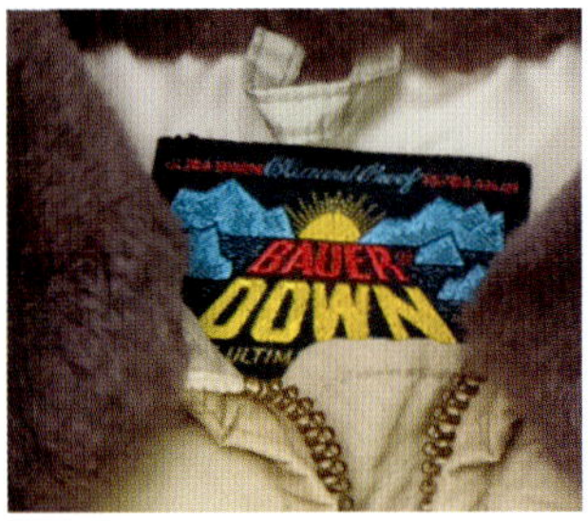

1960's
Eddie Bauer
Blizzard Proof
down jacket

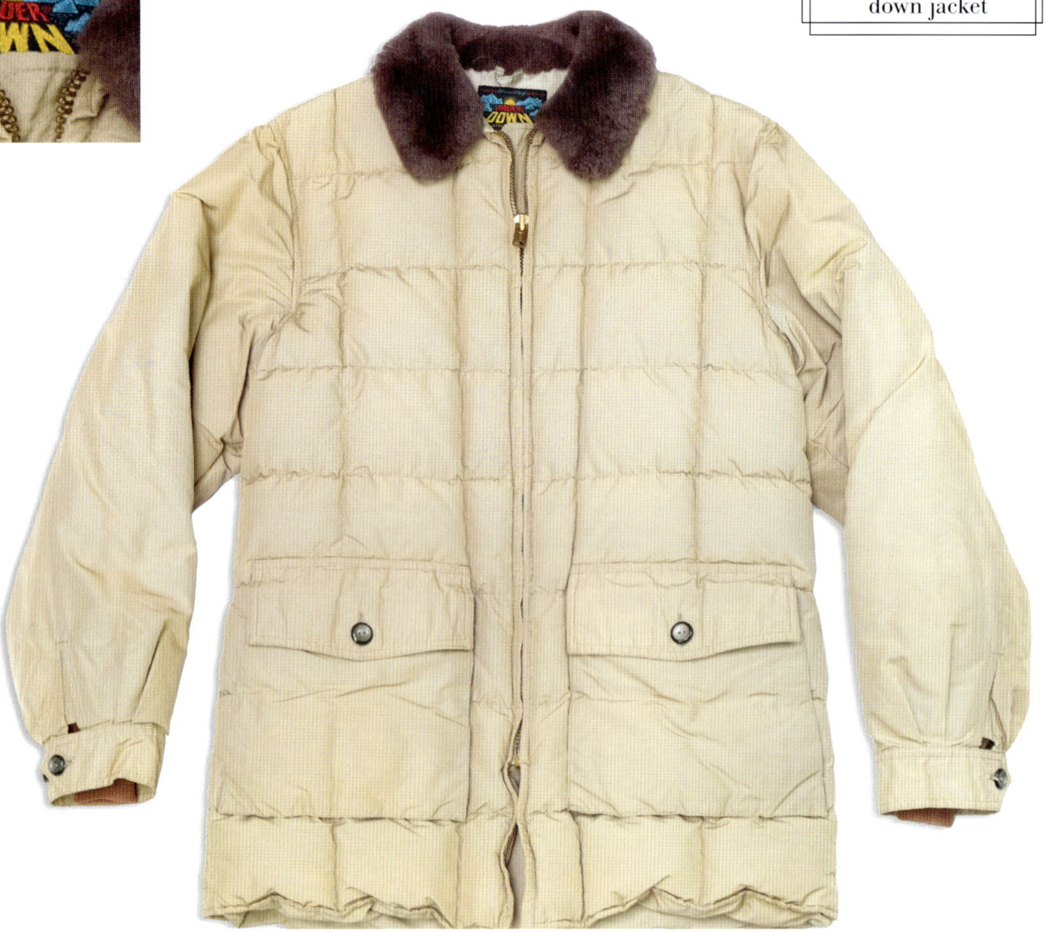

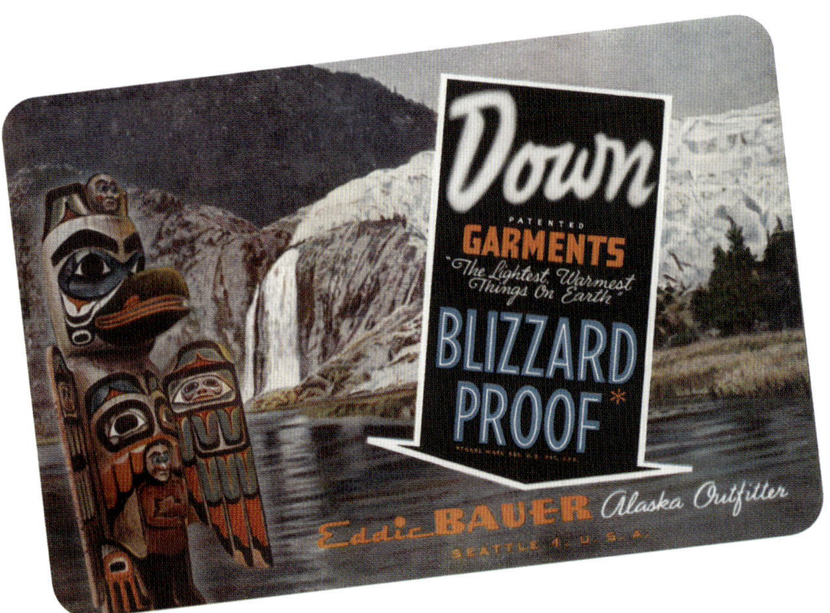

1960's advertising

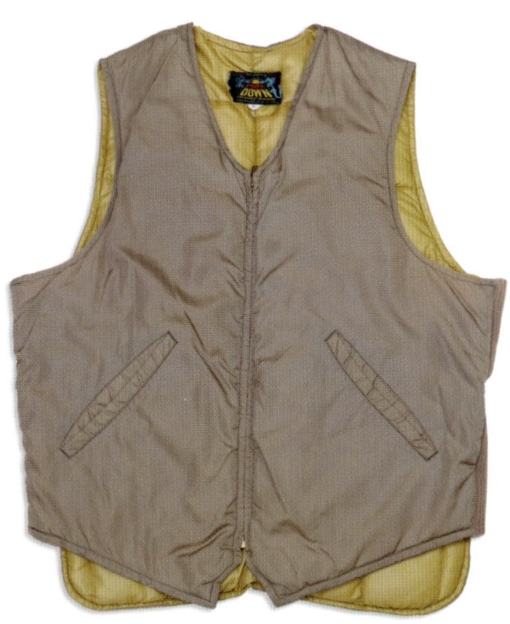

1960's
Eddie Bauer vest
goose down

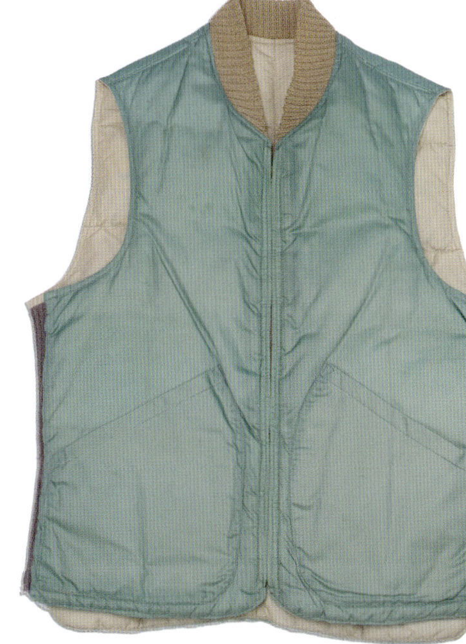

1960's
Eddie Bauer vest
goose down

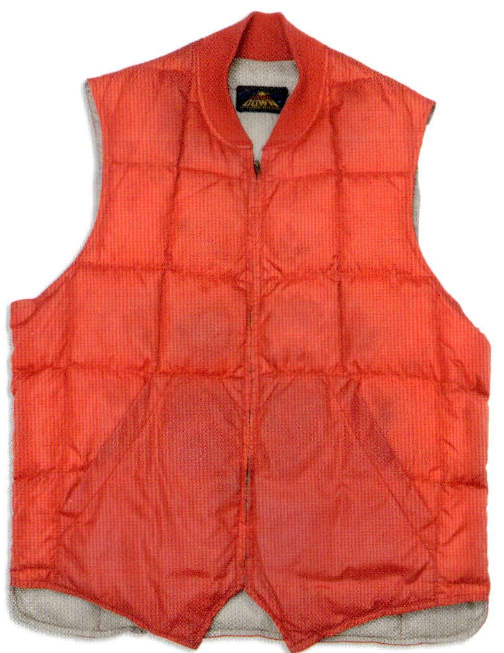

1960's
Eddie Bauer vest
goose down

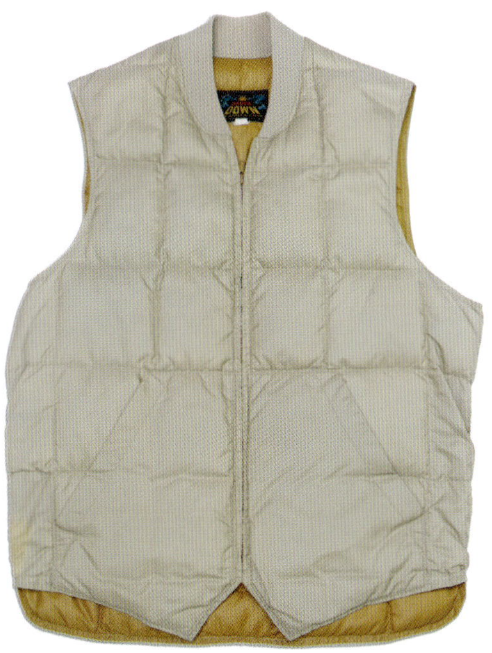

1960's
Eddie Bauer vest
goose down

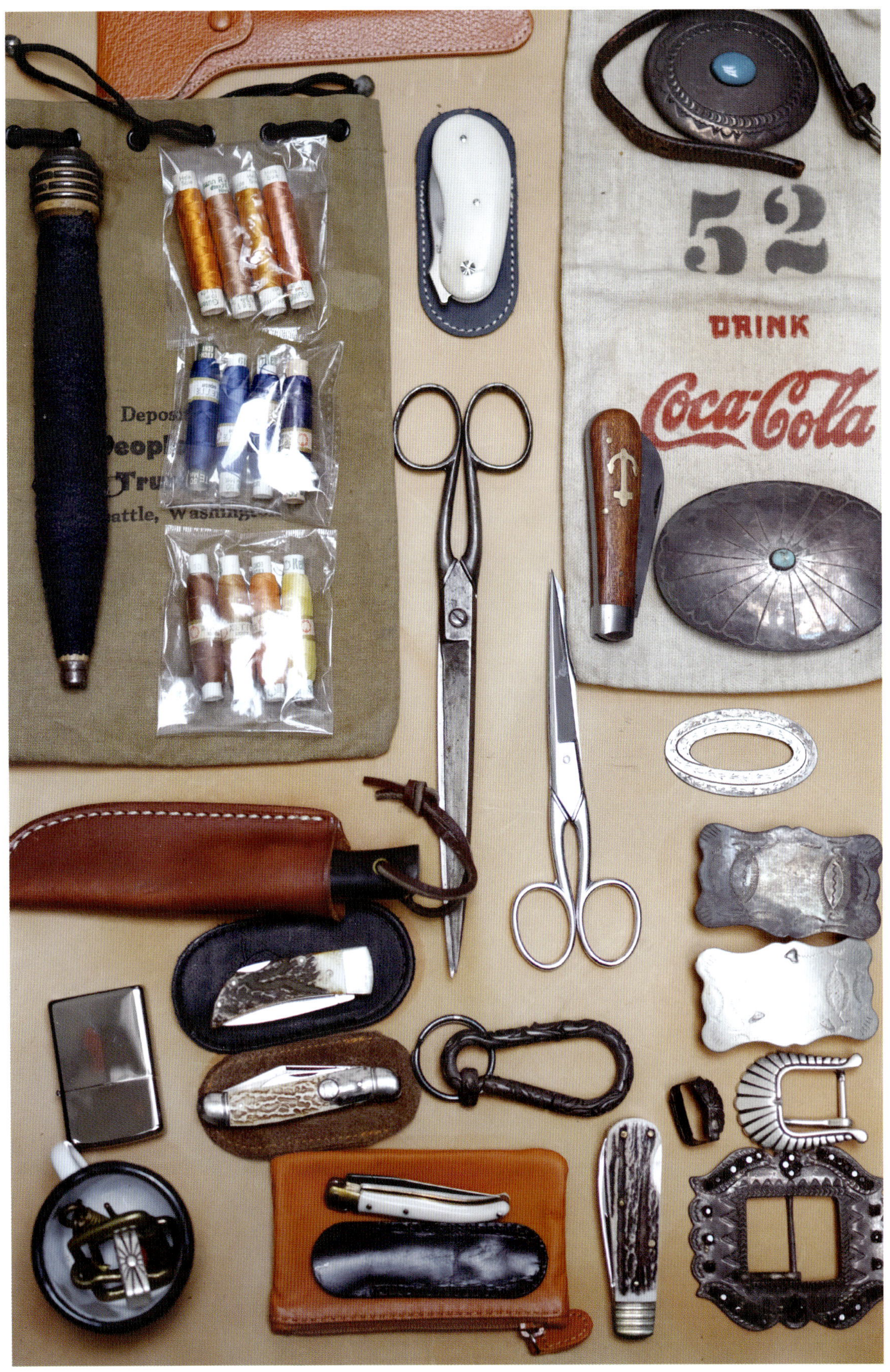

at Alessandro Squarzi archive
Forlì

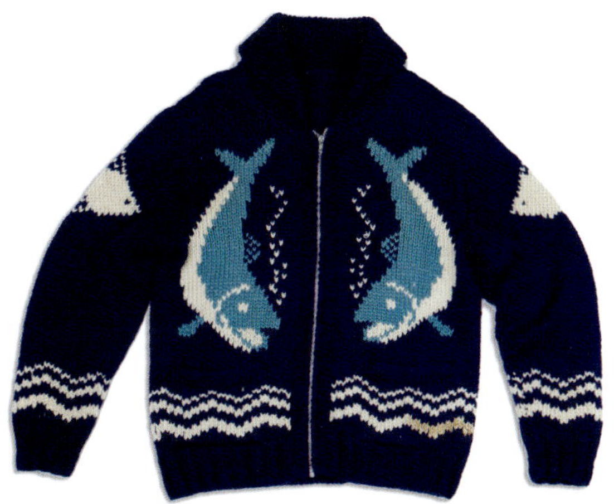

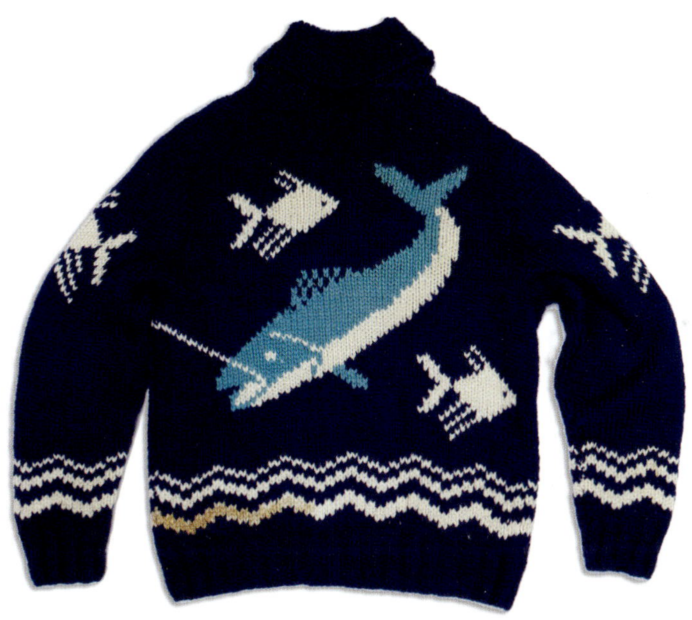

Vintage
unknown "Cowichan"
zipper sweater

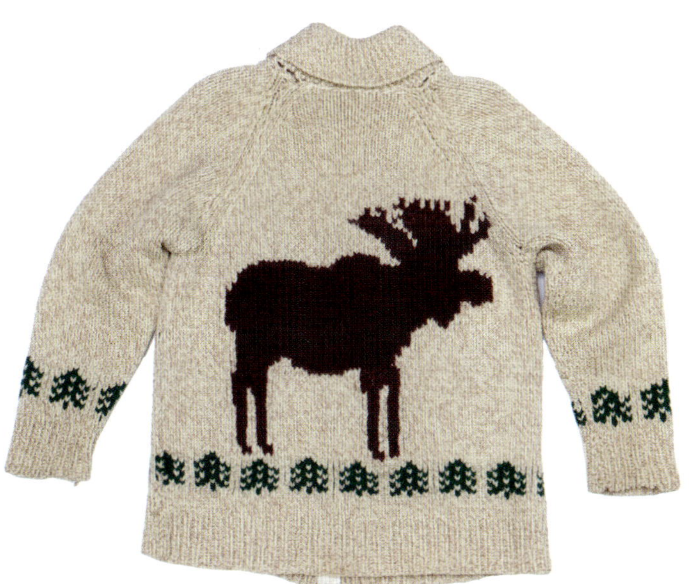

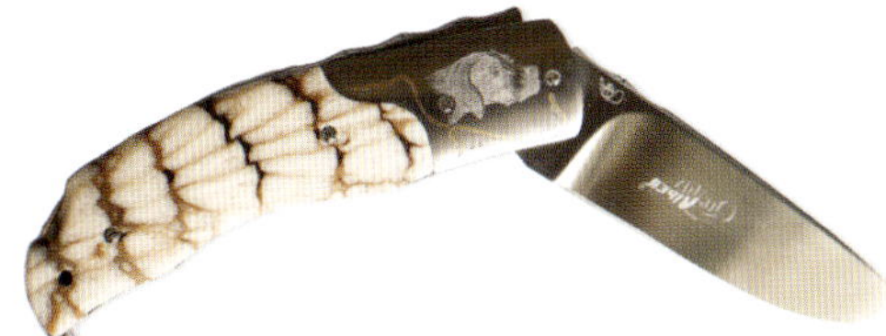

Quality Viper
handcrafted knife
"Straight back"

Vintage
unknown "Cowichan"
zipper sweater

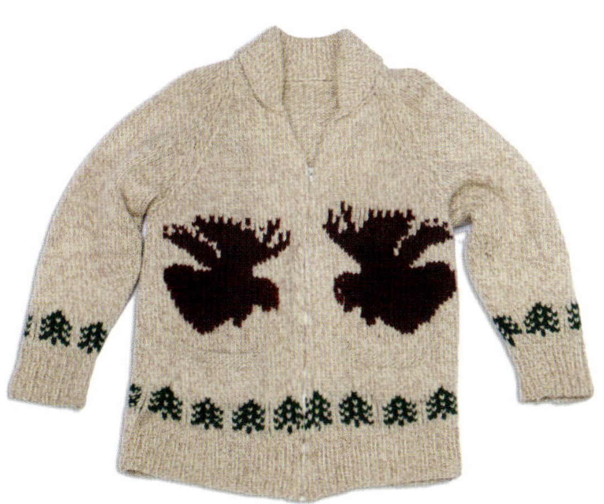

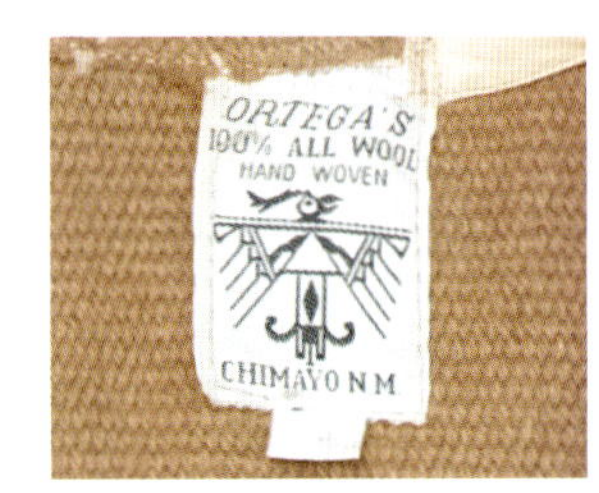

vintage
Ortega's
chimayo vest

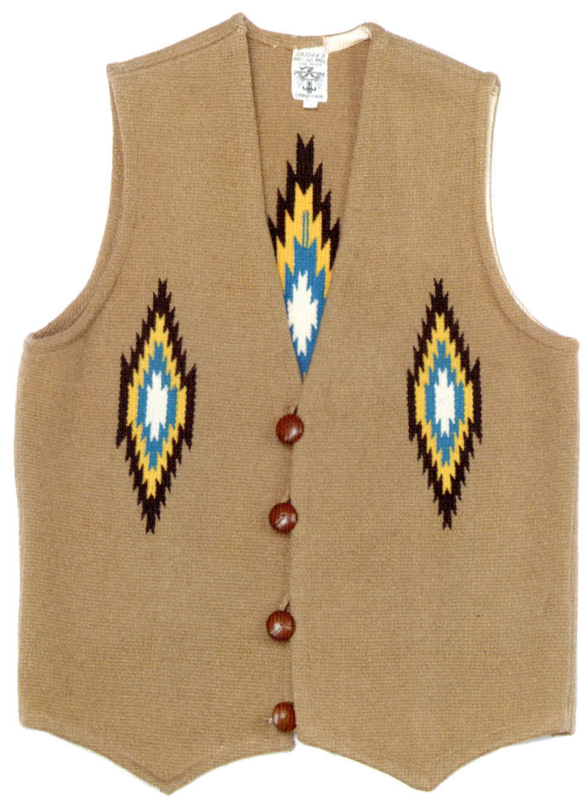

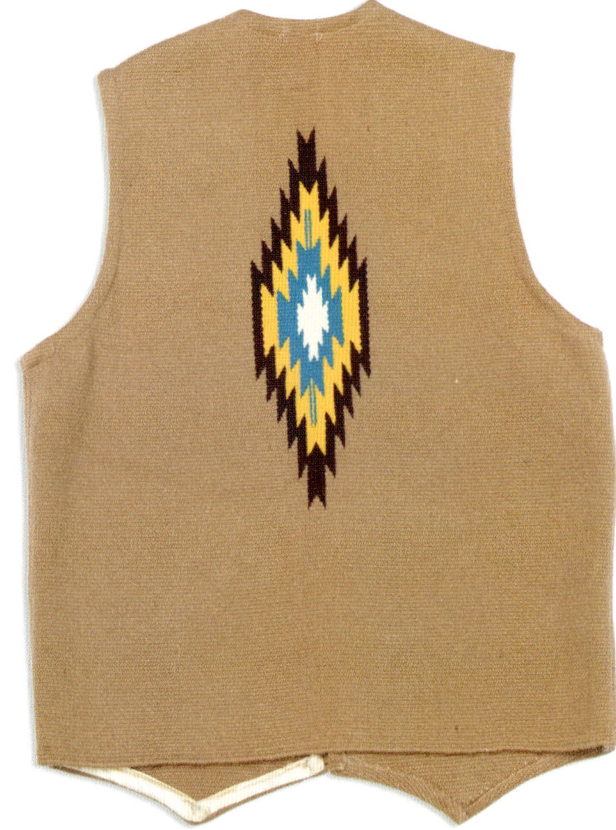

vintage
native American
silver bracelet cuff

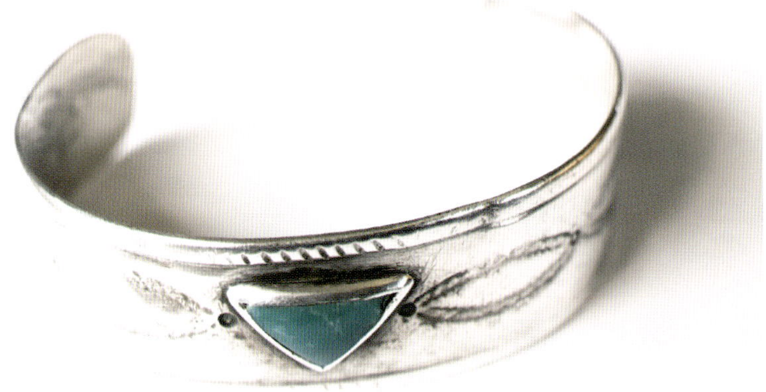

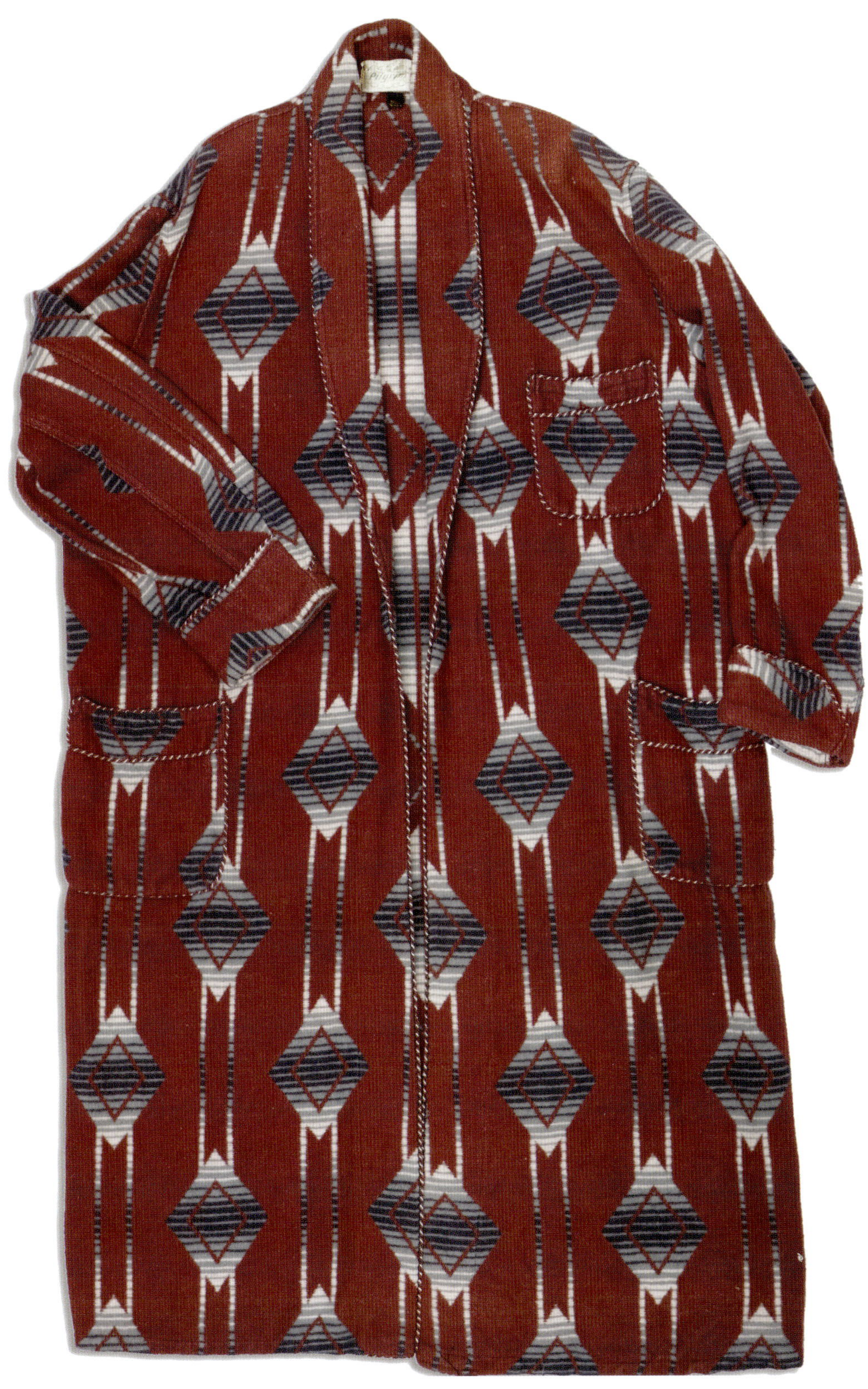

1960's
Pilgrim
men's dressing gown

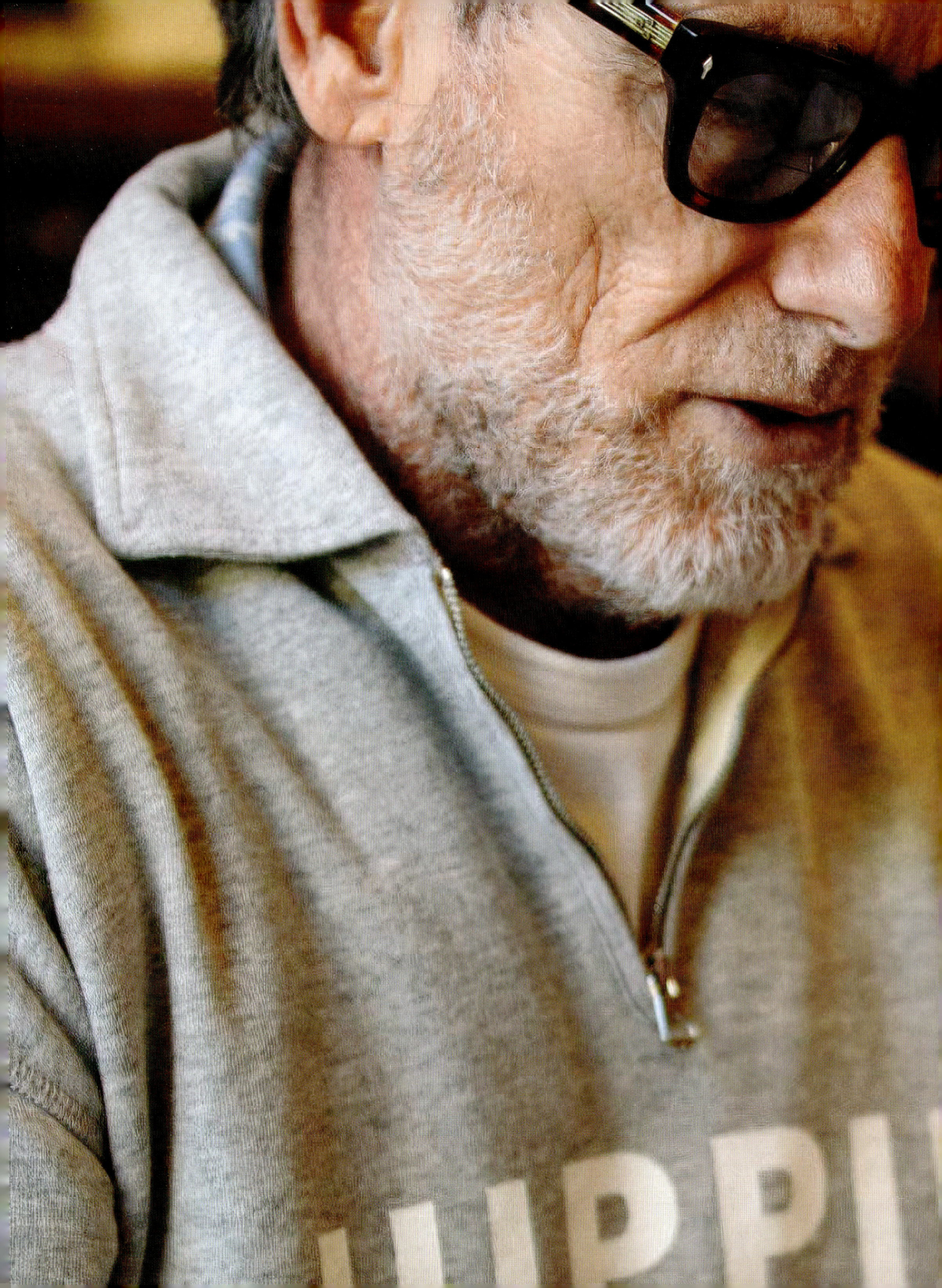
HIPPI

Athletic

CHAPTER

3

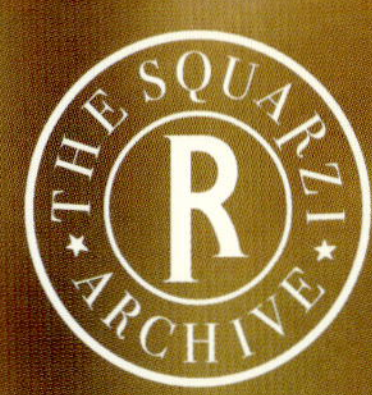

"If you do a job you like,
you don't actually work."

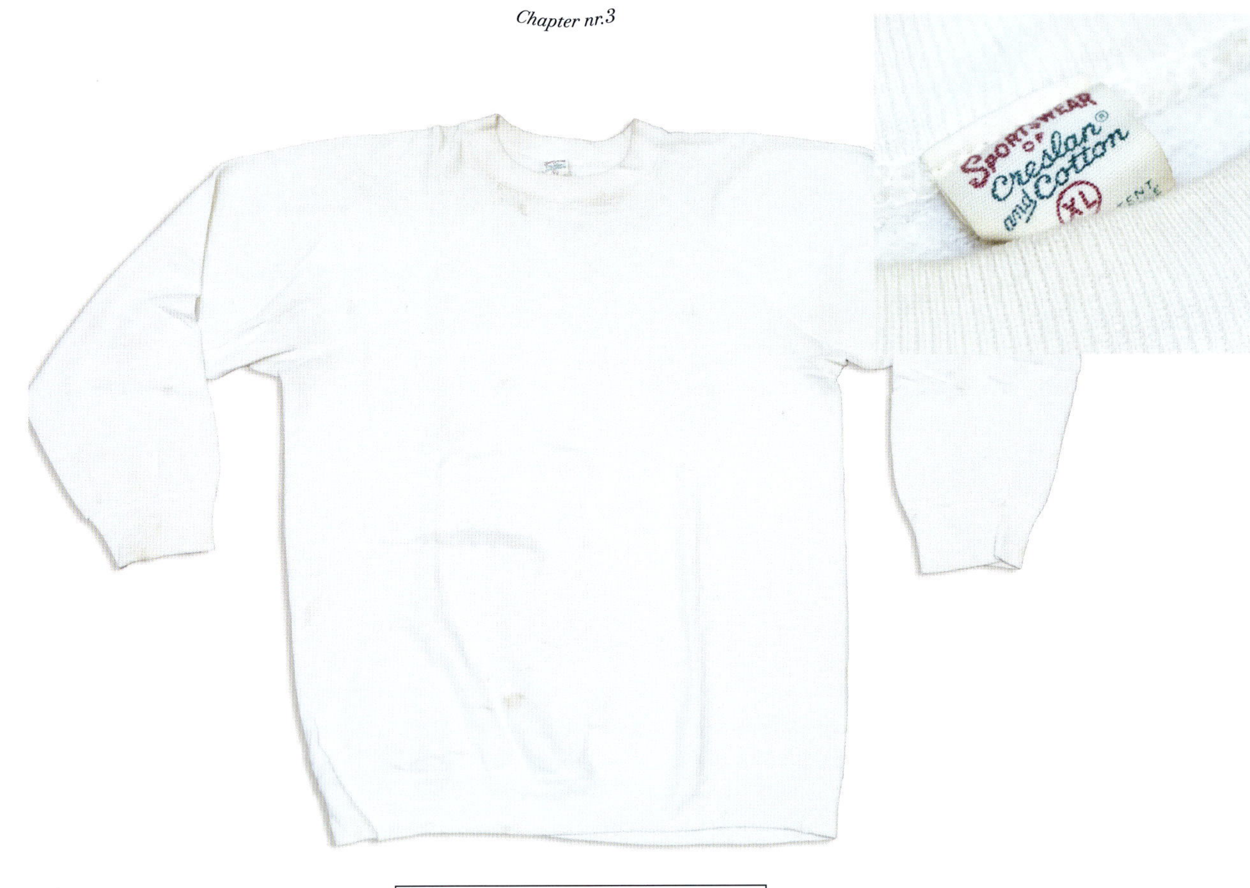

1960's
Sportswear of Creslan and Cotton
crewneck sweatshirt

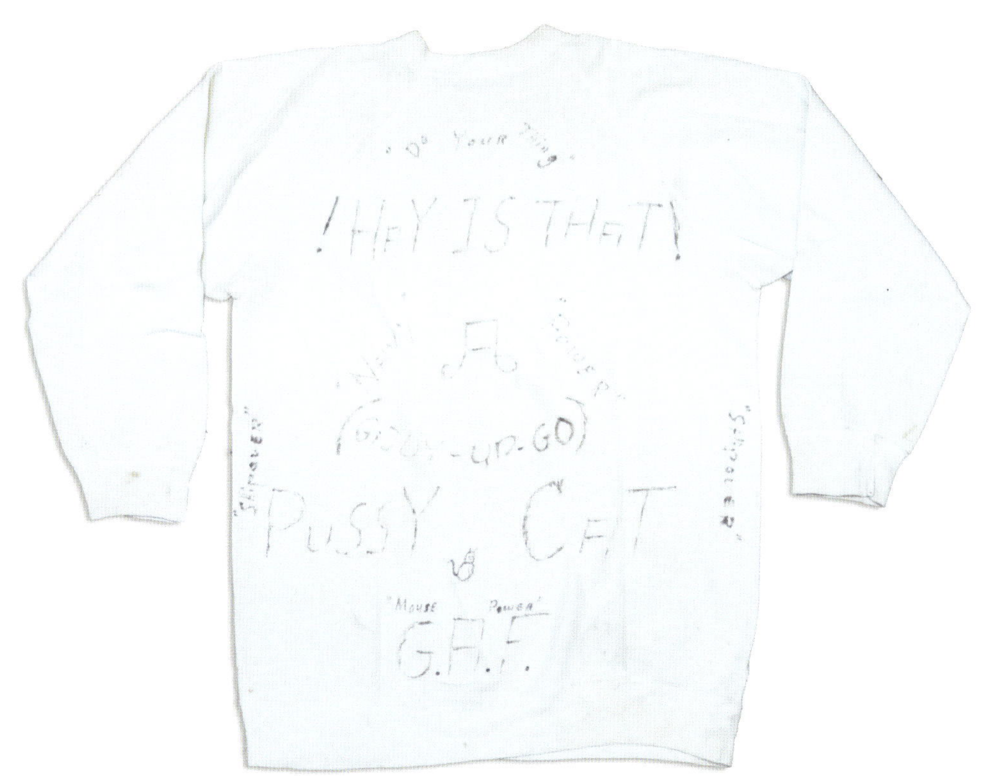

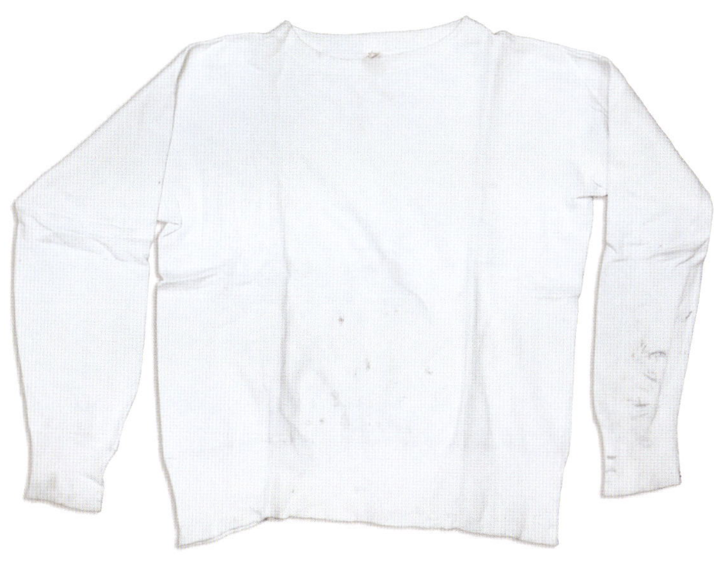

1950's
Pennleigh
crewneck sweatshirt

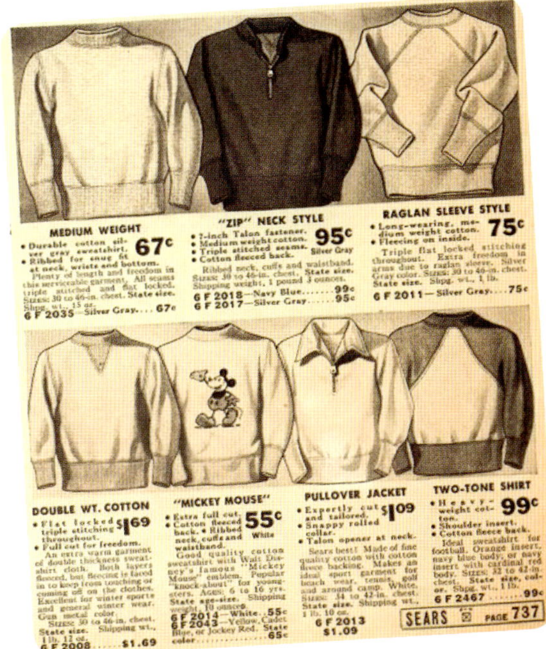

1940's Sears catalogue

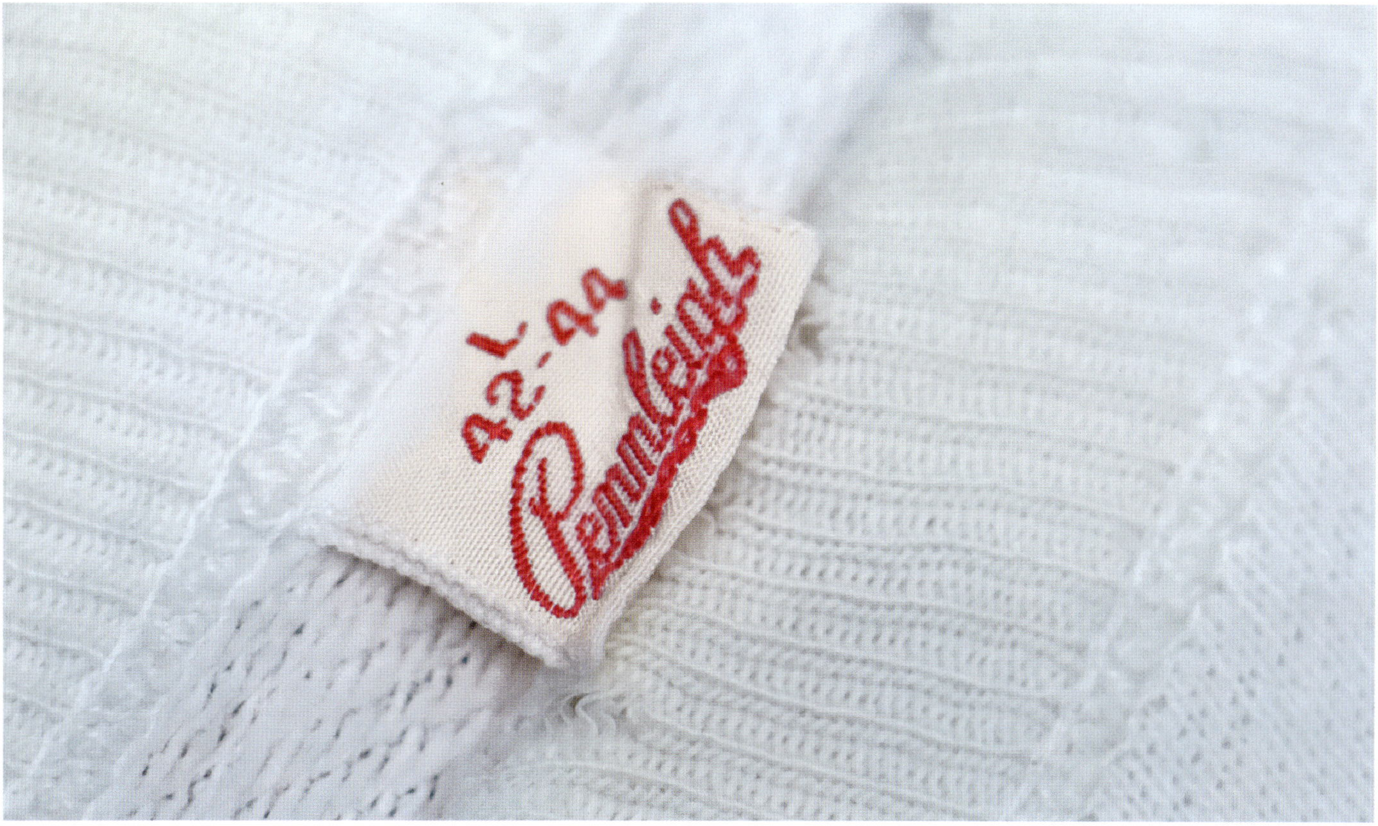

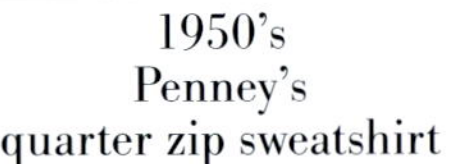

1950's
Penney's
quarter zip sweatshirt

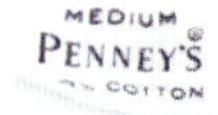

1970's
Sportswear
quarter zip sweatshirt

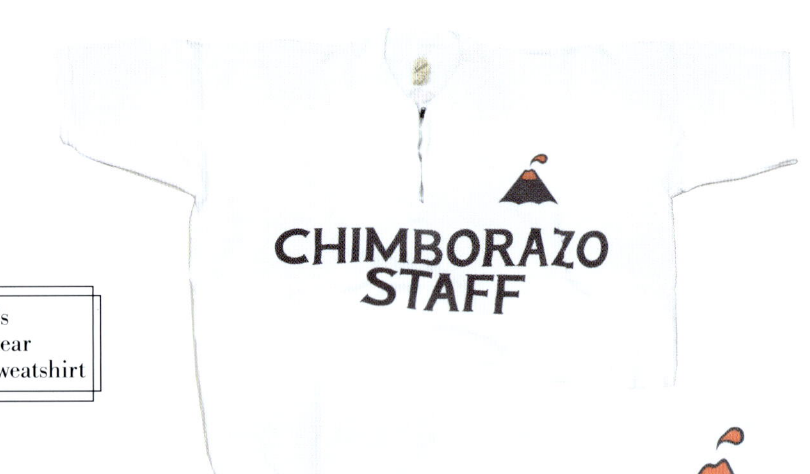

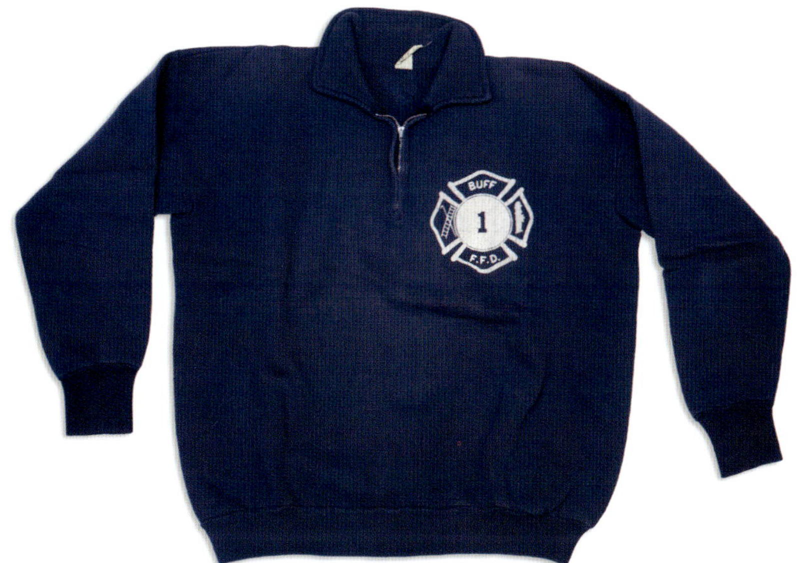

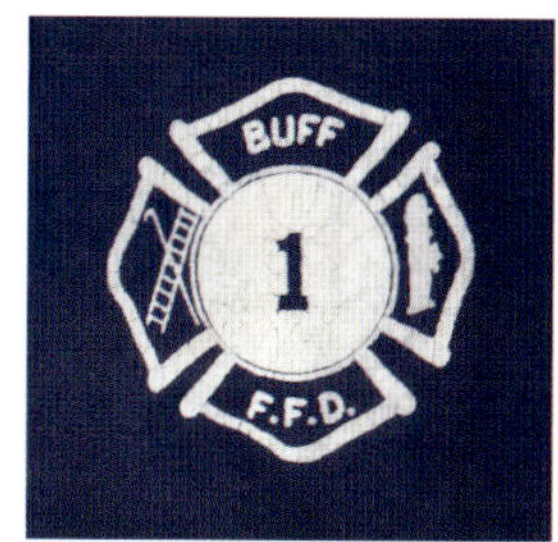

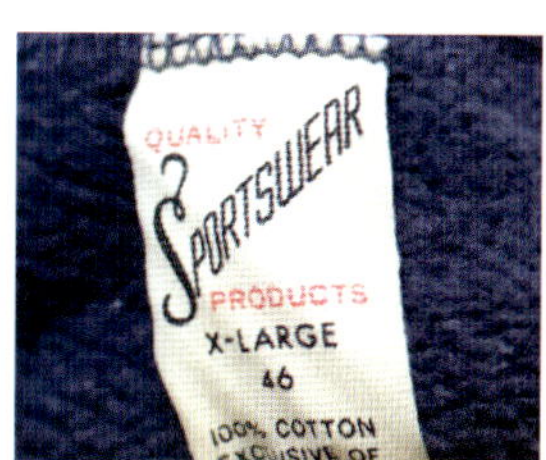

1960's
Sportswear
quarter zip sweatshirt

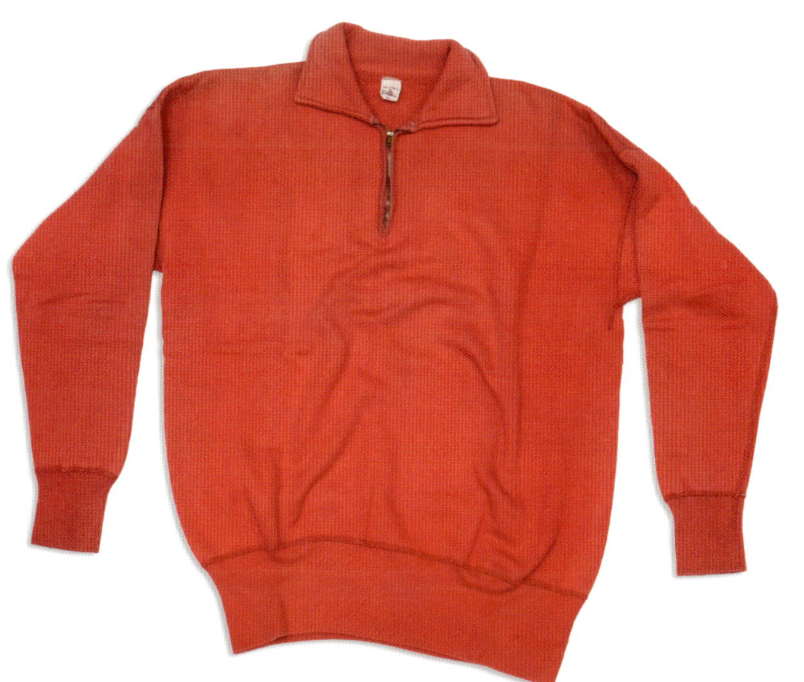

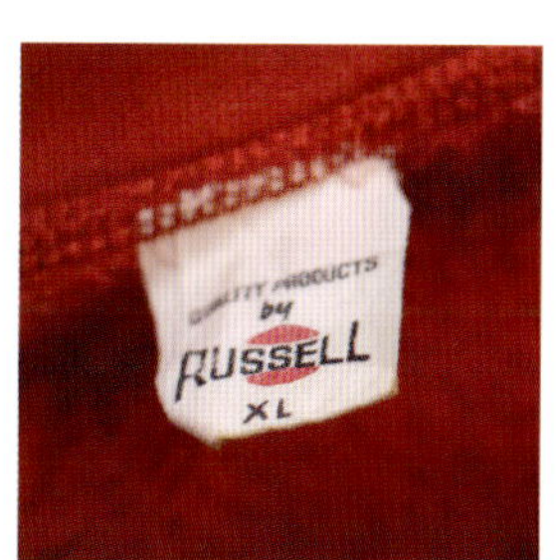

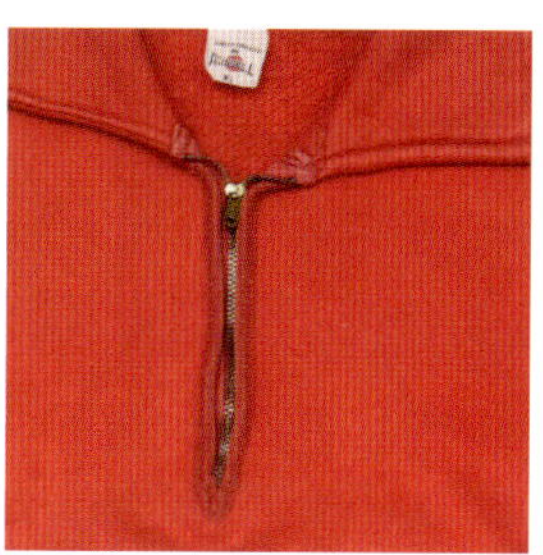

1950's
Russell
quarter zip sweatshirt

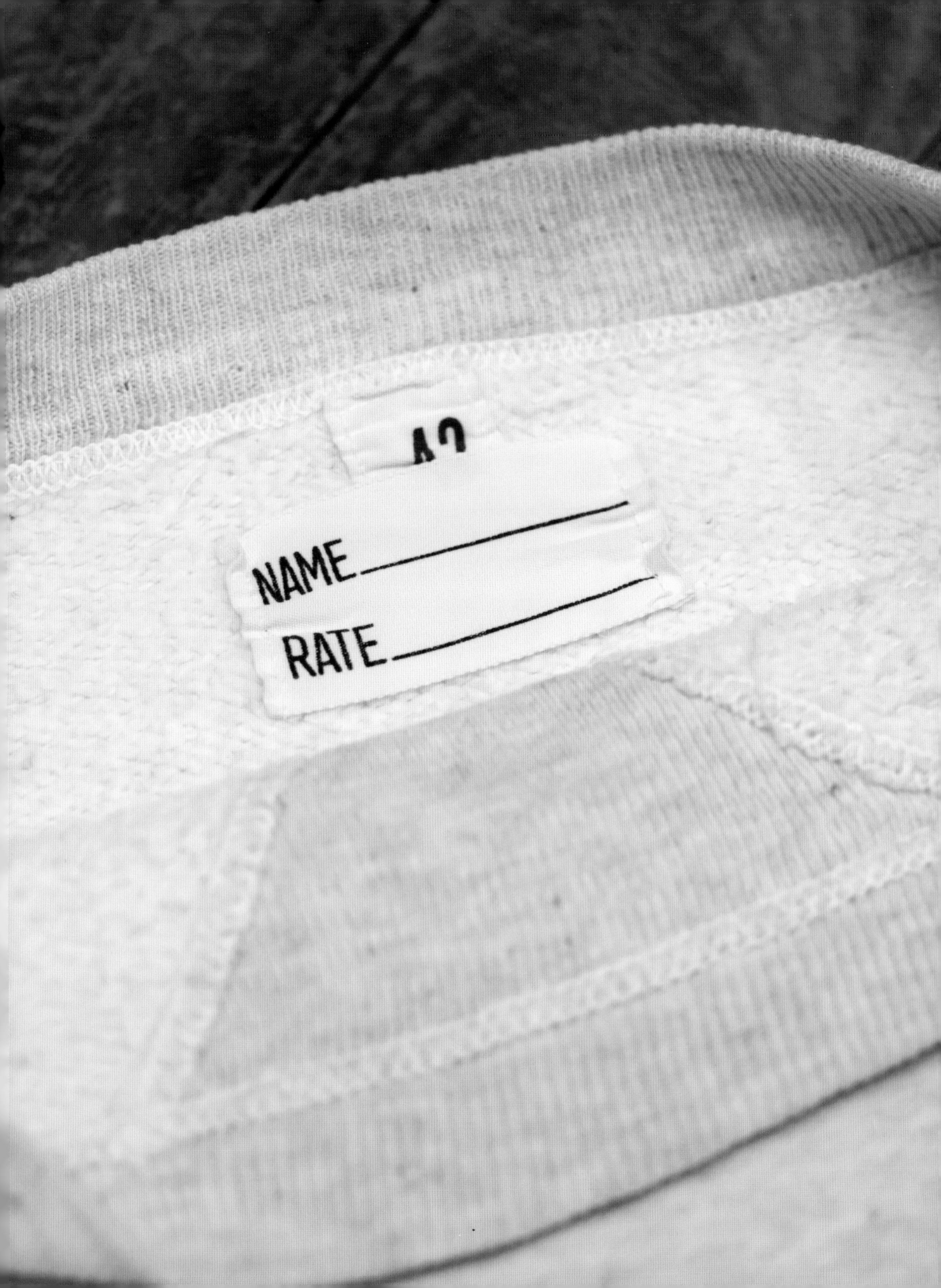
NAME
RATE

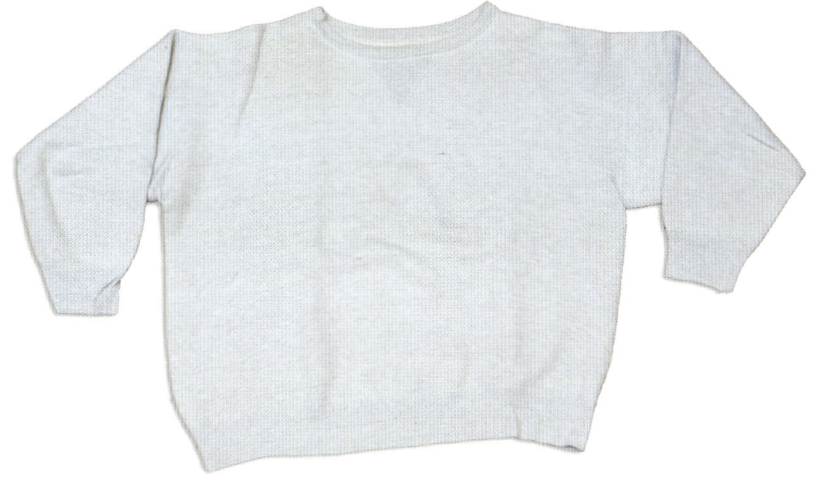

1940's
military sweatshirt
"single V"

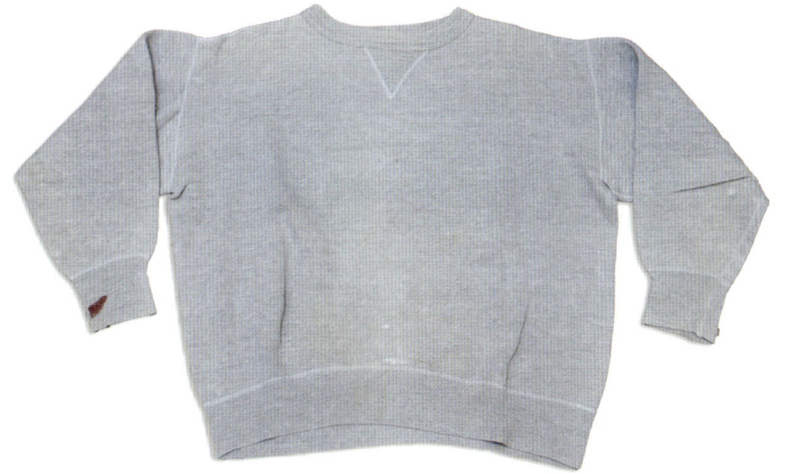

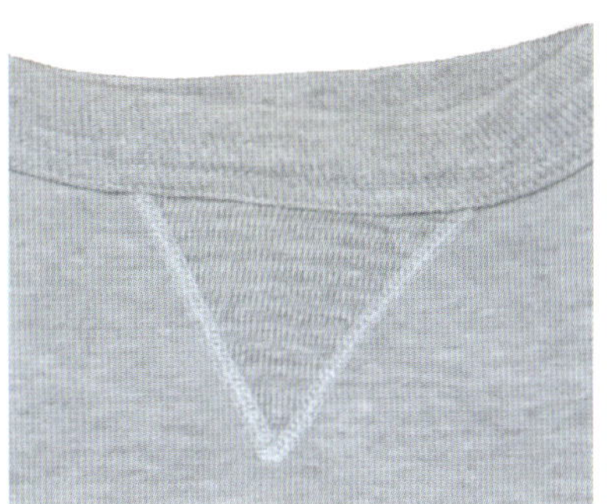

1950's
unknown sweatshirt
"single V"

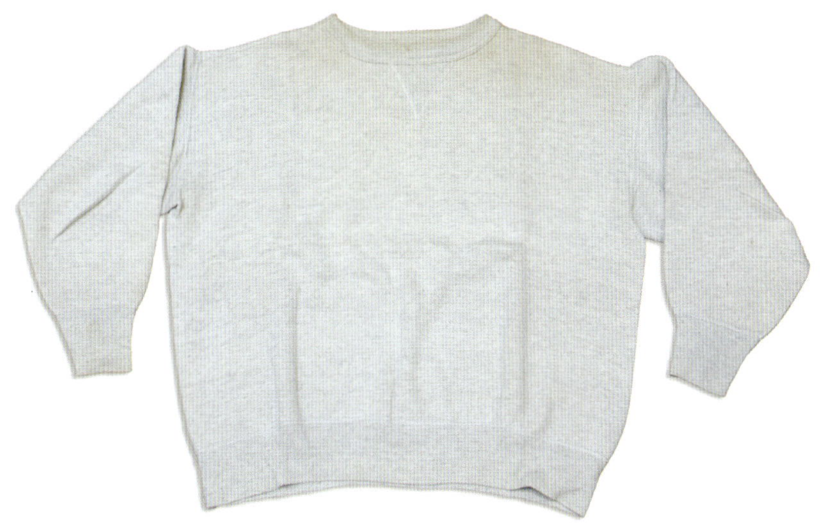

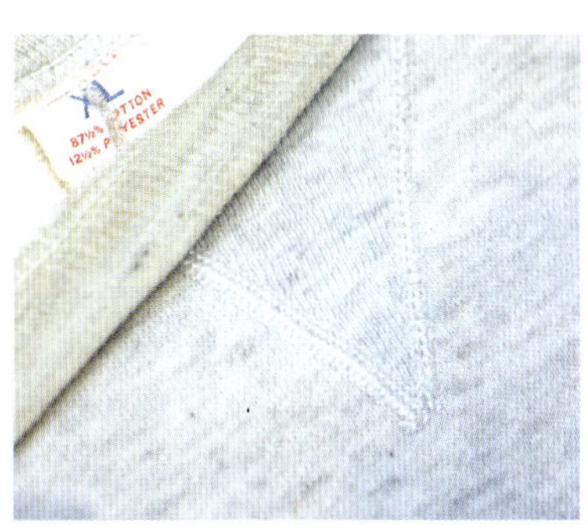

1950's
Russell sweatshirt
"single V"

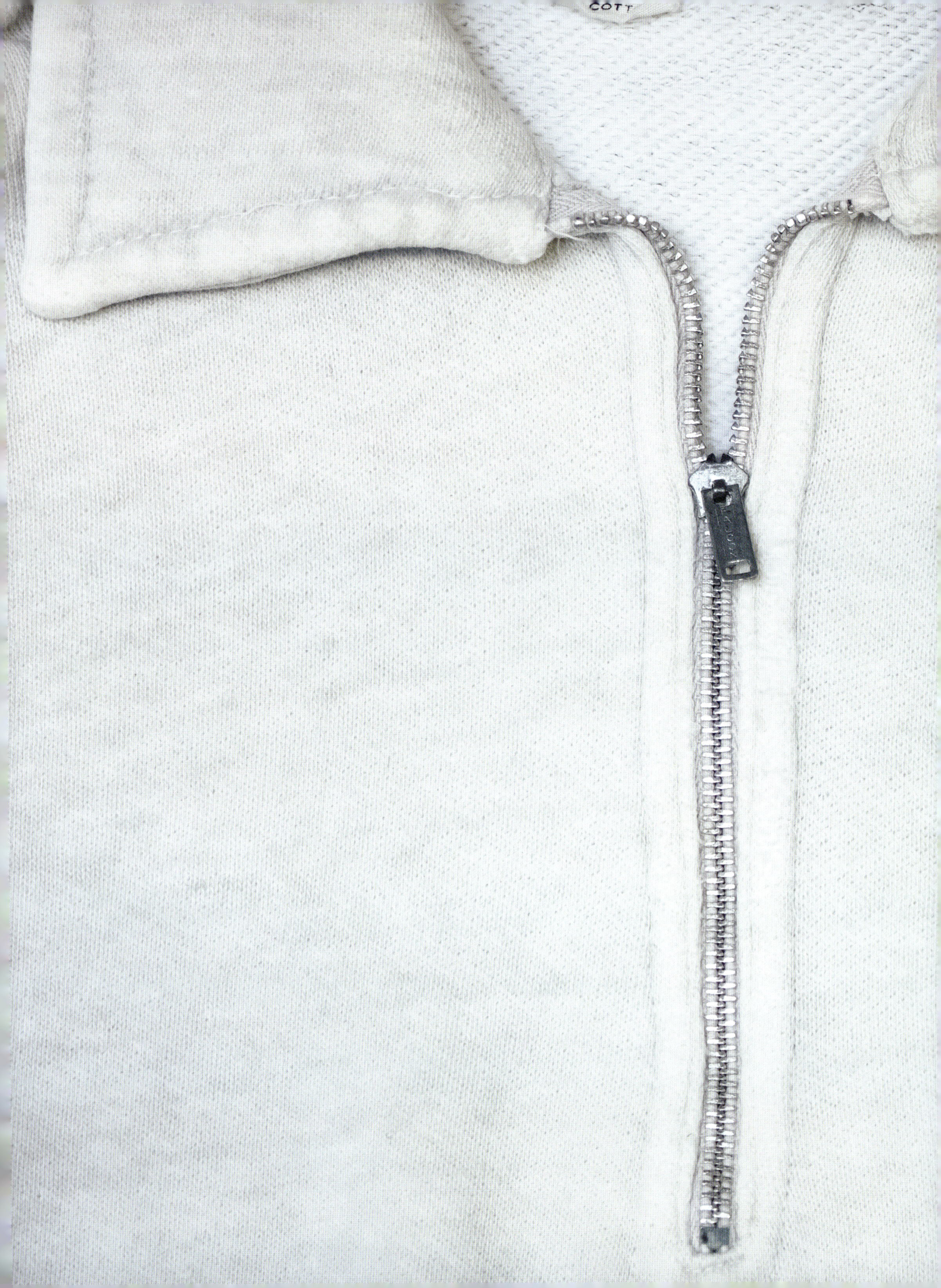

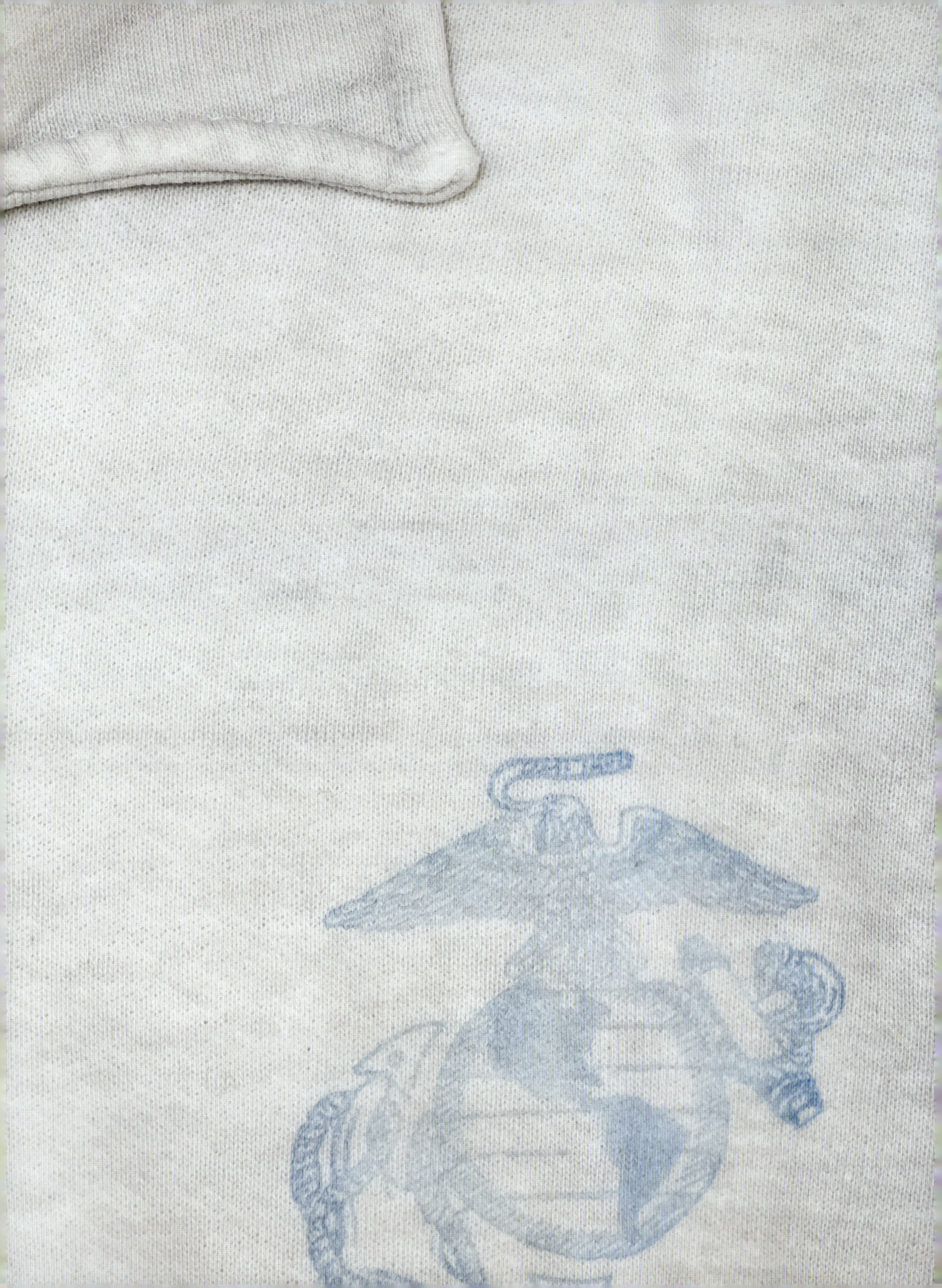

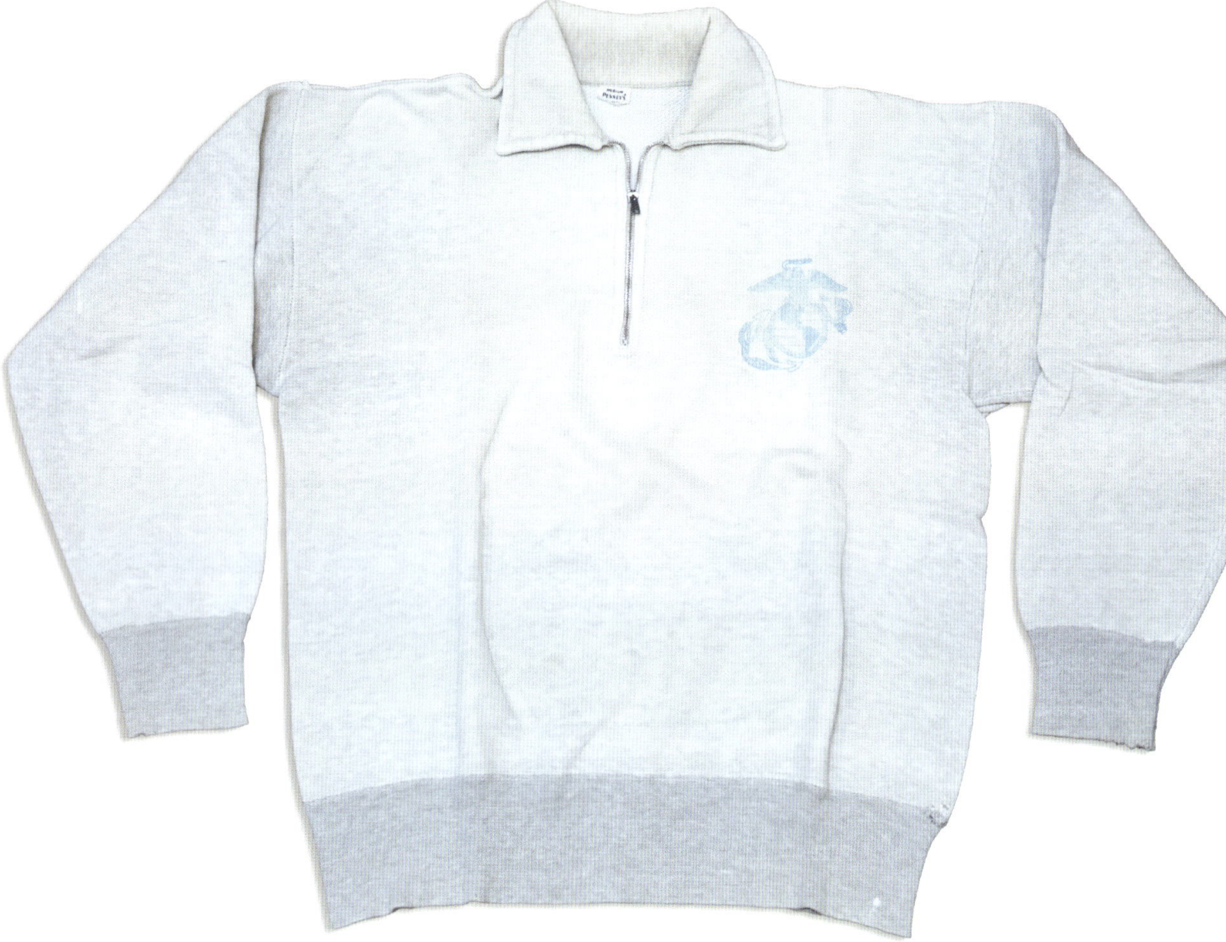

1950's
Penney's
quarter zip sweatshirt
U.S.M.C. "EGA" logo

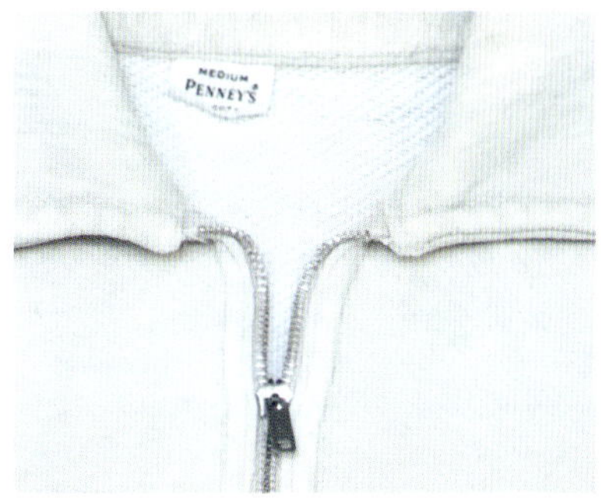

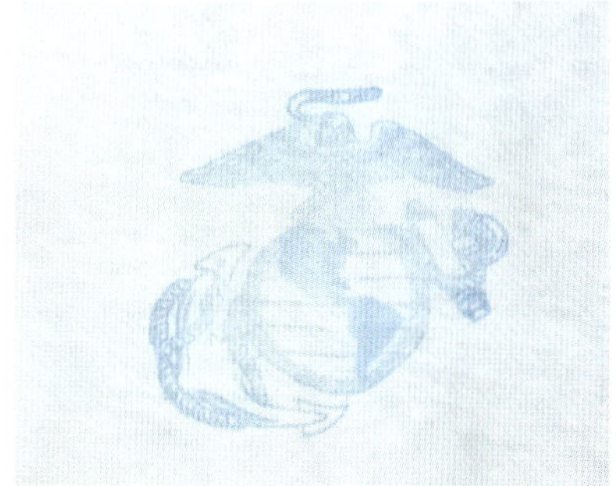

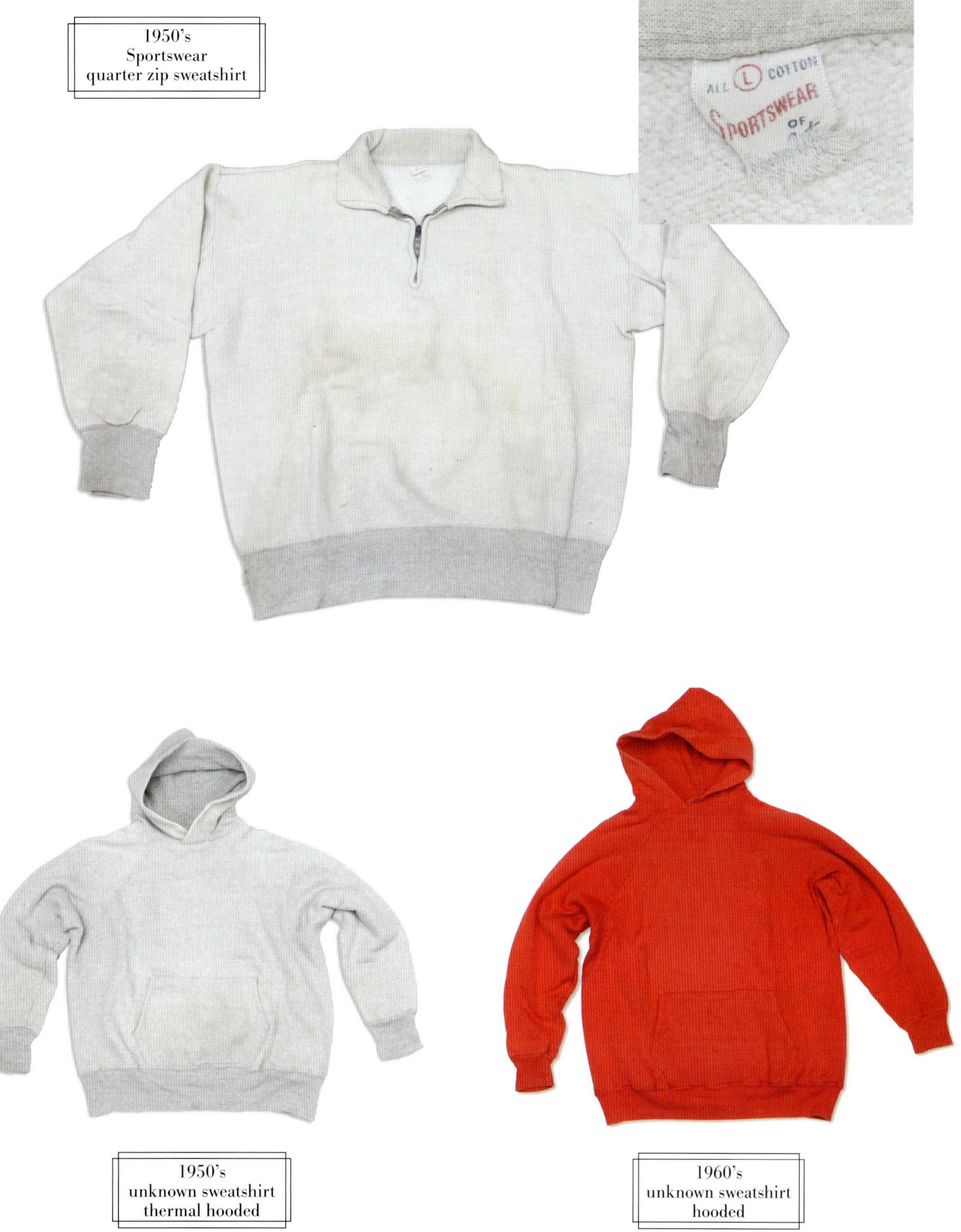

1950's
Sportswear
quarter zip sweatshirt

1950's
unknown sweatshirt
thermal hooded

1960's
unknown sweatshirt
hooded

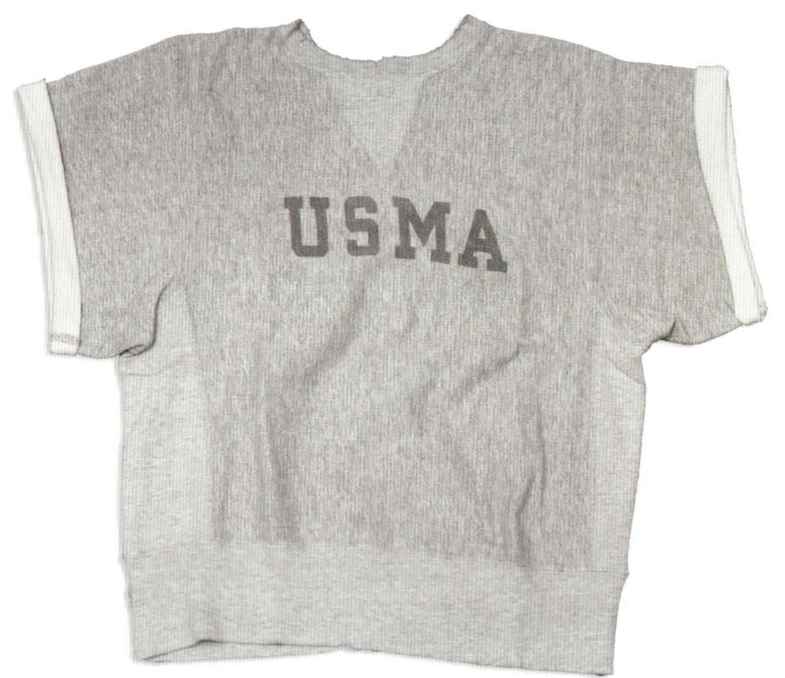

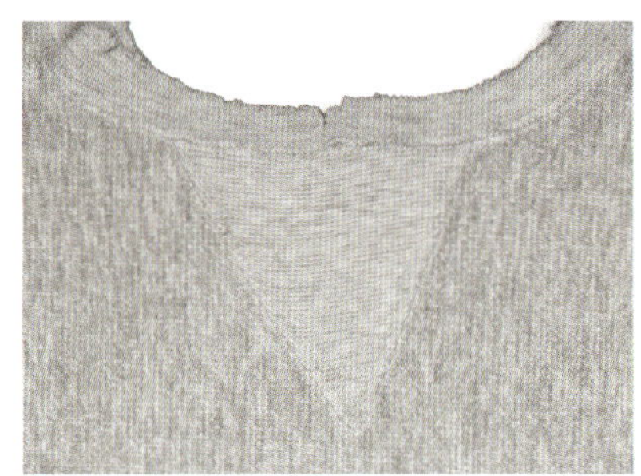

1980's
Champion sweatshirt
reverse wave "USMA"

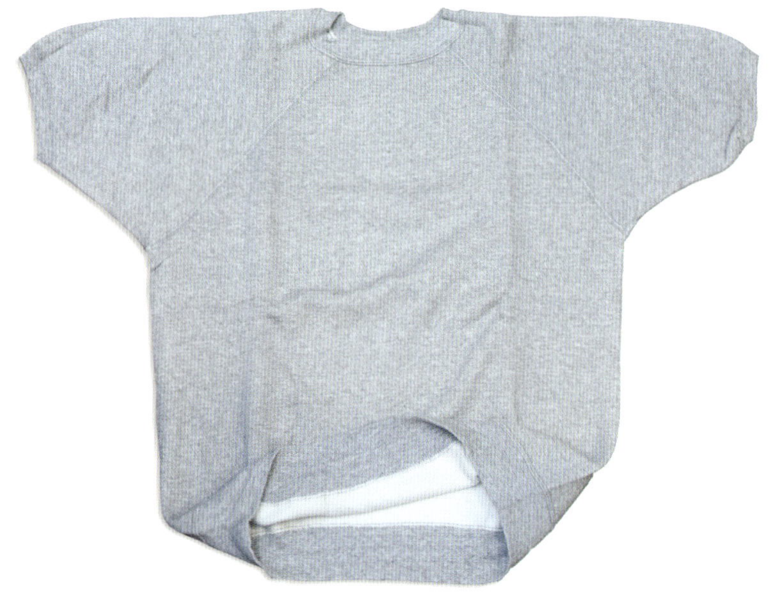

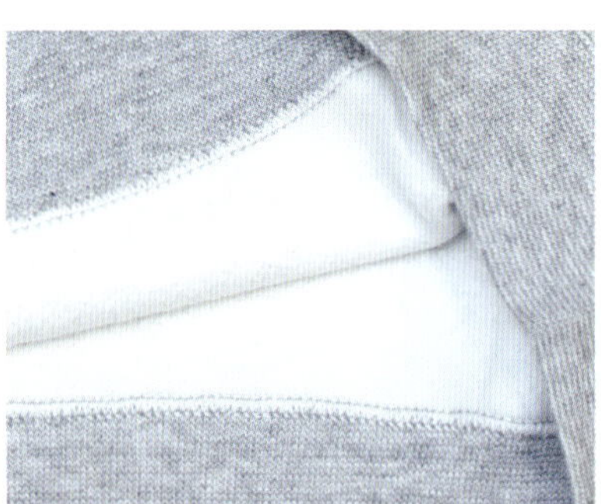

1970's
unknown sweatshirt
crewneck short sleeve

1960's
unknown sweatshirt
crewneck

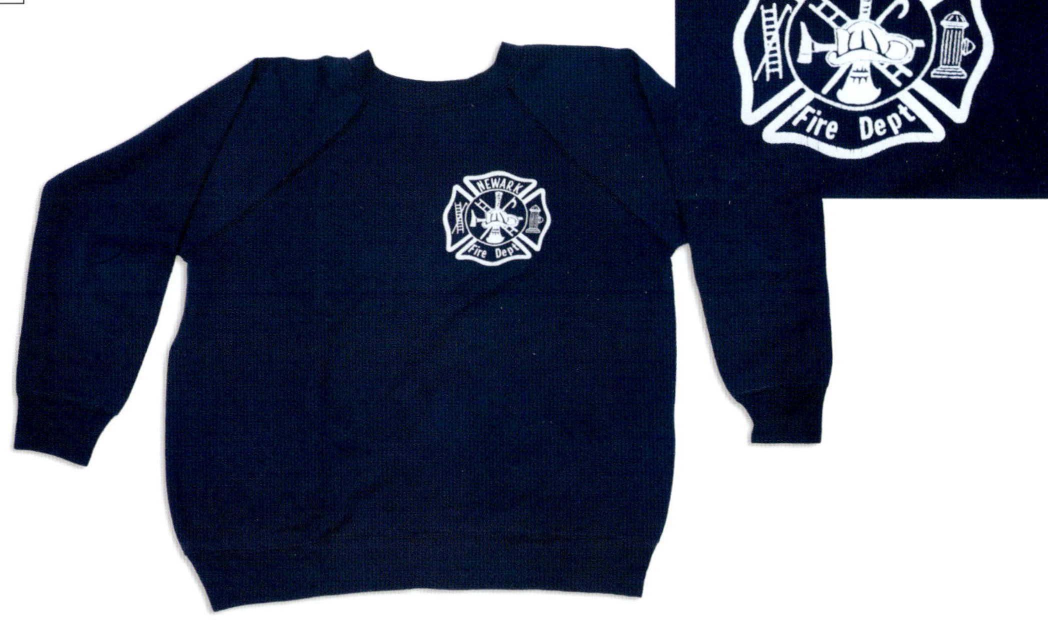

1950's
Russell sweatshirt
"single V"

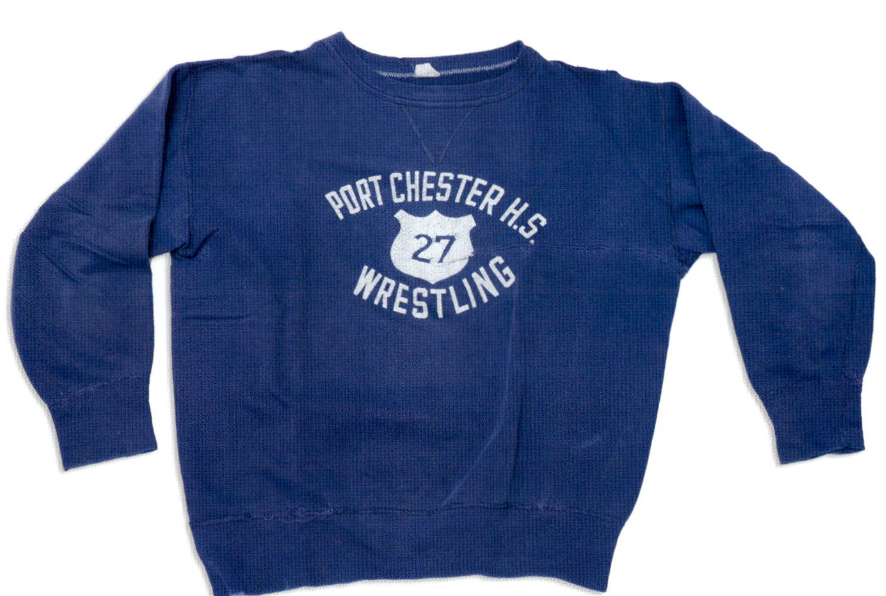

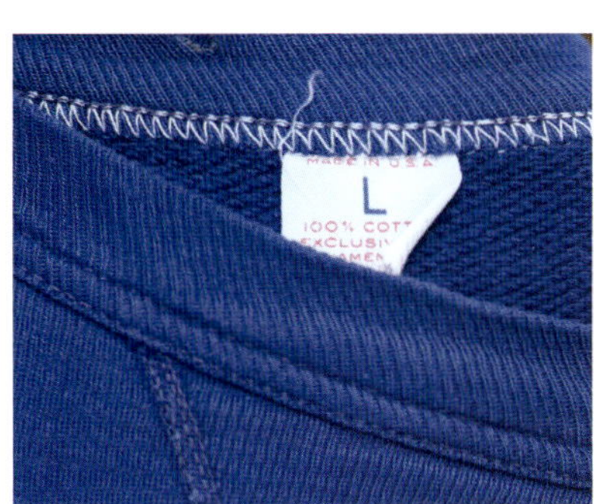

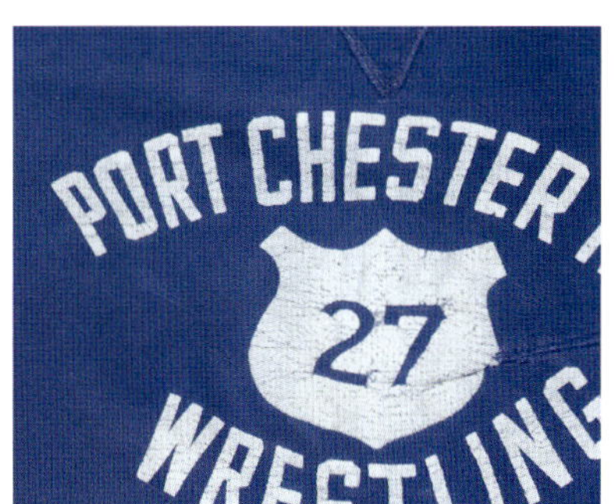

1940's
unknown
stadium jacket

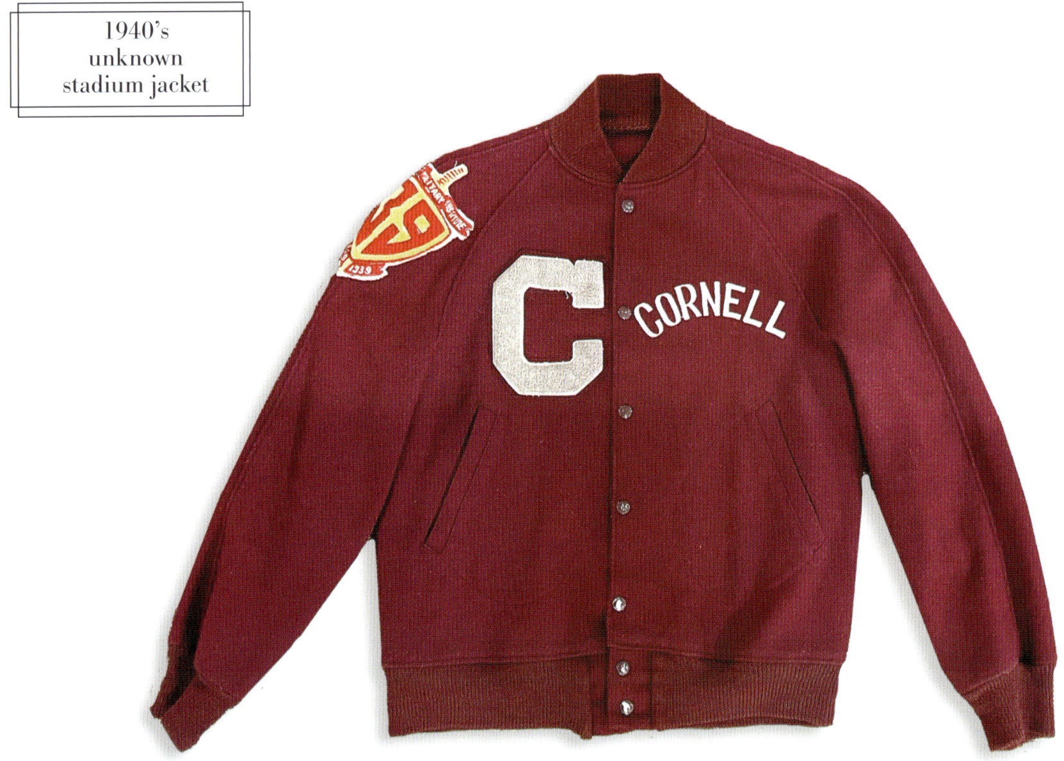

1950's
School Uniform
jacket

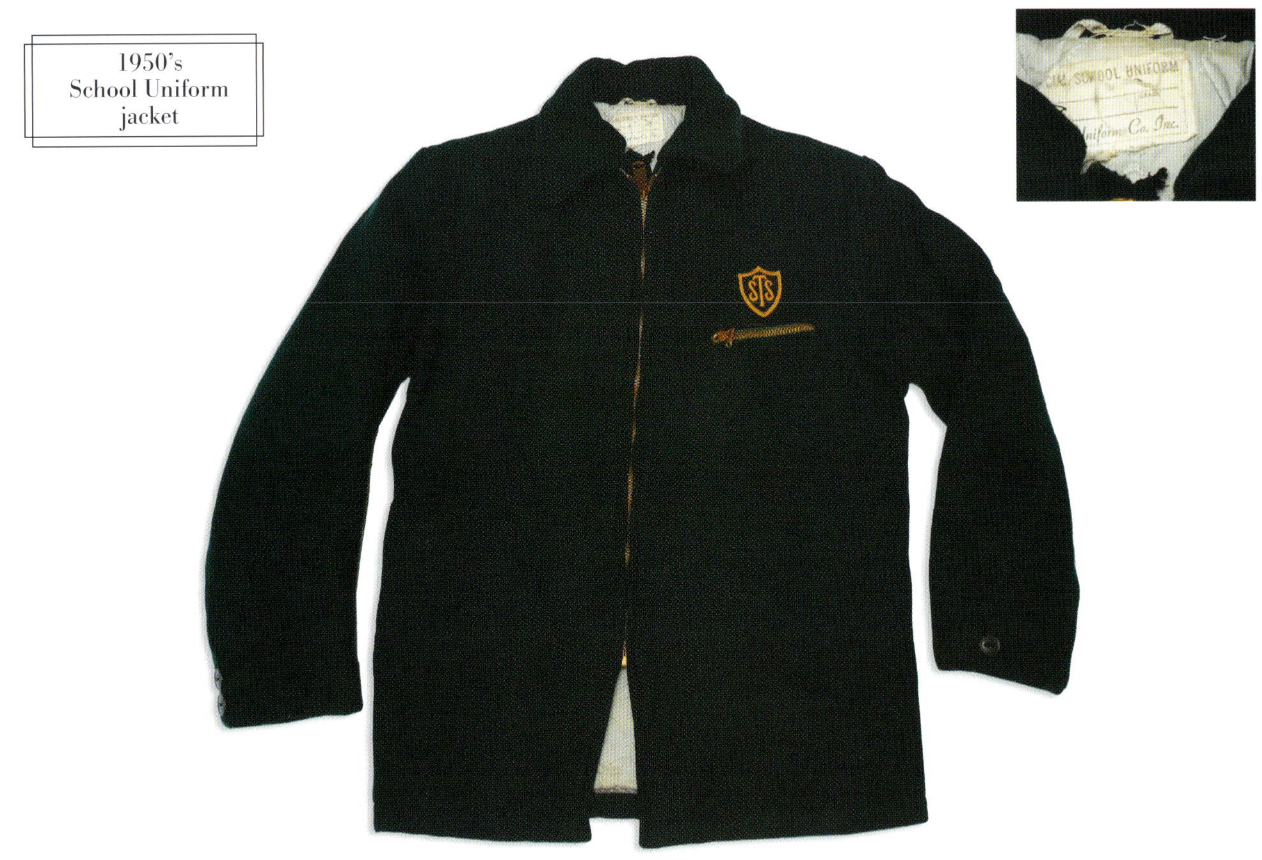

1960's
Sparlings
stadium jacket

1970's
De Long
stadium jacket

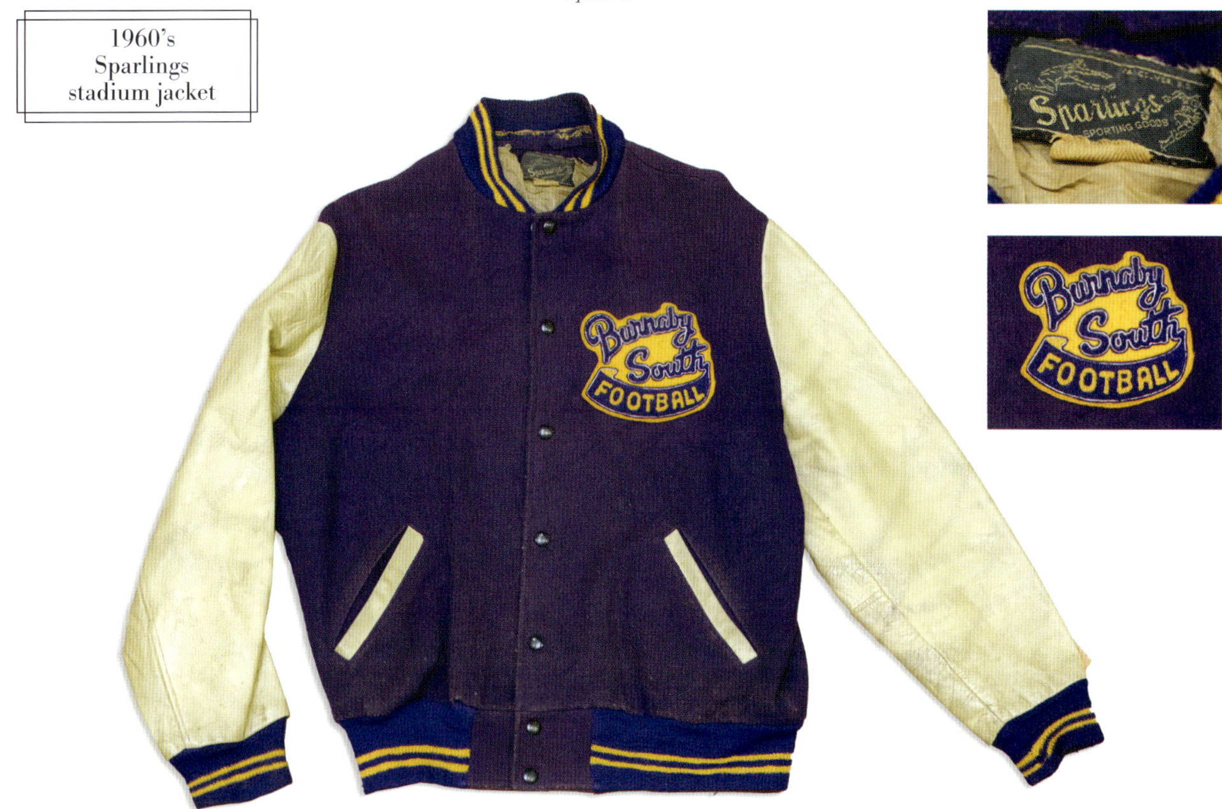

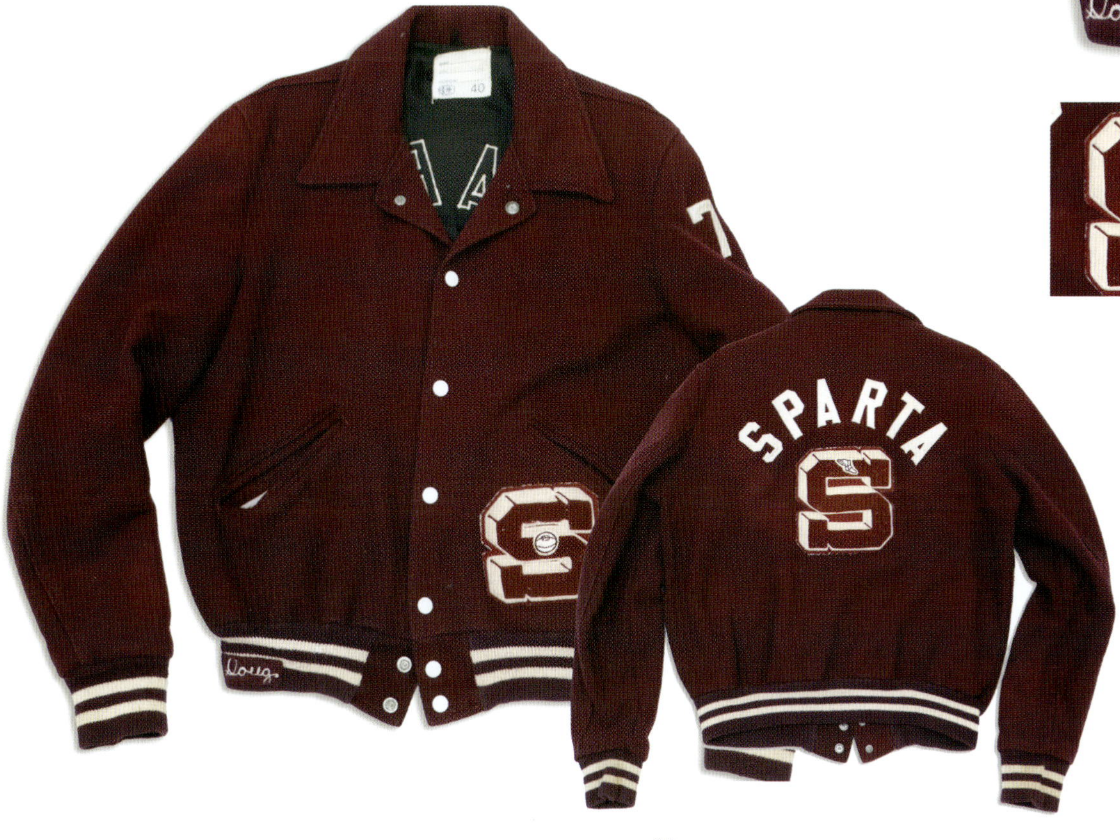

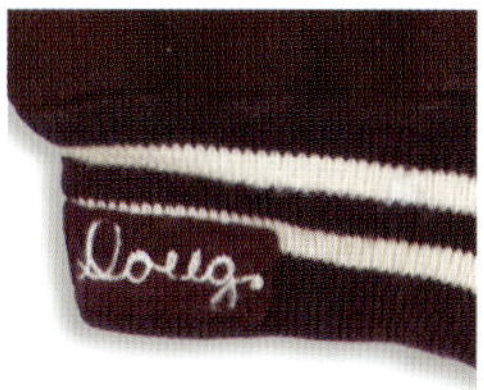

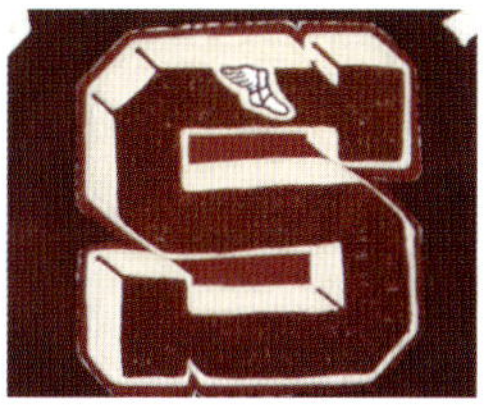

1940's
Butwin
stadium jacket

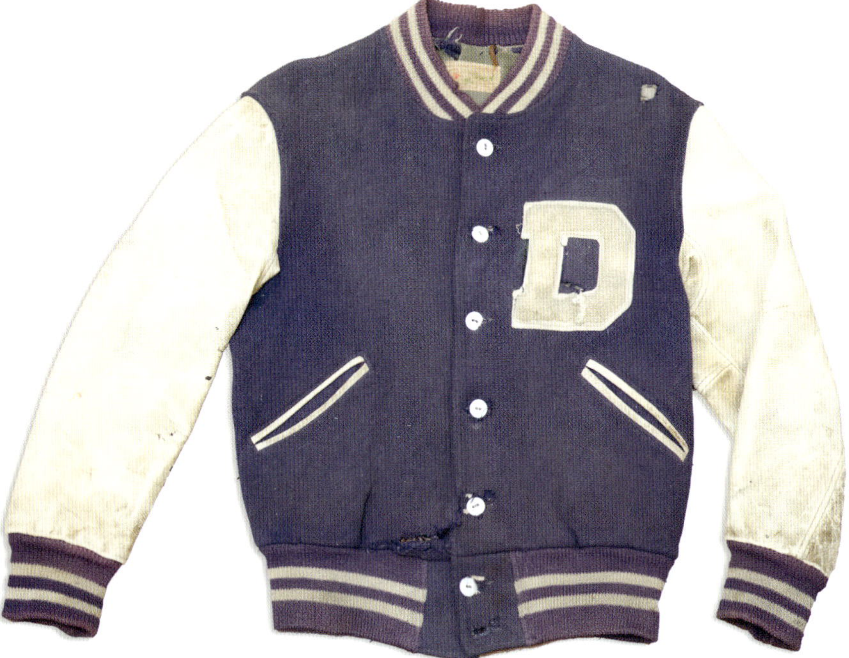

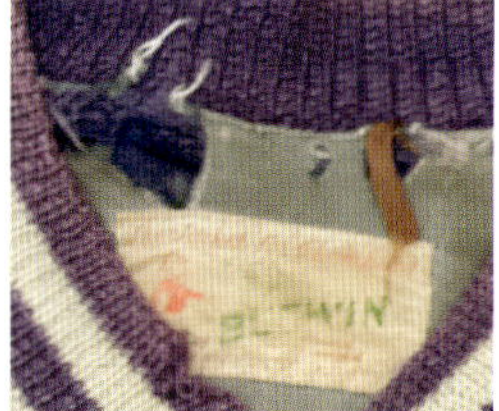

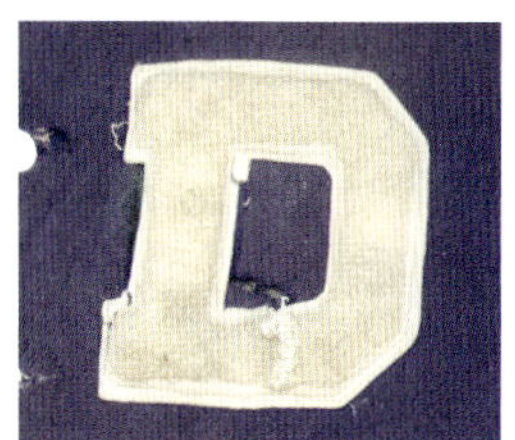

1970's
Naugalite
stadium jacket

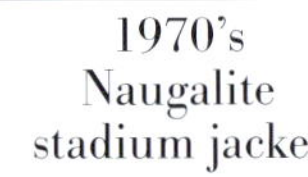

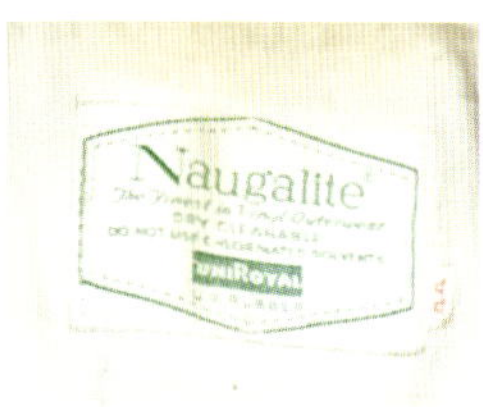

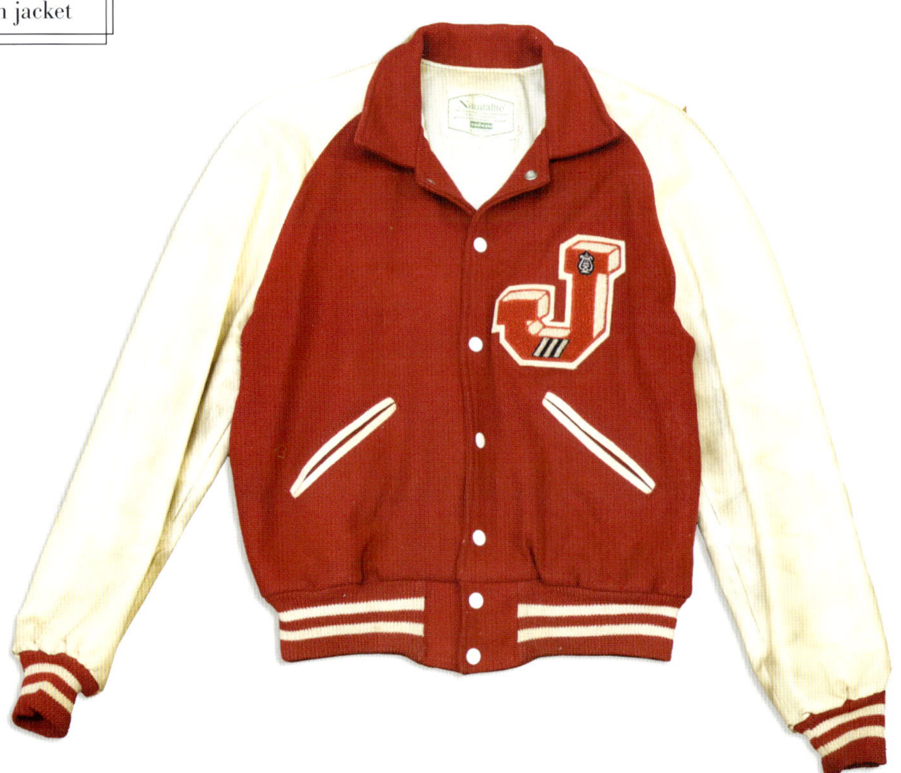

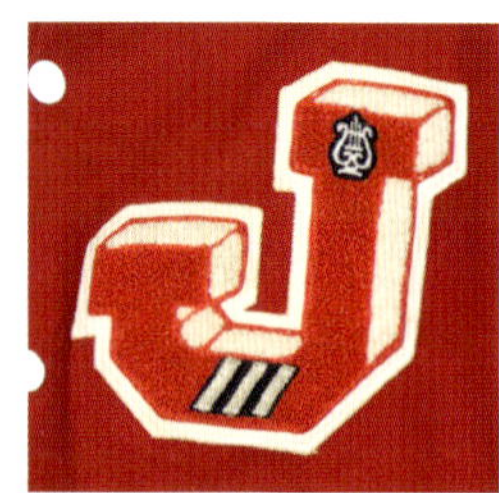

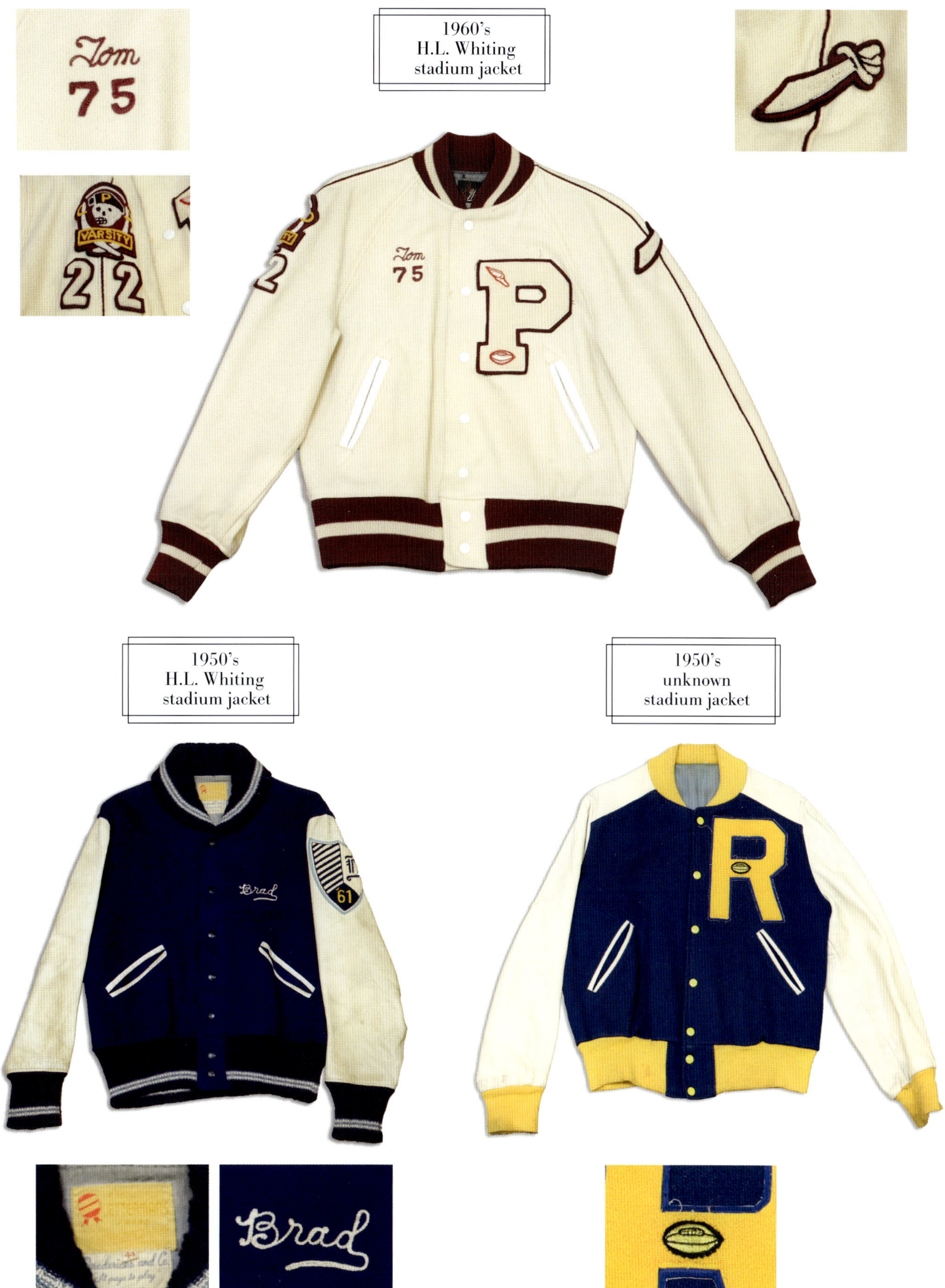
Tom
75
VARSITY
1960's
H.L. Whiting
stadium jacket
1950's
H.L. Whiting
stadium jacket
1950's
unknown
stadium jacket
Brad
Brad

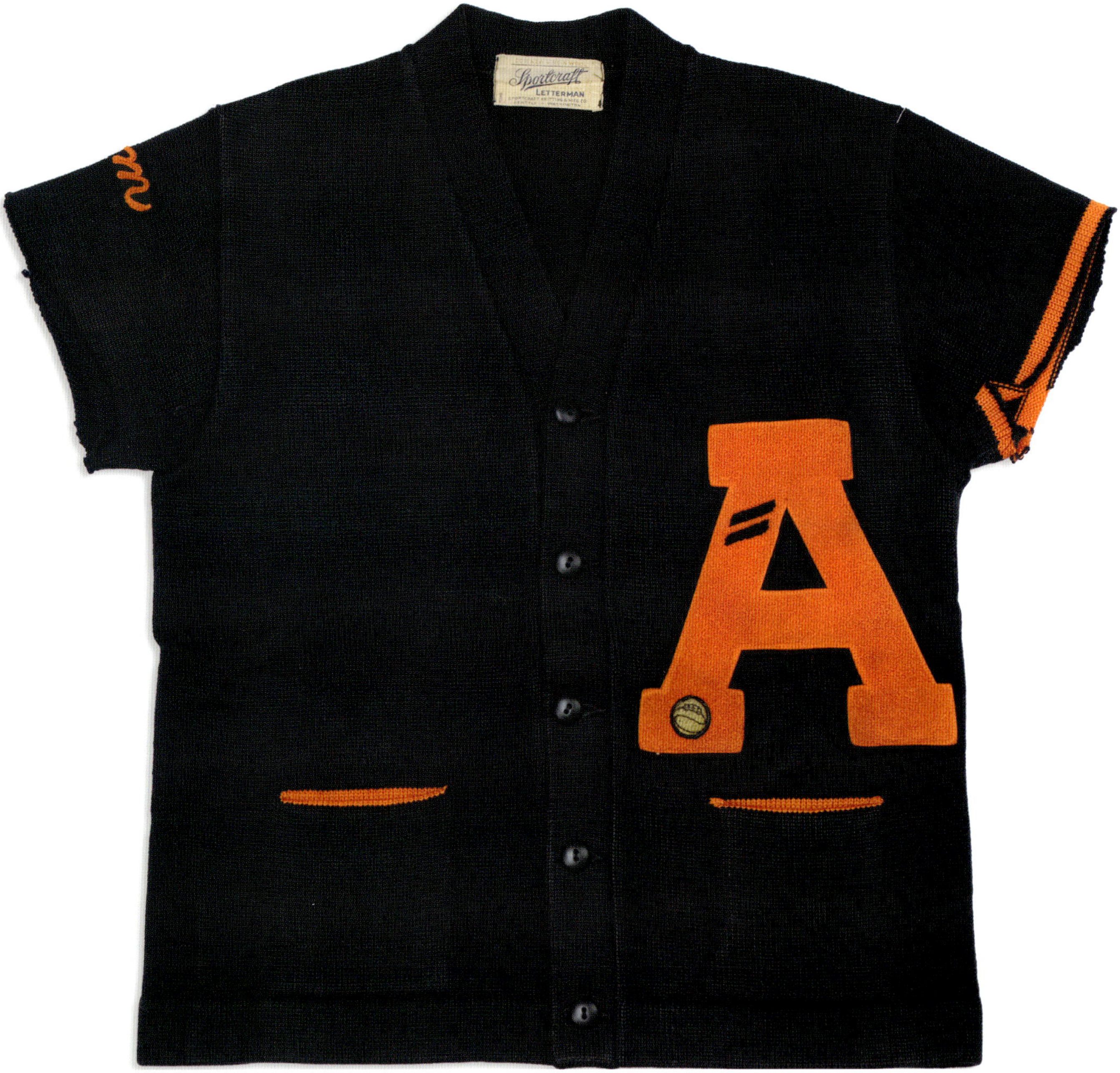

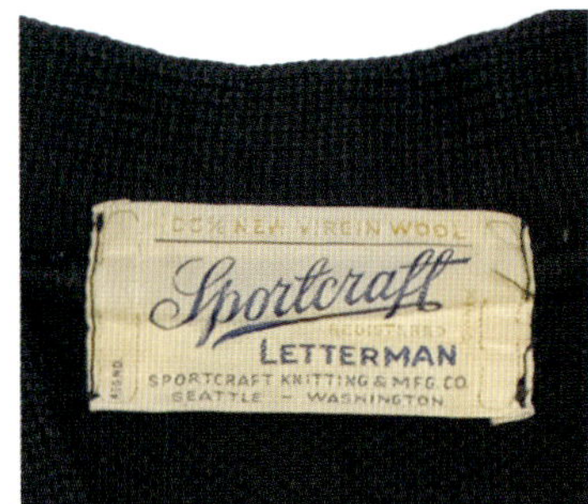

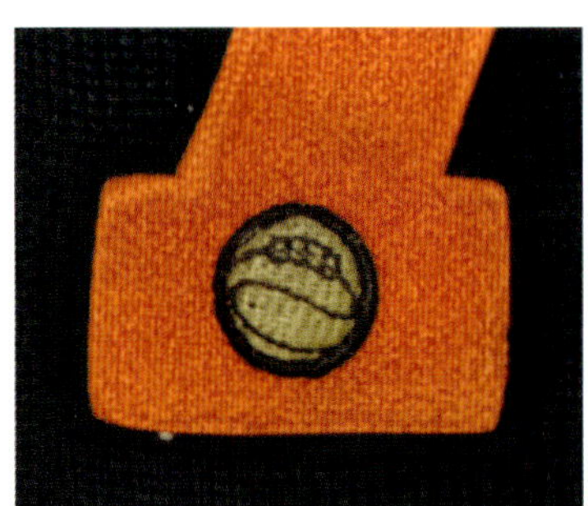

1950's
Sportcraft
letterman cardigan

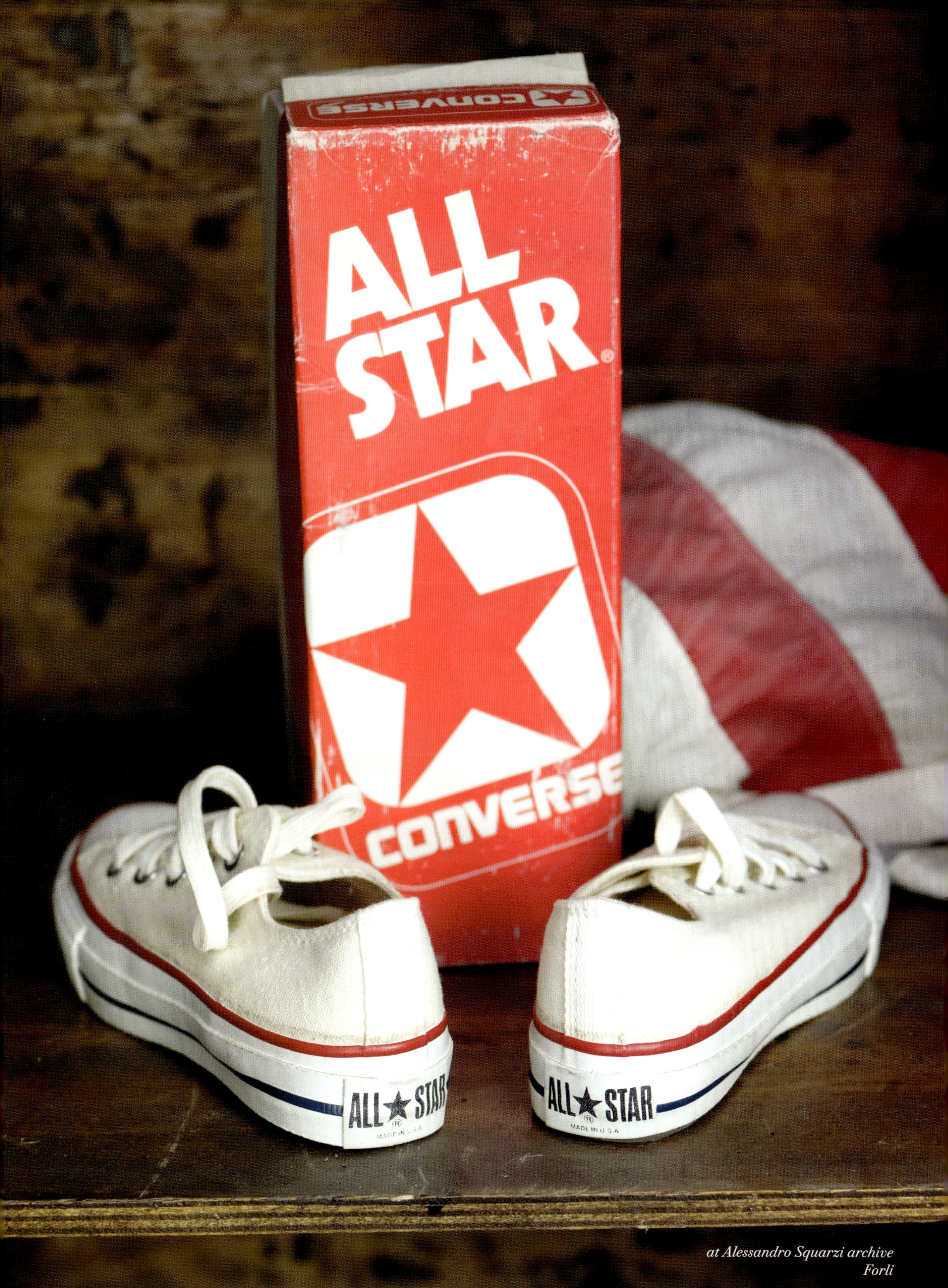

at Alessandro Squarzi archive
Forlì

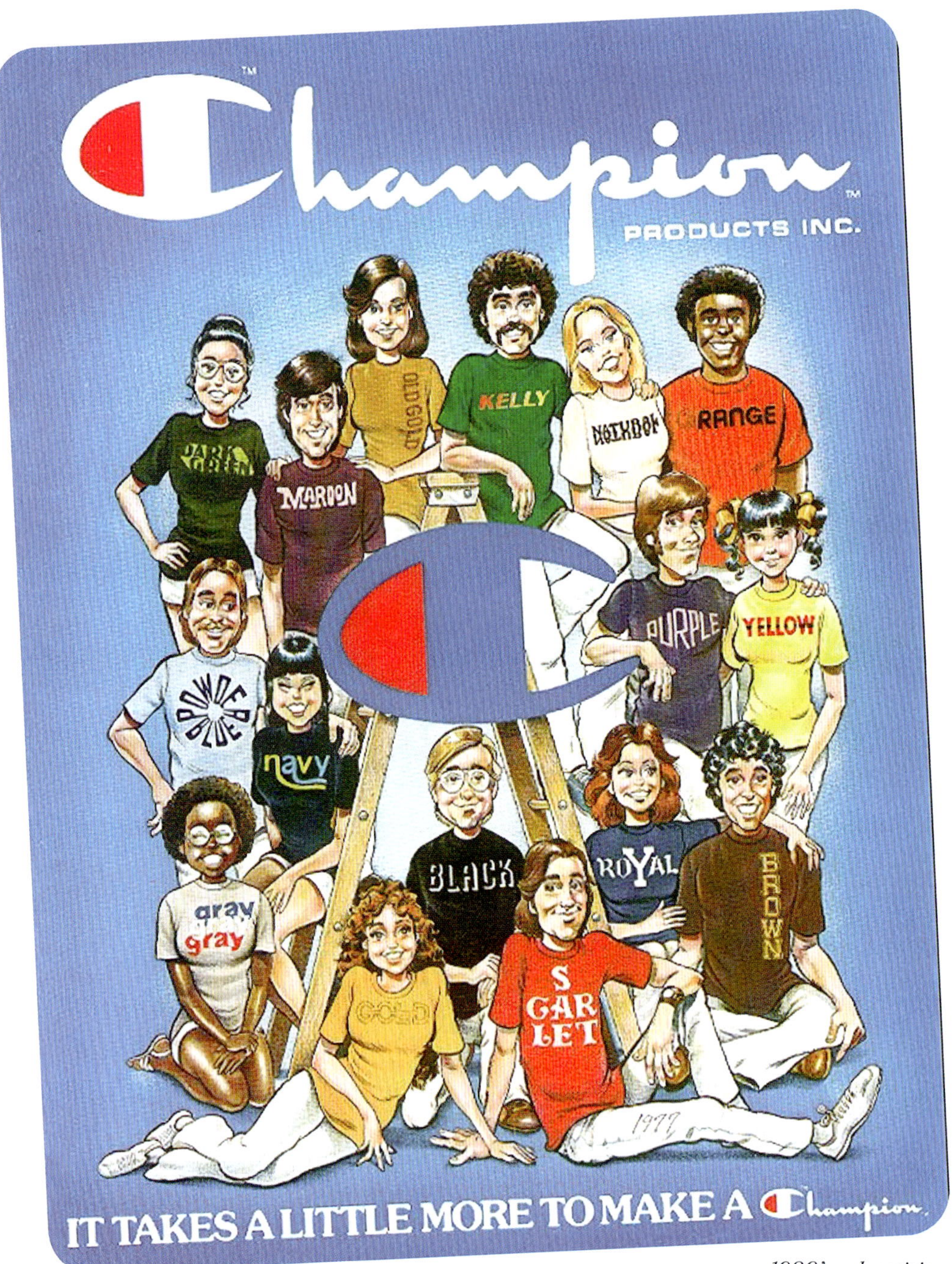

1980's advertising

1970's
Champion ringer T-shirt
"Blue bar"

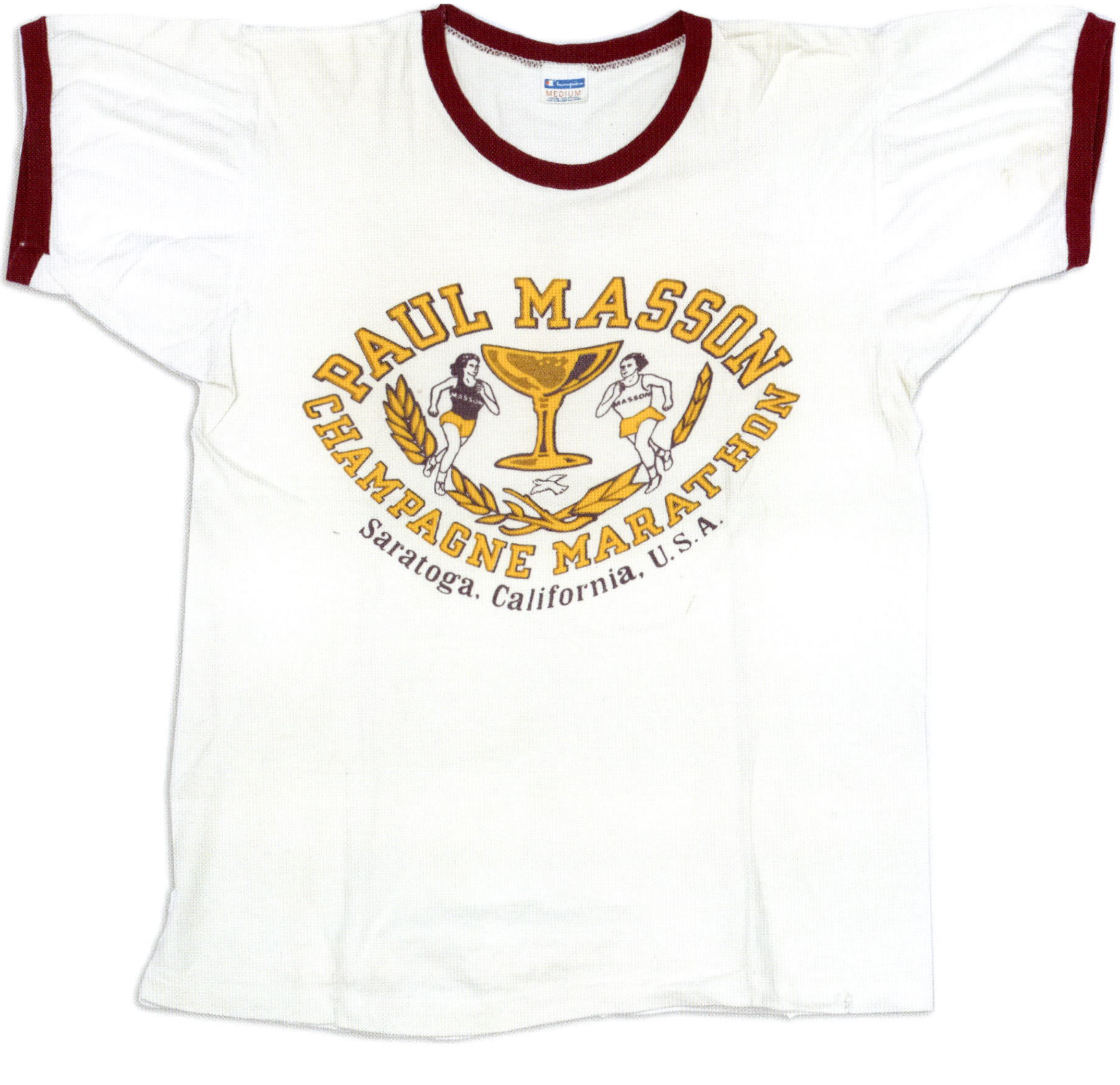

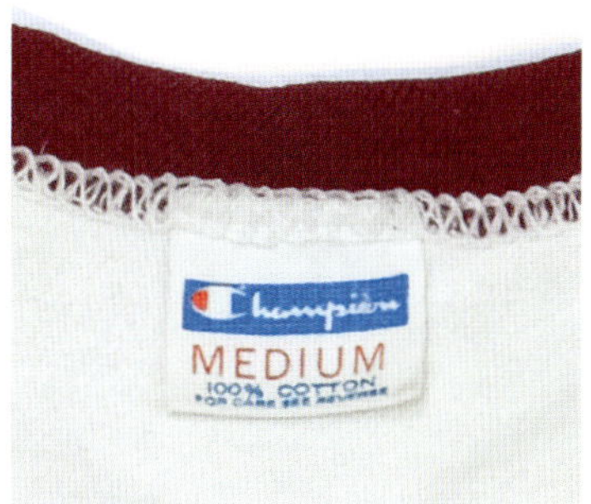

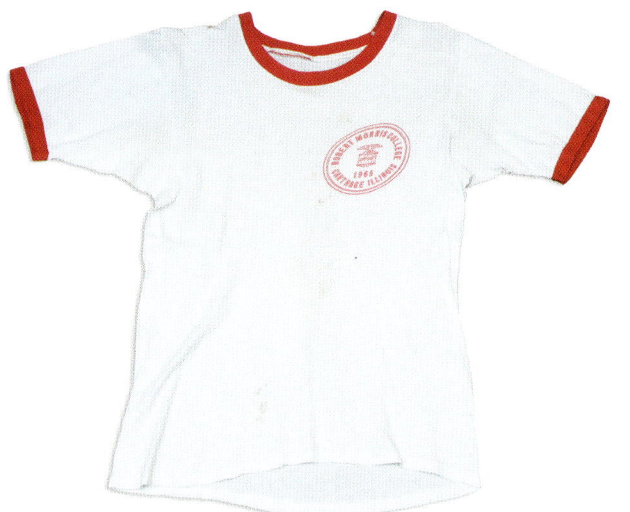

1960's
unknown
ringer T-shirt

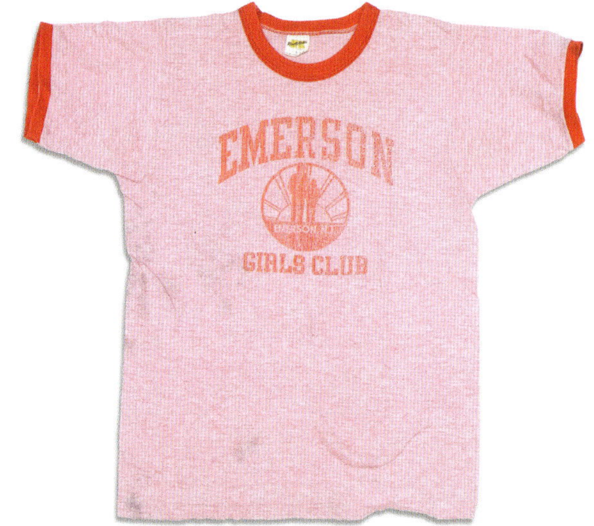

1970's
Russell Athletic
ringer T-shirt

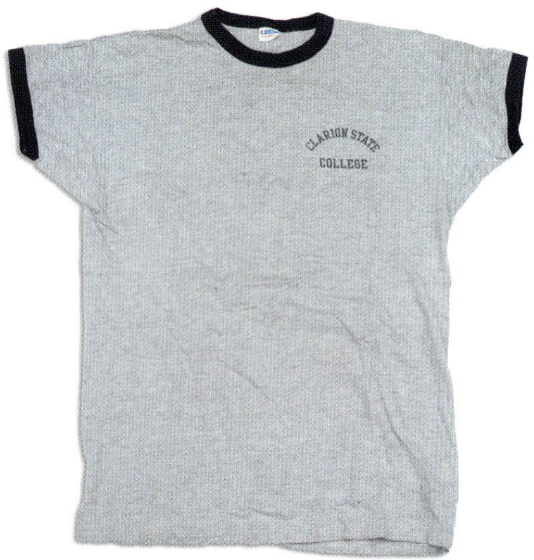

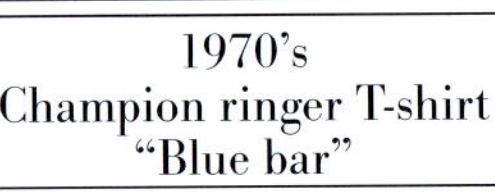

1970's
Champion ringer T-shirt
"Blue bar"

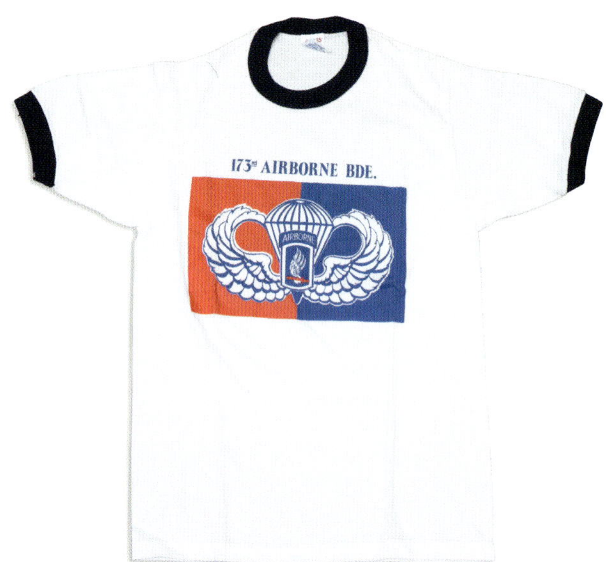

1980's
Jerzees
ringer T-shirt

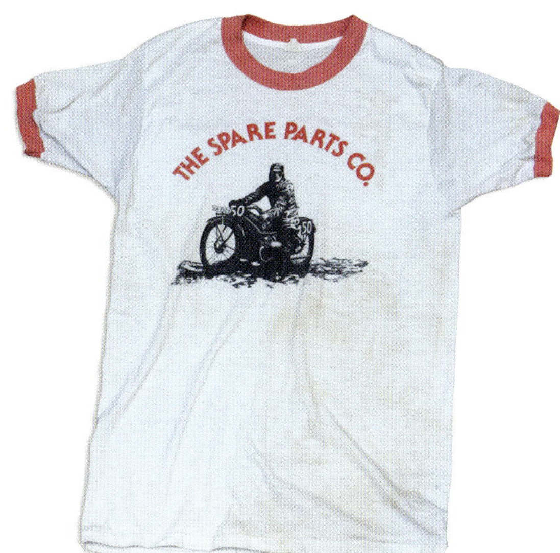

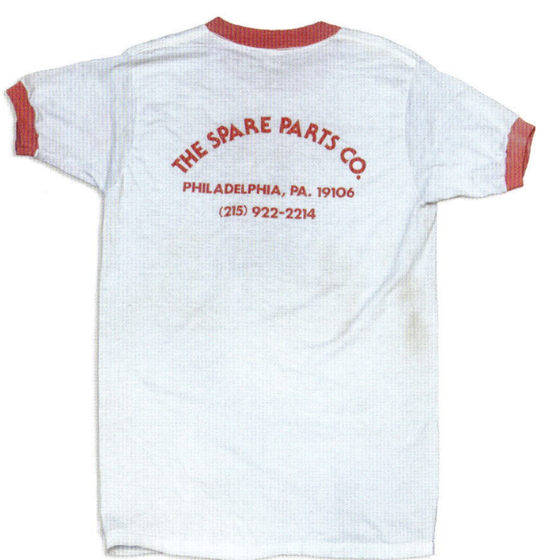

1980's
unknown
ringer T-shirt

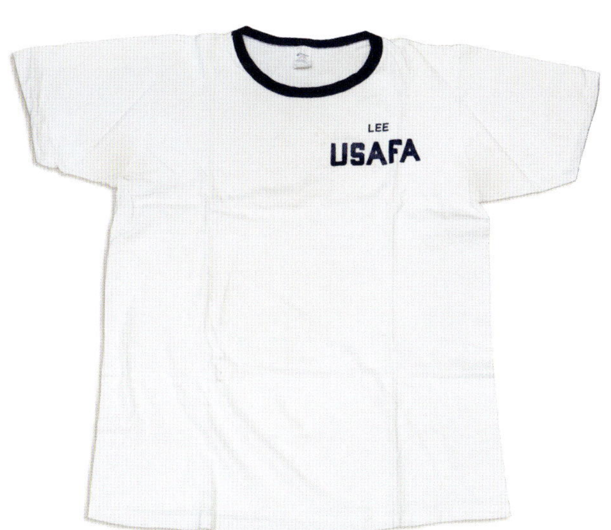

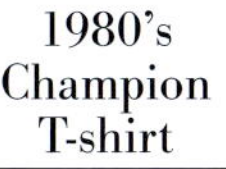

1980's
Champion
T-shirt

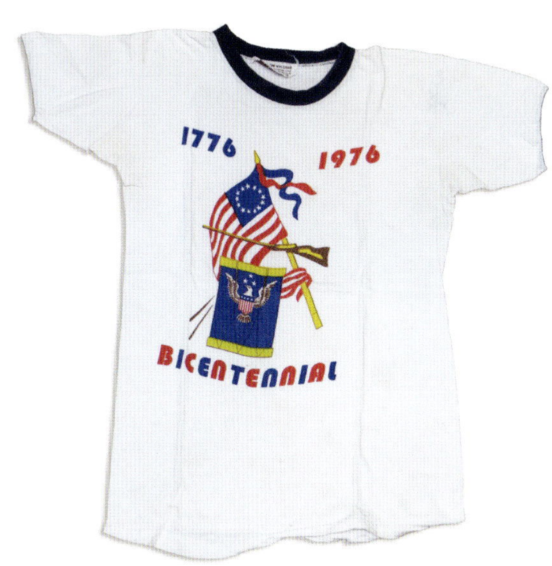

1970's
commemorative
T-shirt

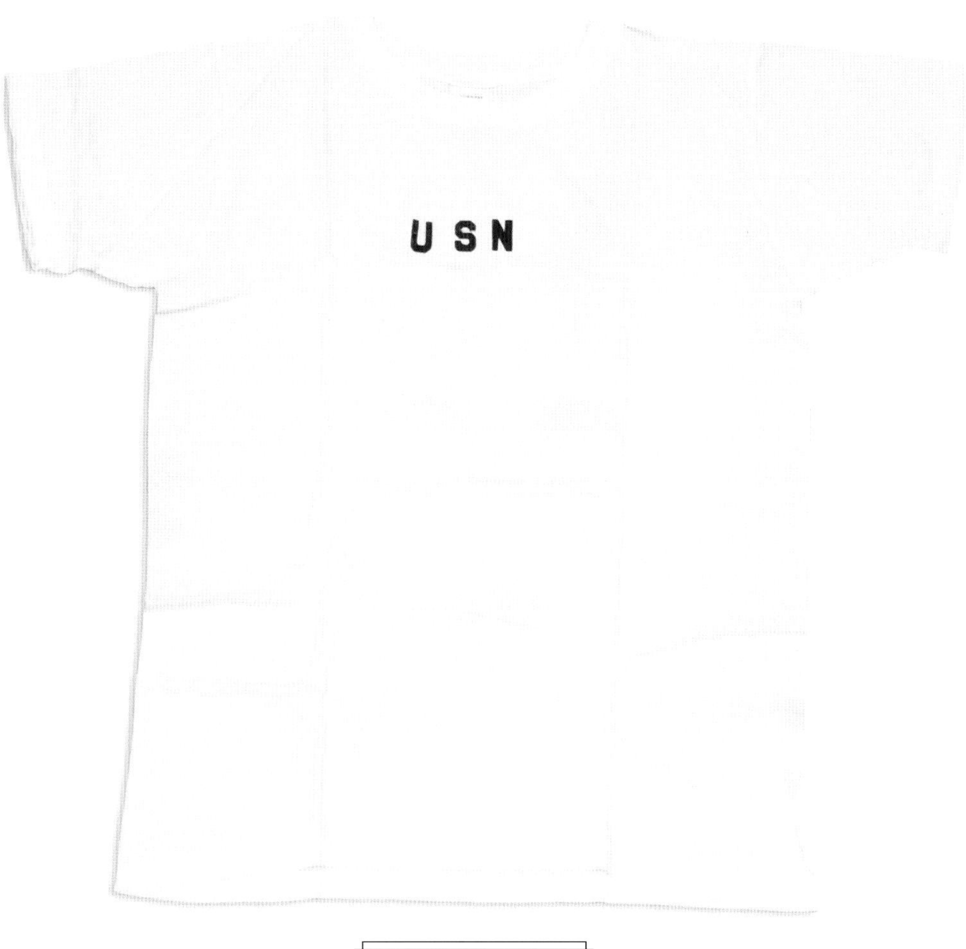

1970's
unknown
T-shirt

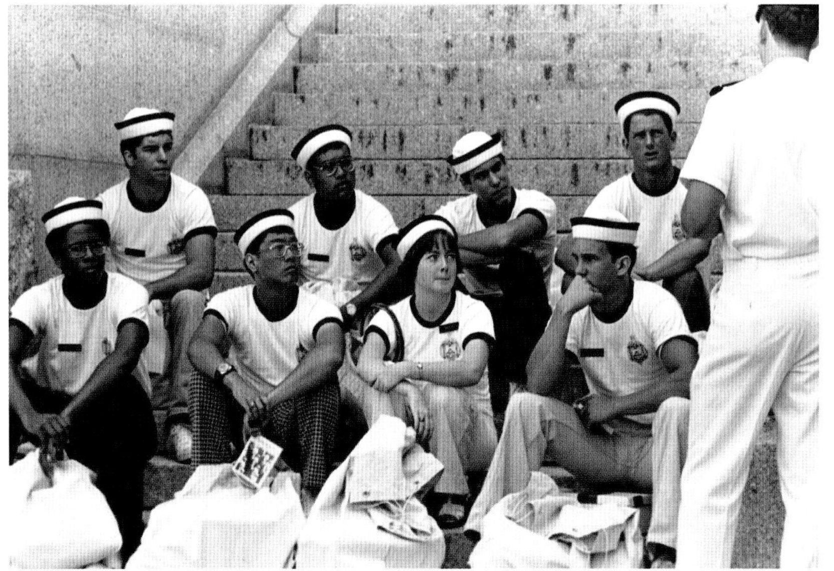

U.S. Naval Academy 1976

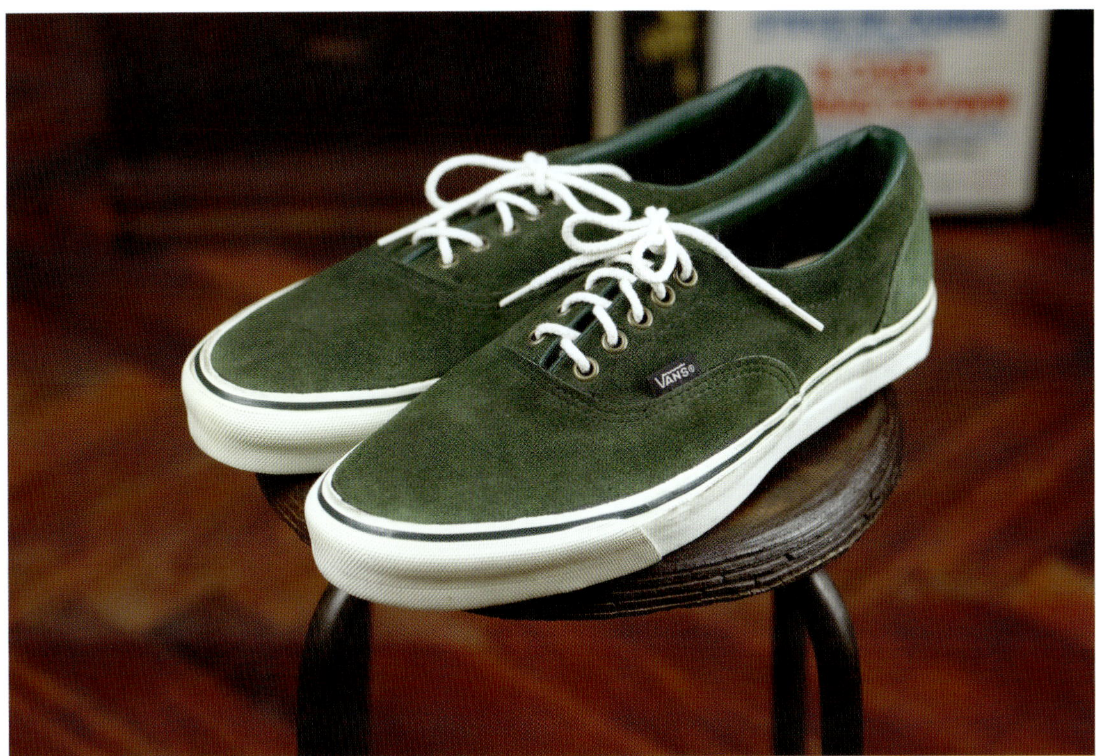

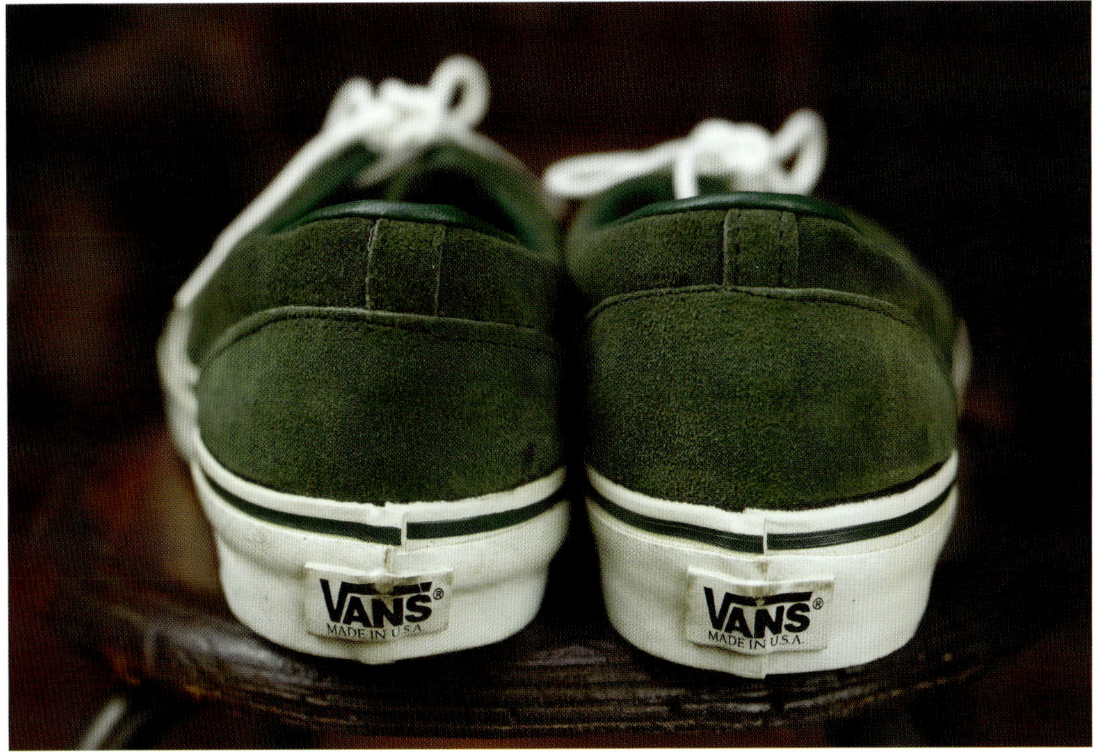

1990's
VANS Authentic
"Made in U.S.A."

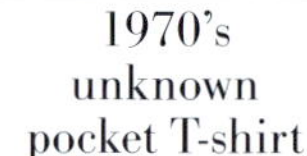

1970's
unknown
pocket T-shirt

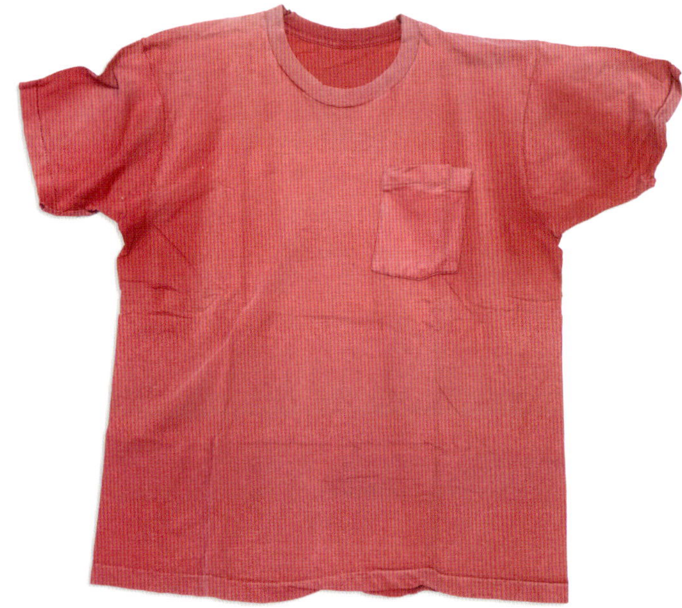

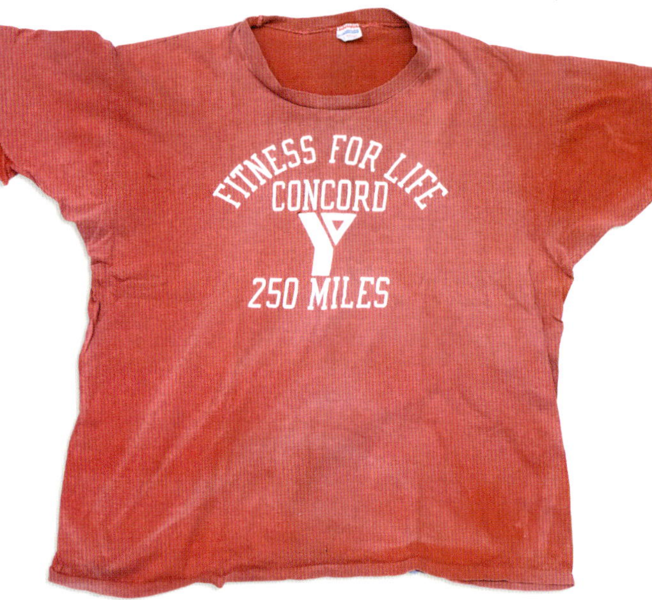

1970's
Champion T-shirt
"Blue bar"

1980's
unknown
pocket T-shirt

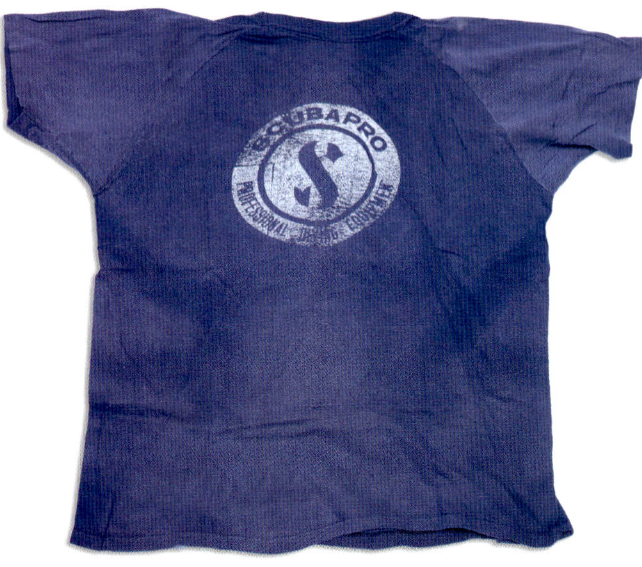

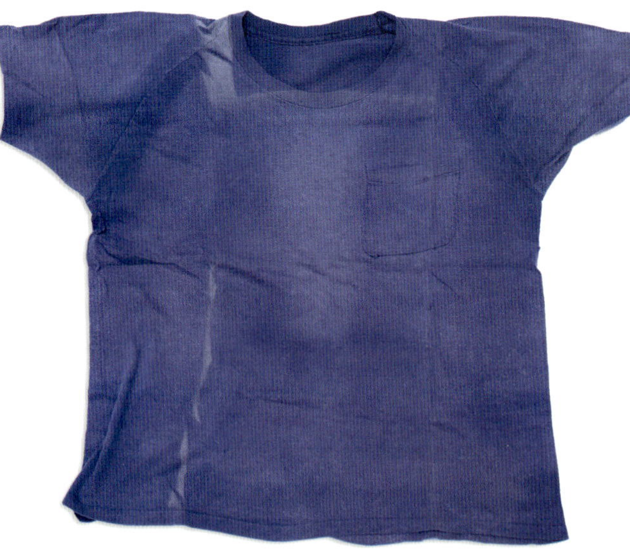

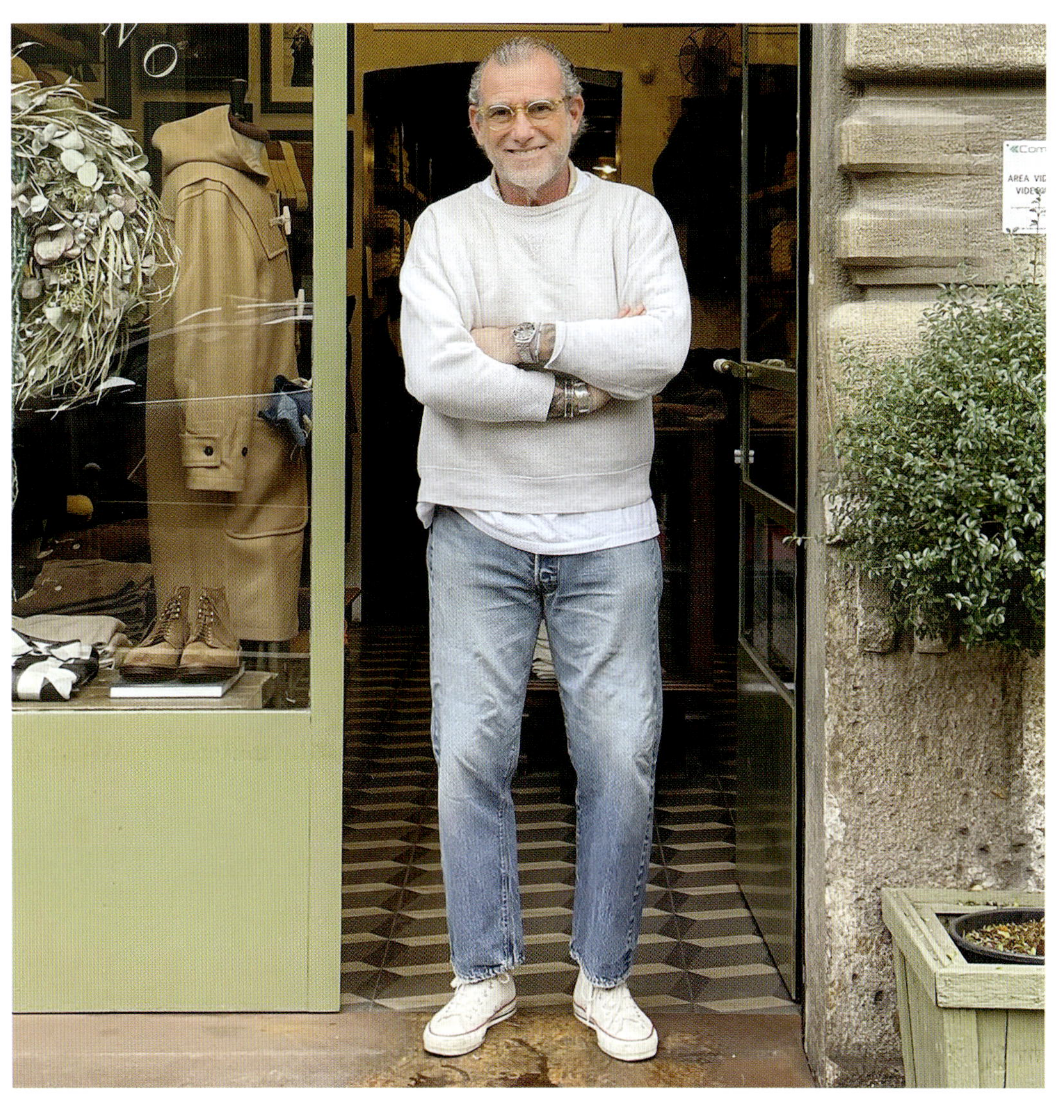

at Fortela store, Milano
Alessandro Squarzi photo archive

Military

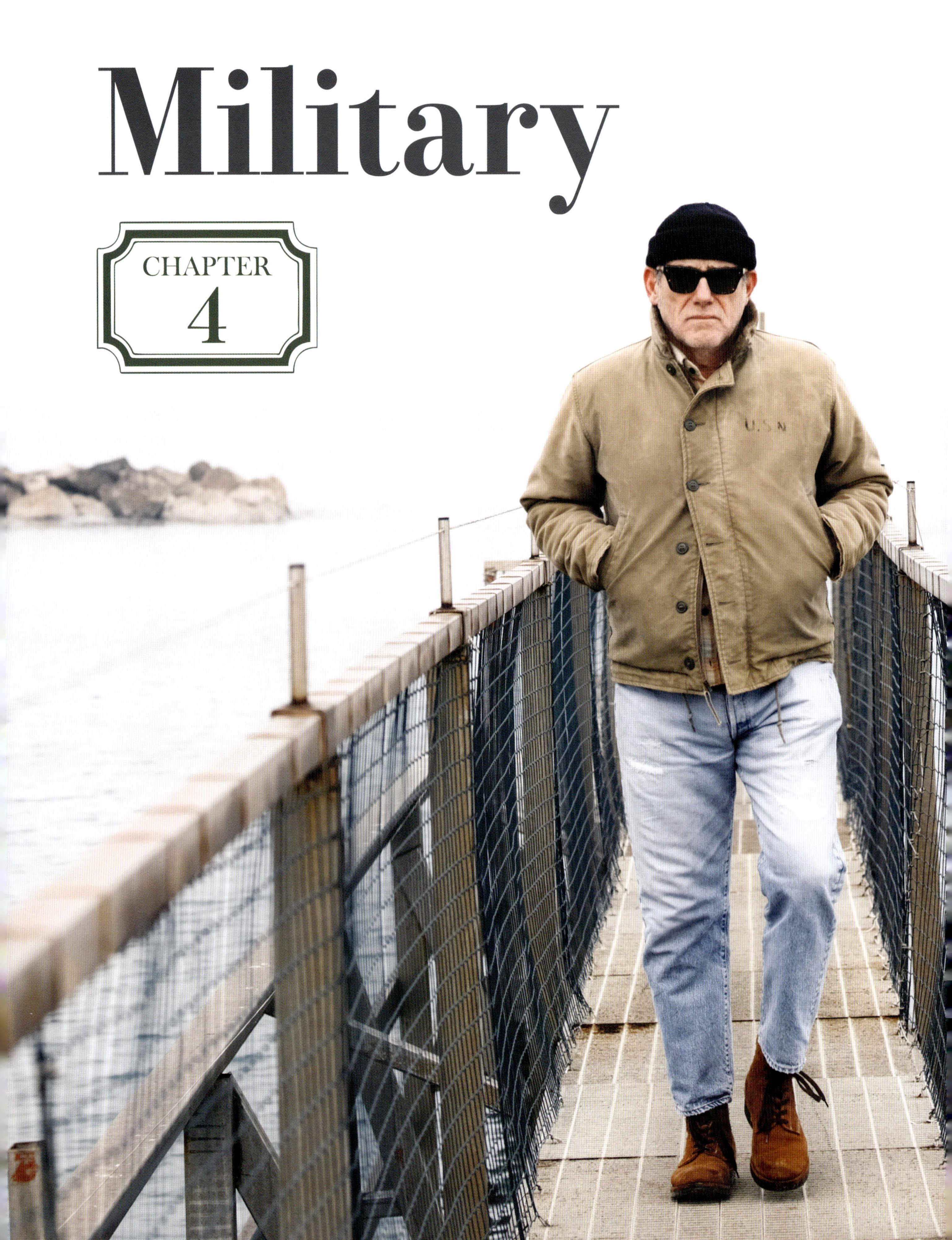

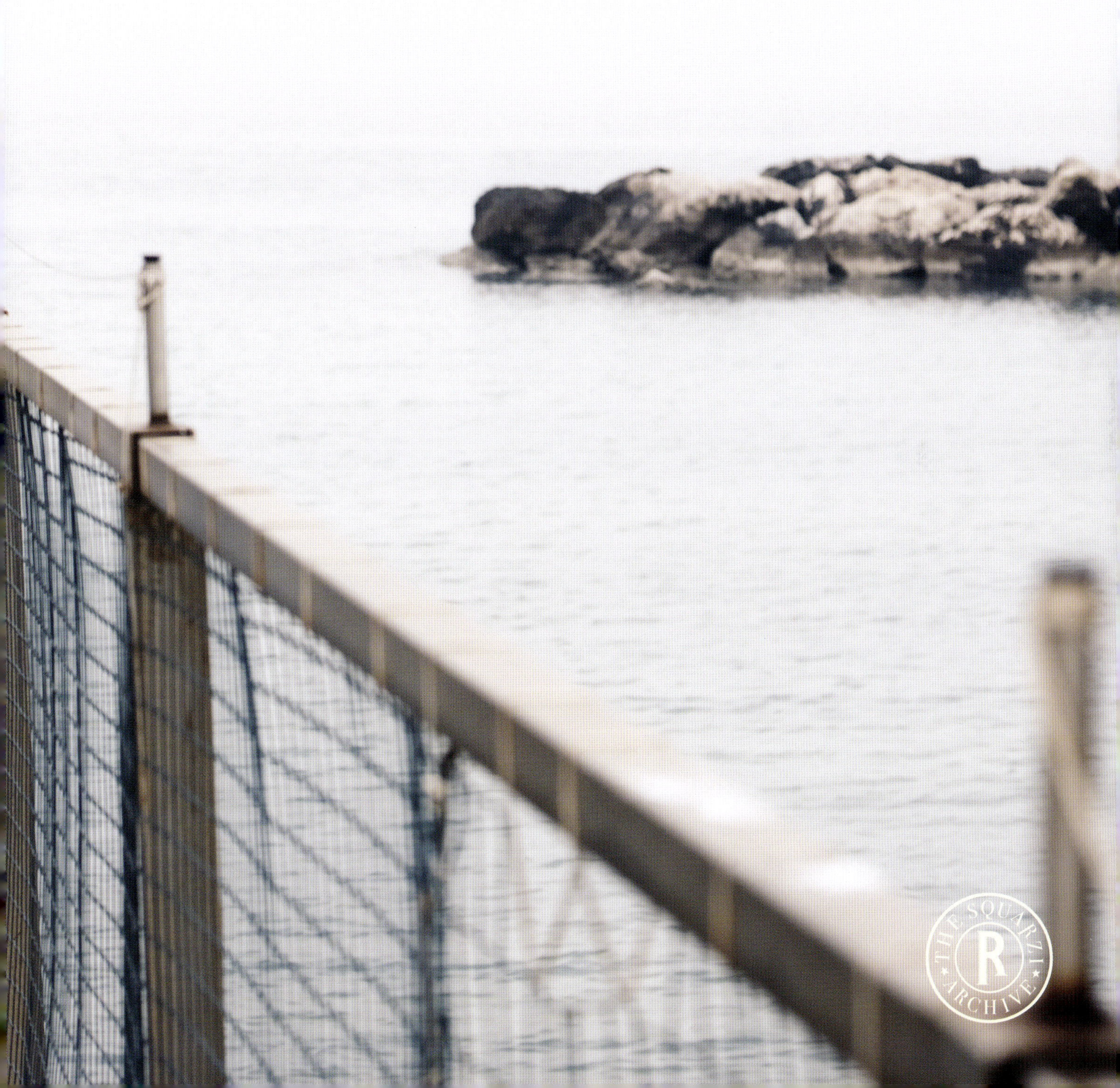

"Anything that has a history
will never go unnoticed."

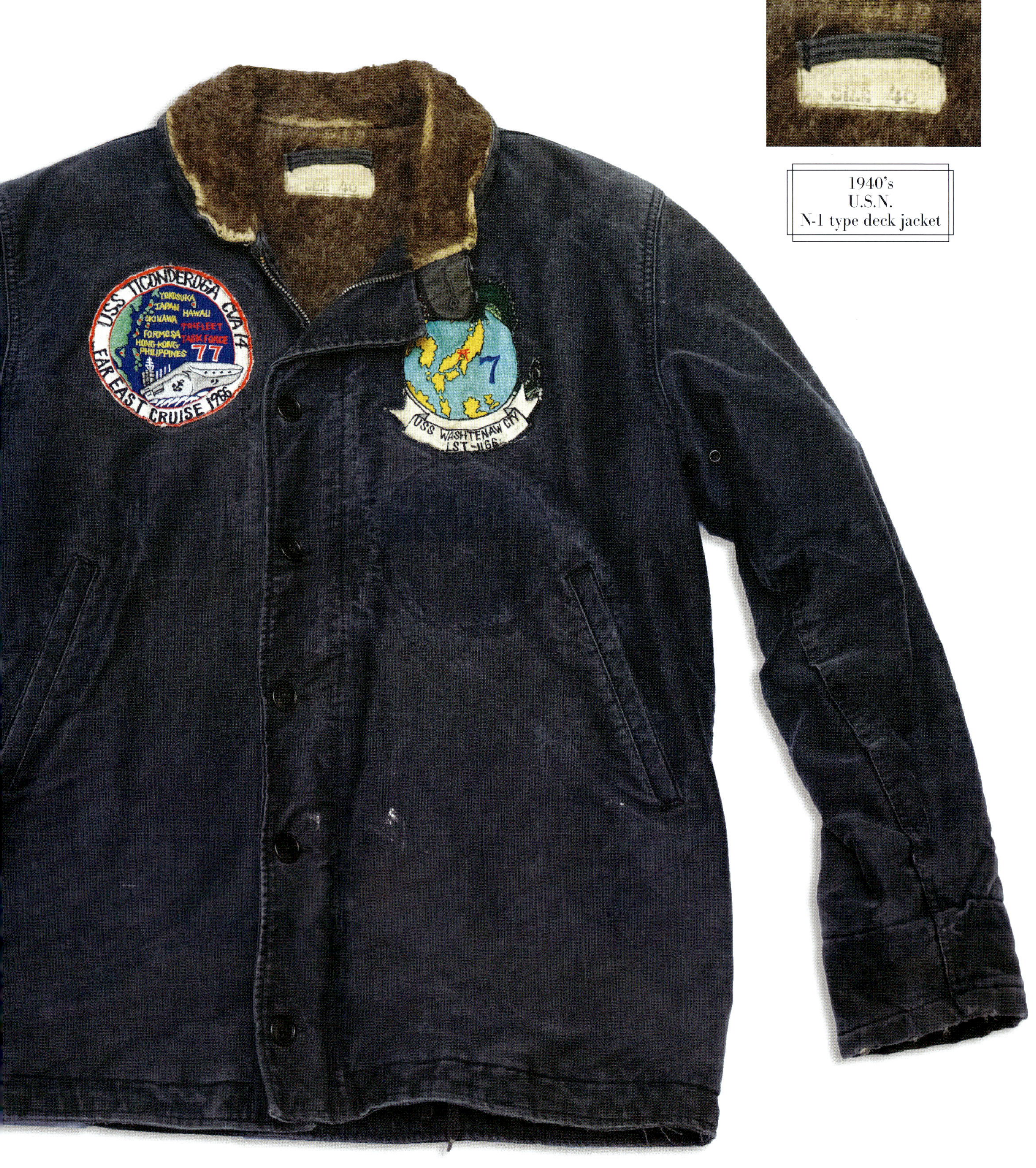

1940's
U.S.N.
N-1 type deck jacket

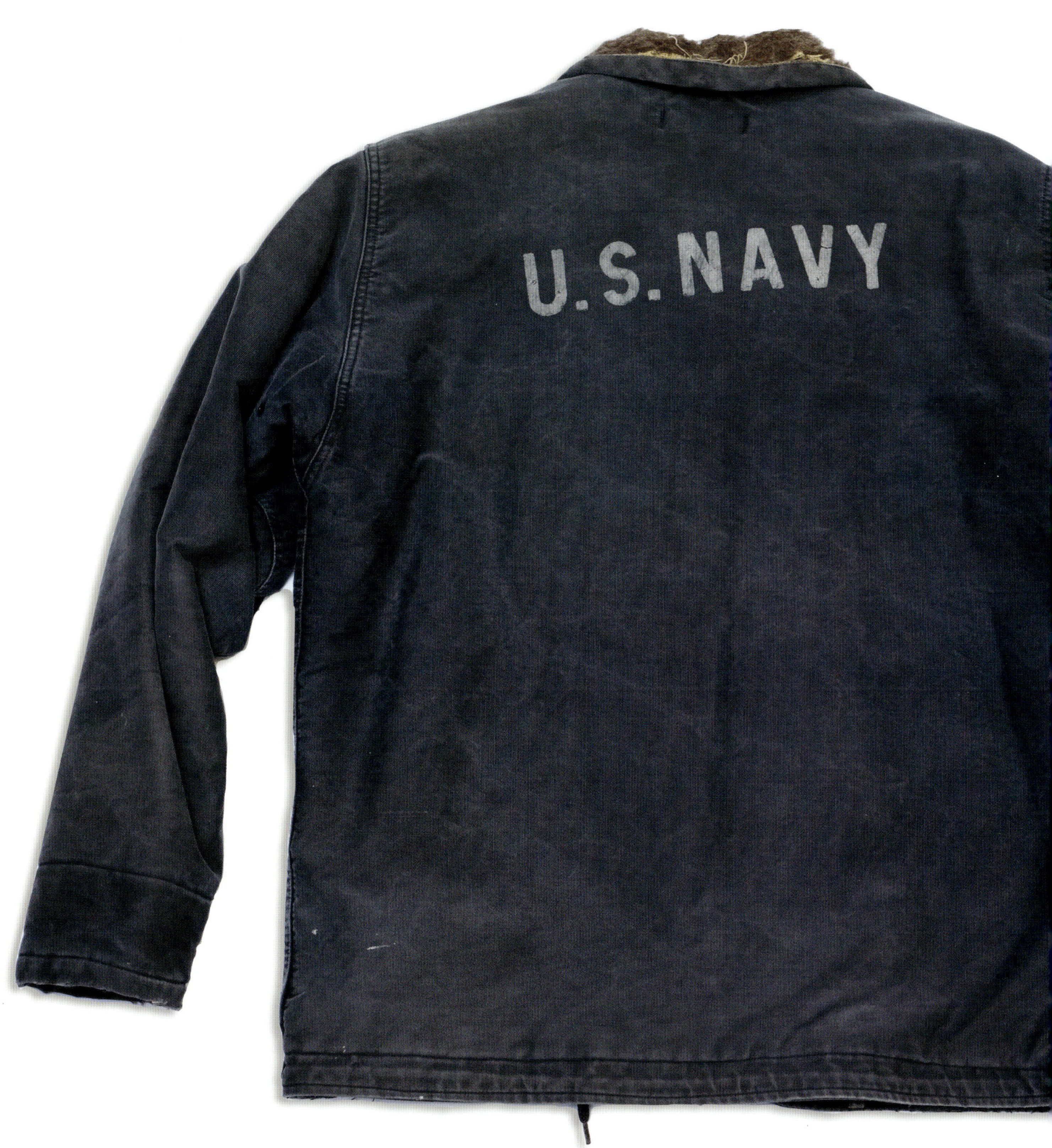

U.S.NAVY

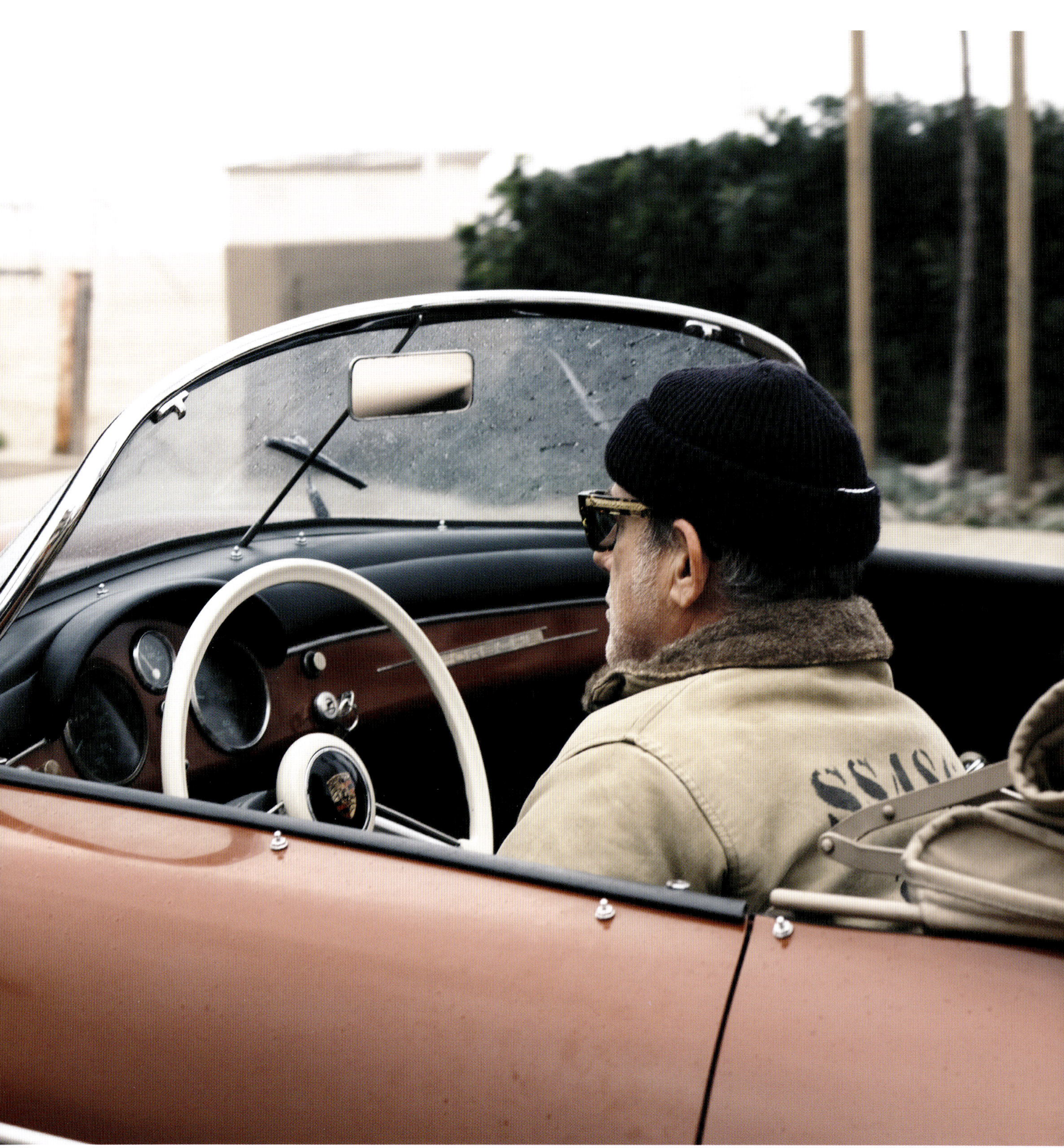

at Alessandro Squarzi home
Rimini

1940's
U.S.N.
N-1 type deck jacket

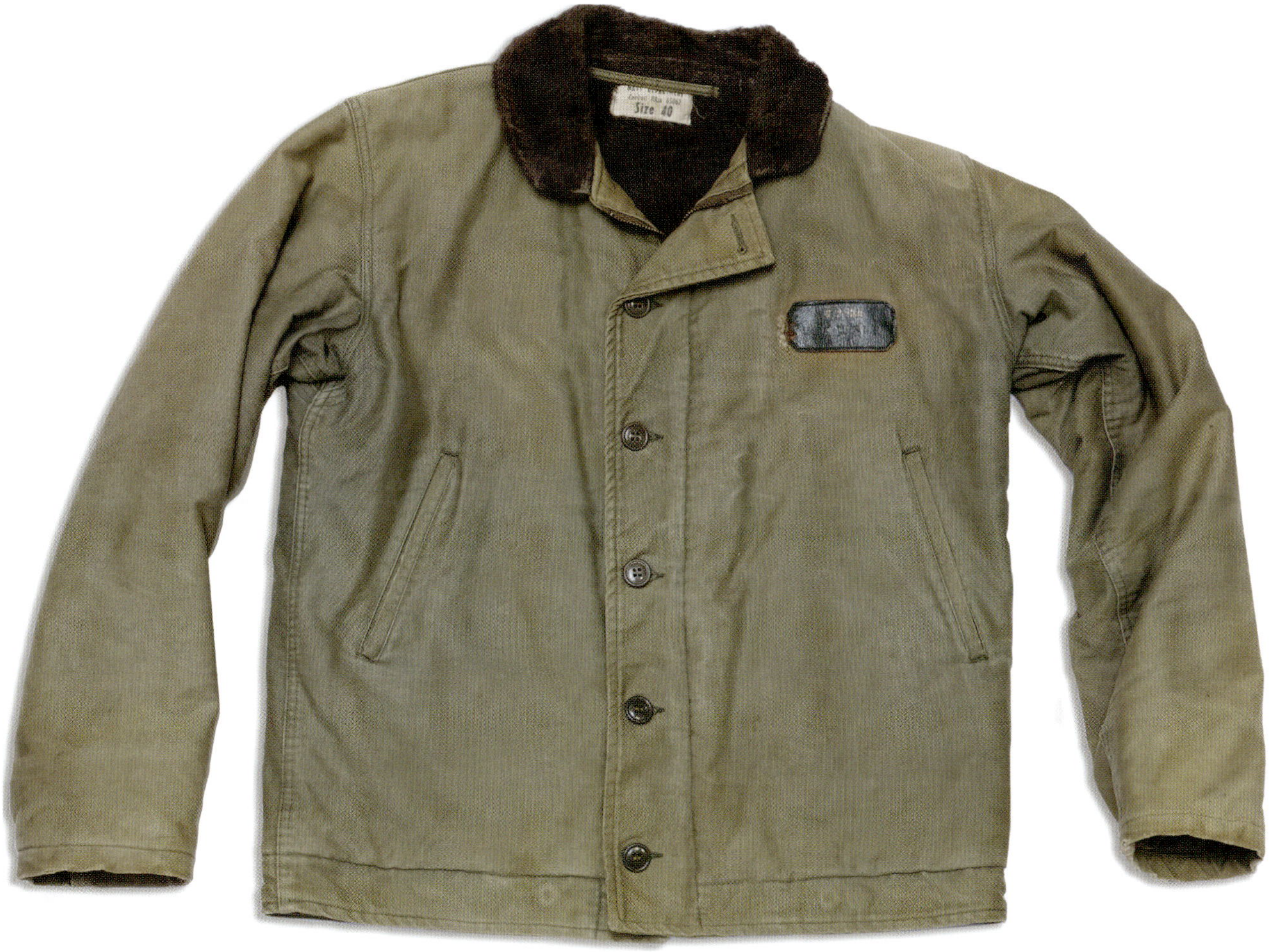

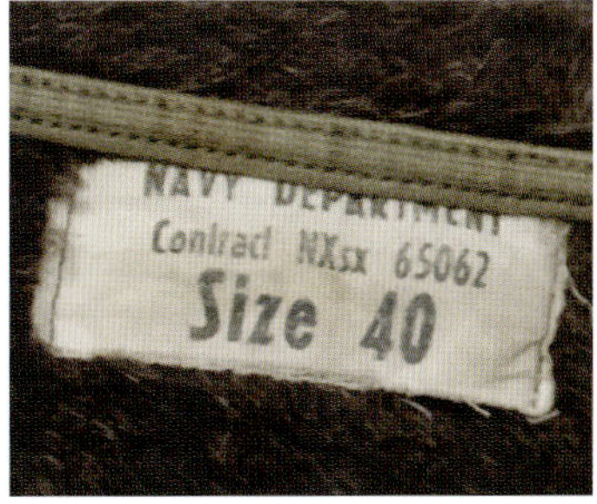

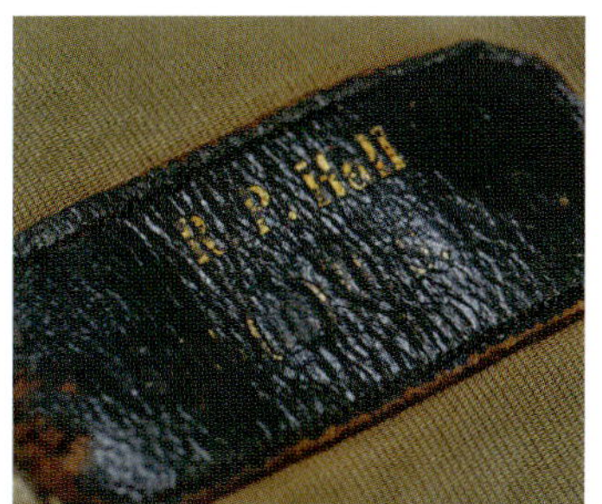

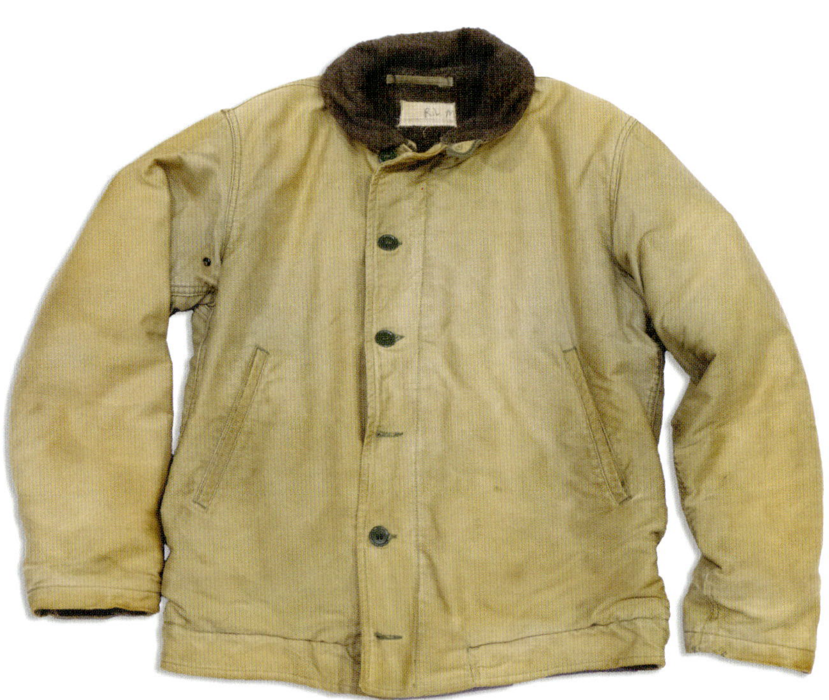

1940's
U.S.N.
N-1 type deck jacket

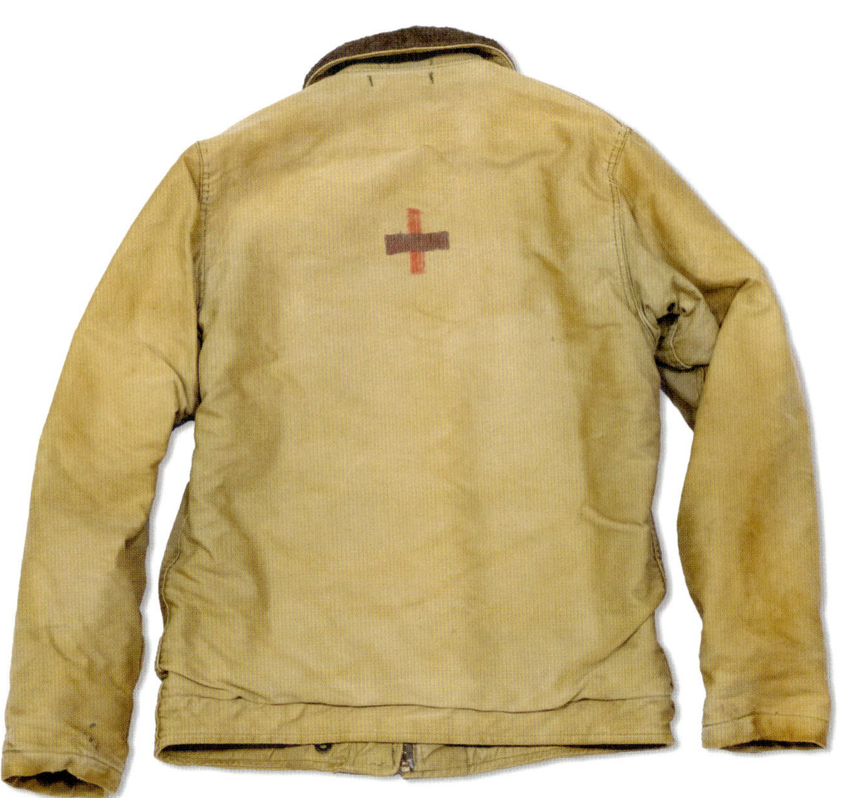

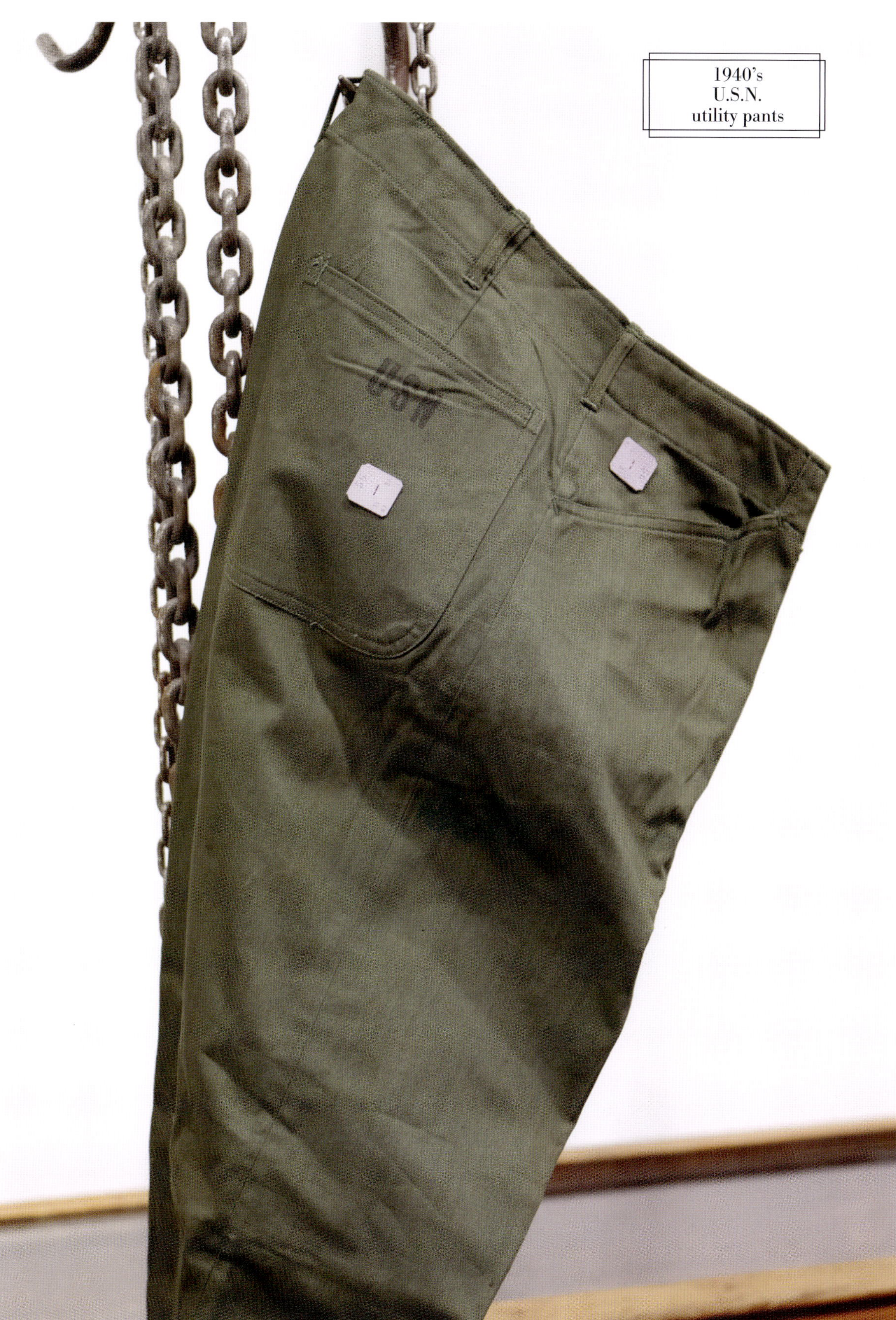

1940's
U.S.N.
utility pants

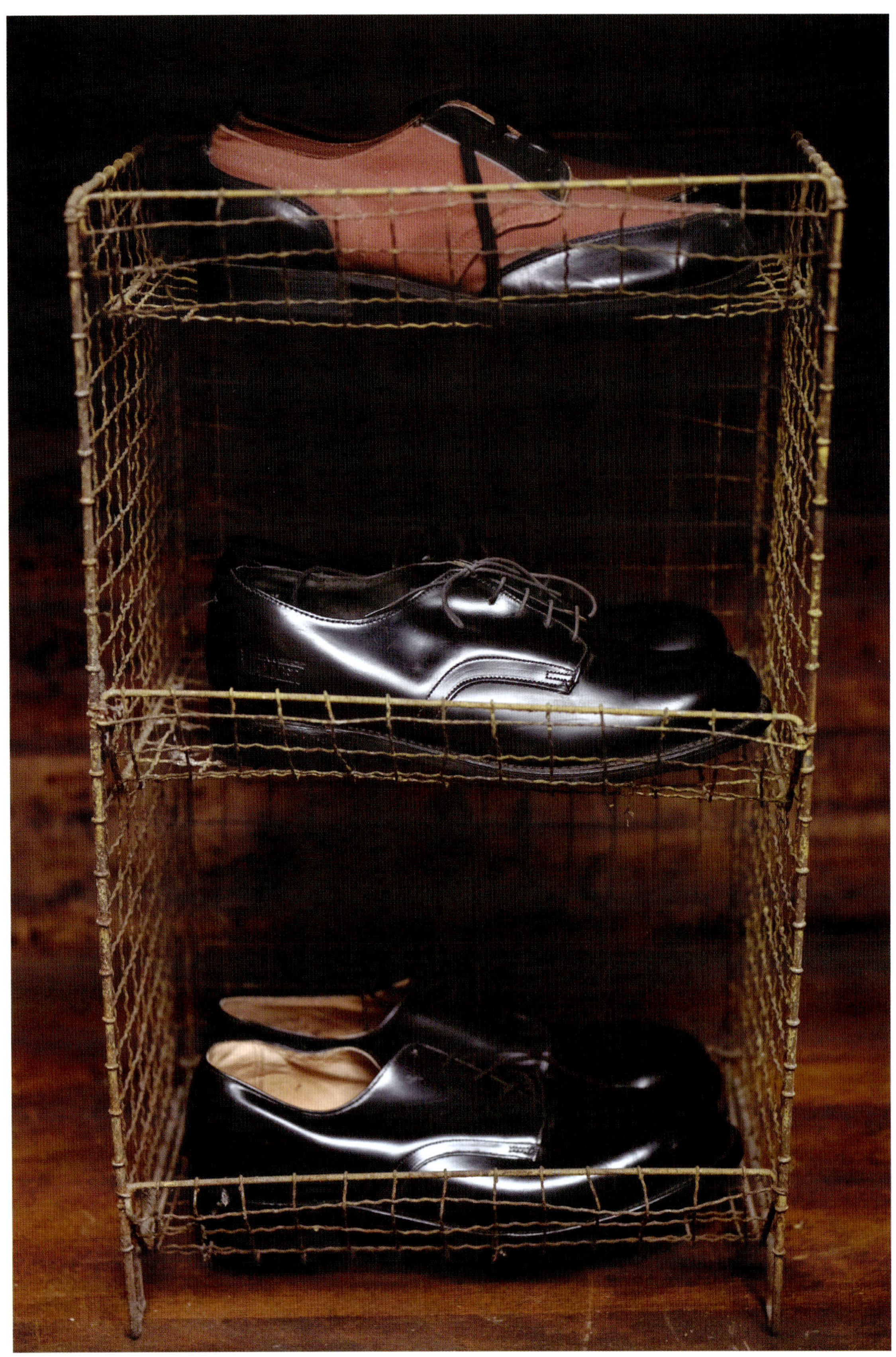

at Alessandro Squarzi archive
Forlì

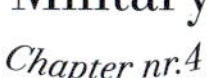

1950's
Marine Nationale
blouson de pont

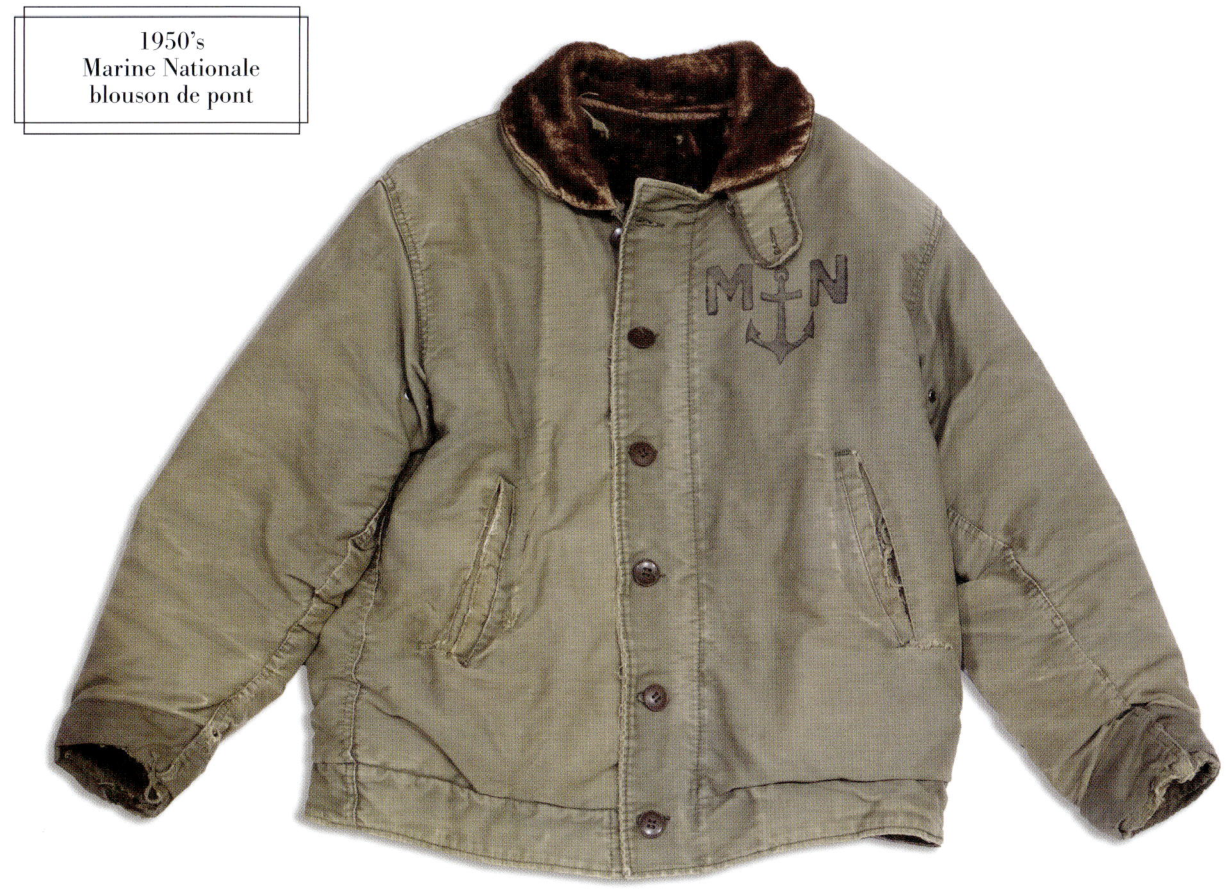

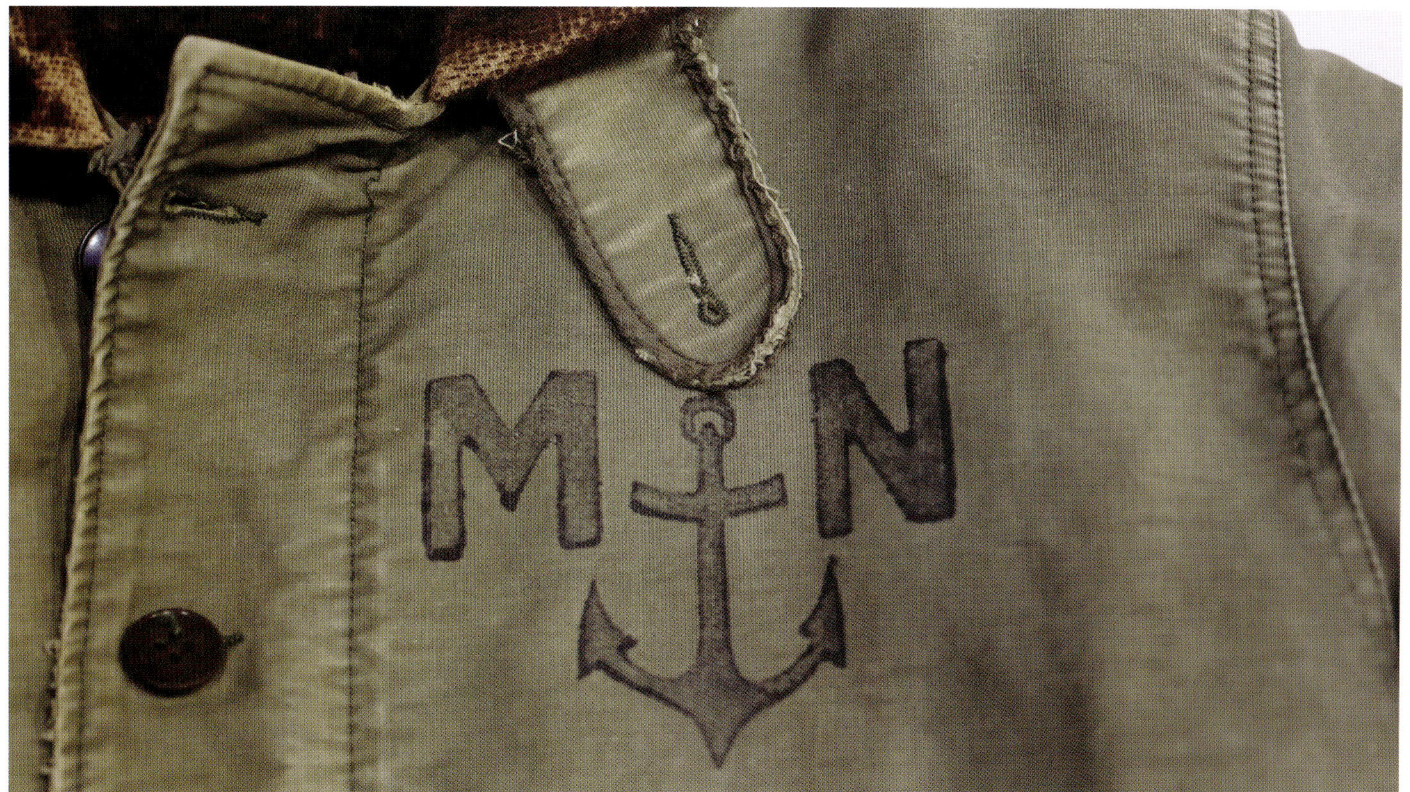

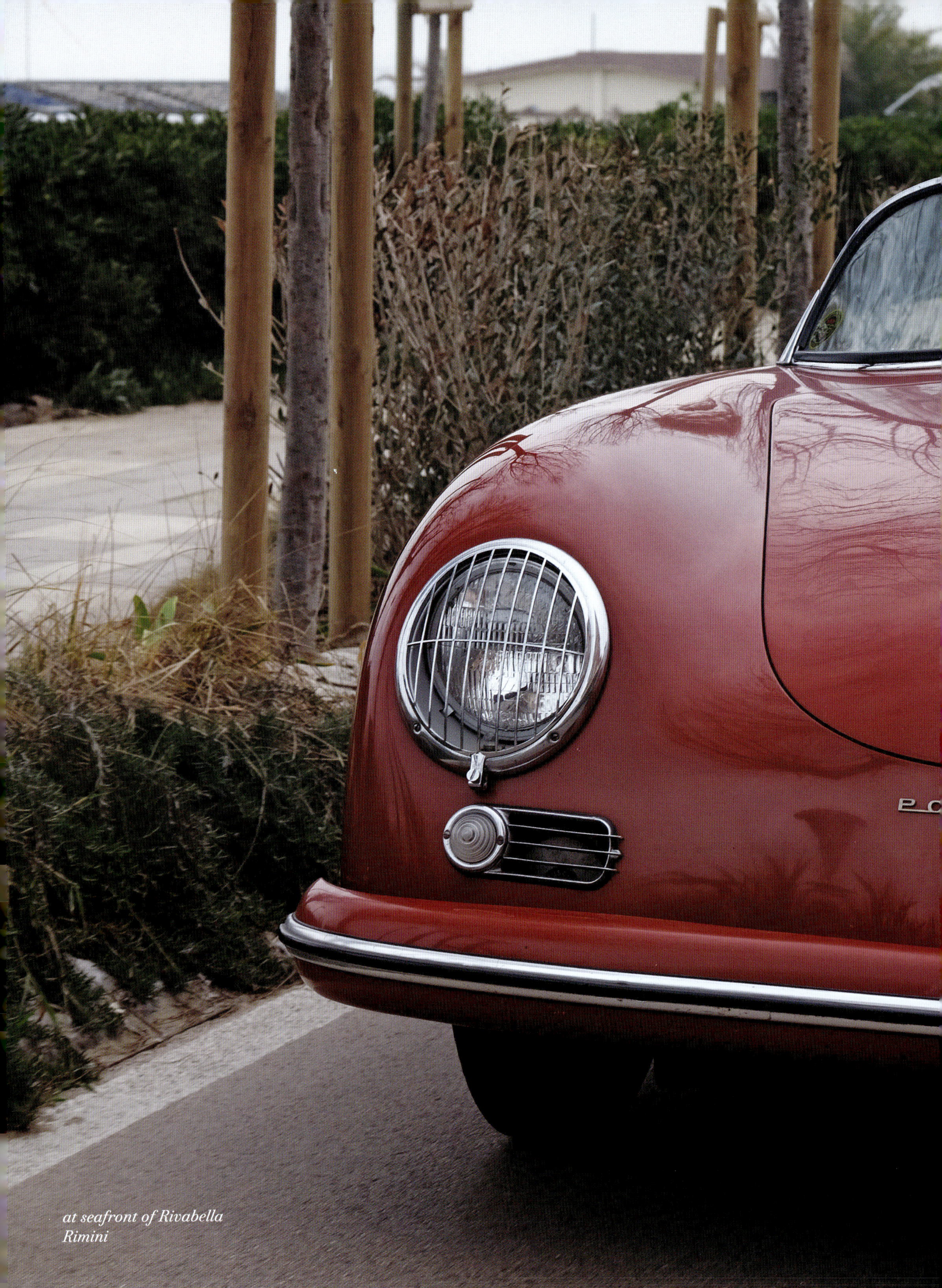

*at seafront of Rivabella
Rimini*

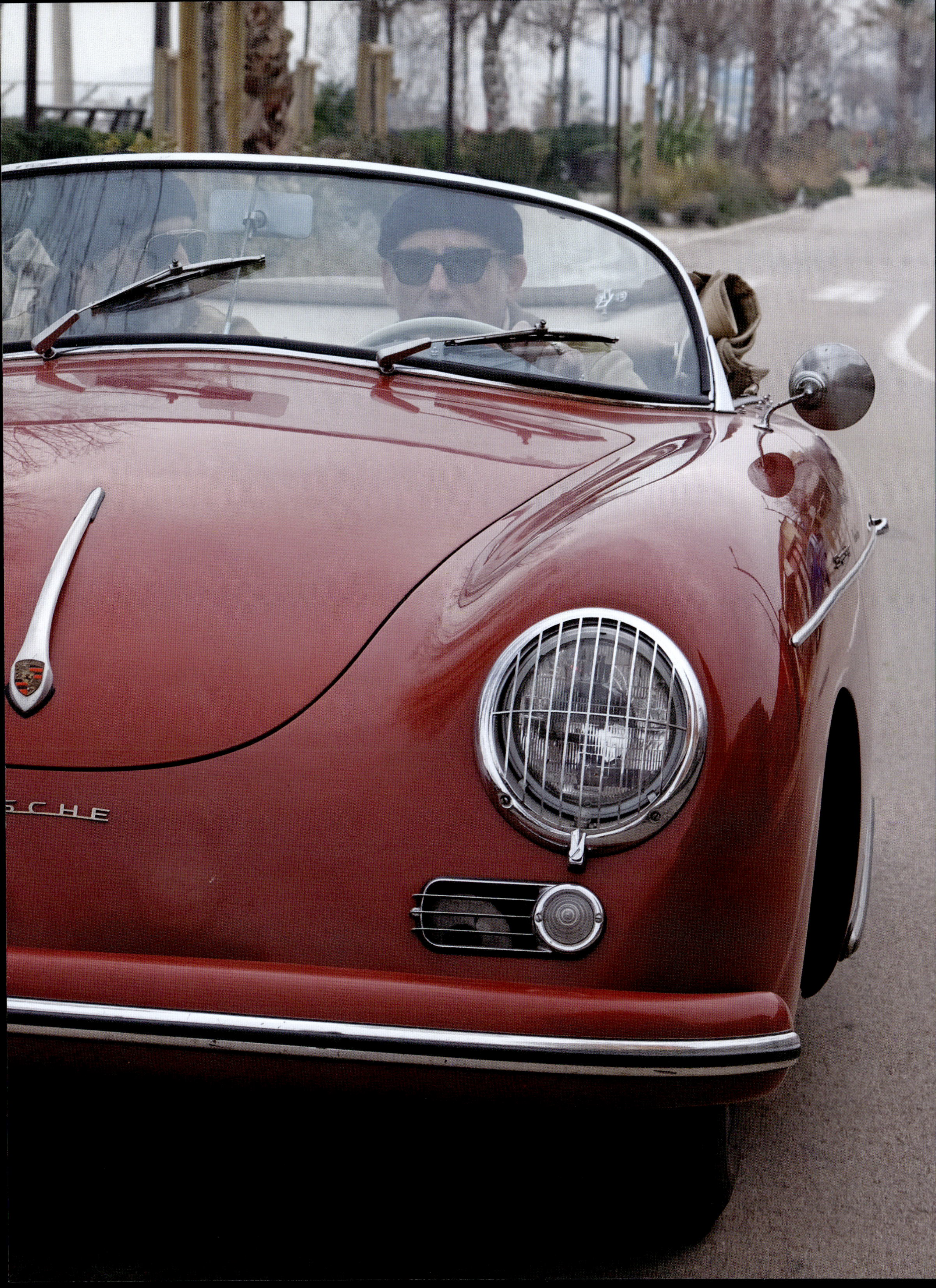

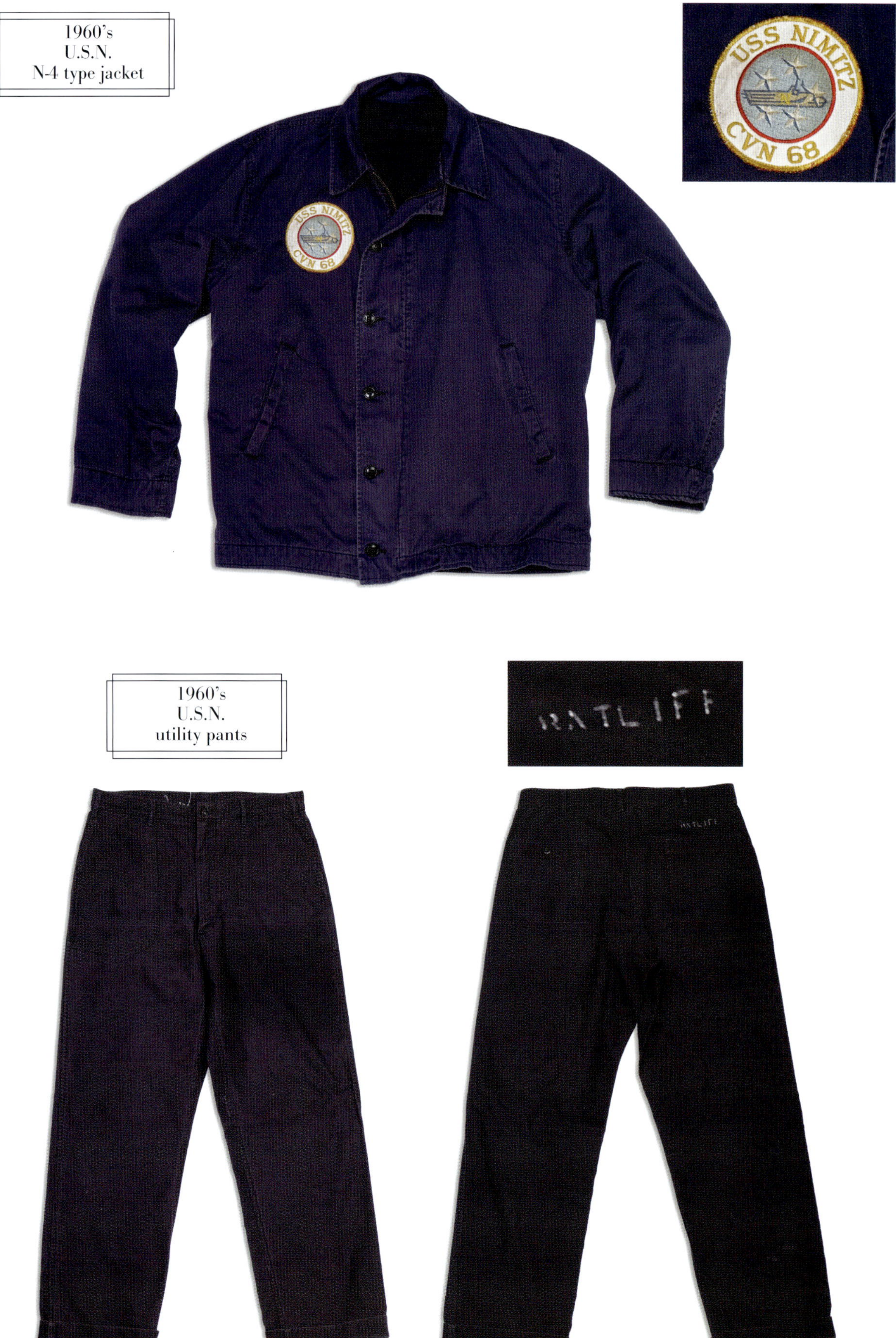

1960's
U.S.N.
N-4 type jacket

1960's
U.S.N.
utility pants

1950's
U.S.ARMY
vest

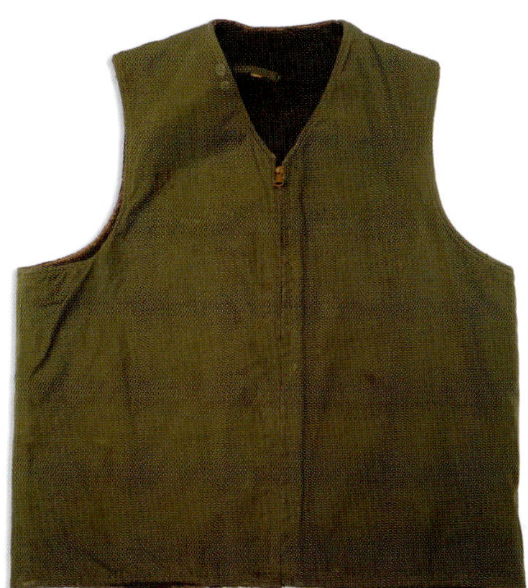

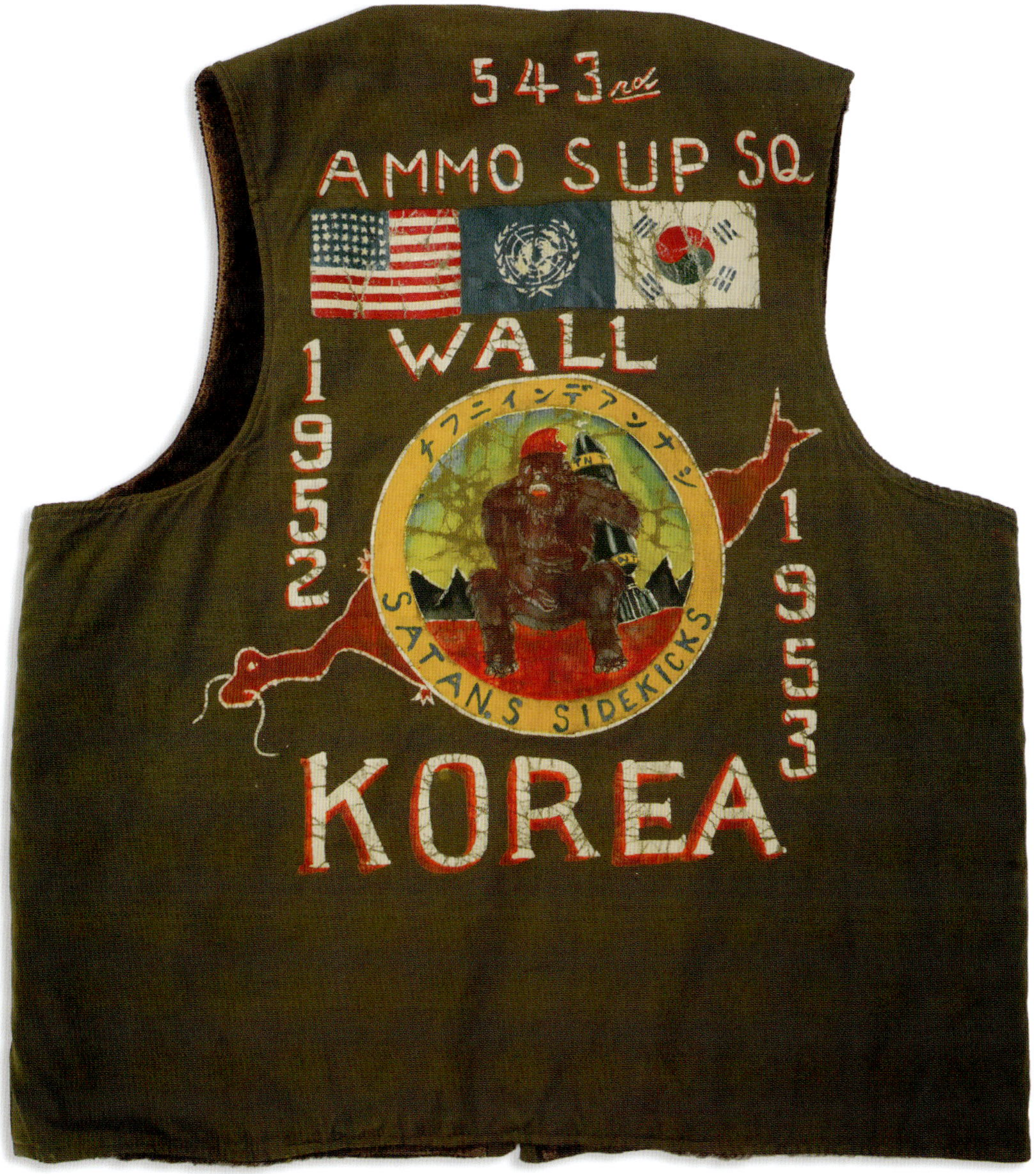

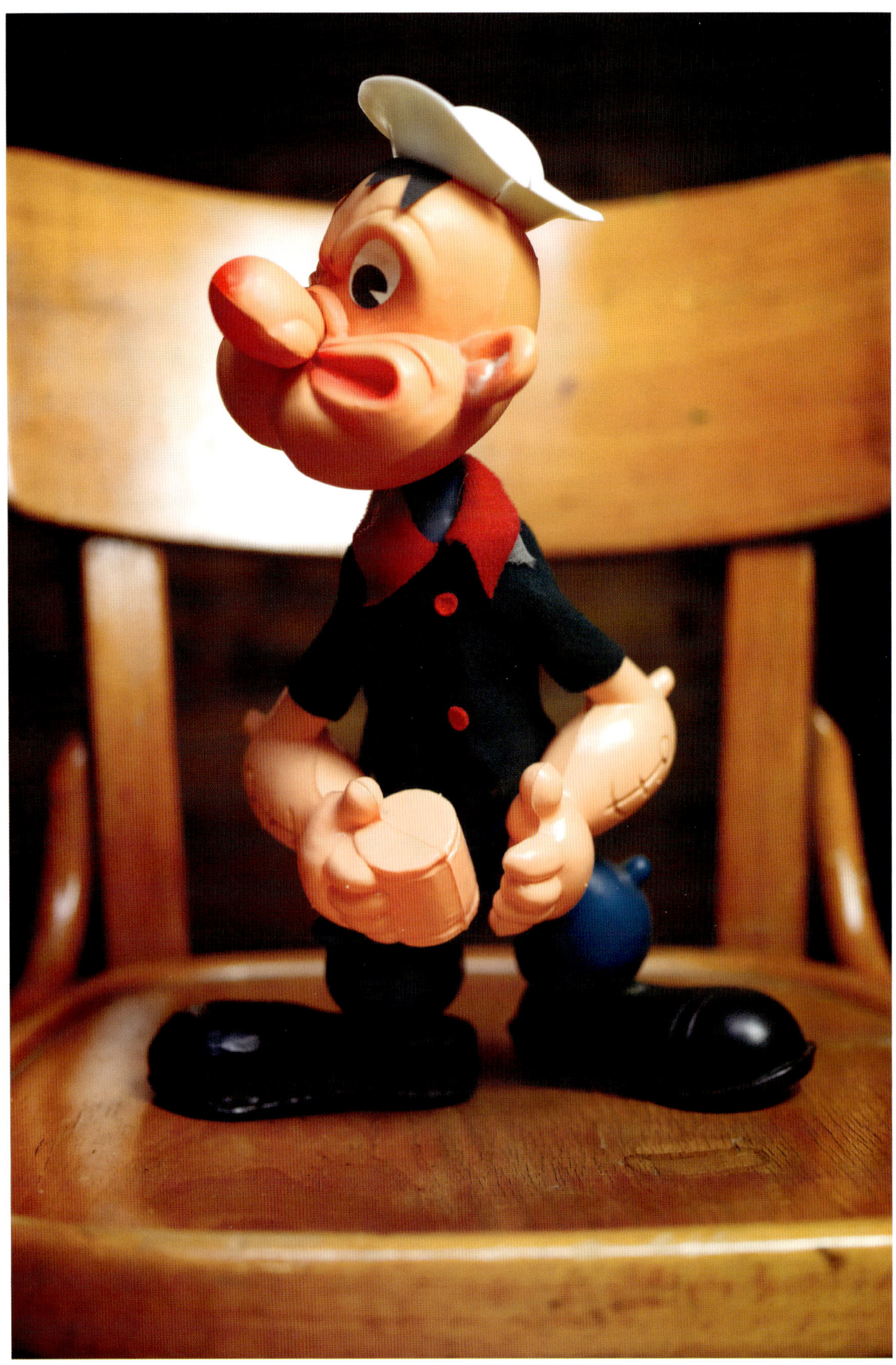

at Alessandro Squarzi archive
Forlì

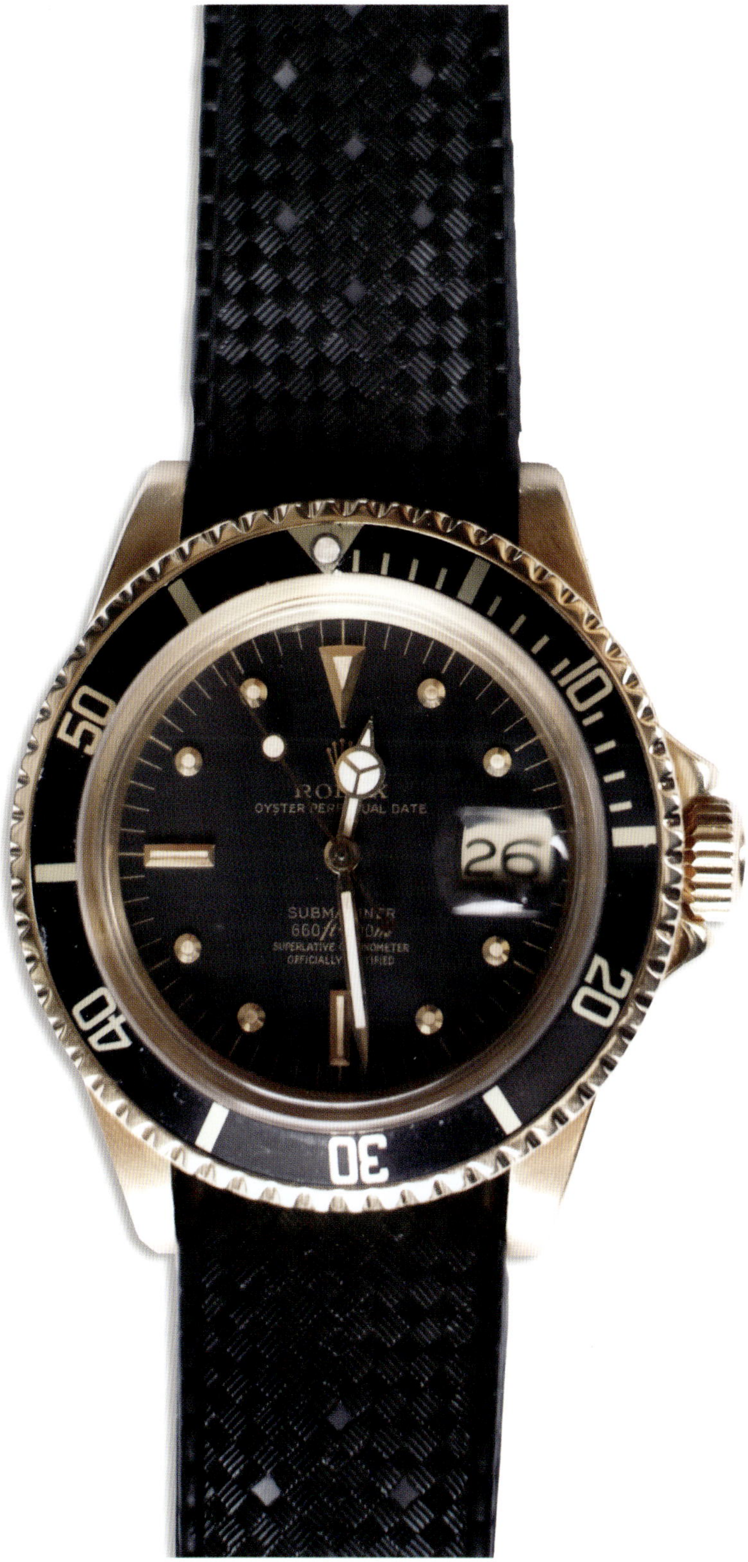

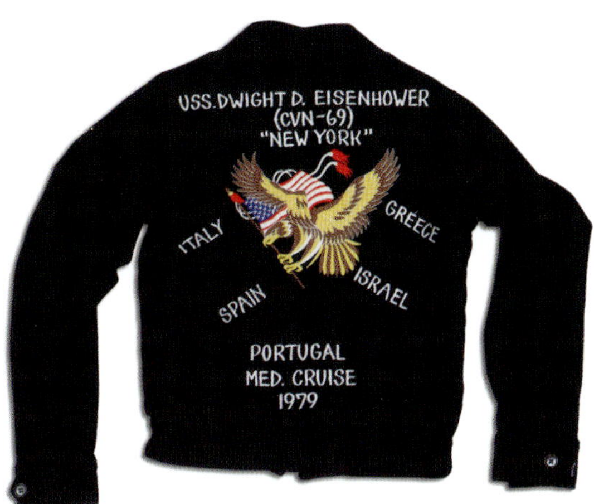

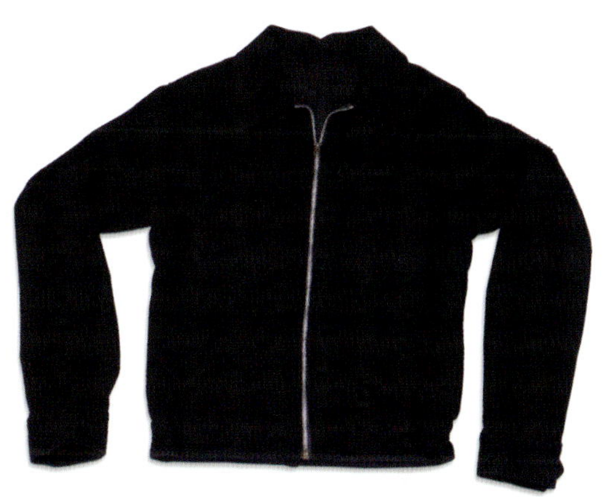

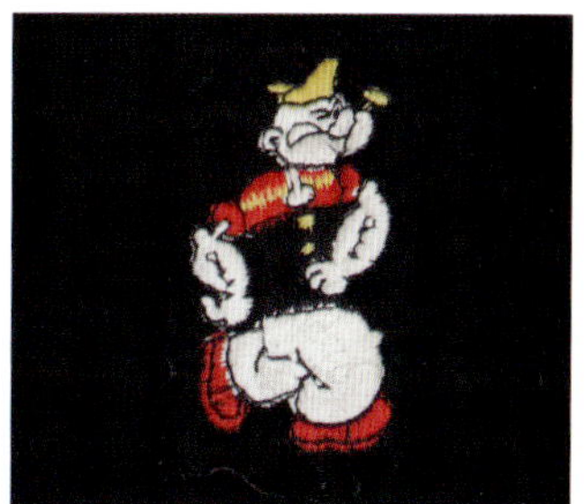

1968
Rolex Submariner
Ref. 1680

1970's
Navy
souvenir jacket

1940's
U.S.M.C.
herringbone twill (hbt) pants

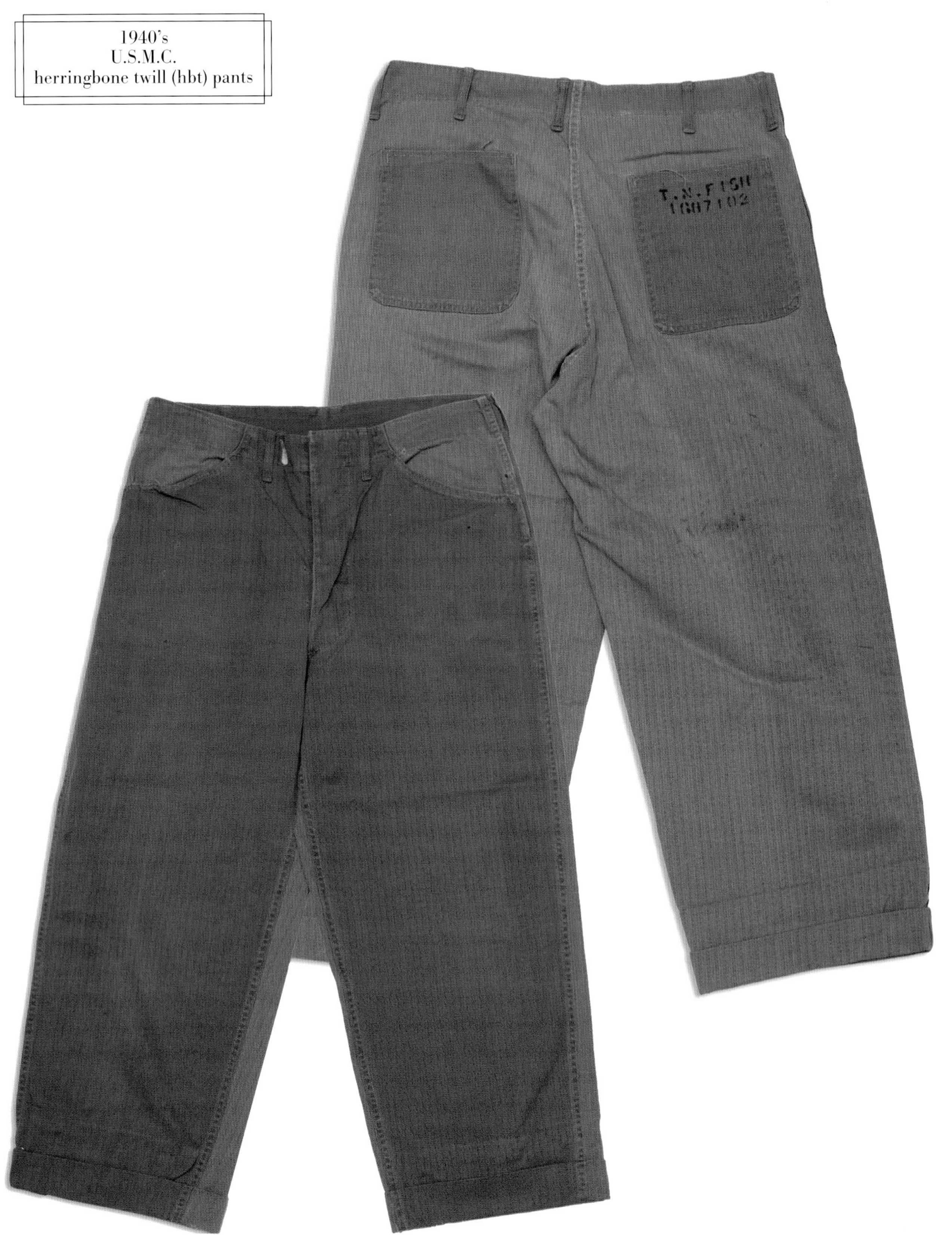

1940's
U.S.M.C. shirt
P-44 type frogskin hbt

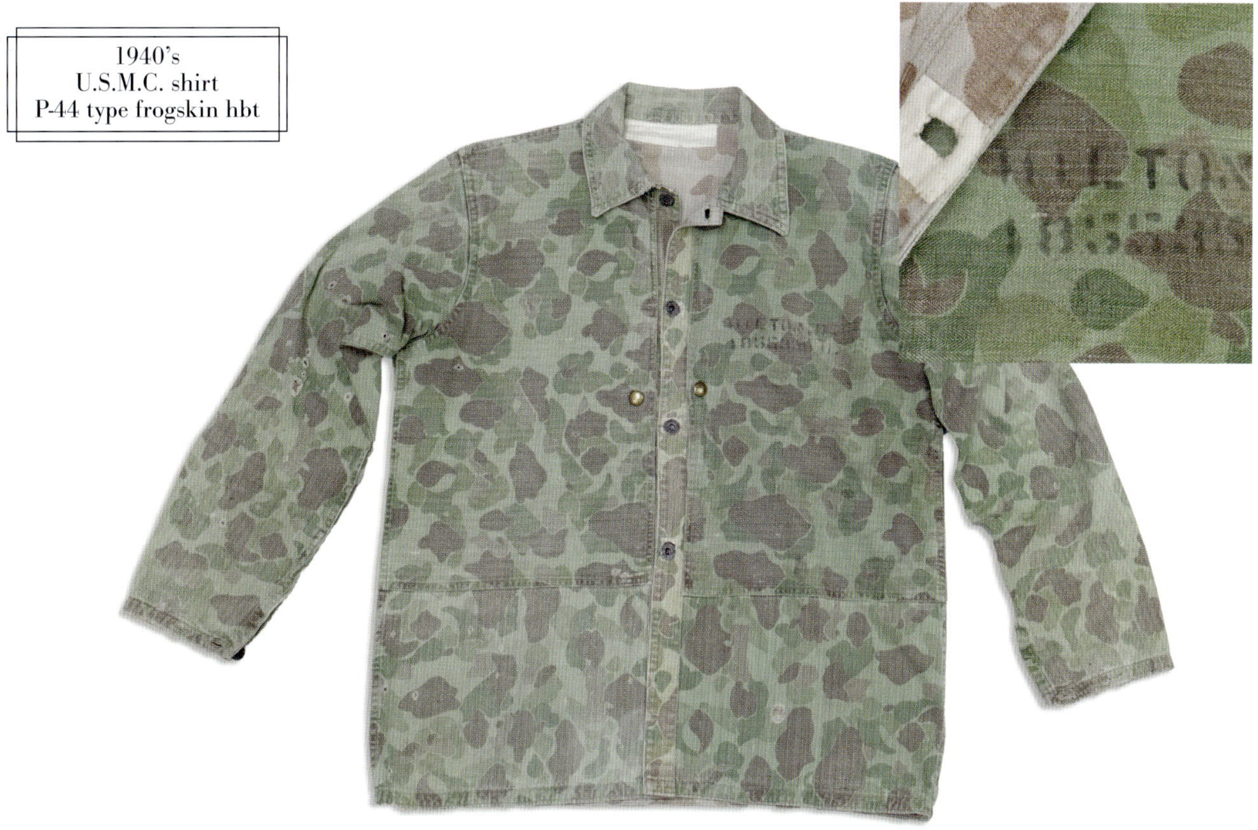

1940's
U.S.M.C. shirt
P-44 type frogskin hbt

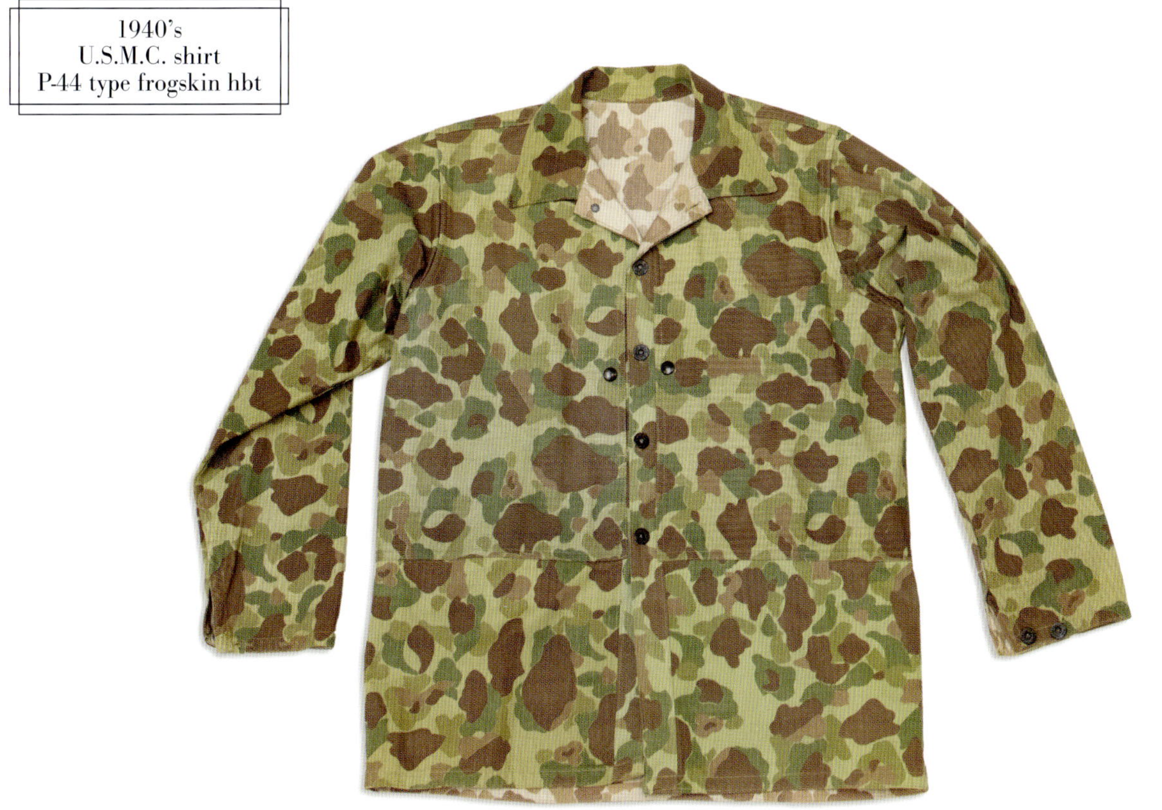

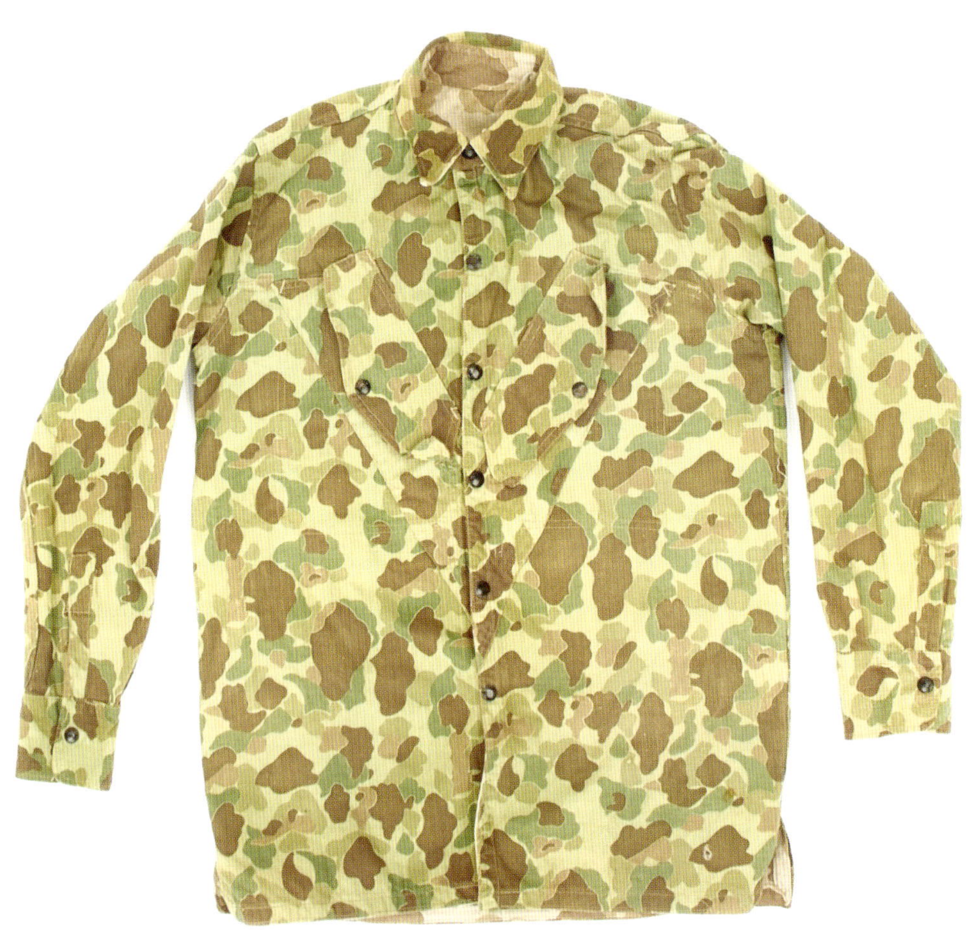

1940's
U.S.M.C. Paramarine jacket
frogskin hbt

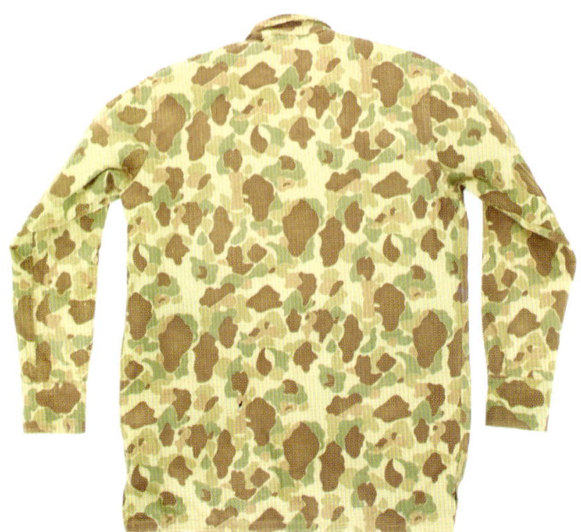

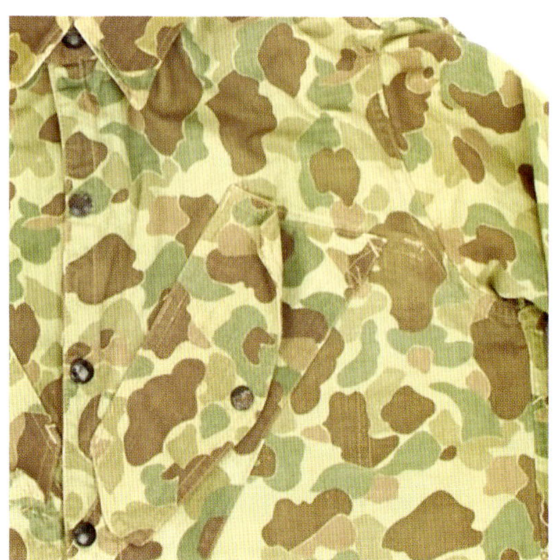

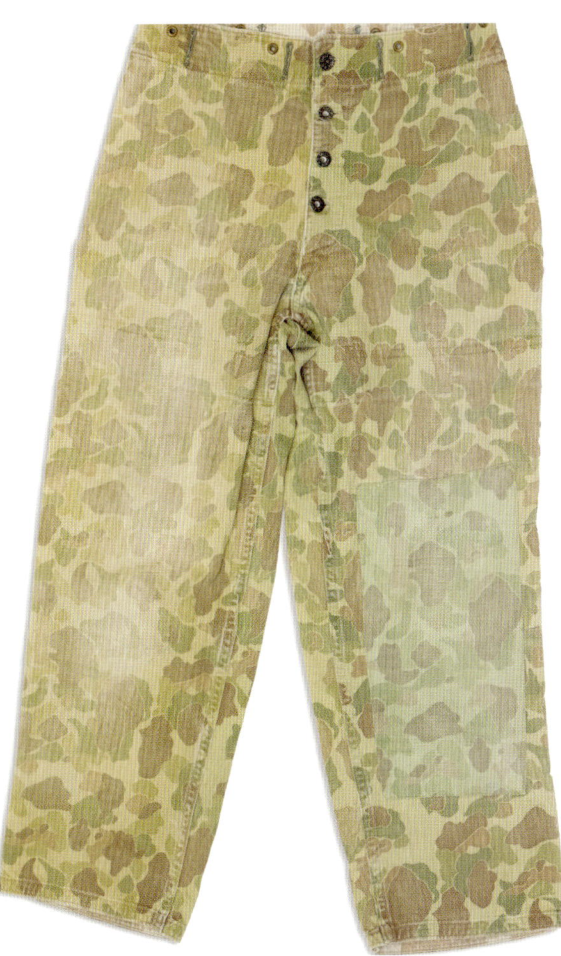 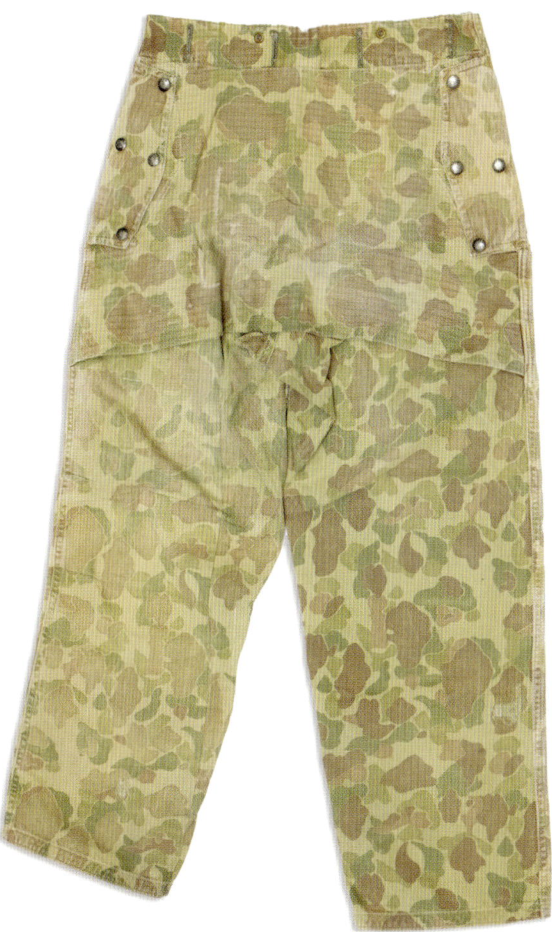

1940's
U.S.M.C. Paramarine pants
frogskin hbt

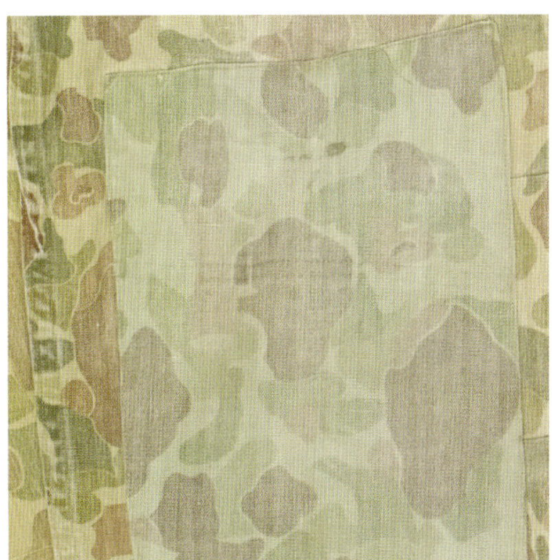 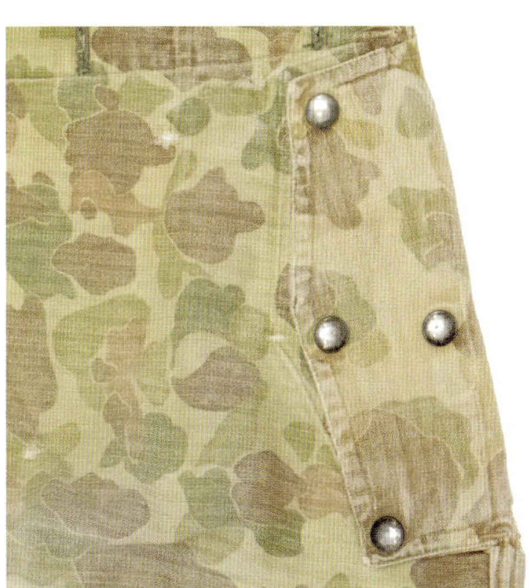

1940's
U.S.M.C. shirt
hbt P-44 type

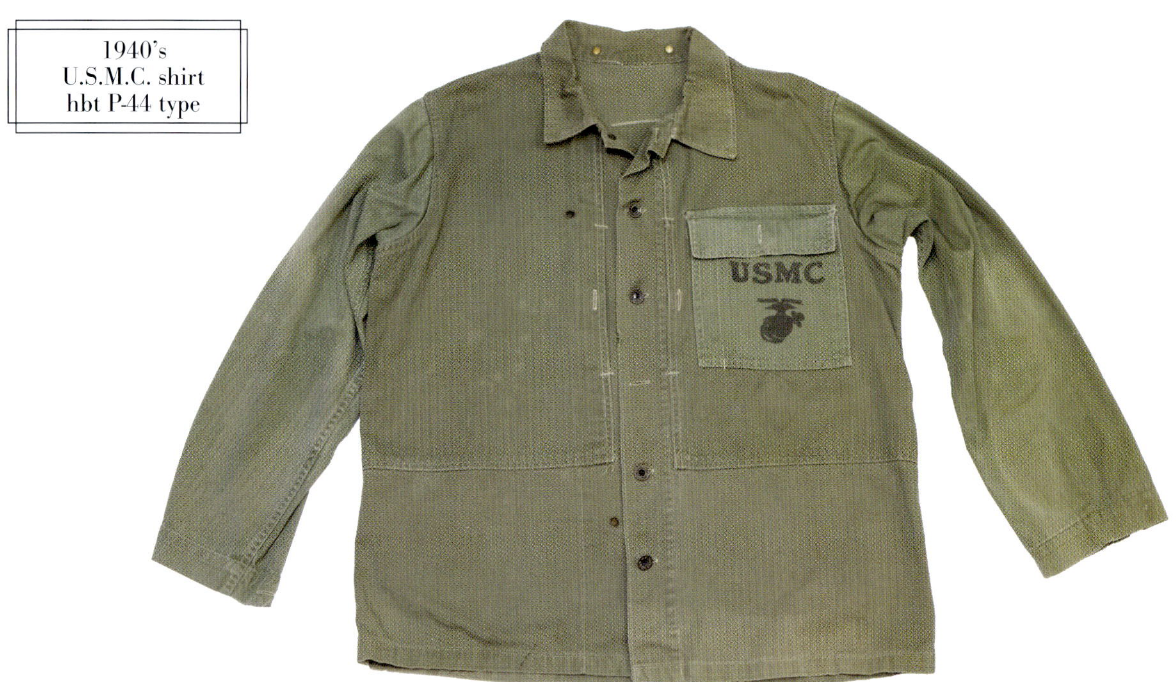

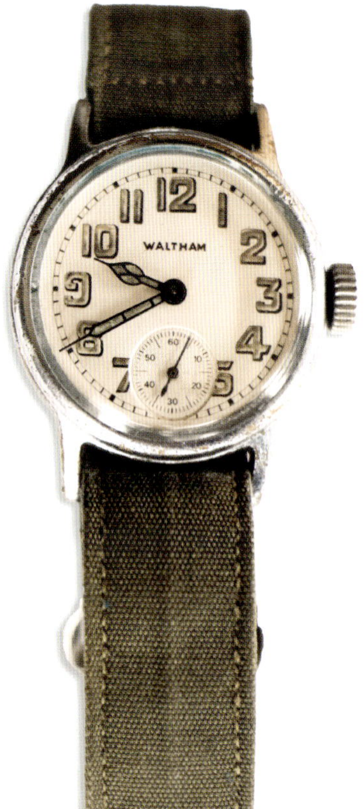

1940's
Waltham
wrist watch

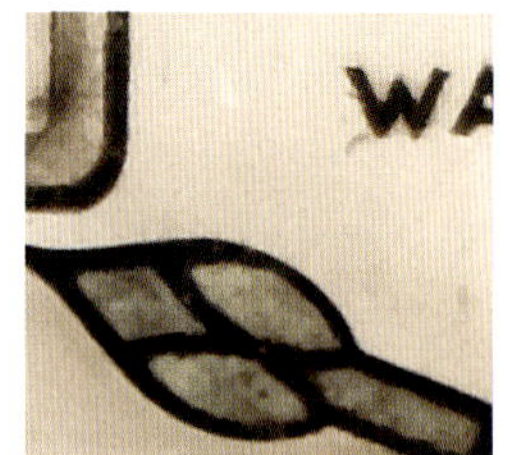

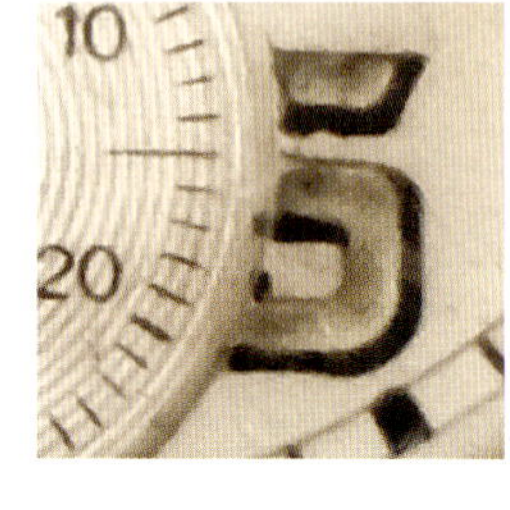

1940's
U.S. ARMY shirt
hbt type II

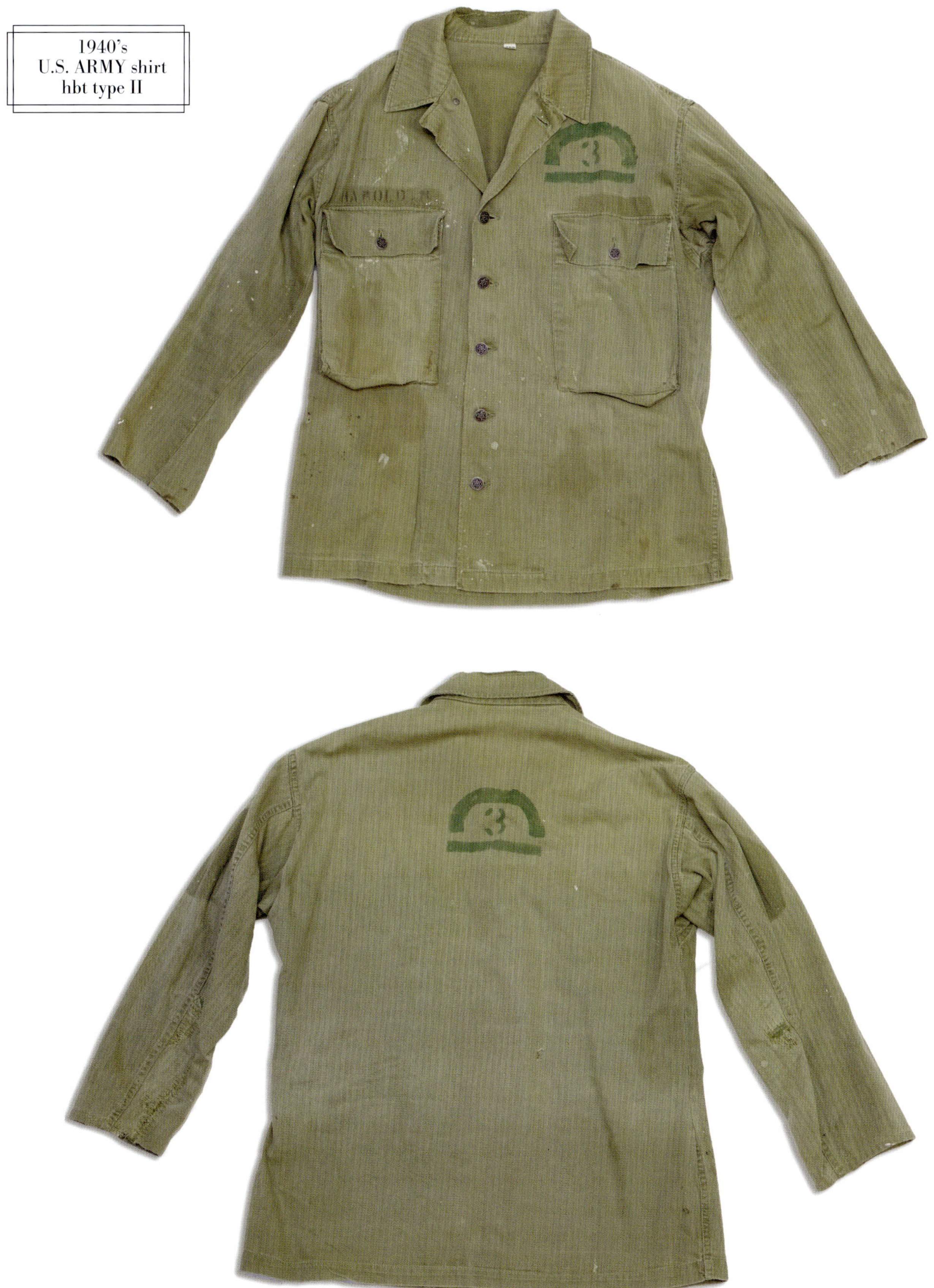

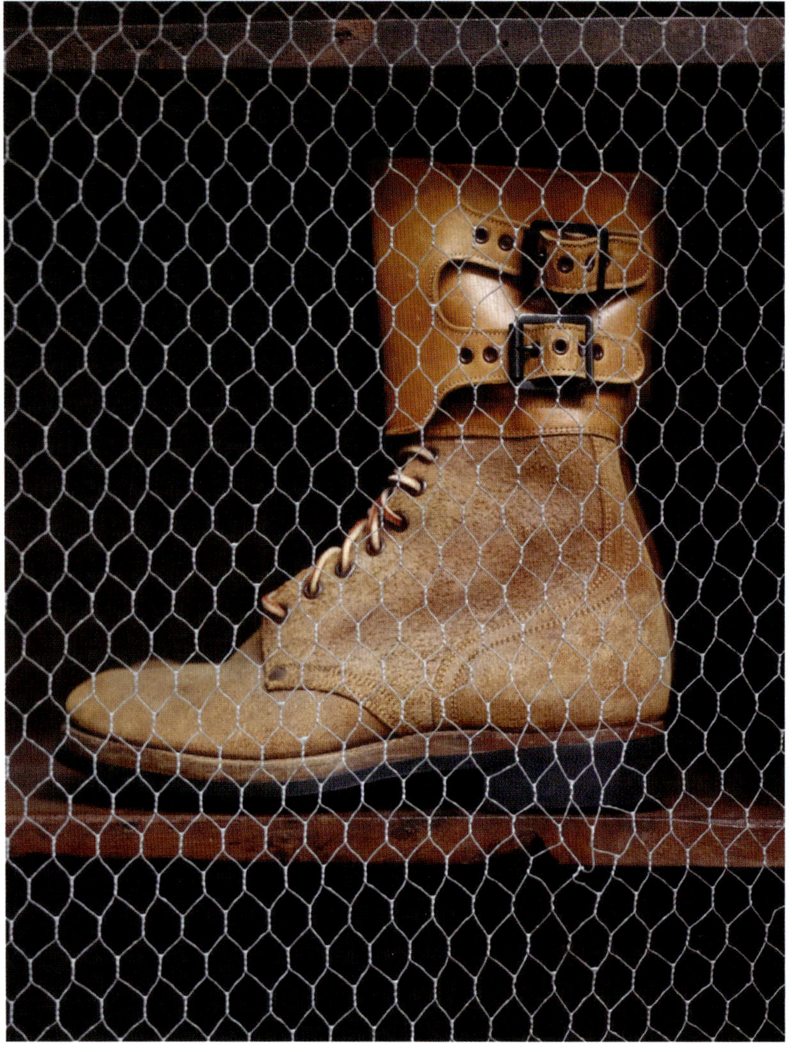

1944
U.S. ARMY
buckle boots

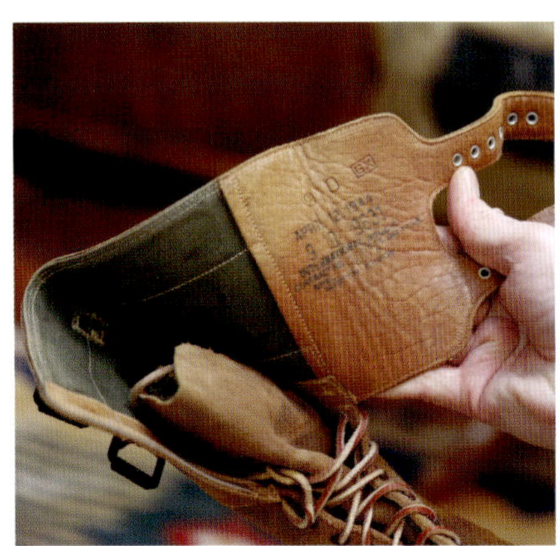

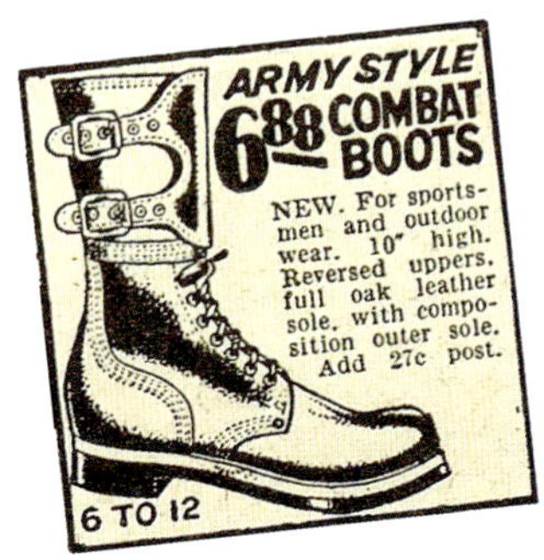

1940's advertising

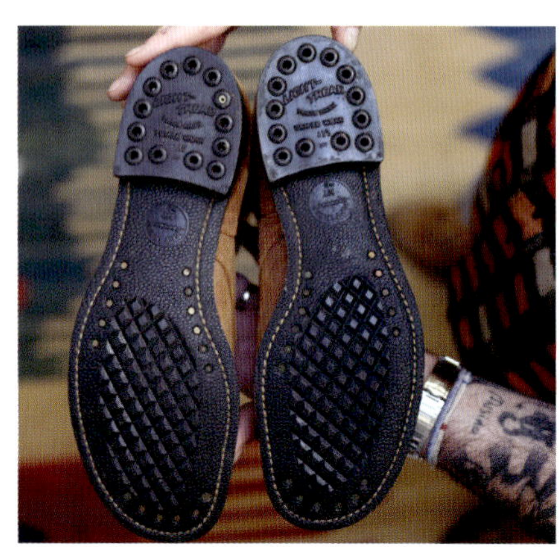

1980's
U.S.M.C.
souvenir jacket

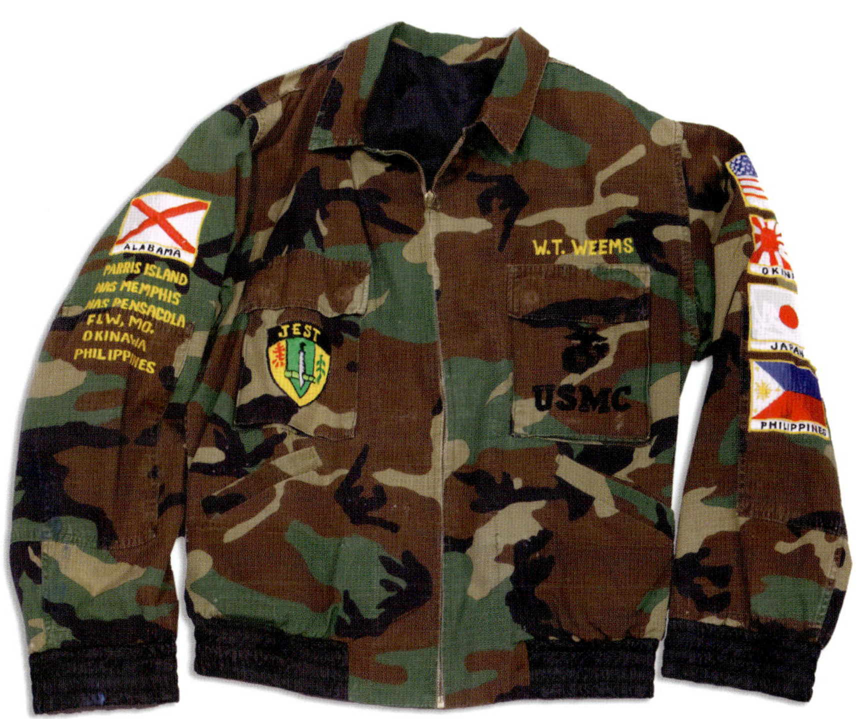

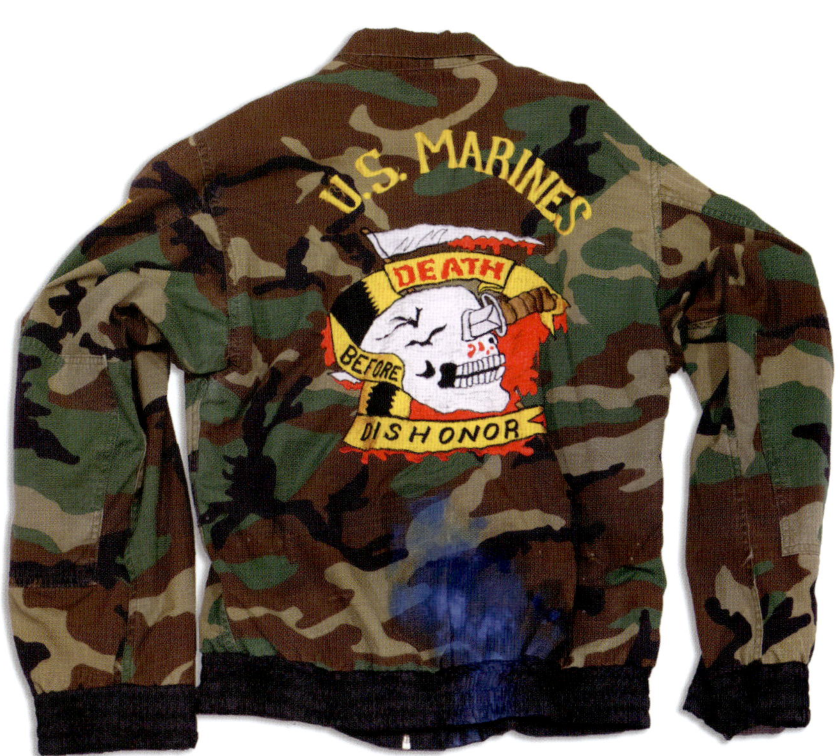

1940's
U.S.A.A.F.
B-4 type Officer bag

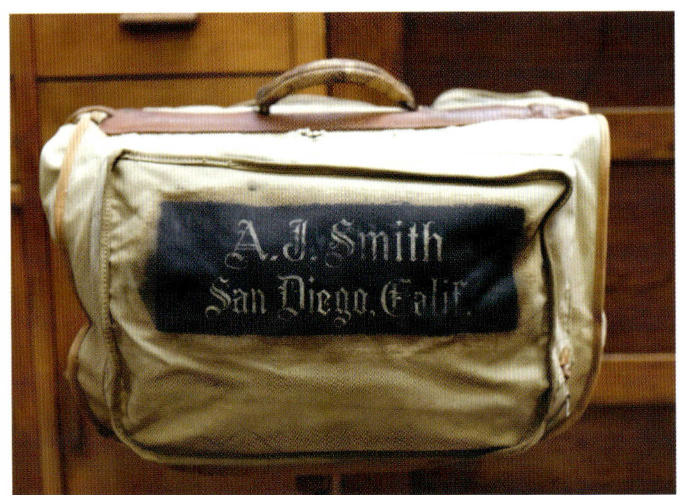

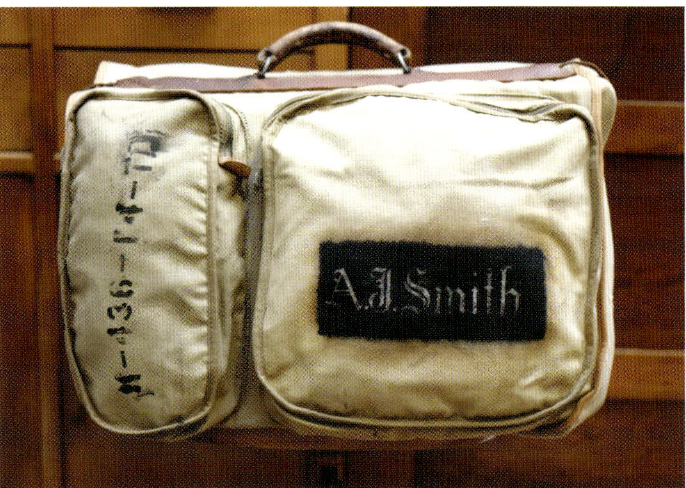

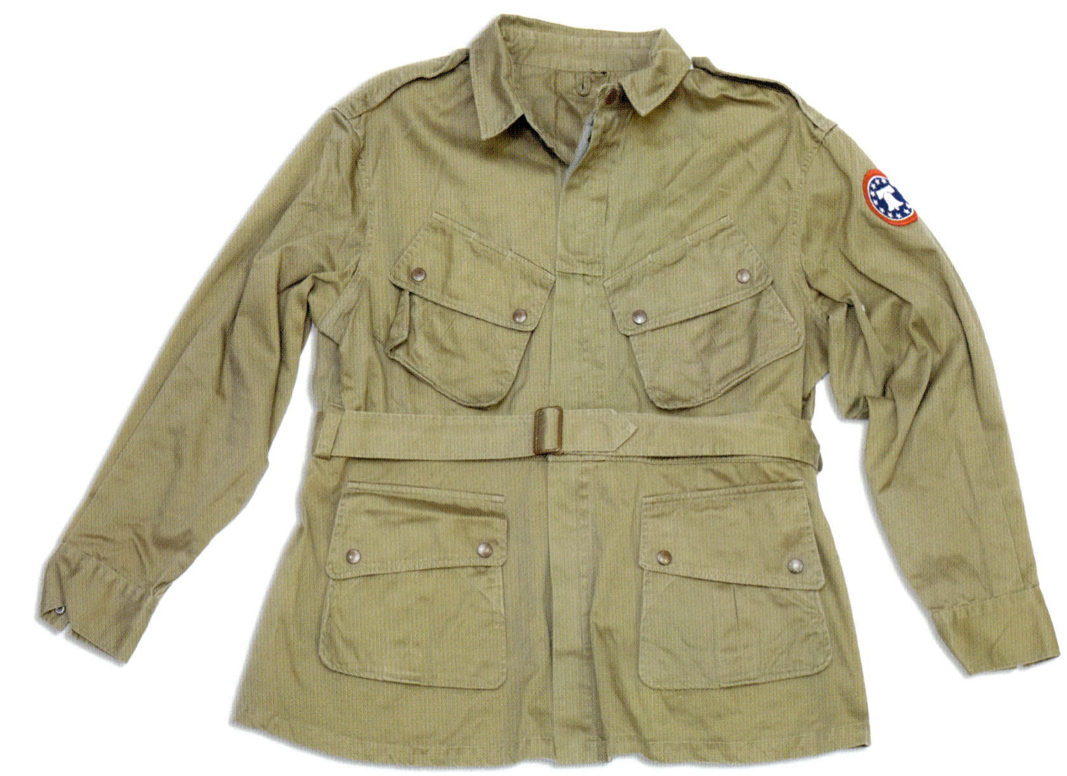

1940's
U.S.ARMY
M-42 type jacket

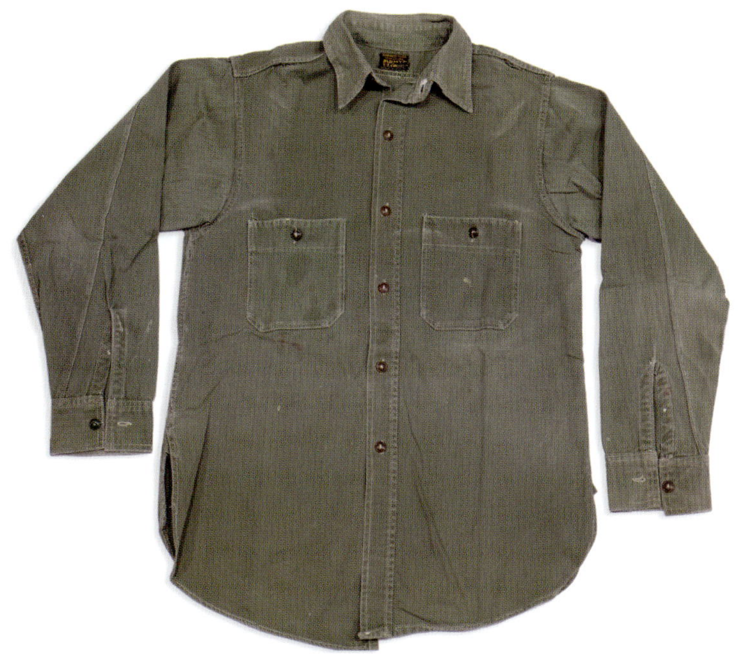

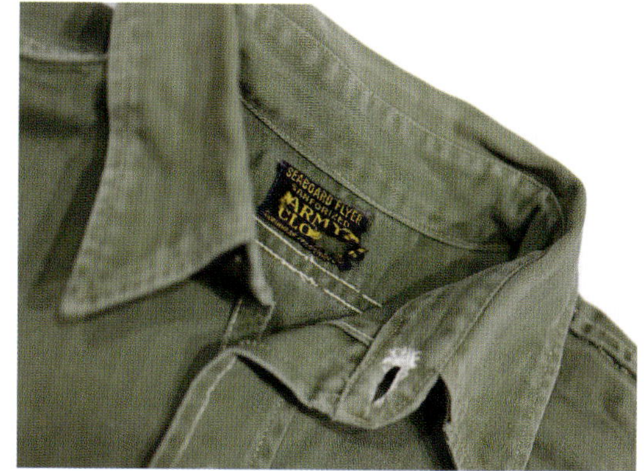

1940's
Army Clothes
private purchase shirt

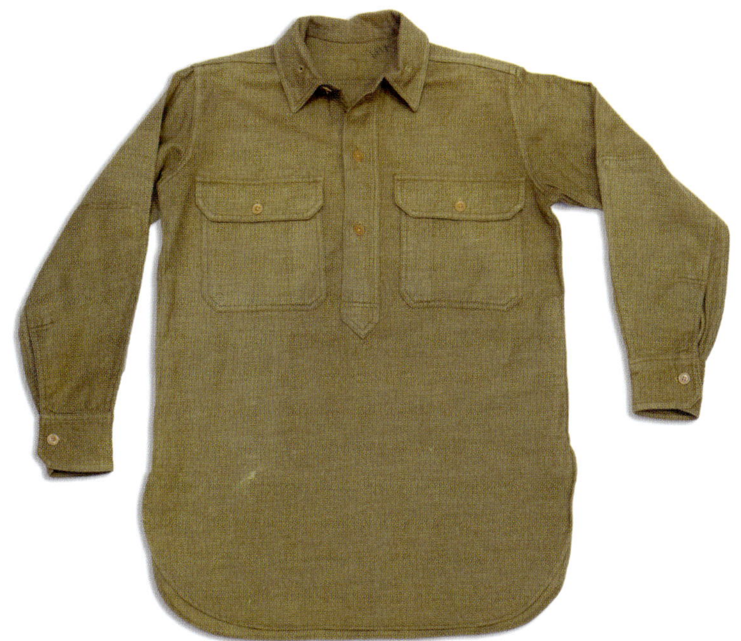

1910's
U.S. ARMY
M-1917 type wool shirt

1940's
U.S.A.A.F.
kit bag

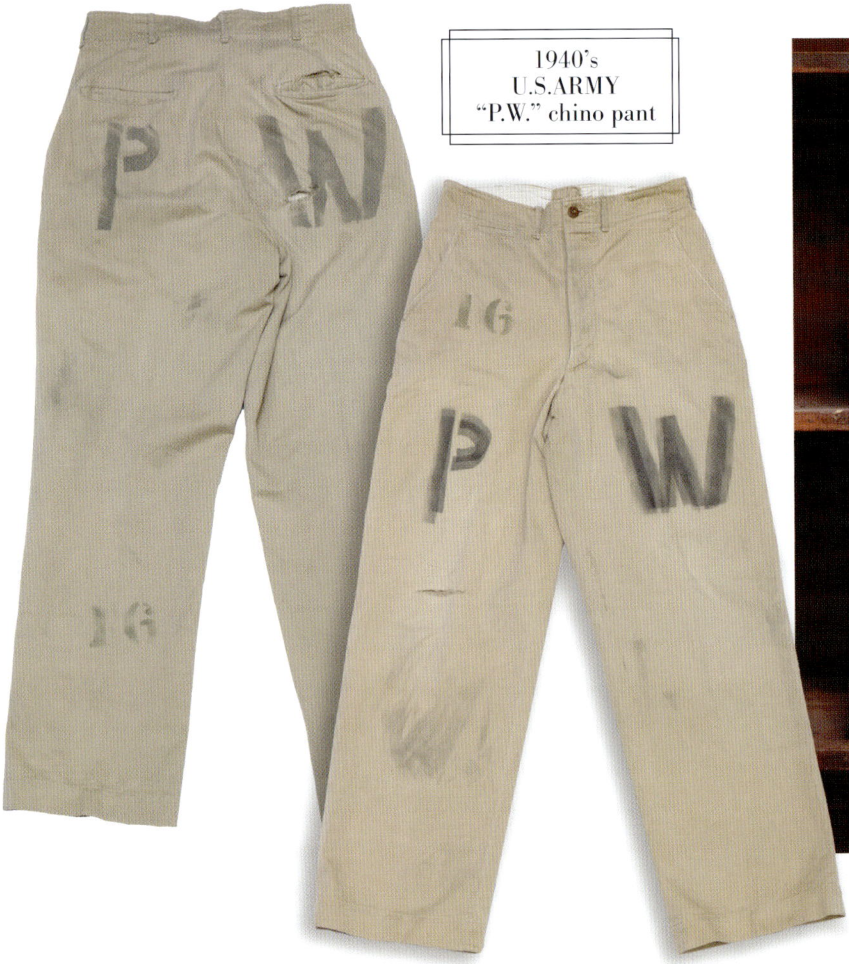

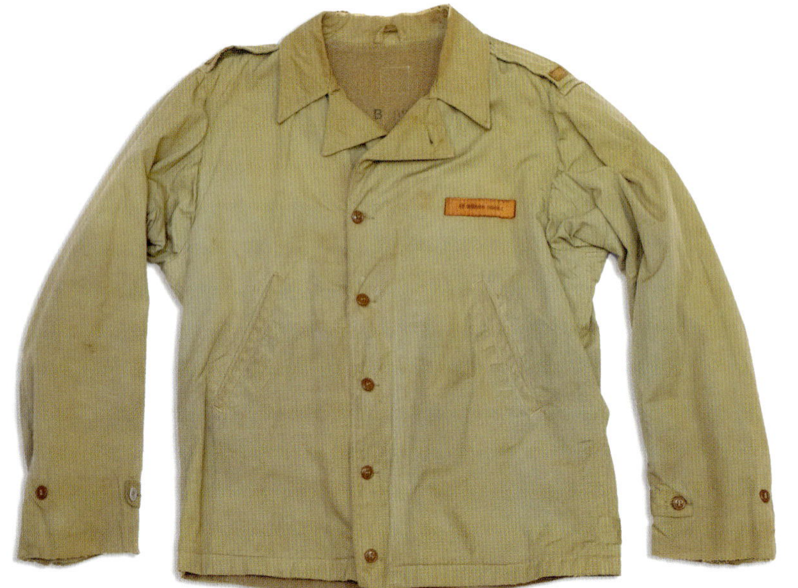

1940's
U.S.ARMY
"P.W." chino pant

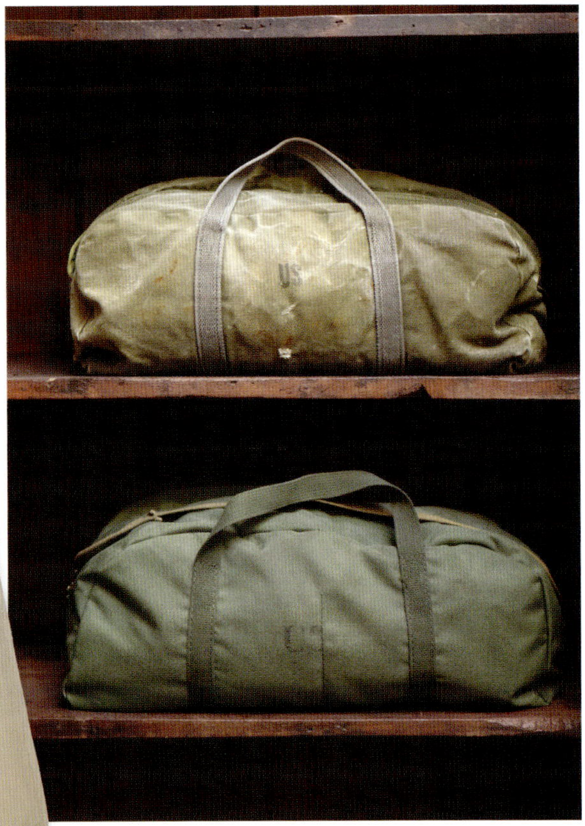

1940's - 1960's
U.S.ARMY
duffle bags

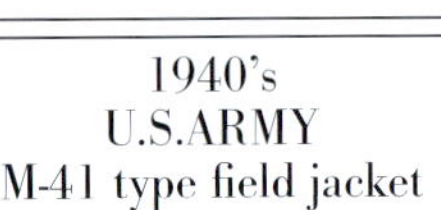

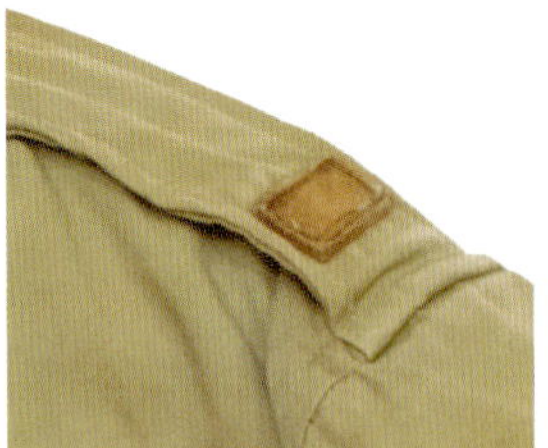

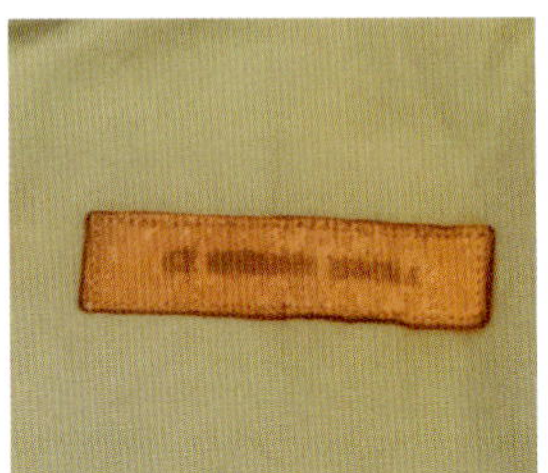

1940's
U.S.ARMY
M-41 type field jacket

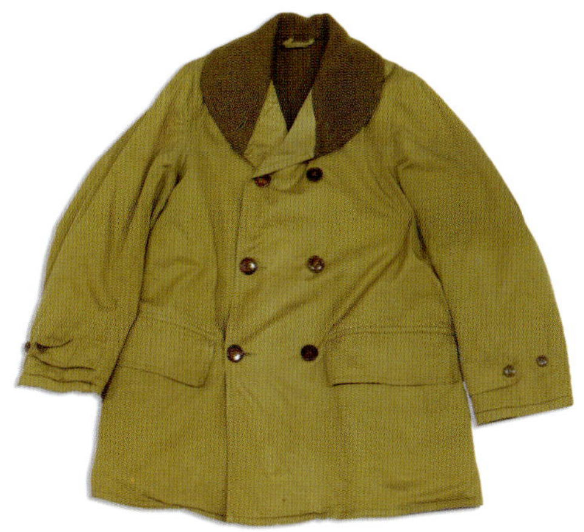

1940's
U.S. ARMY
Makinaw Jeep Coat

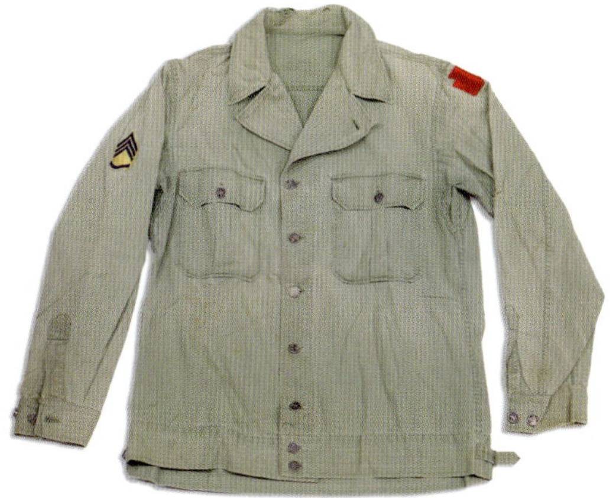

1940's
U.S.ARMY
1st type hbt shirt

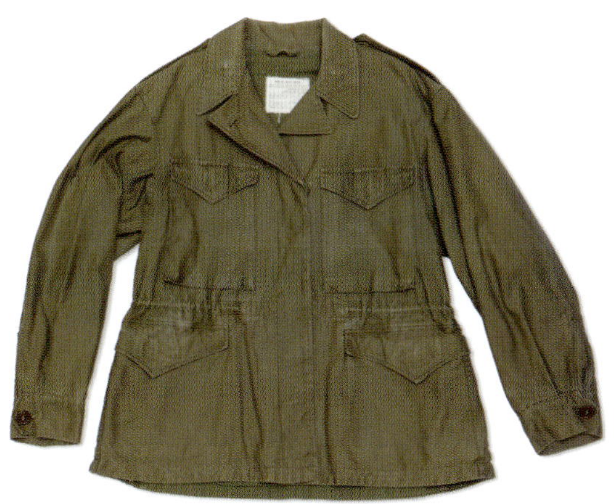

1940's
U.S.ARMY
M-43 type field jacket

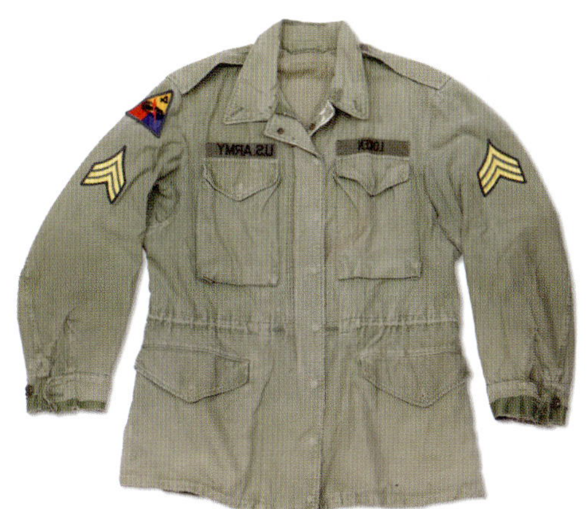

1950's
U.S.ARMY
M-51 type field jacket

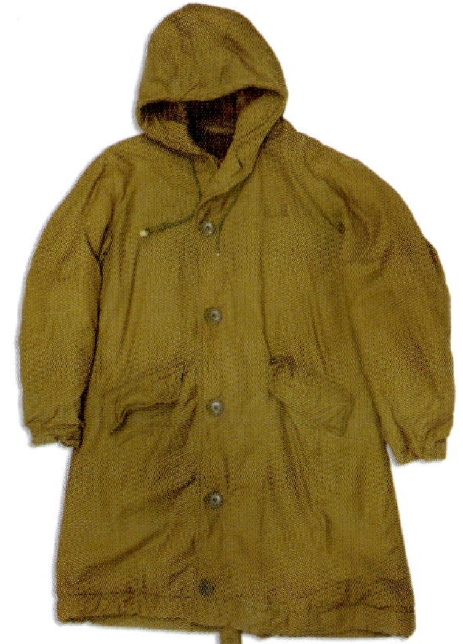

1940's
U.S.N.
N-1 type Deck Parka

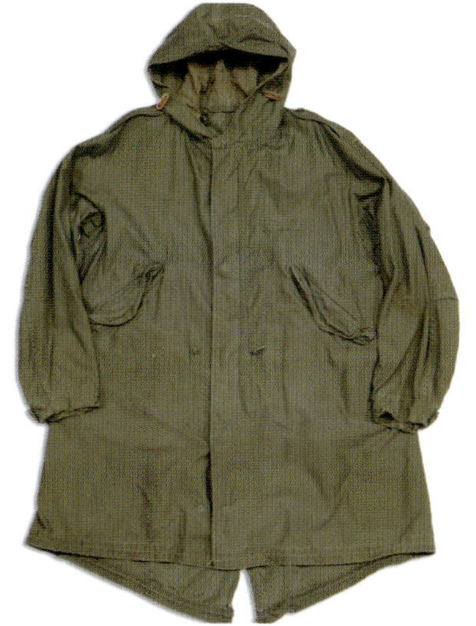

1950's
U.S.ARMY
M-51type Fishtail parka

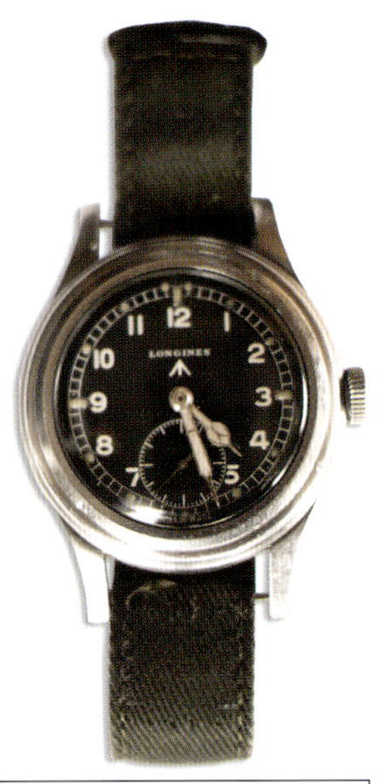

1940's
LONGINES
Royal Army wrist watch

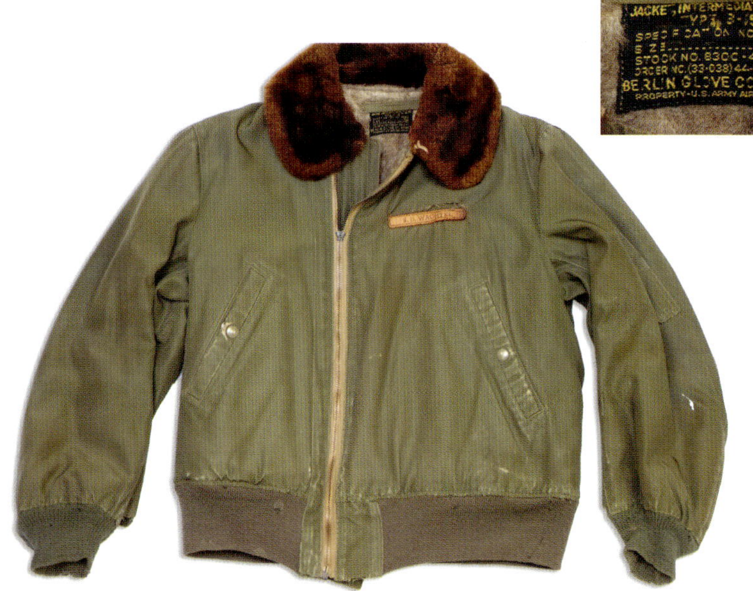

1940's
U.S.A.A.F.
B-15 type flight jacket

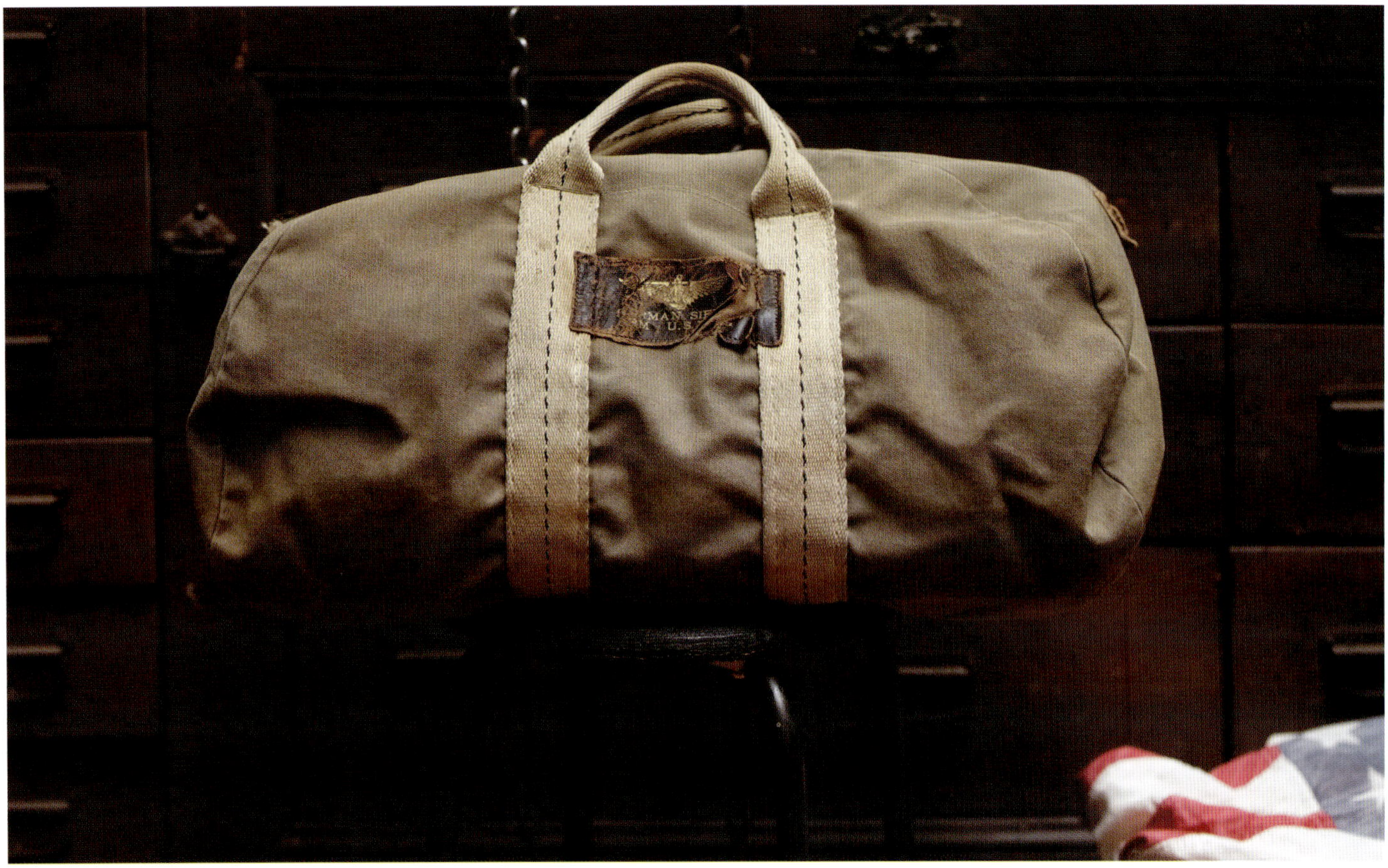

1940's
U.S.N.
pilot bag

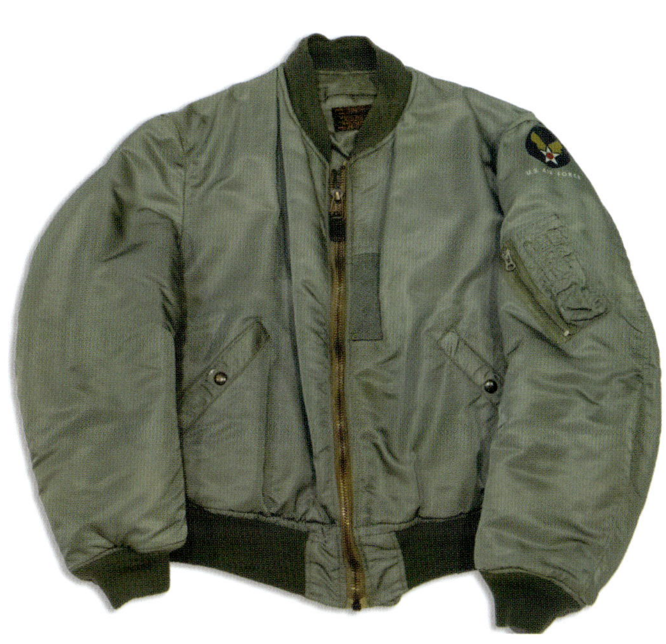

1950's
U.S.A.F.
M-A1 type flight jacket

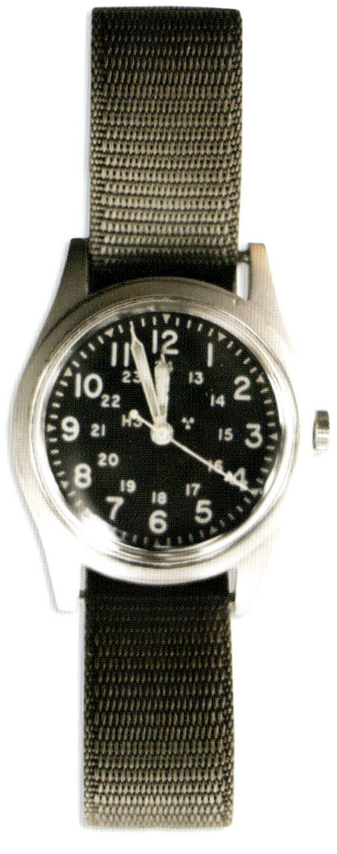

1960's
U.S. ARMY
Wrist watch

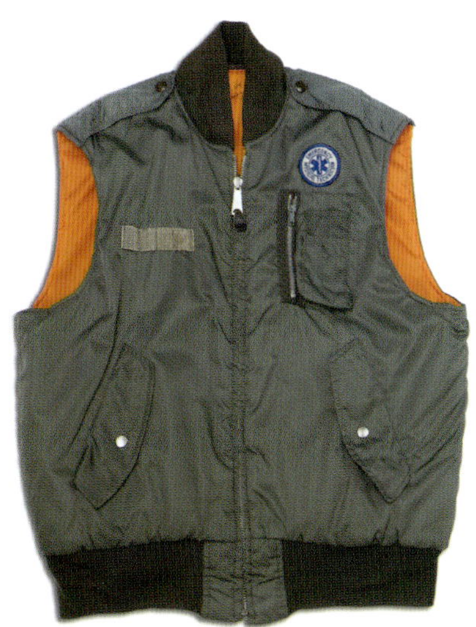

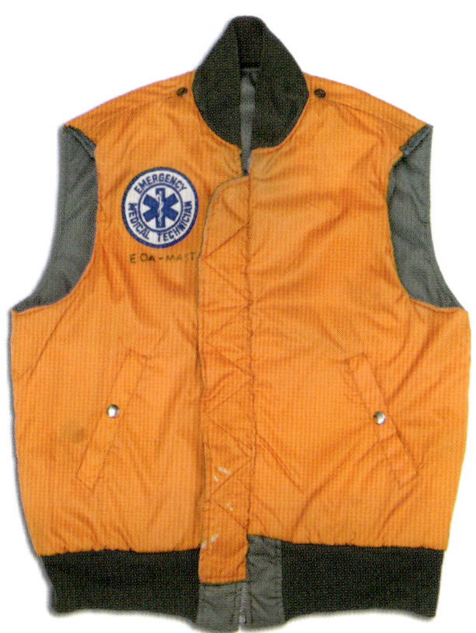

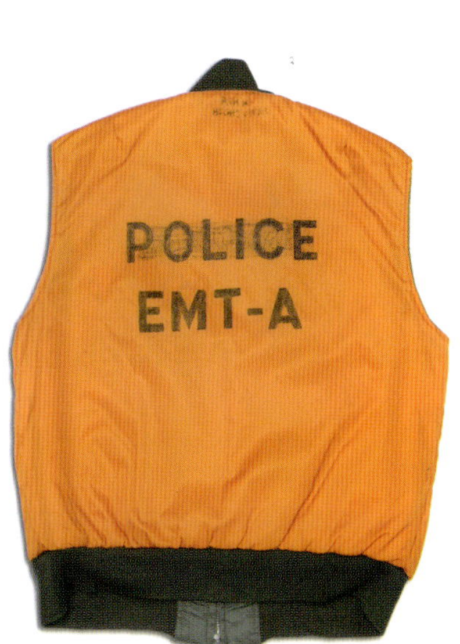

1960's
U.S.A.F.
custom bomber vest

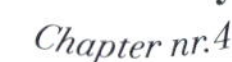

1950's
U.S.ARMY
hbt shirt

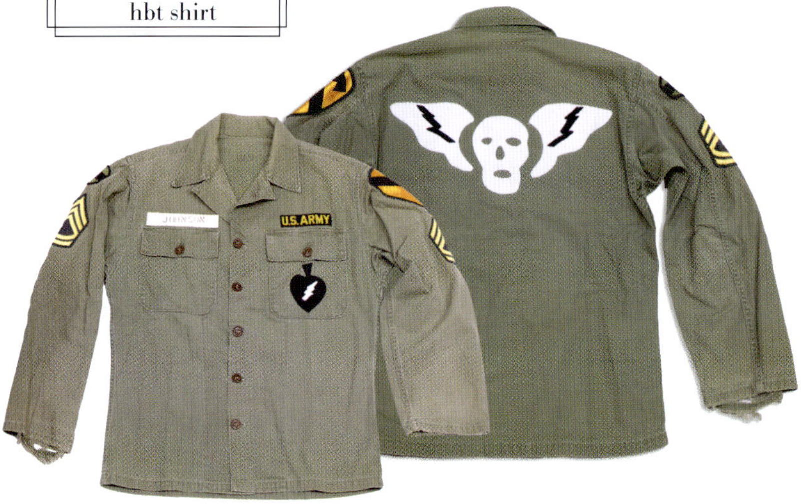

1940's
U.S.A.A.F.
aviator kit bag

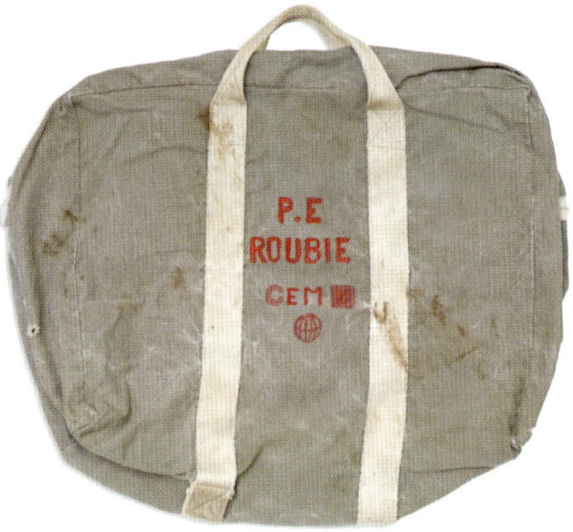

1960's
ARMY
sateen kid utility shirt

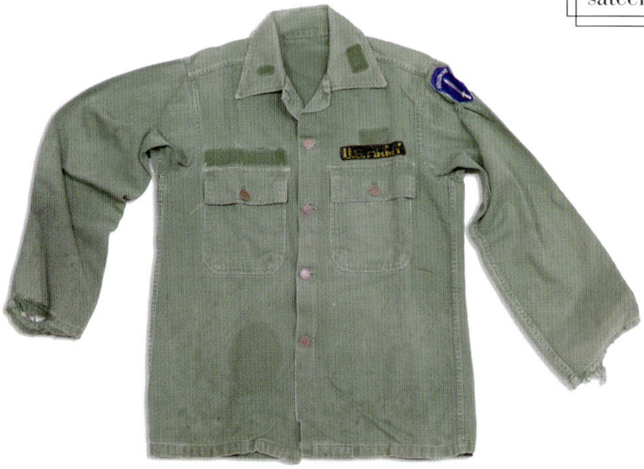

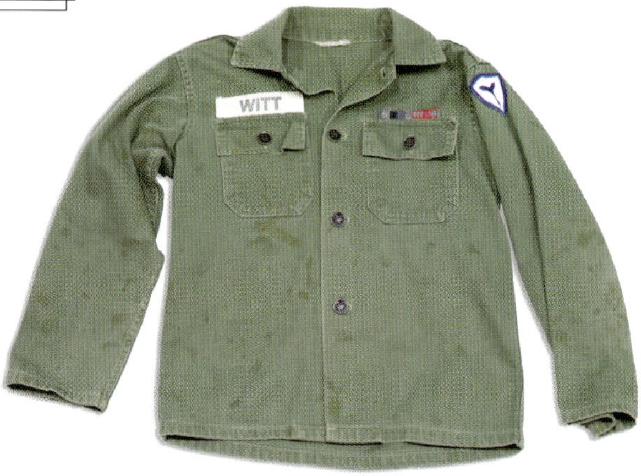

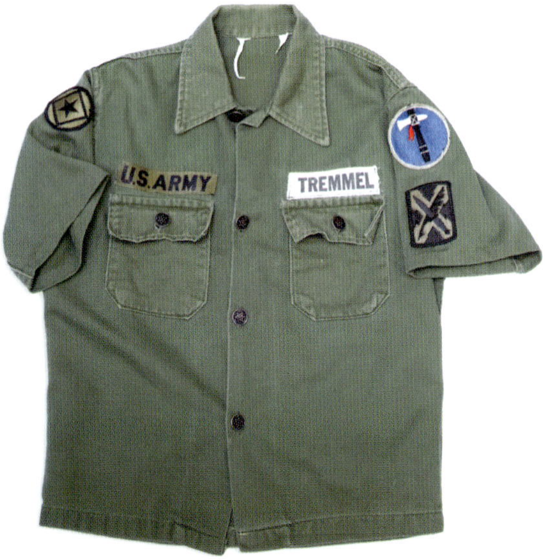

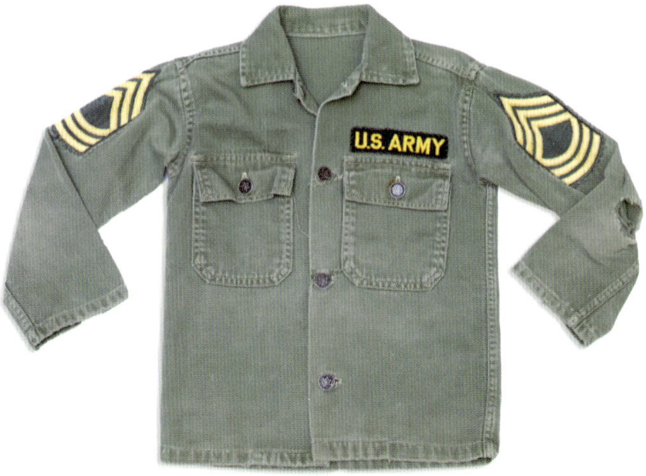

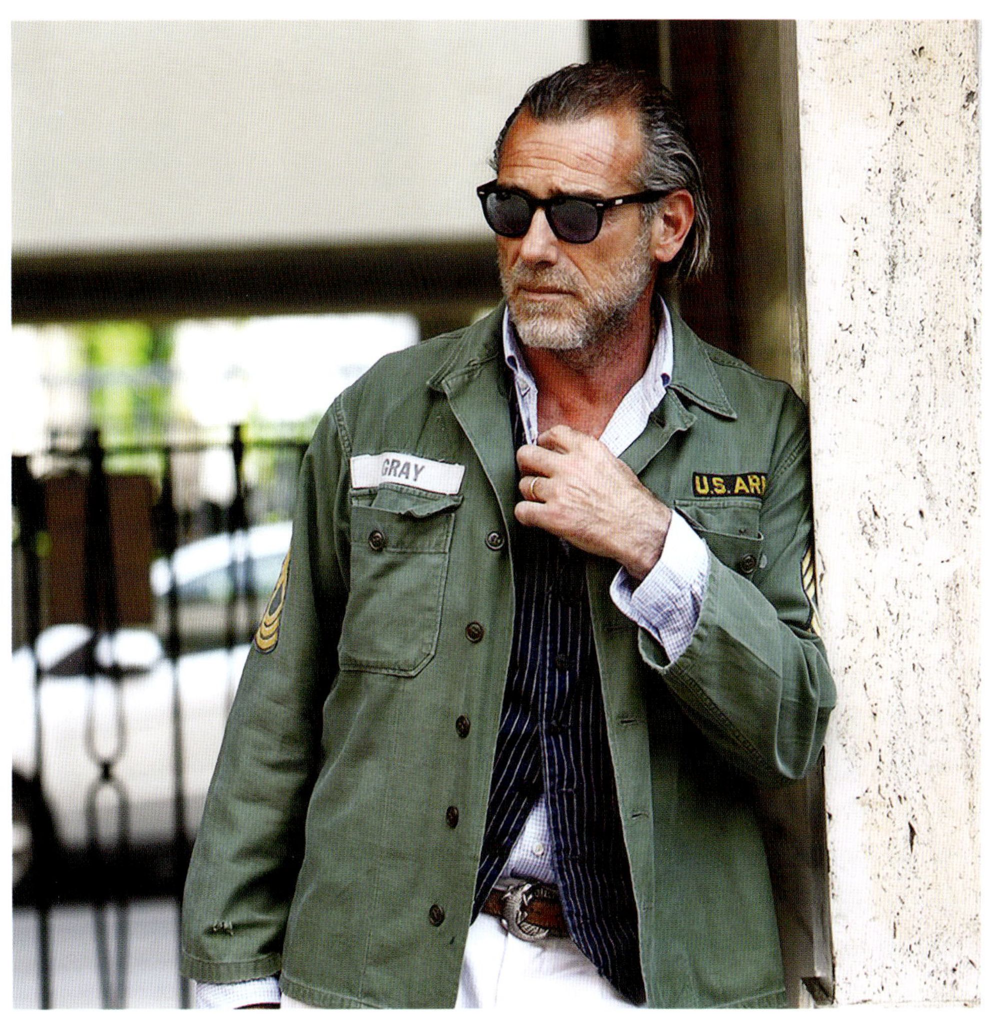

Downtown, Milano
Alessandro Squarzi photo archive
Courtesy of Guerrism

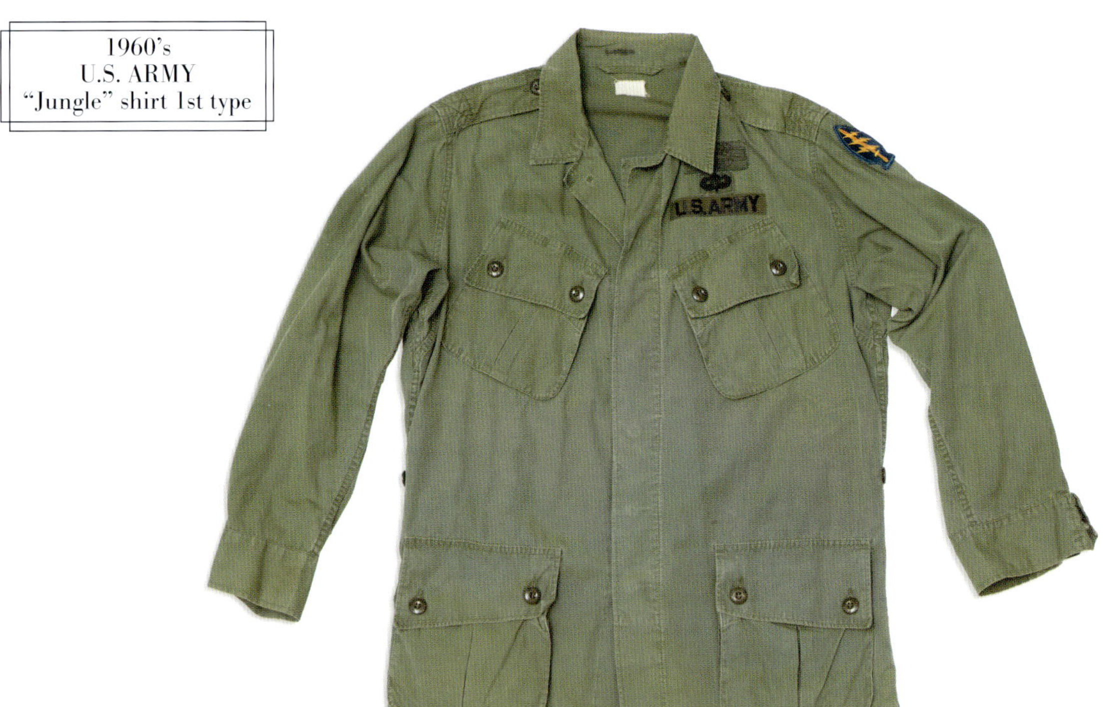

1960's
U.S. ARMY
"Jungle" shirt 1st type

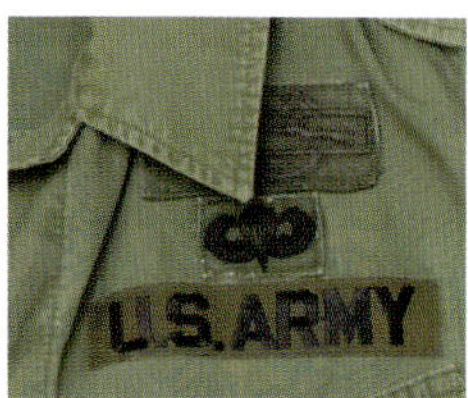

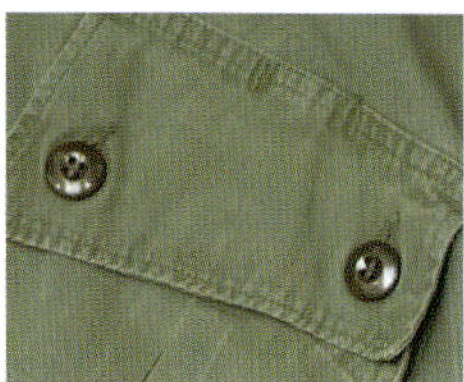

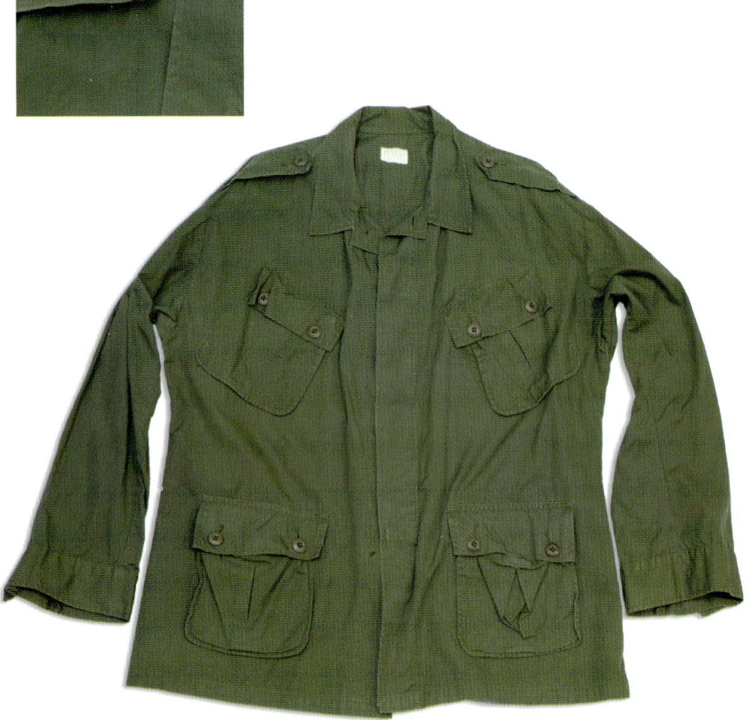

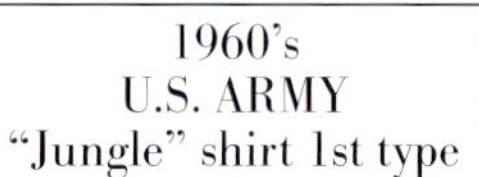

1960's
U.S. ARMY
"Jungle" shirt 1st type

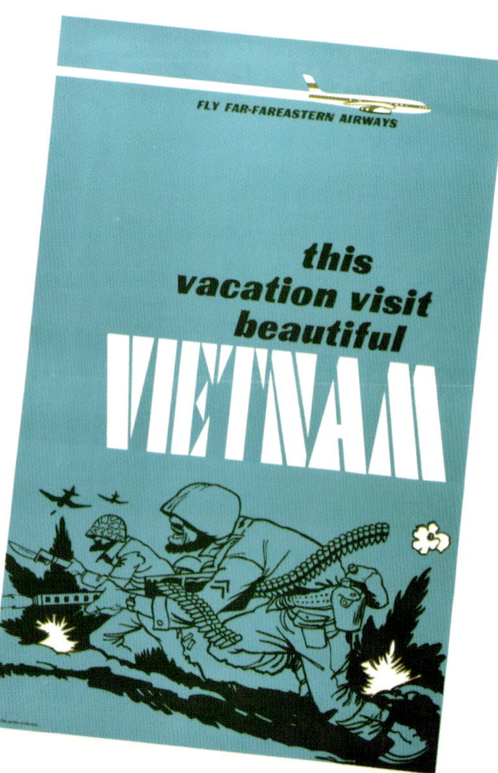

*Original Vintage Poster Fly Far-FarEastern
Airways Vietnam Anti War US Soldiers*

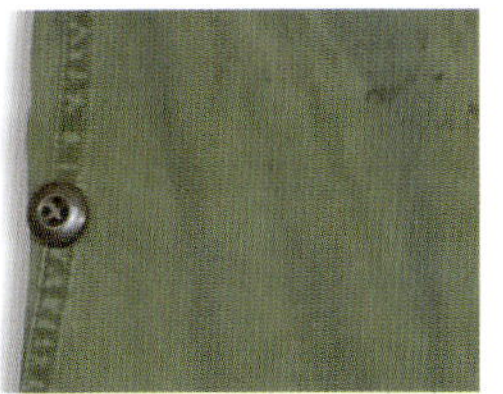

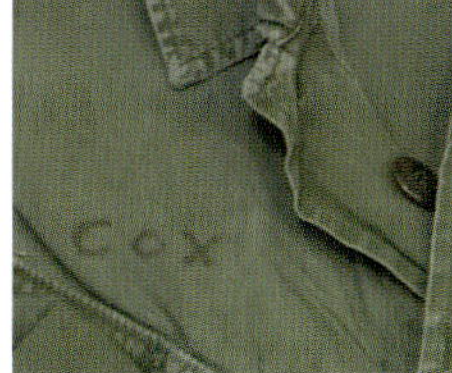

1960's
U.S. ARMY
"Jungle"shirt 2nd type

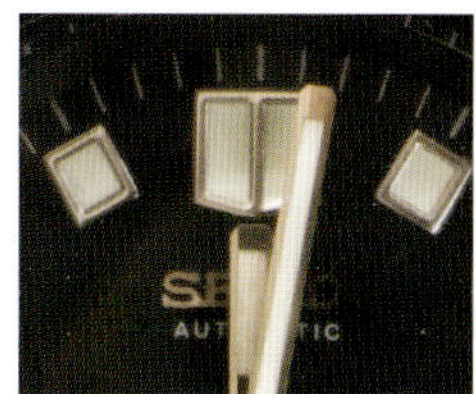

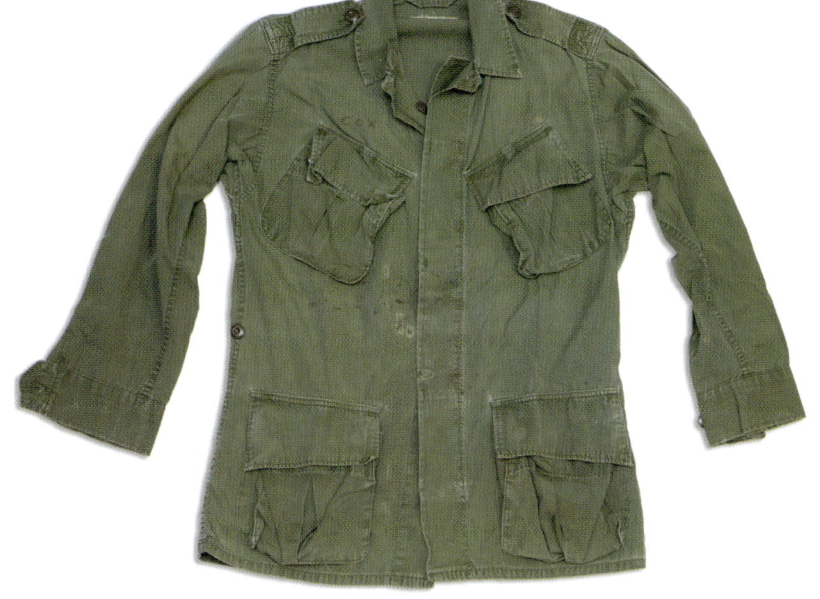

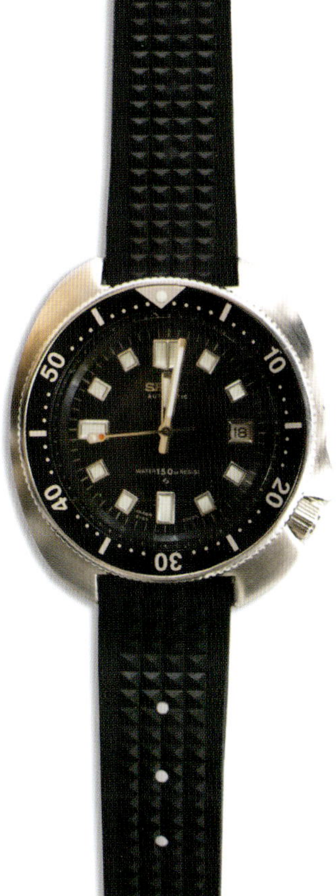

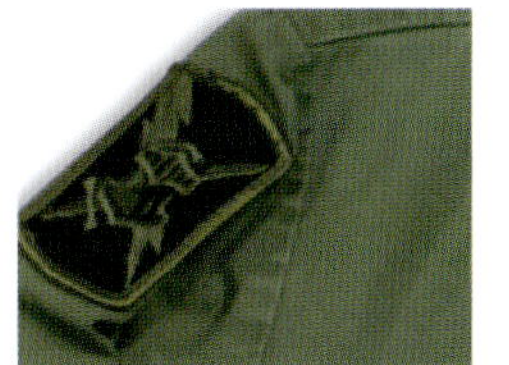

1960's
U.S. ARMY
"Jungle"shirt 3rd type

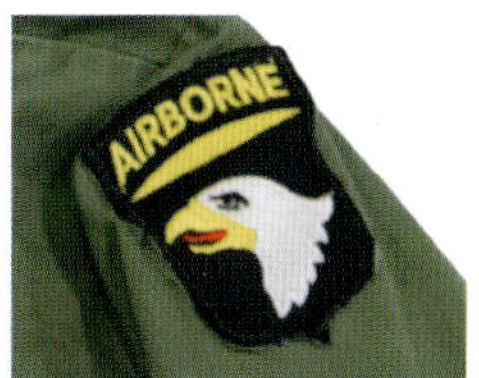

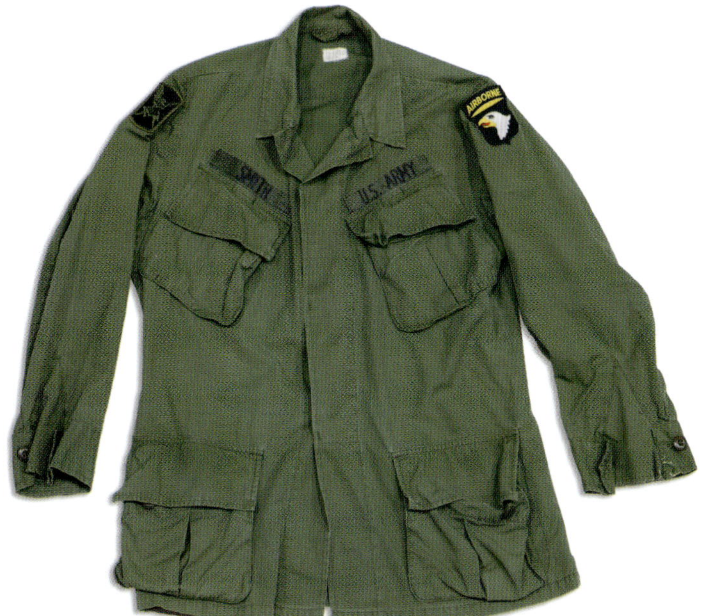

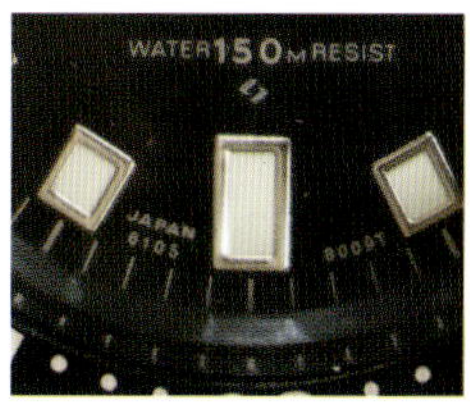

1960's
Seiko 6105
Wrist watch

1960's
U.S. ARMY
M-65 type "tiger stripe"

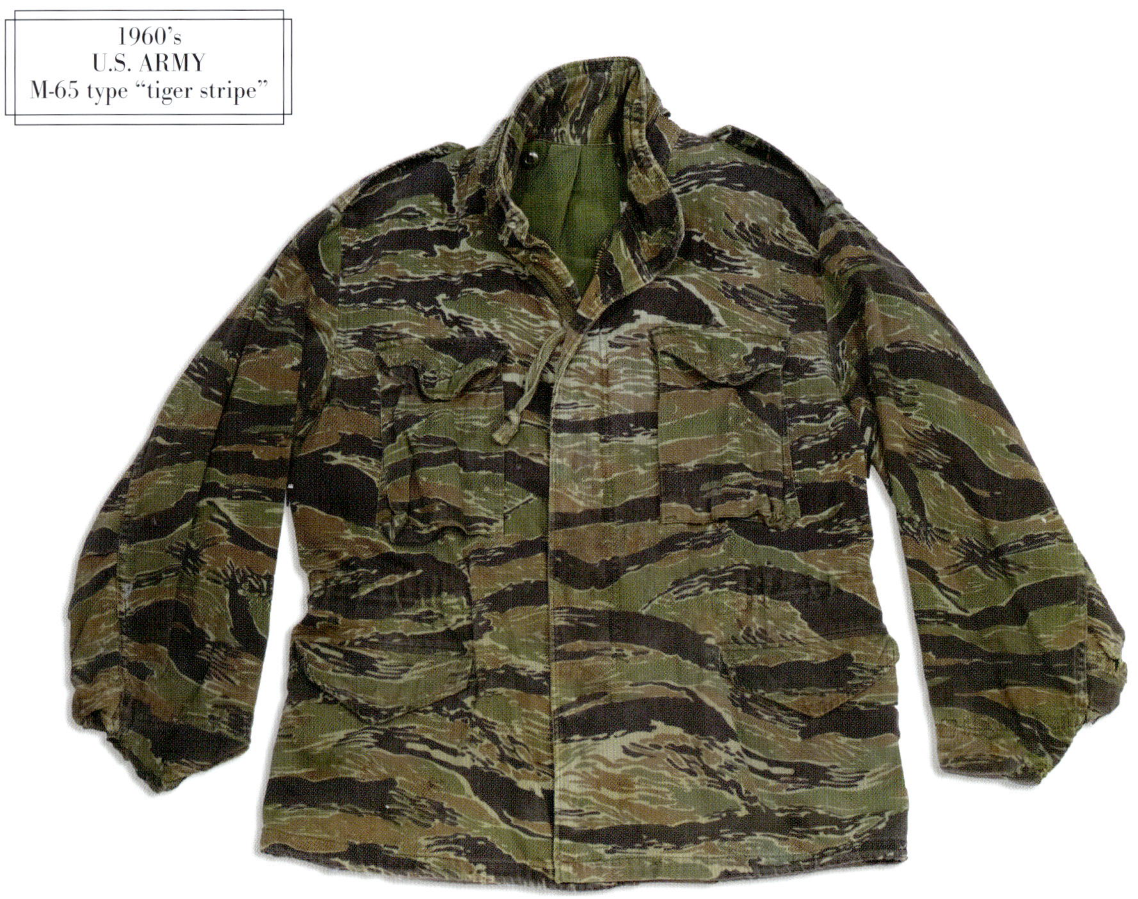

1960's
U.S. ARMY
Fatigue pants "cutted"

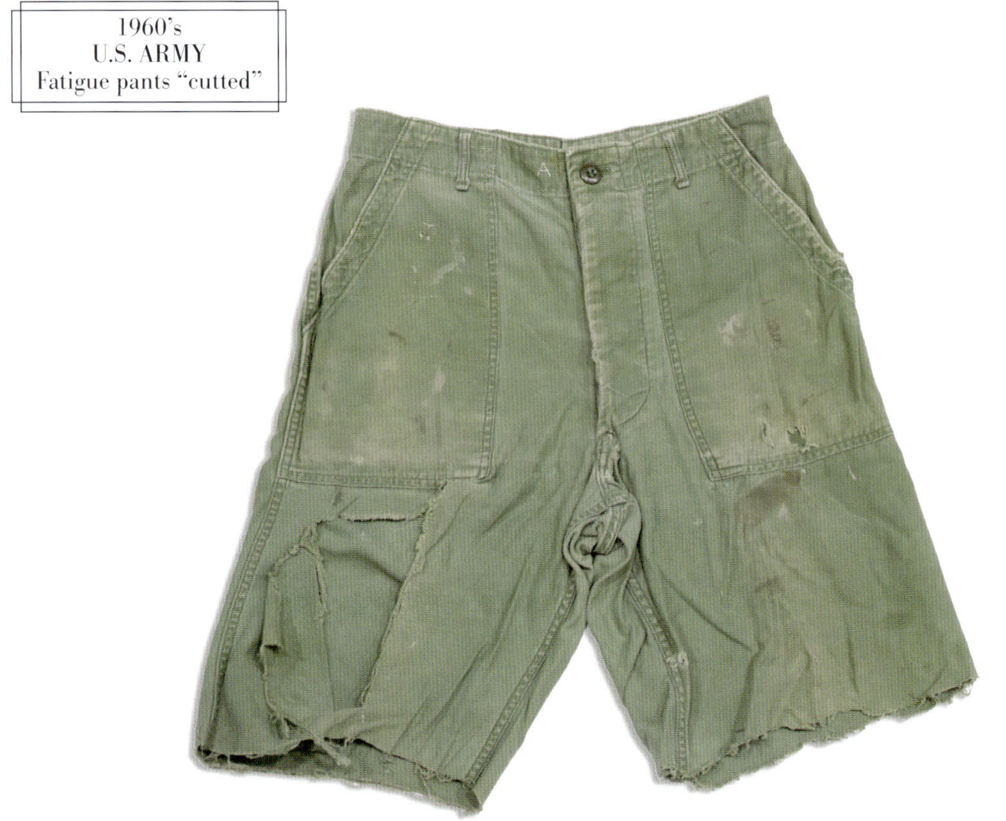

Vintage
Royal Navy
duffle coat

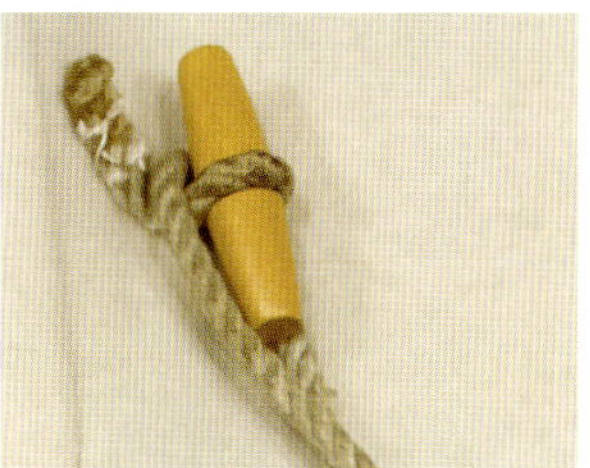

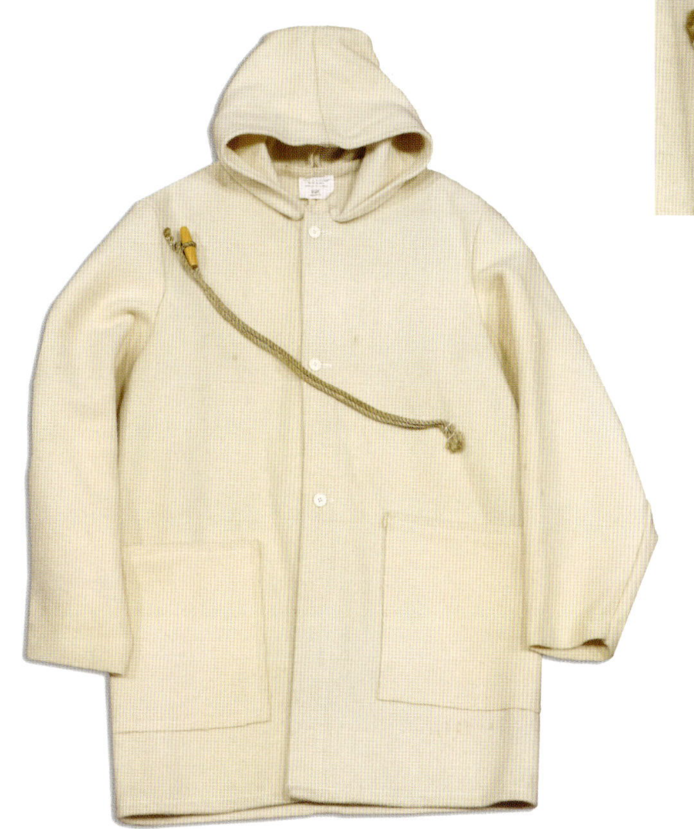

Vintage
Royal Navy
wool jacket

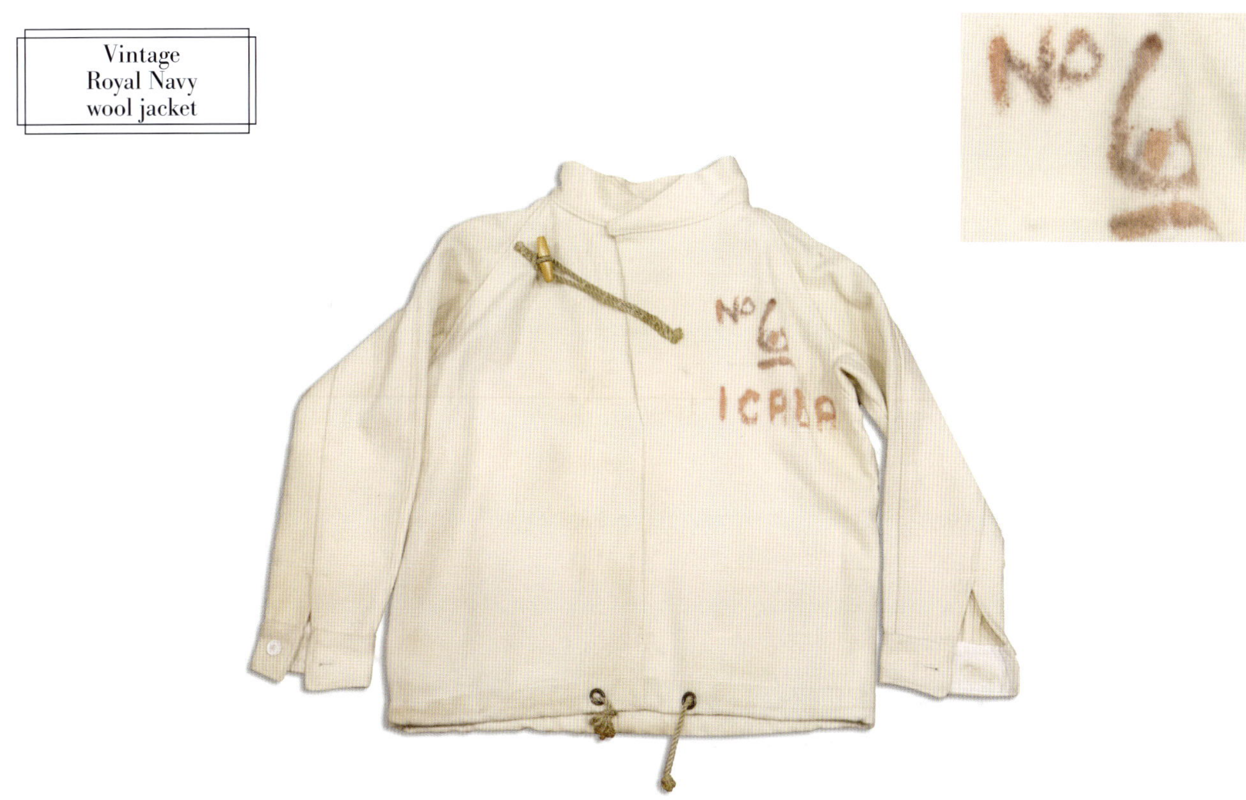

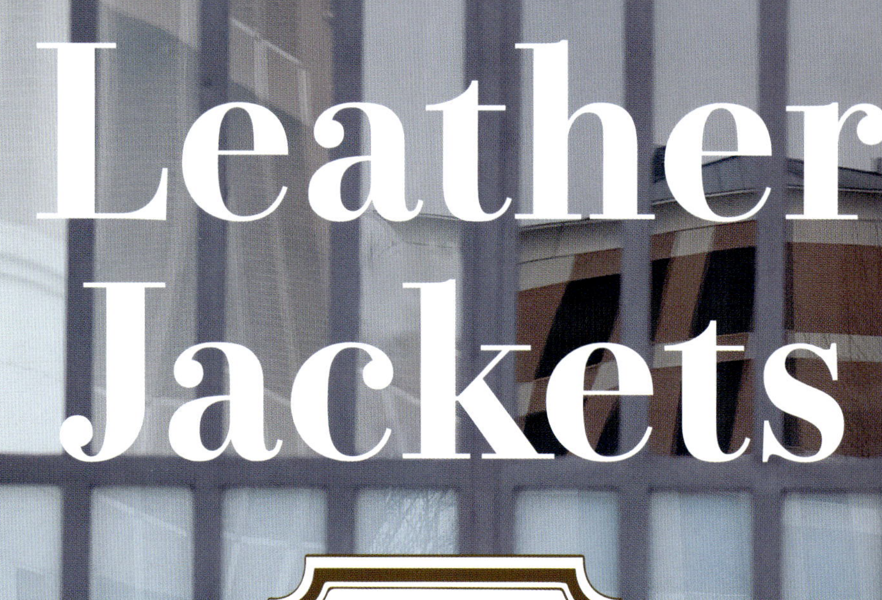

Leather Jackets

Sportswear
Motorcycle
& Military

*"Today, 40% of the clothes produced in the world
end up in pulp with the label still attached."*

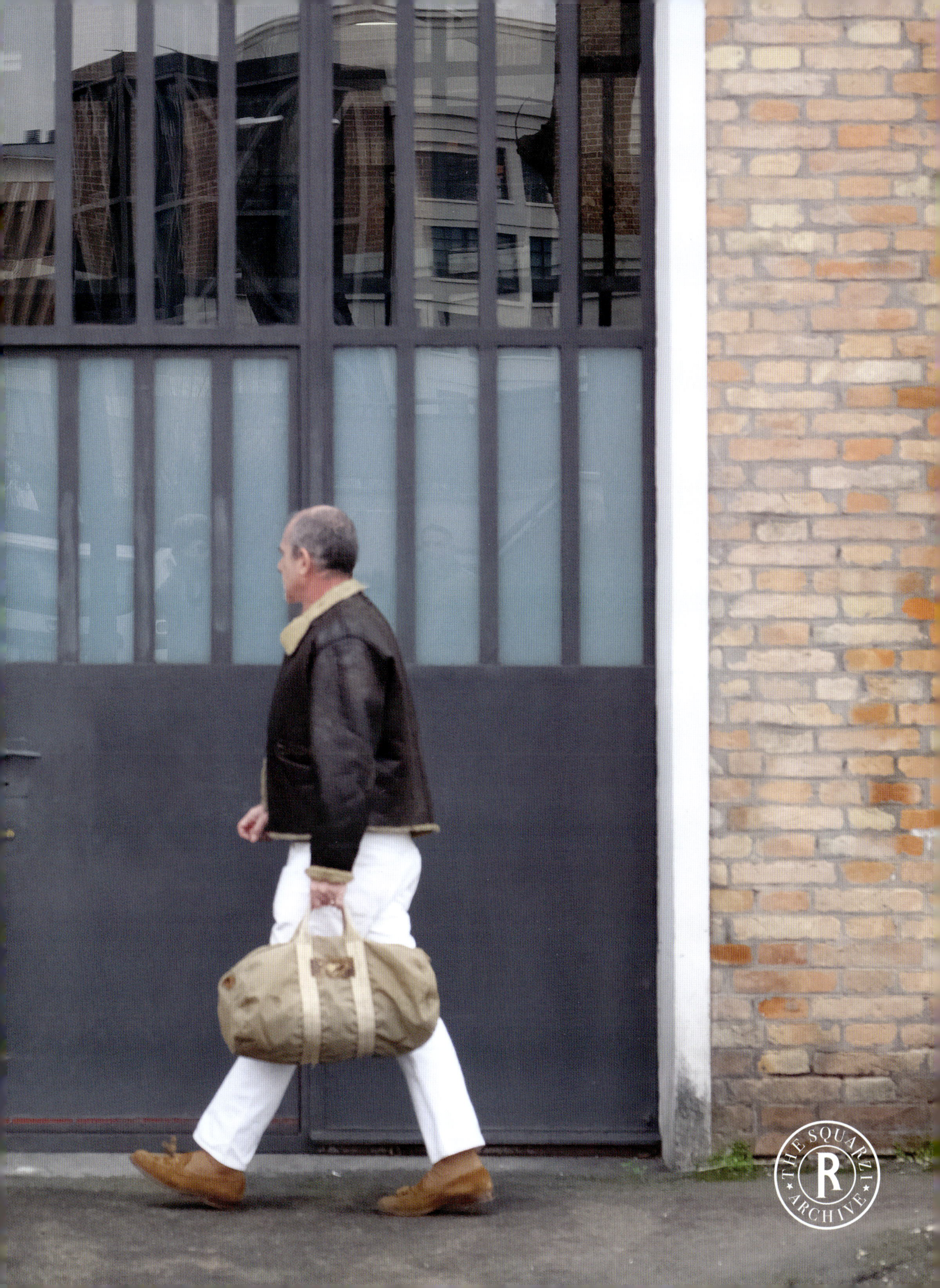

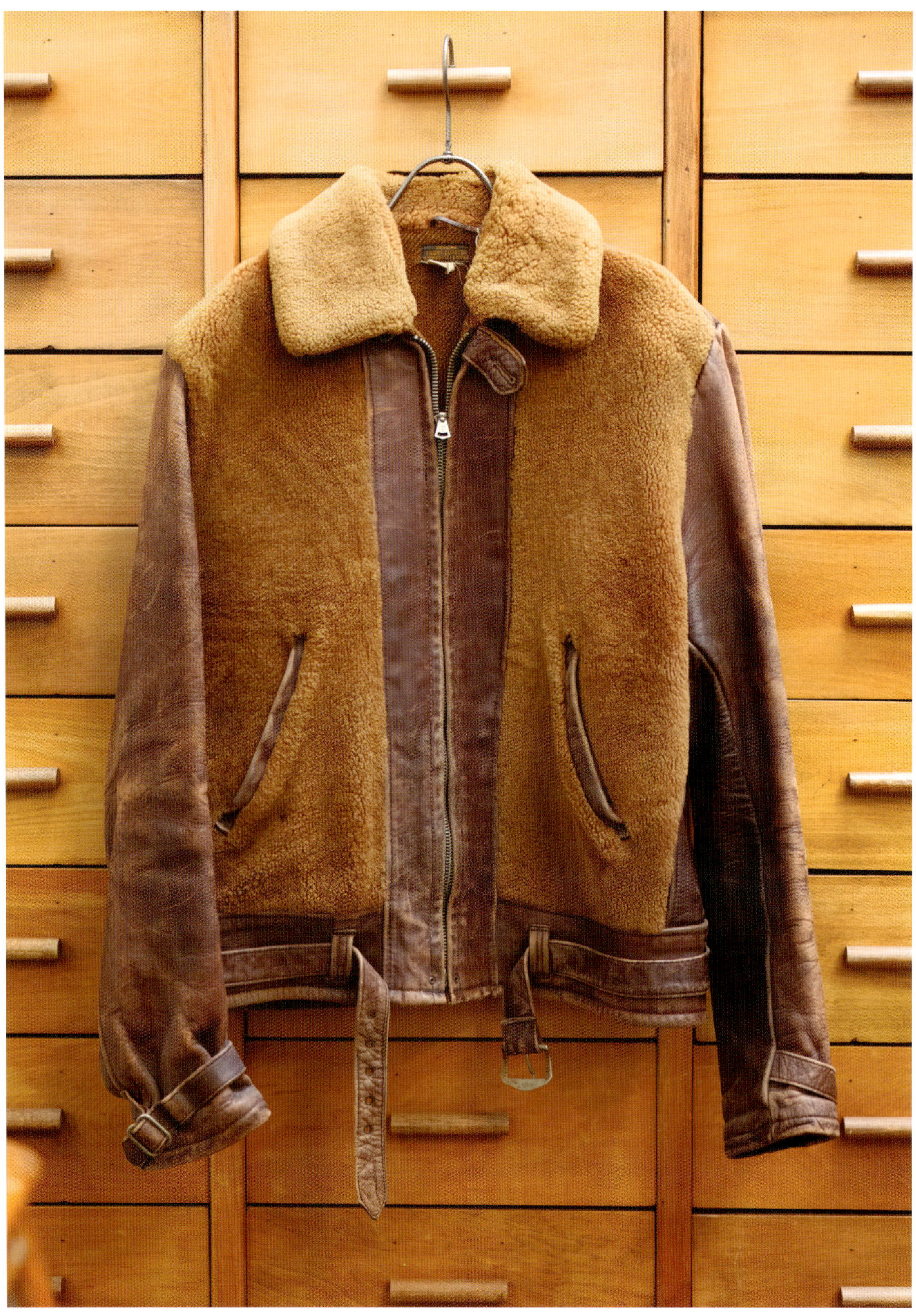

1930's
unknown
"Grizzly" jacket

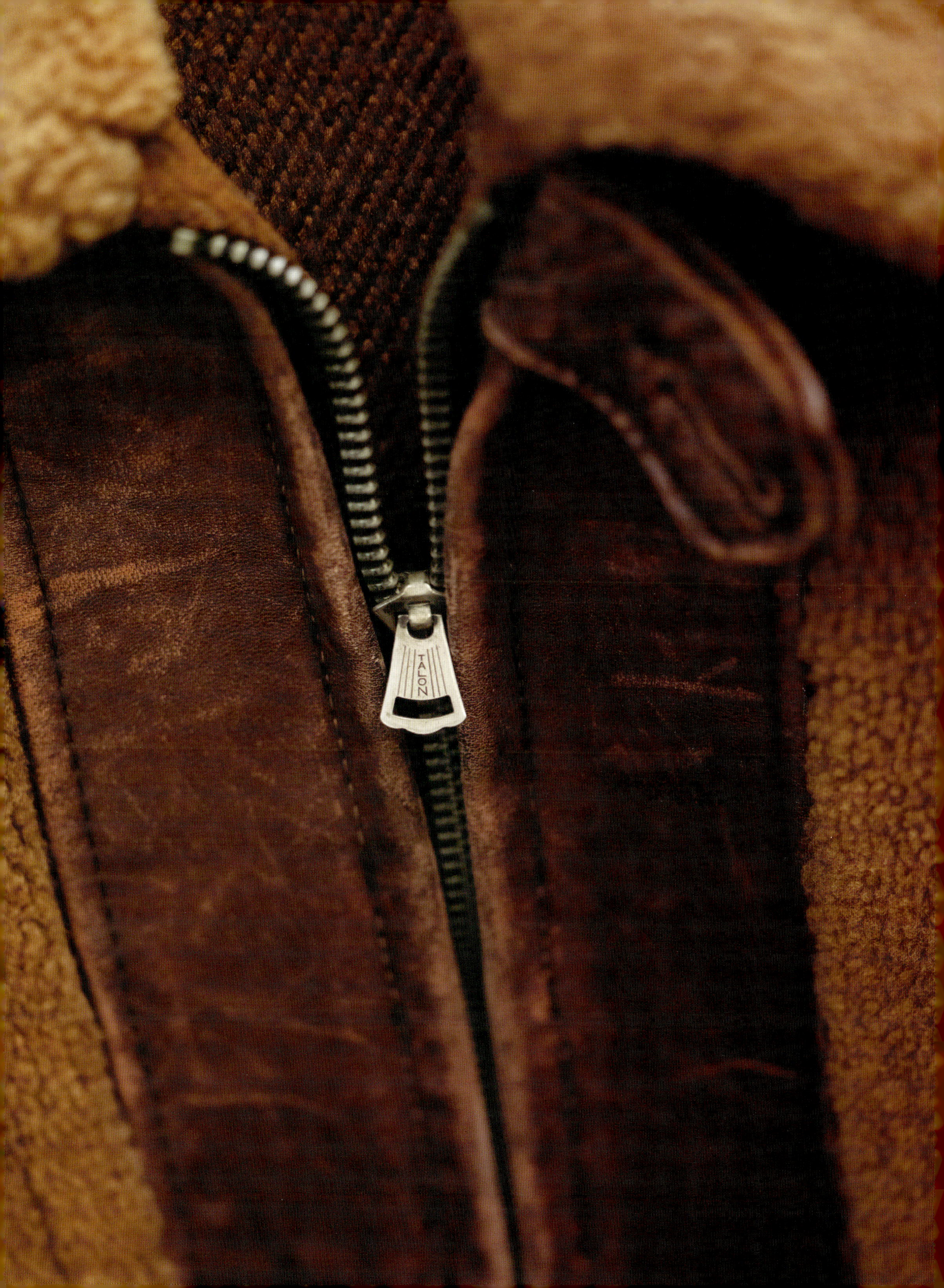

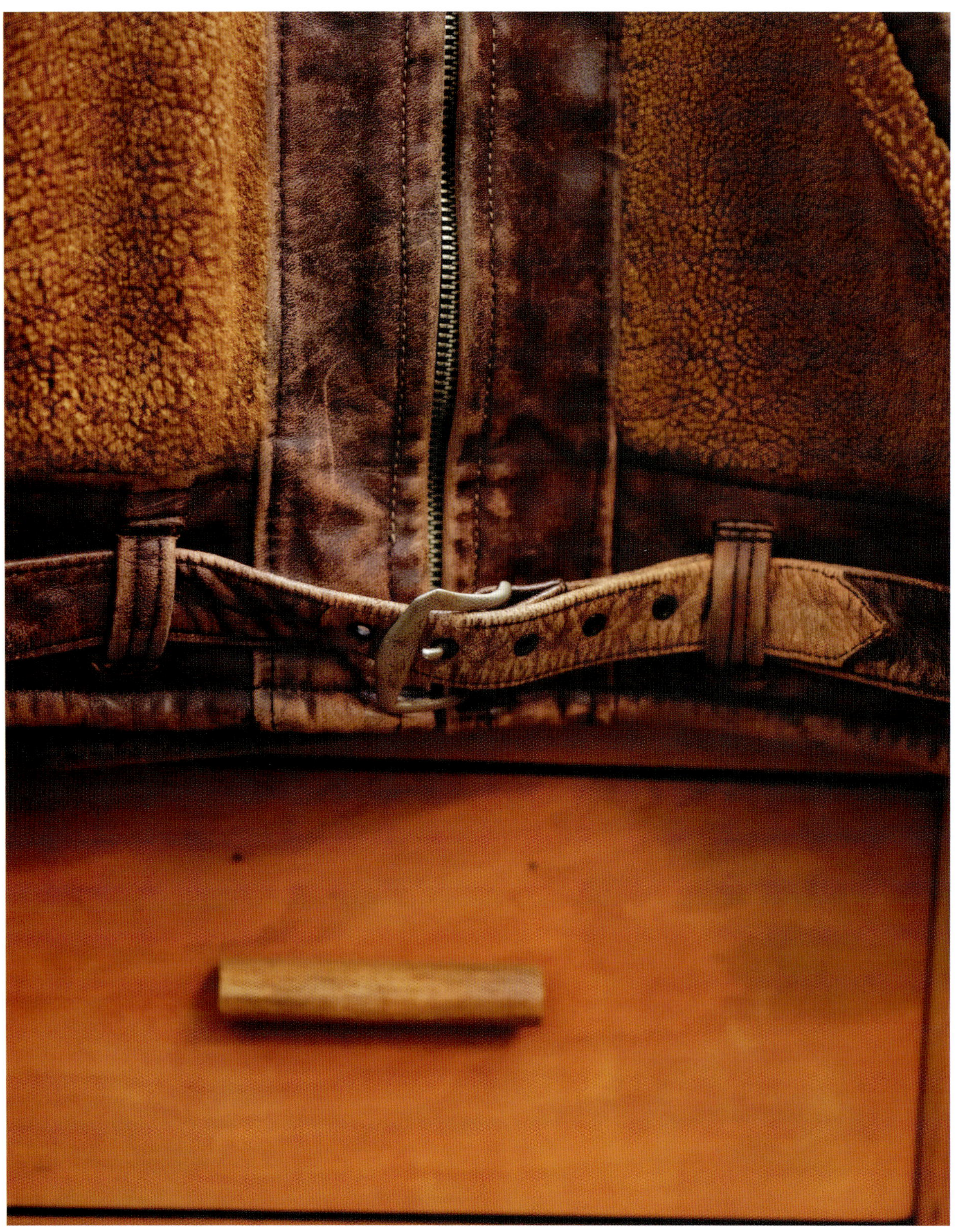

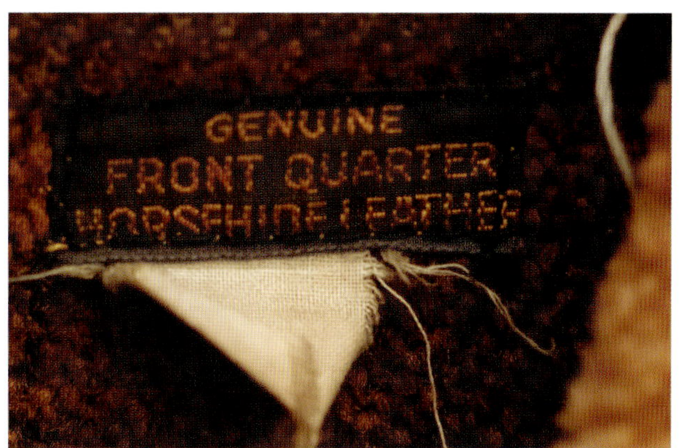
GENUINE
FRONT QUARTER
HORSEHIDE LEATHER

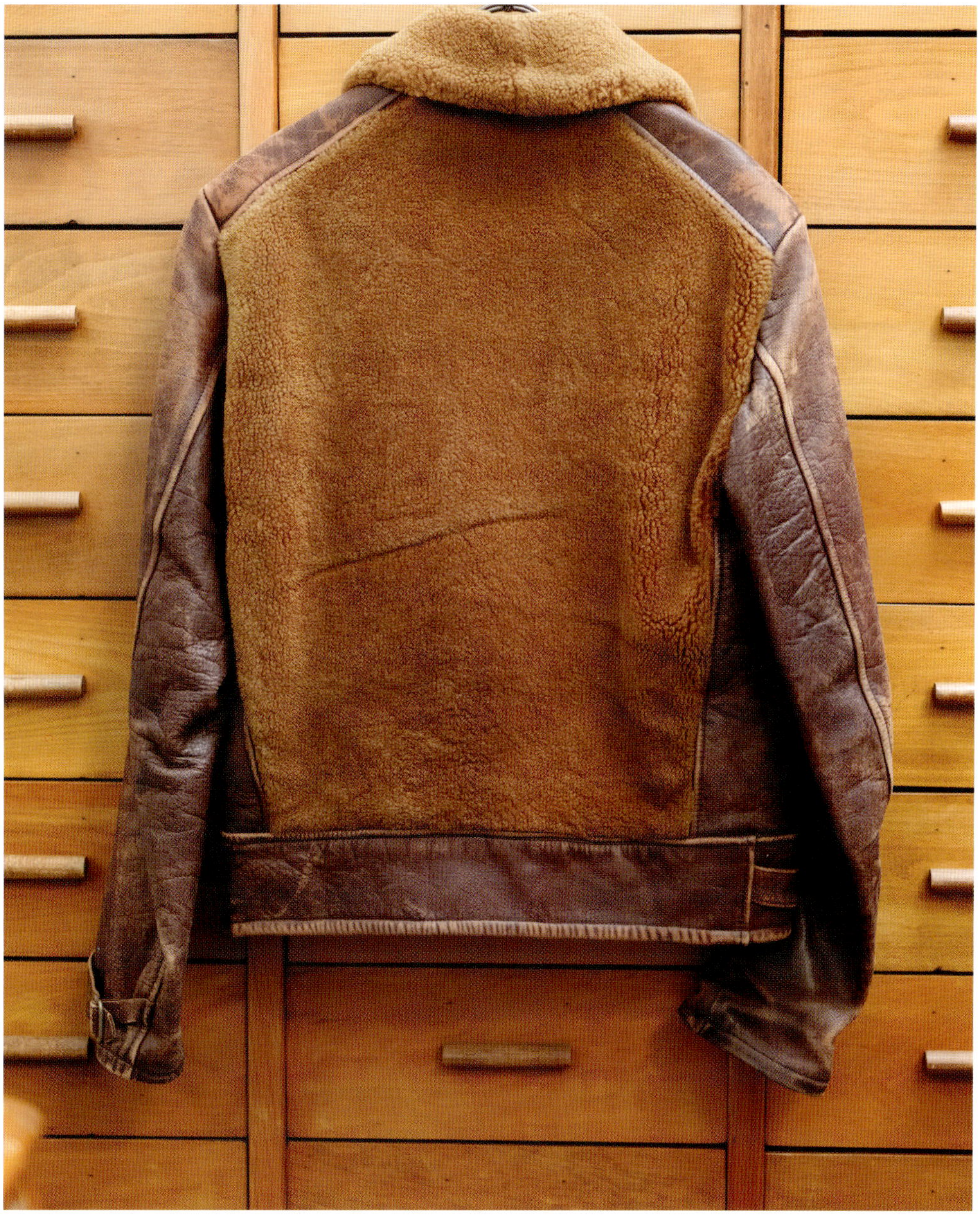

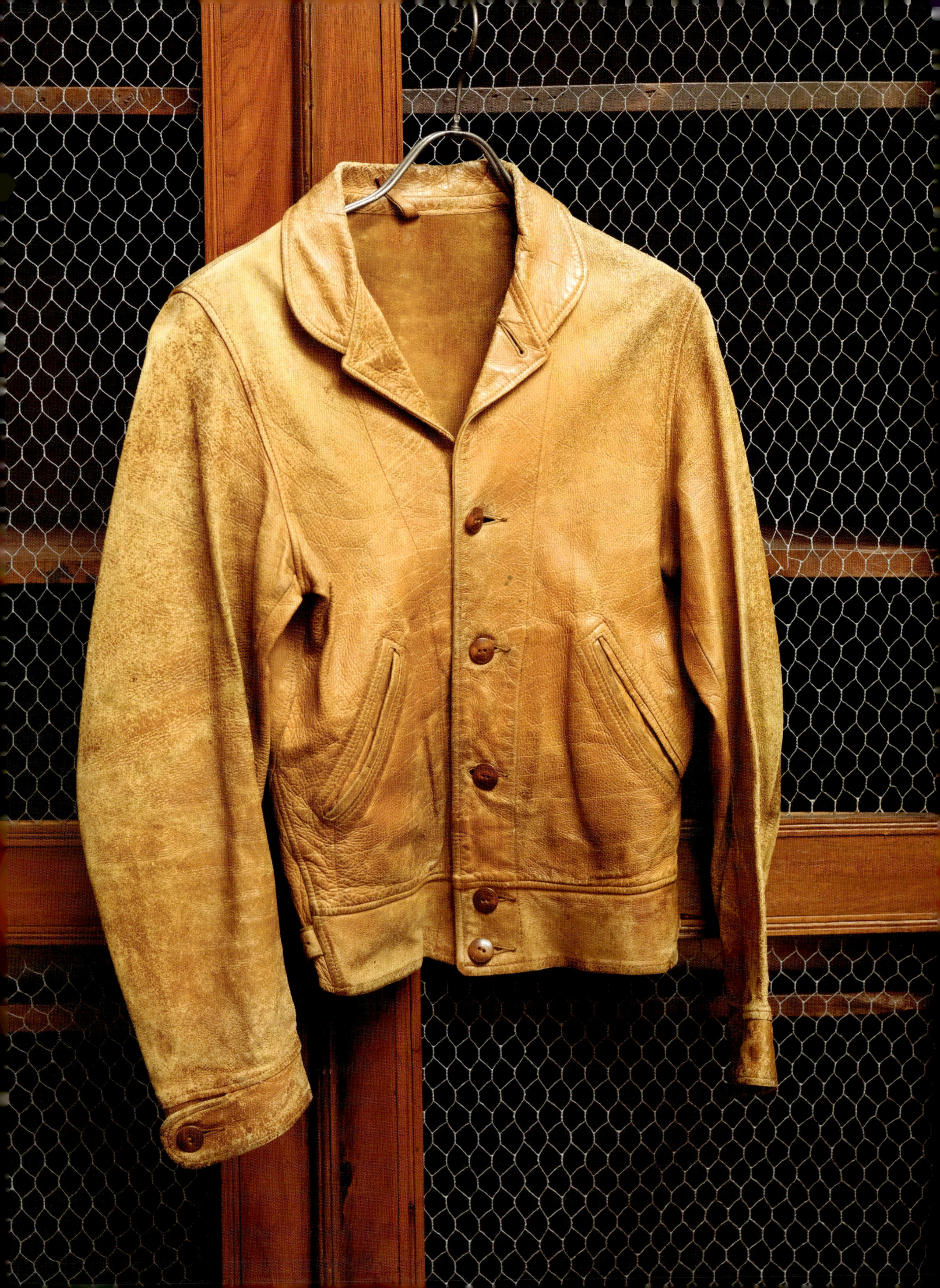

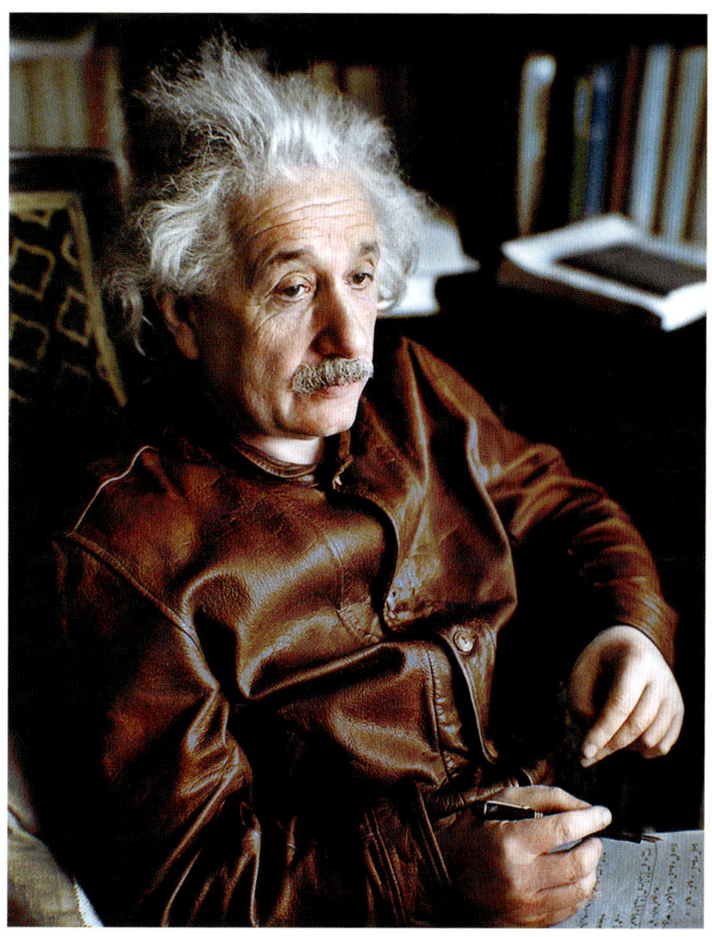

Albert Einstein, 1930's

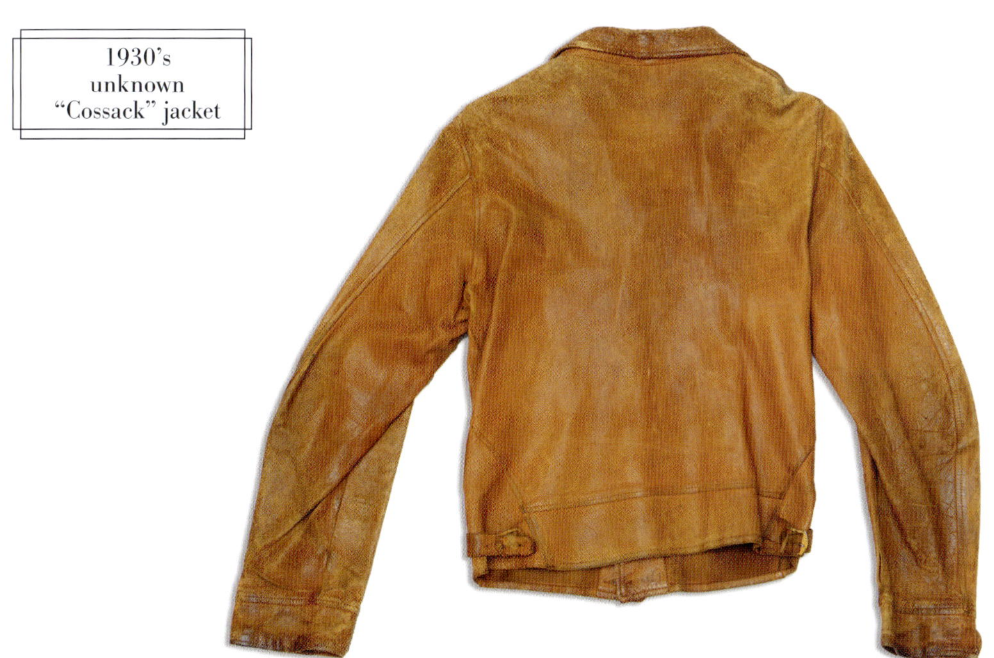

1930's
unknown
"Cossack" jacket

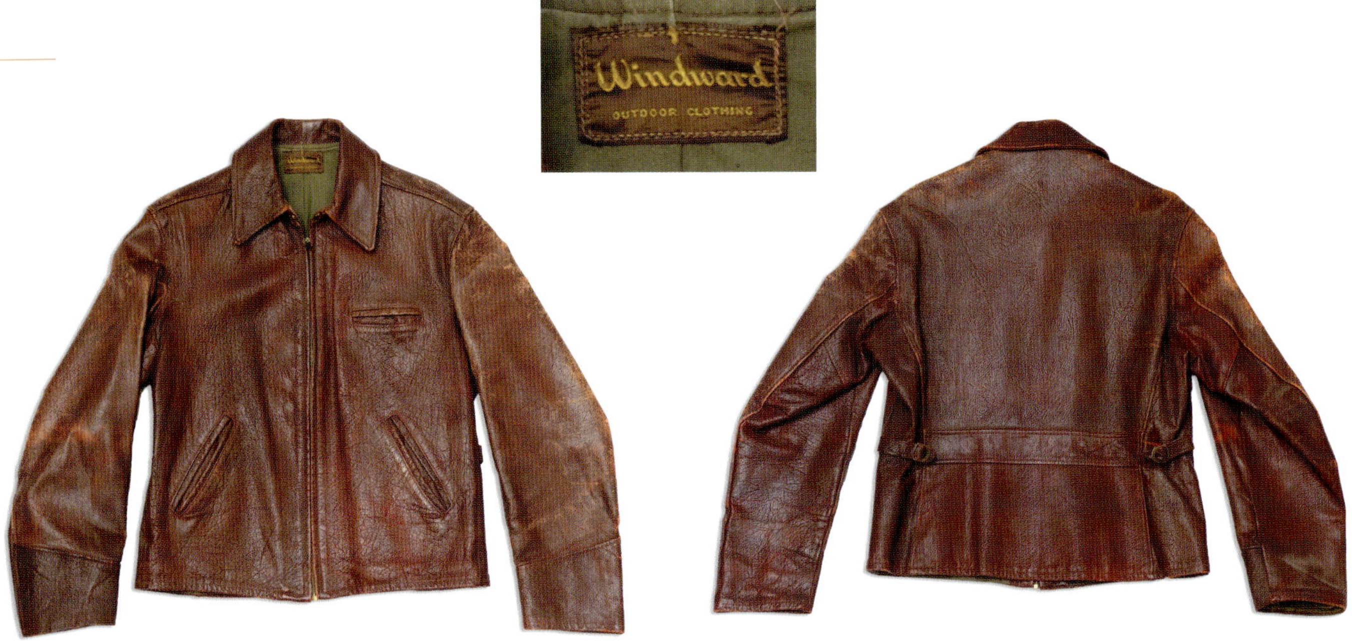

1940's
Windward sport jacket
"Half belt"

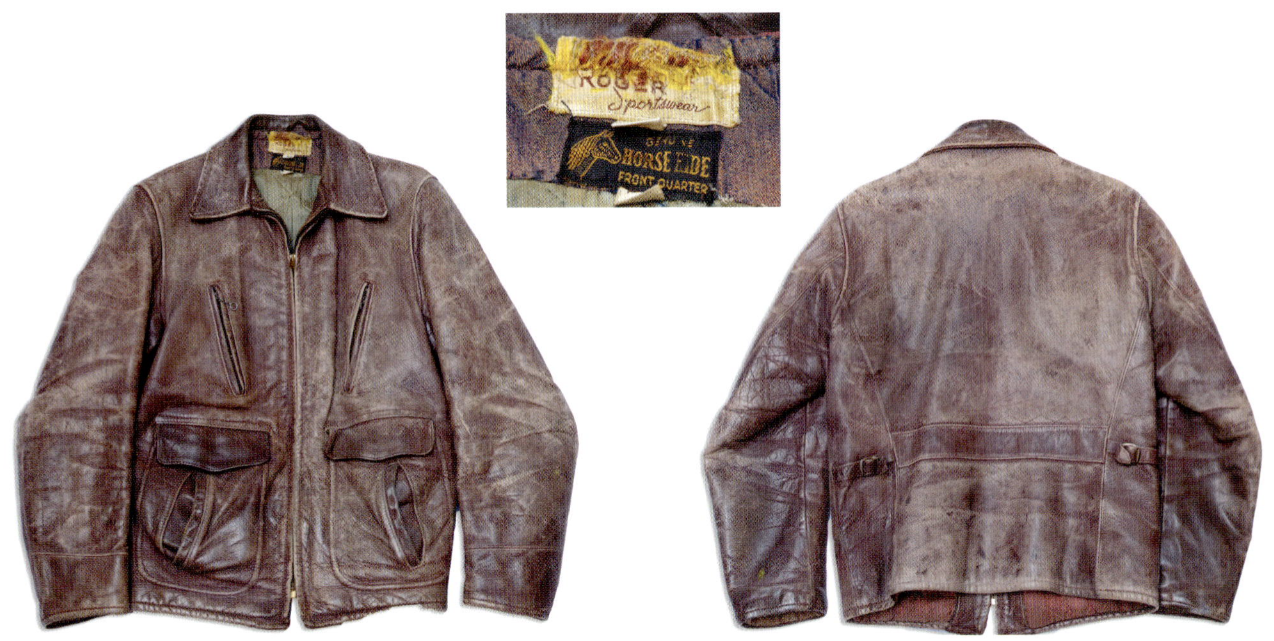

1950's
Roger Sportswear jacket
"Half belt"

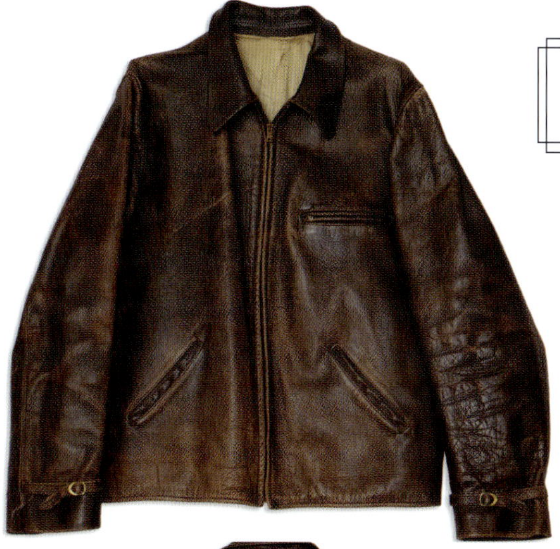

1950's
unknown
sport jacket

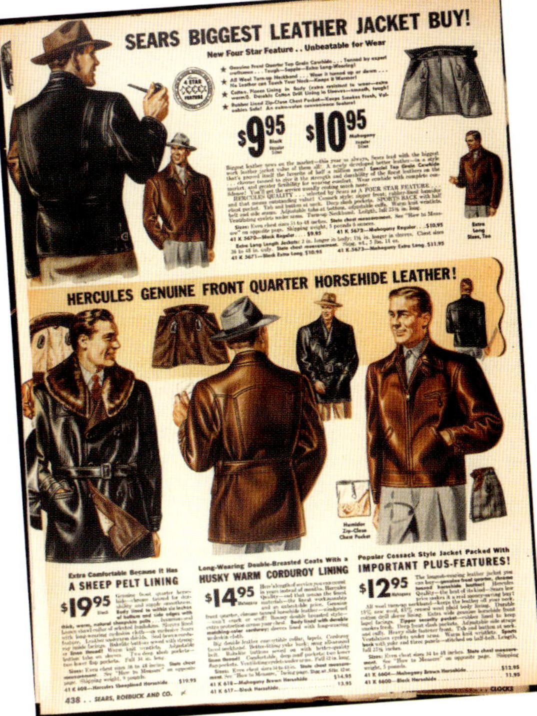

1930's Sears catalogue

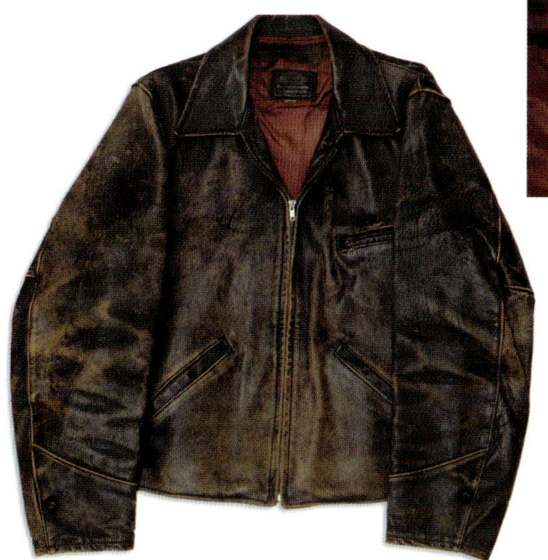

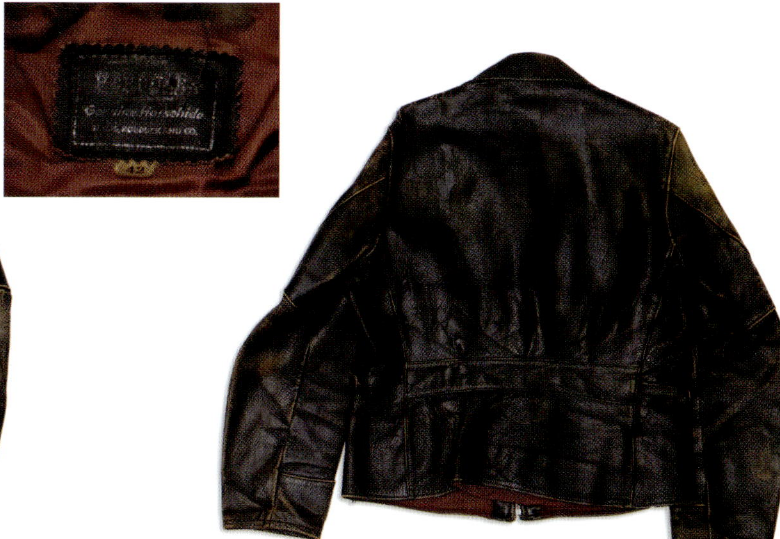

1950's
Hercules
sport jacket

1940's
unknown
sport jacket

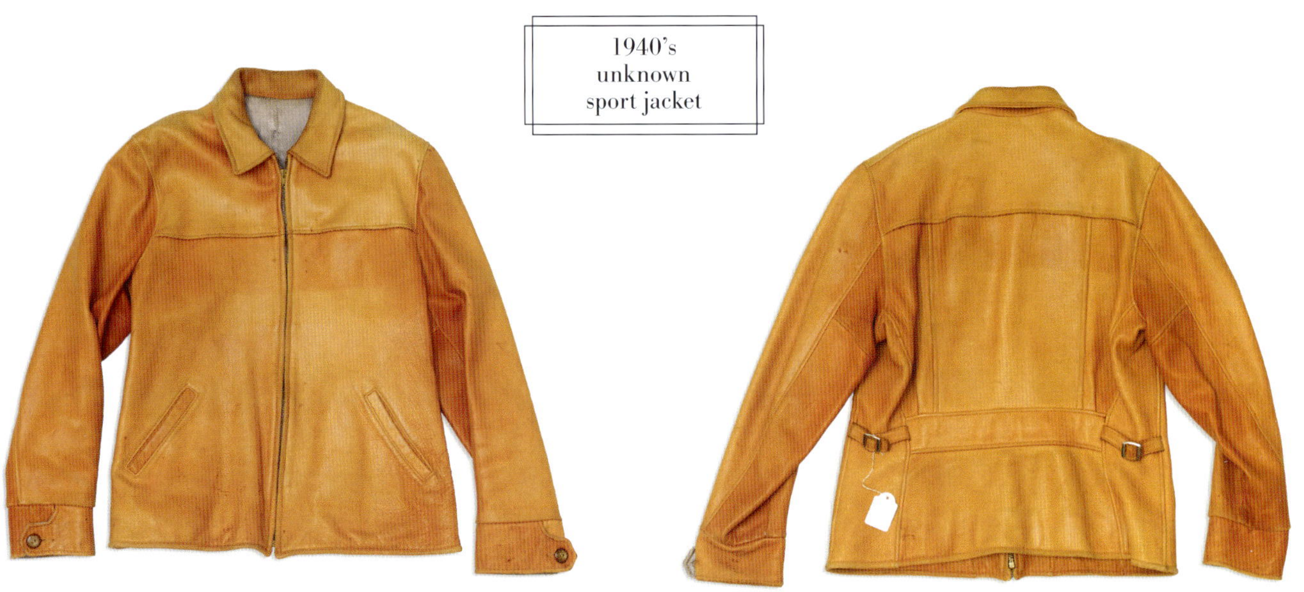

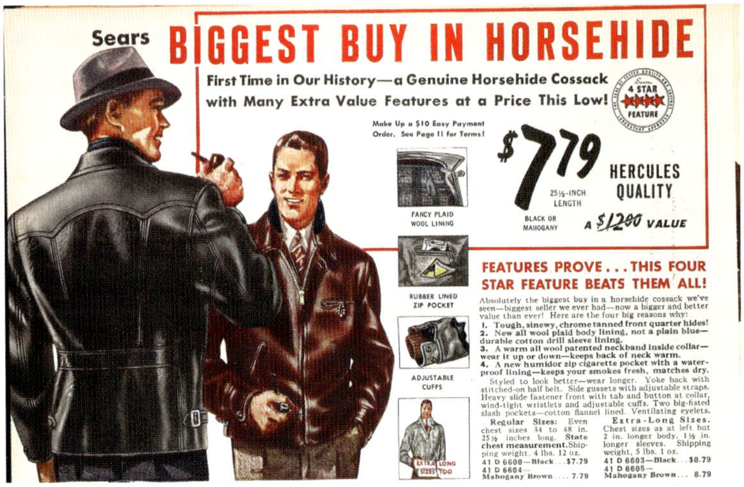

1930's Sears catalogue

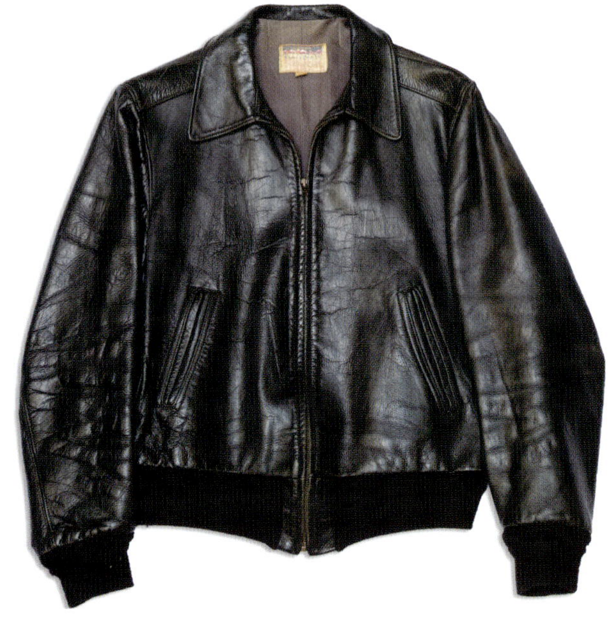

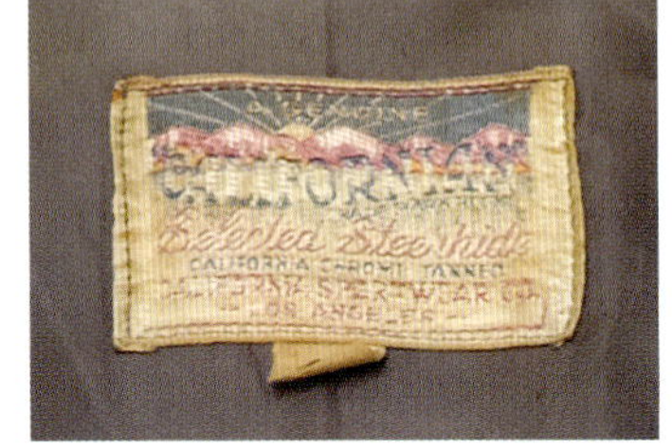

1950's
Californian
sport jacket

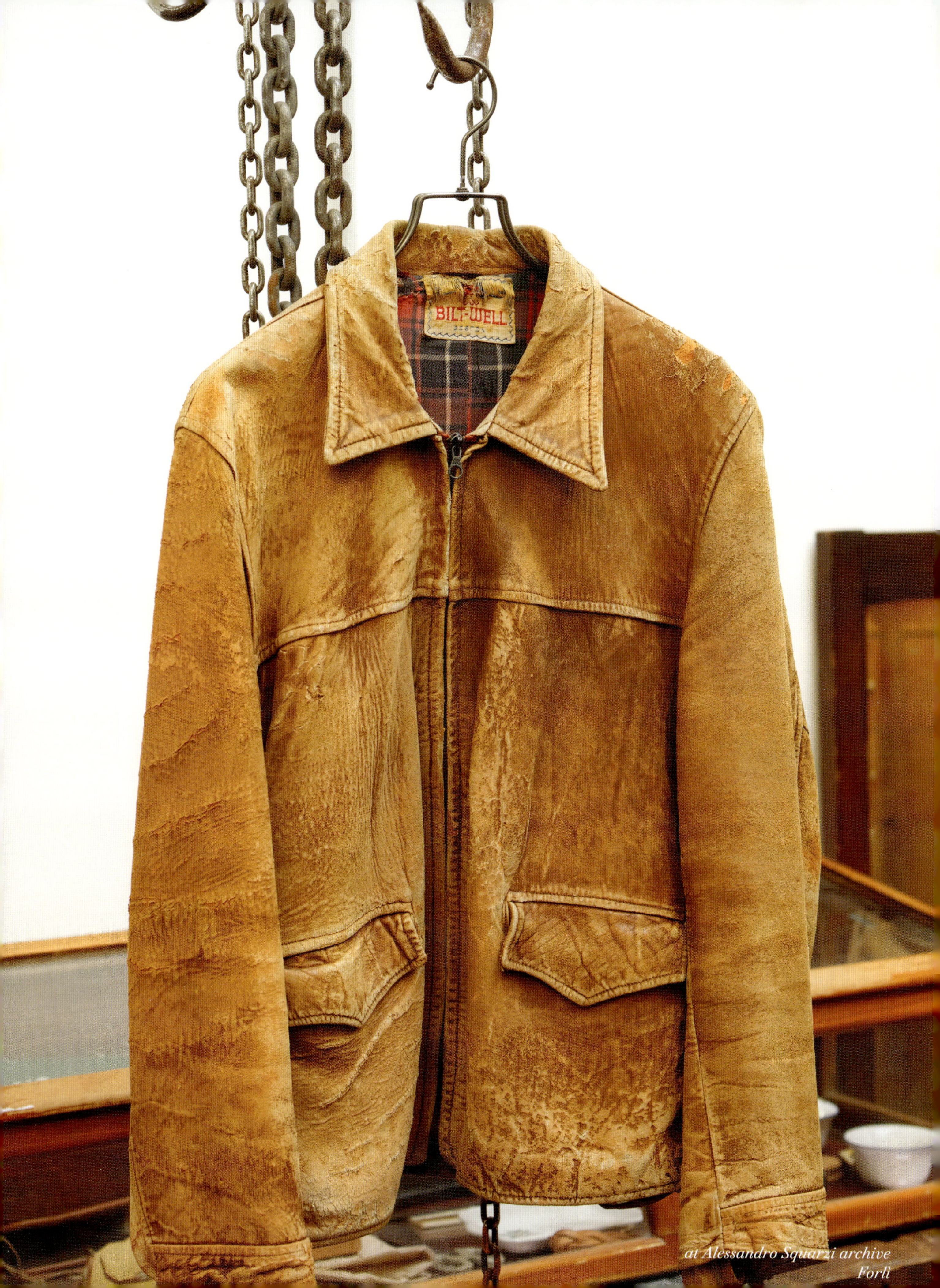
BILT-WELL

at Alessandro Squarzi archive
Forlì

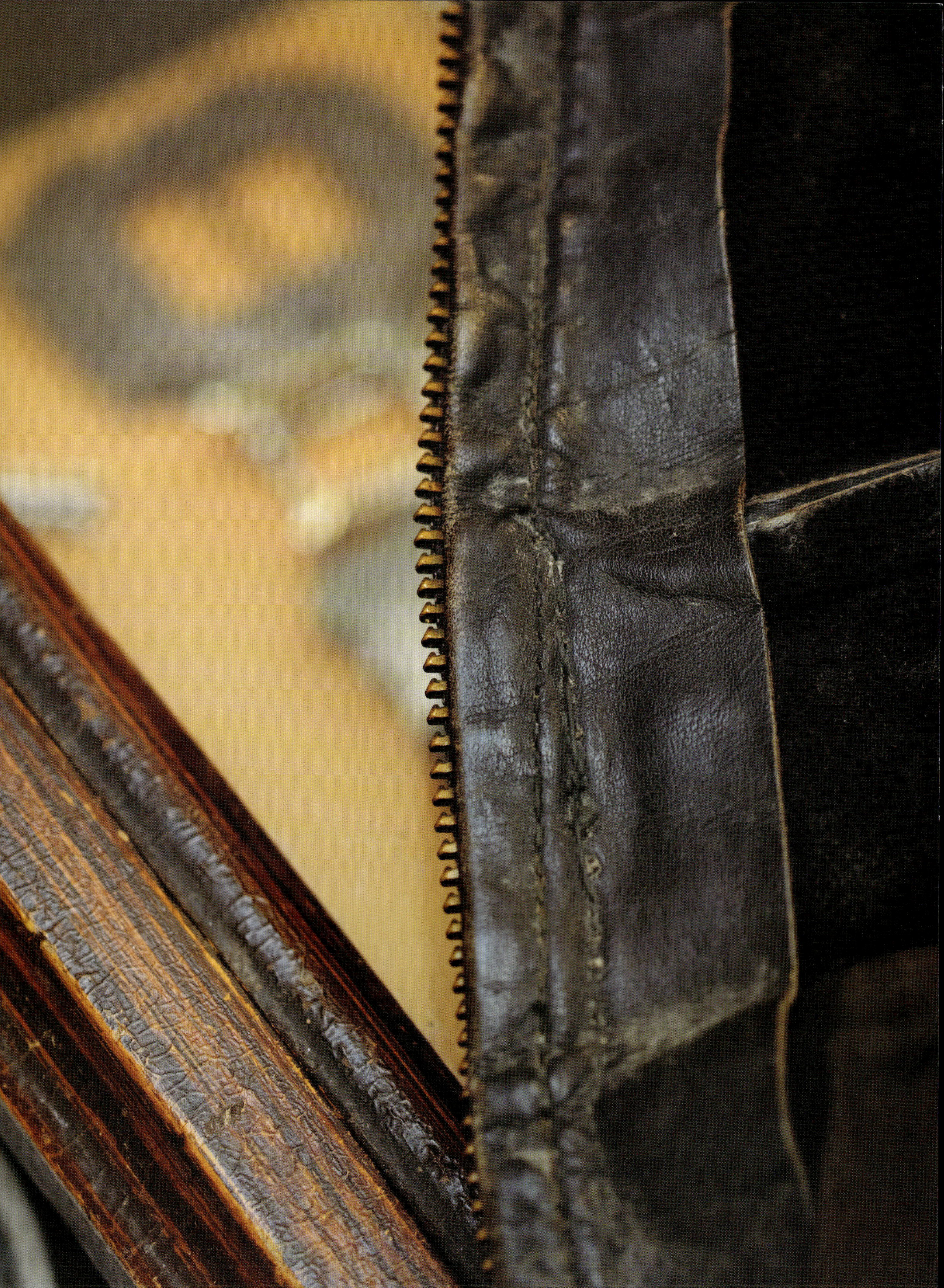

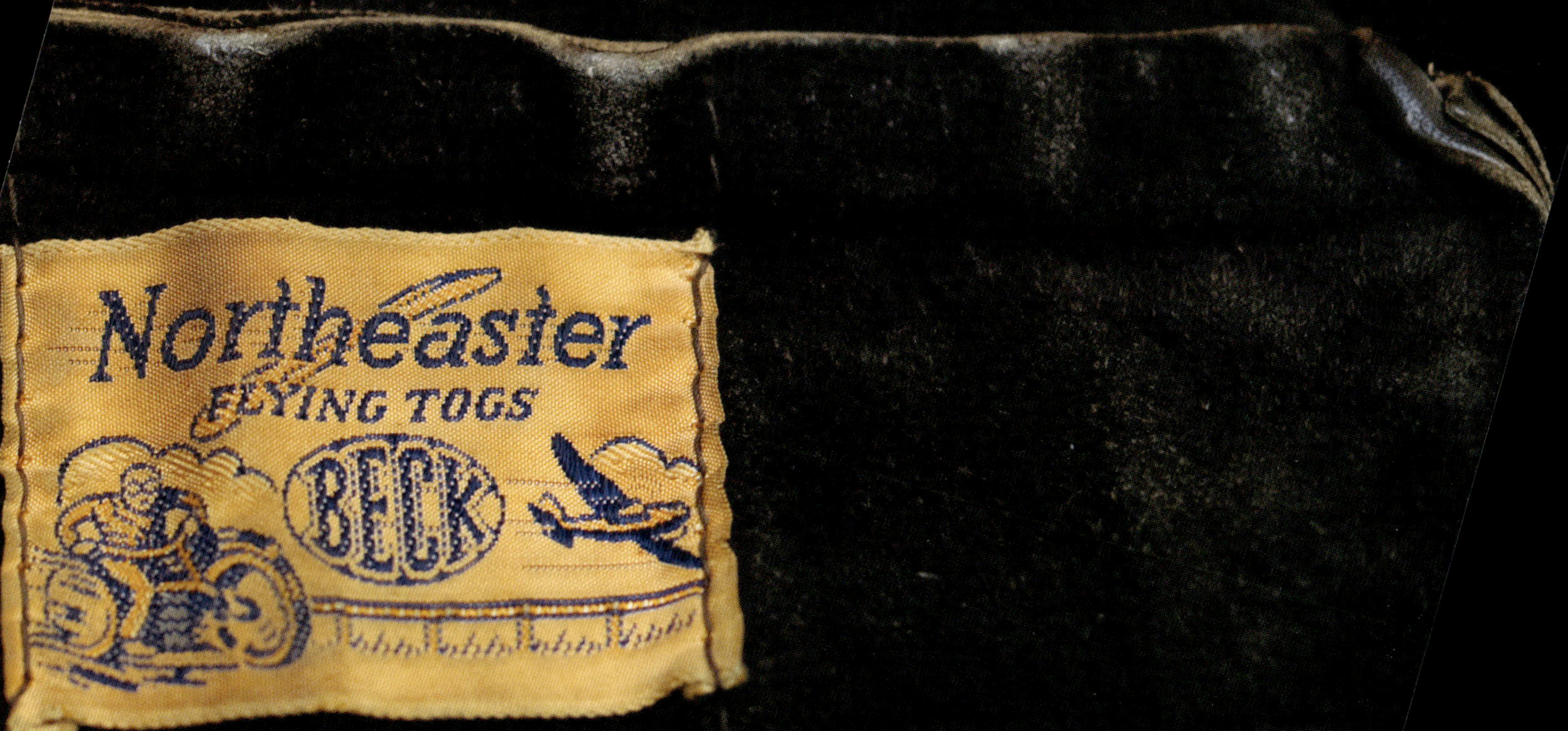

Northeaster
FLYING TOGS
BECK

1940's
Beck 333
rider jacket

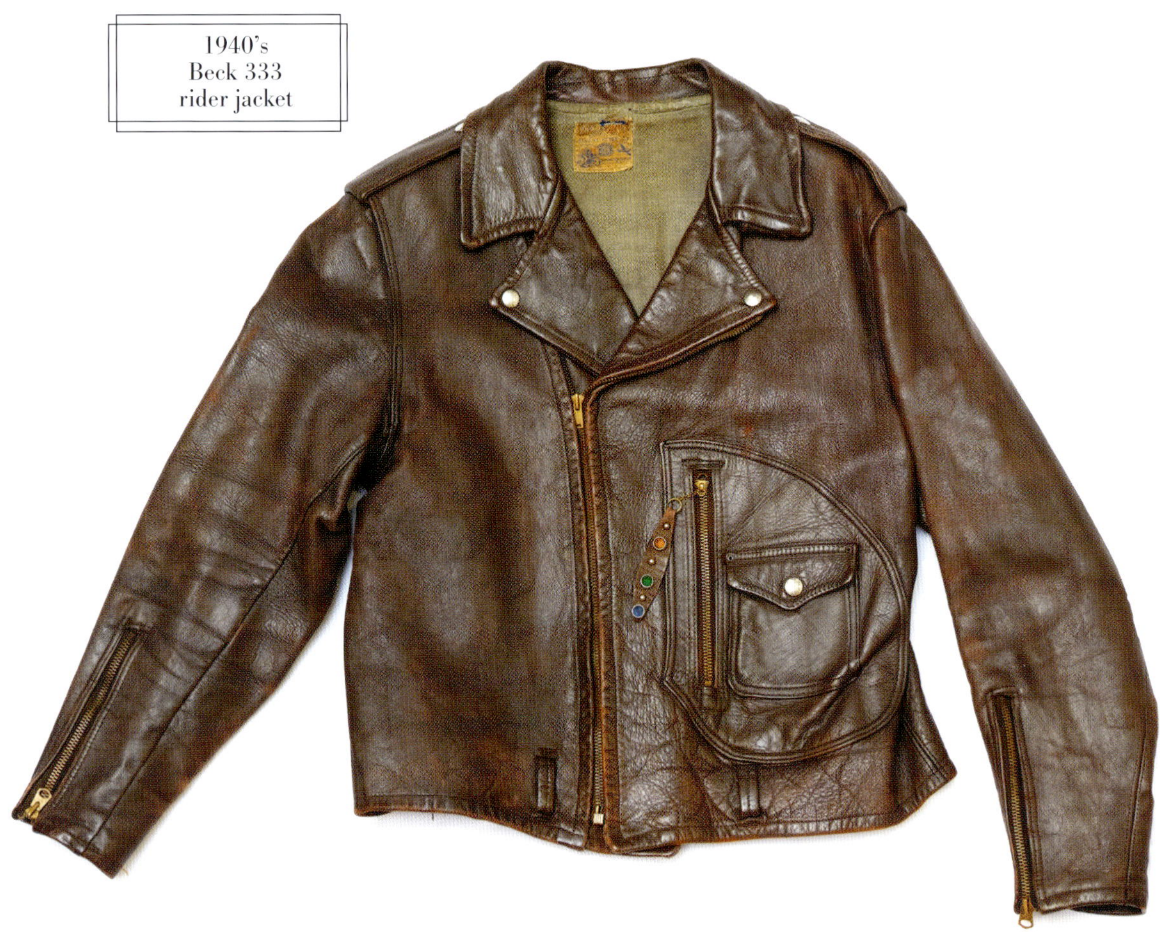

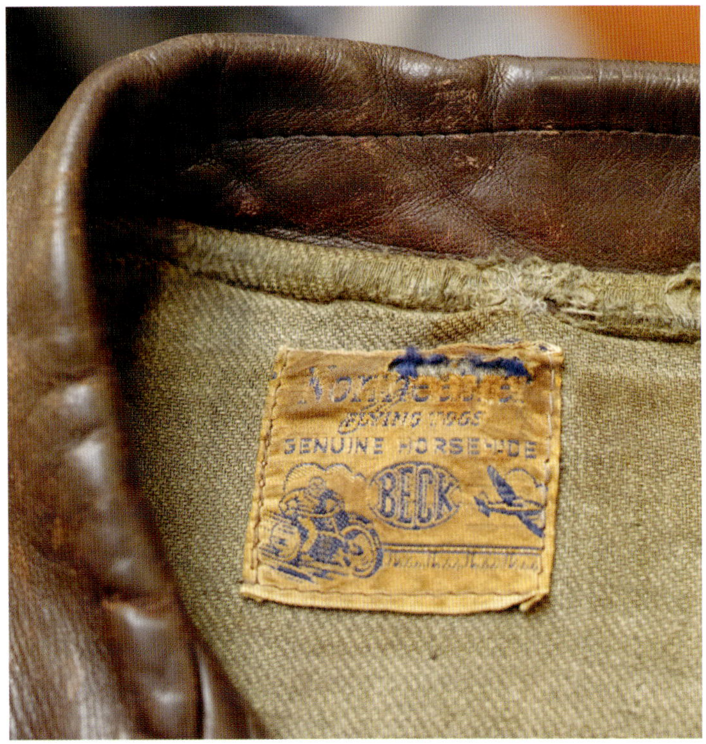

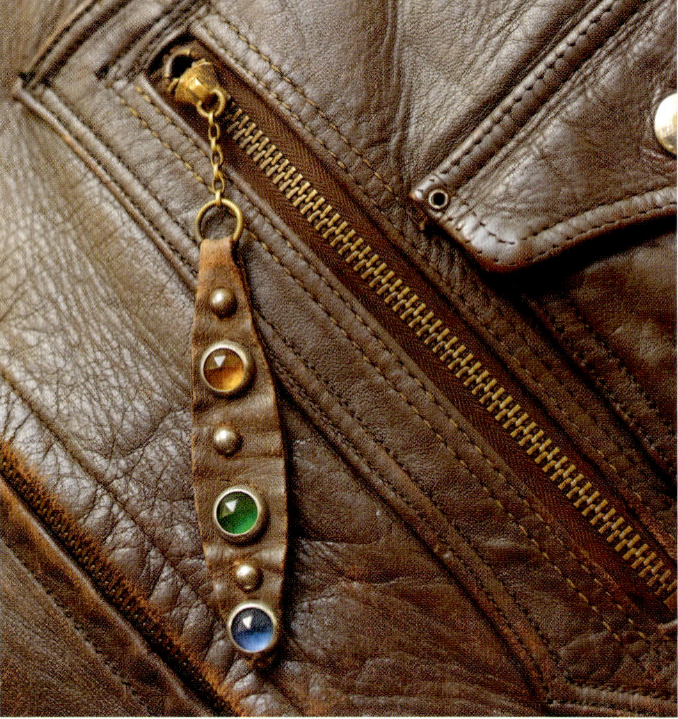

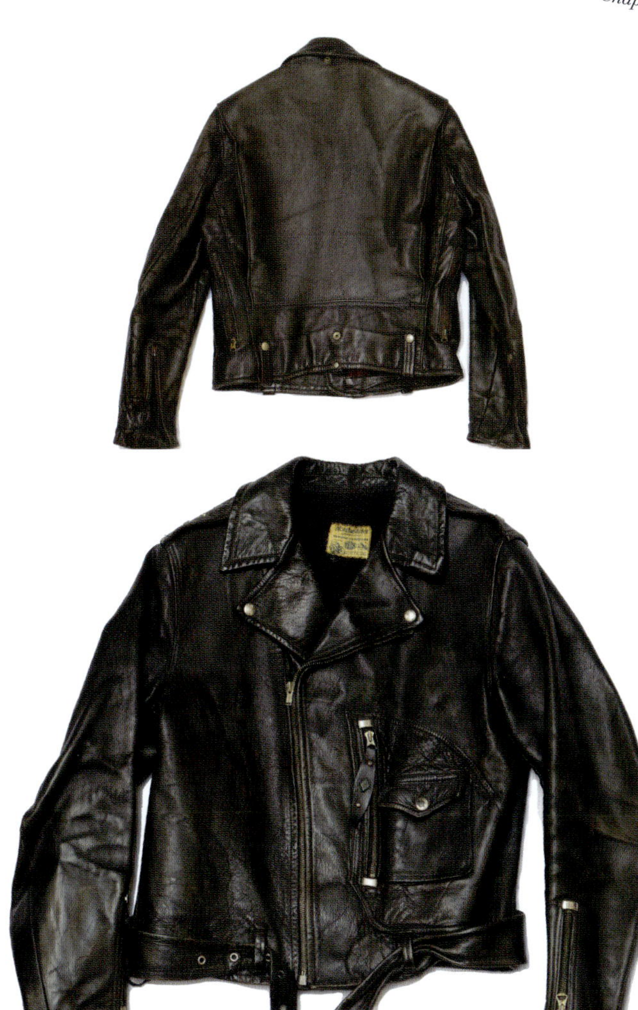

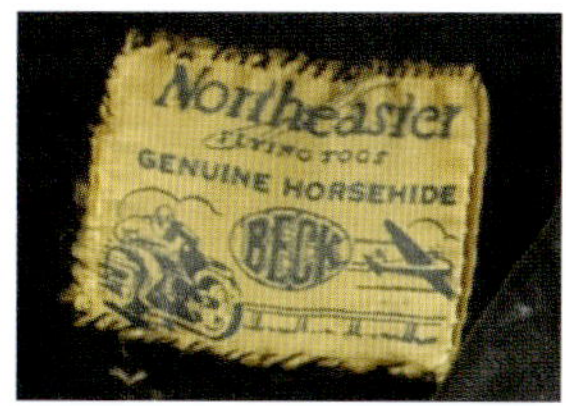

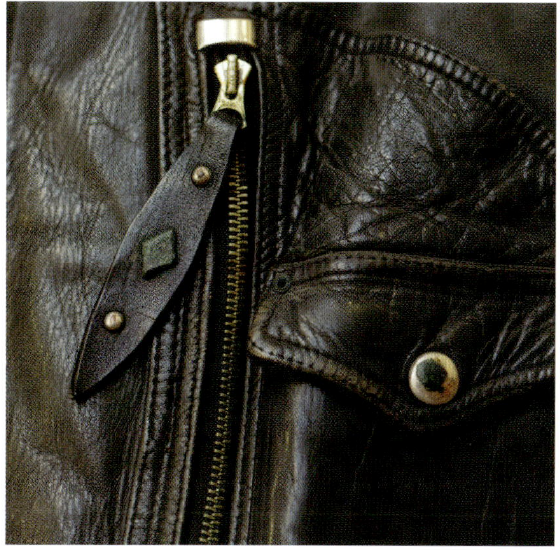

1940's
Beck 333
rider jacket

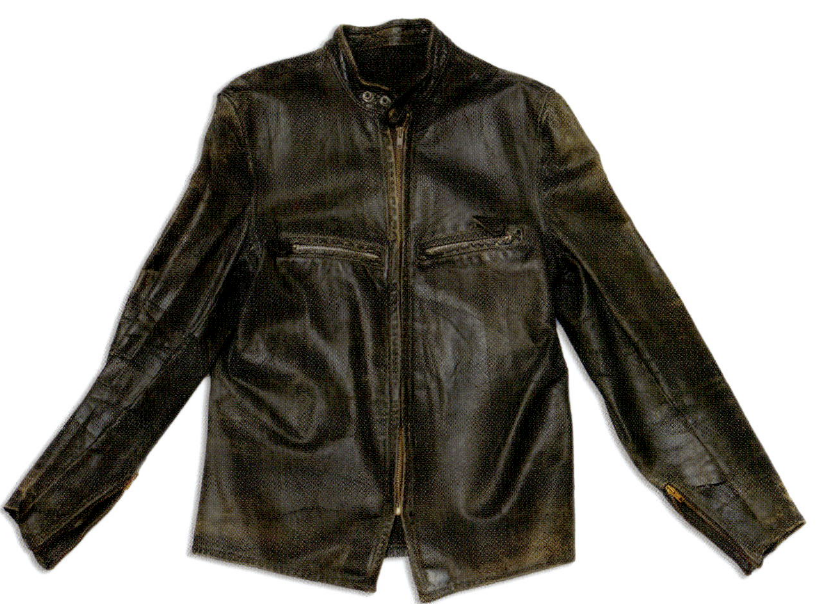

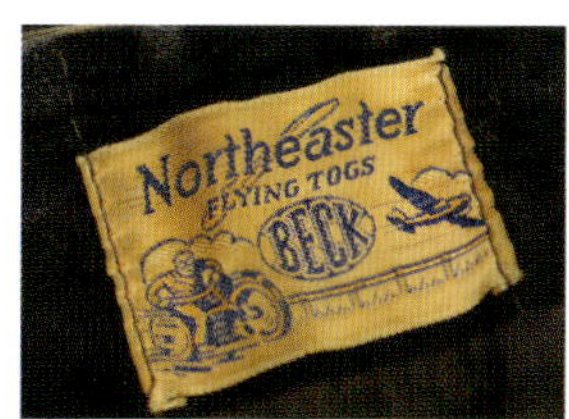

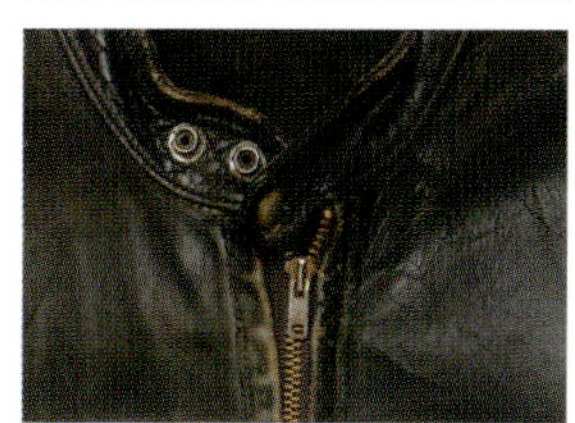

1950's
Beck 666
"Single Riders" jacket

1950's
Buco J-21
rider jacket

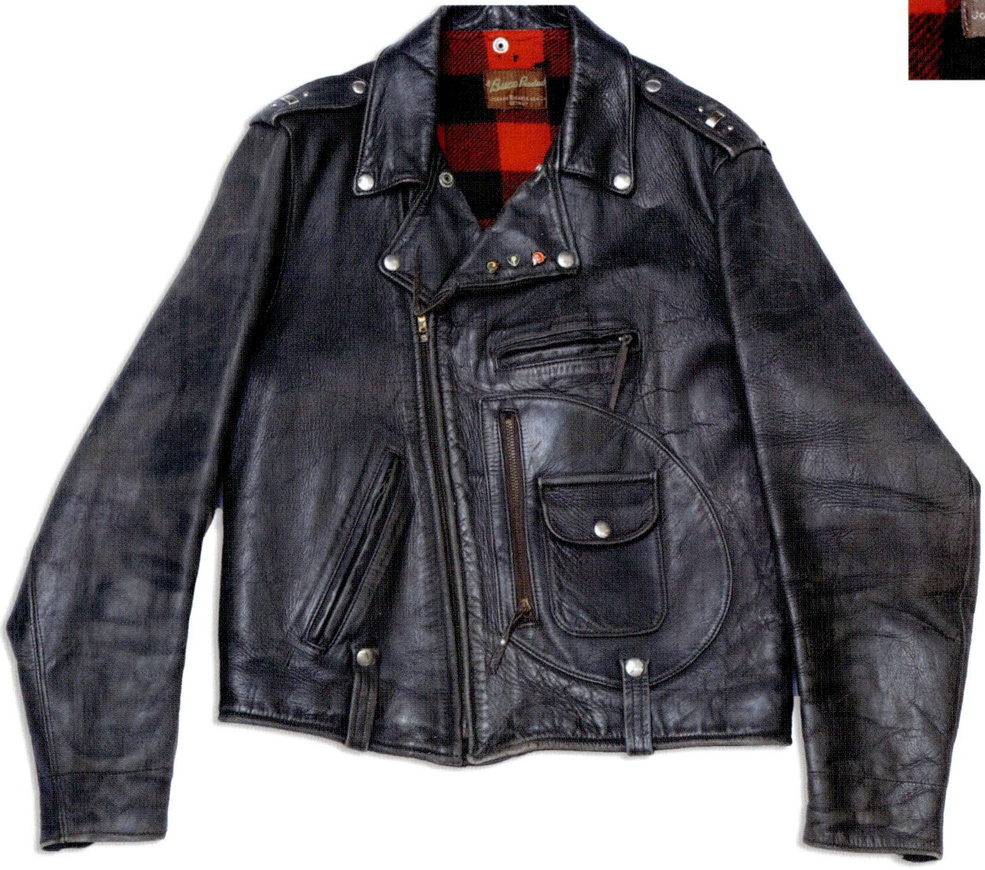

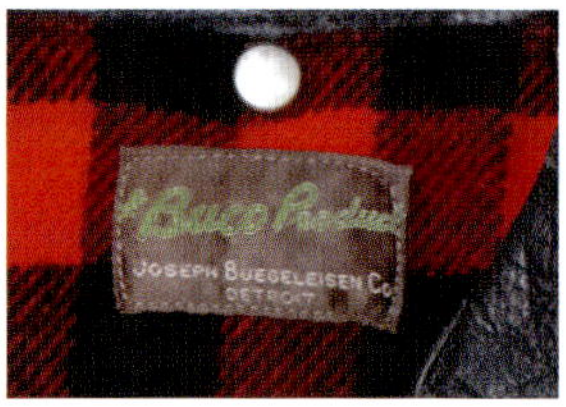

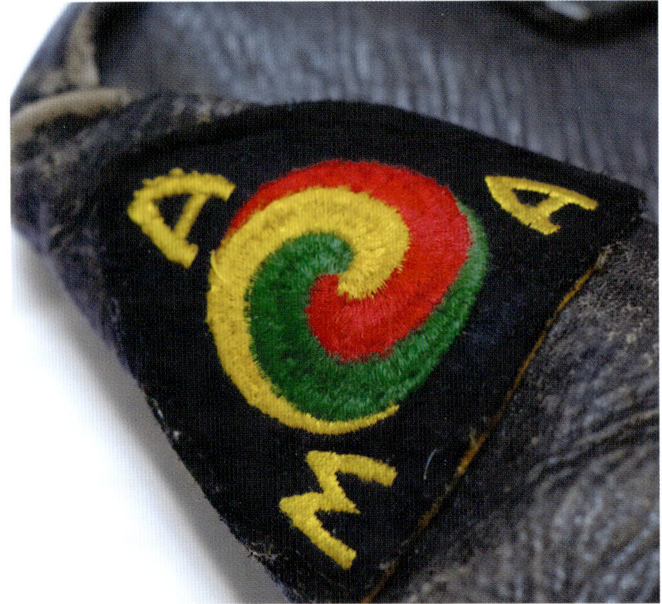

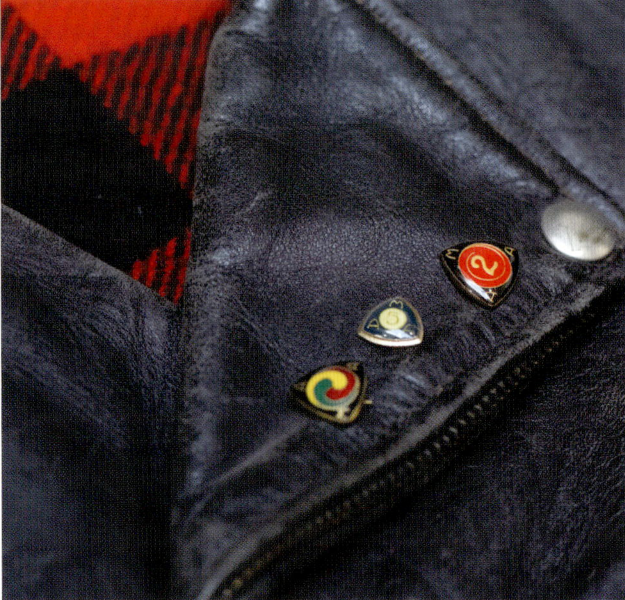

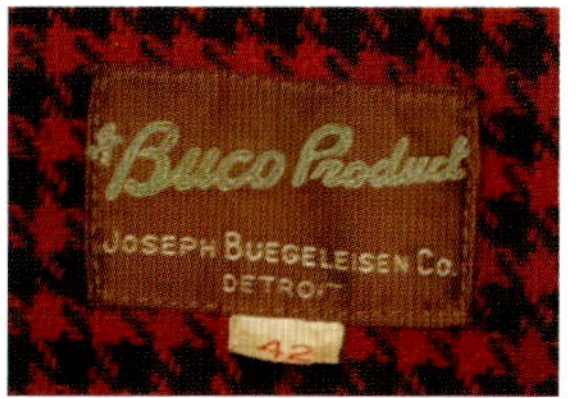

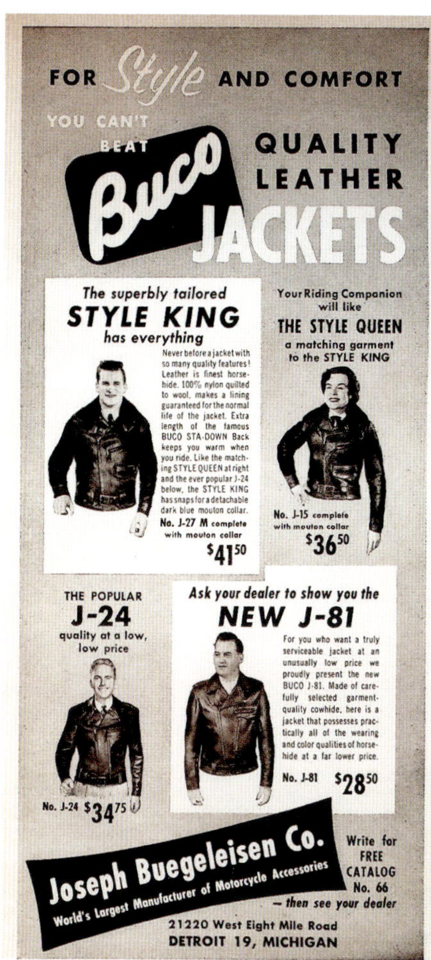

1950's advertising

1950's
Buco J-22
rider jacket

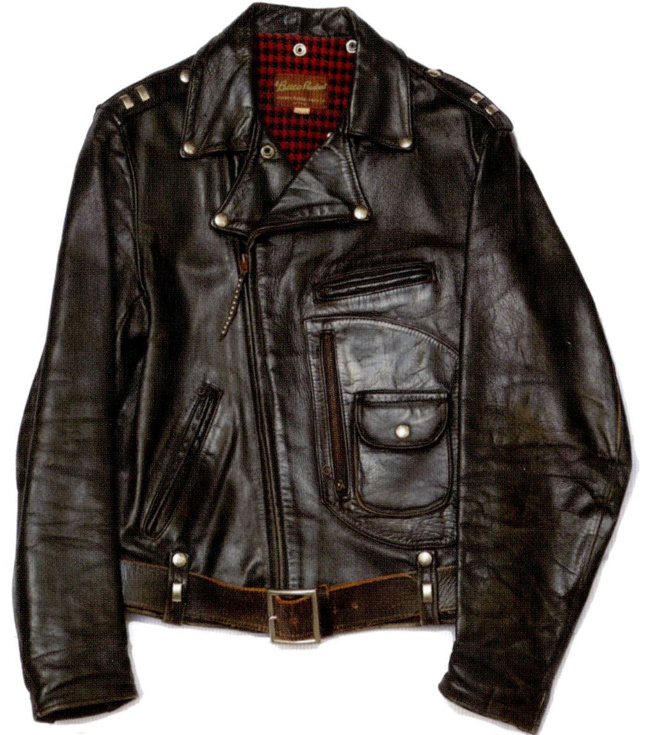

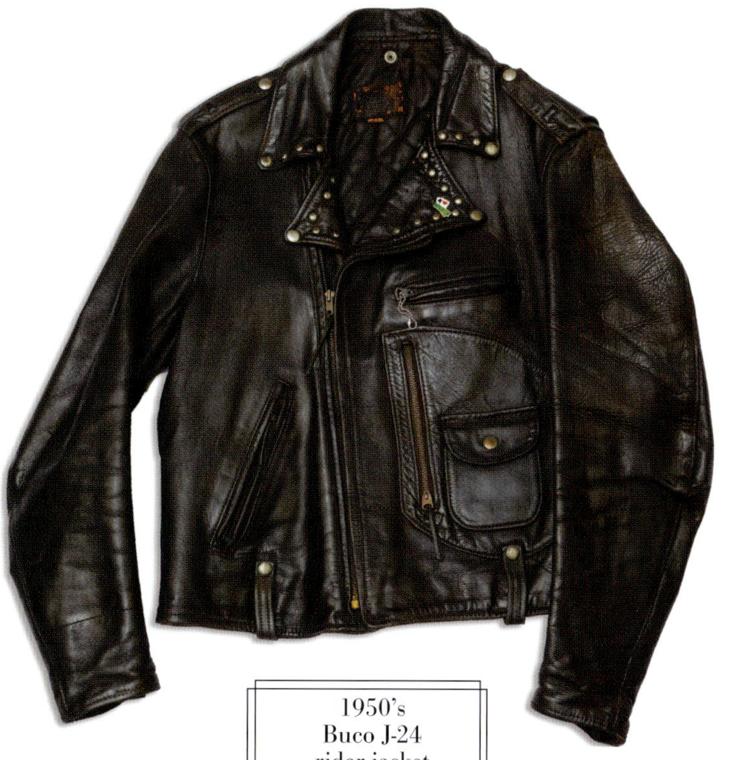

1950's
Buco J-24
rider jacket

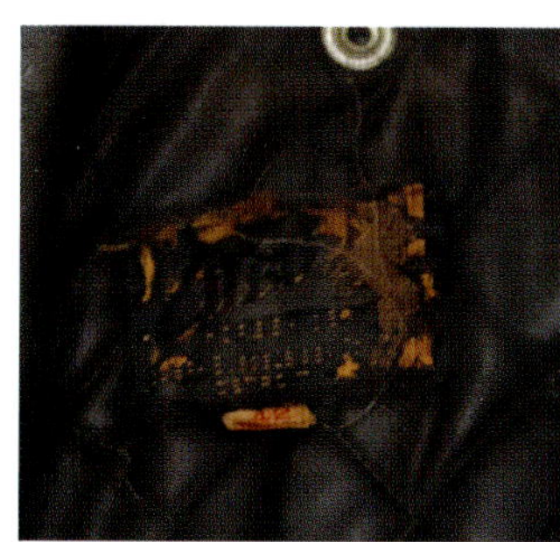

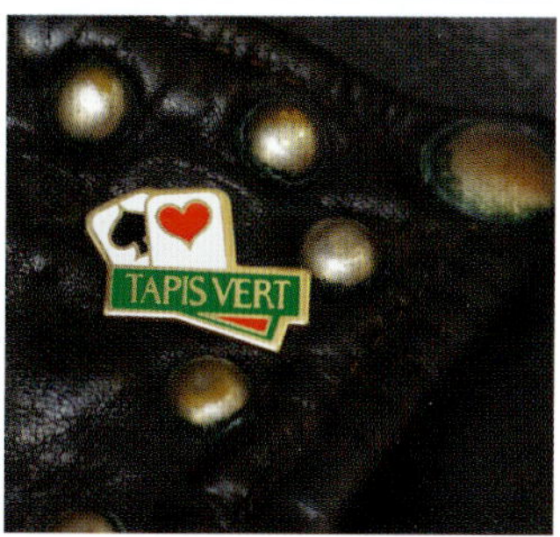

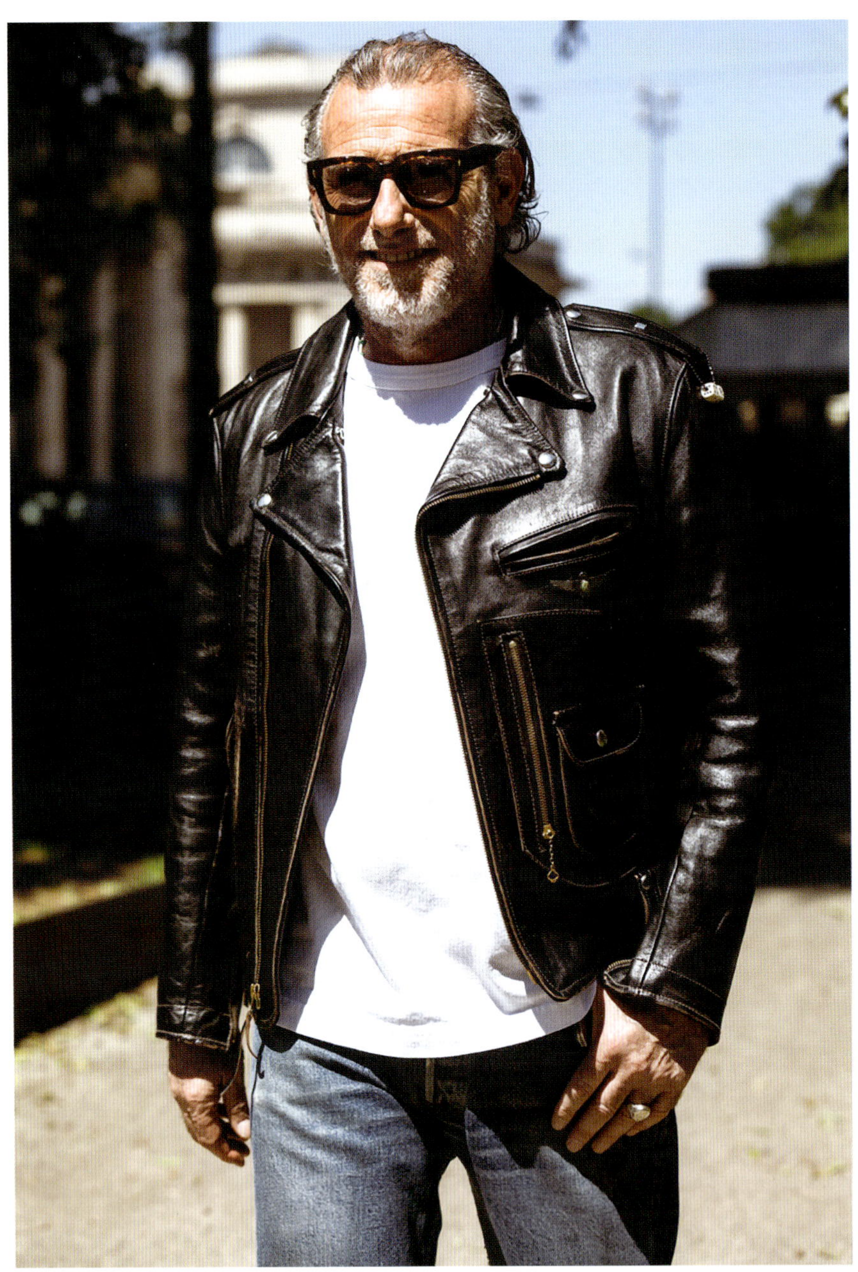

Downtown, Milano
Alessandro Squarzi photo archive

mid 50's
Buco J-21
rider jacket

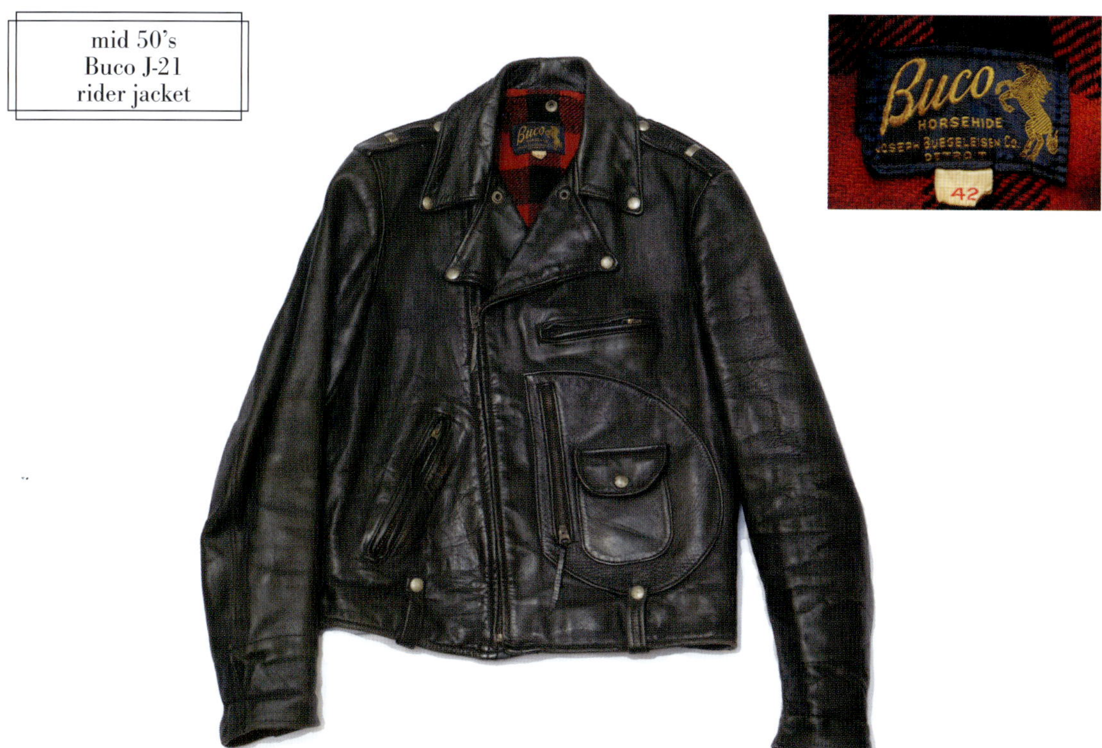

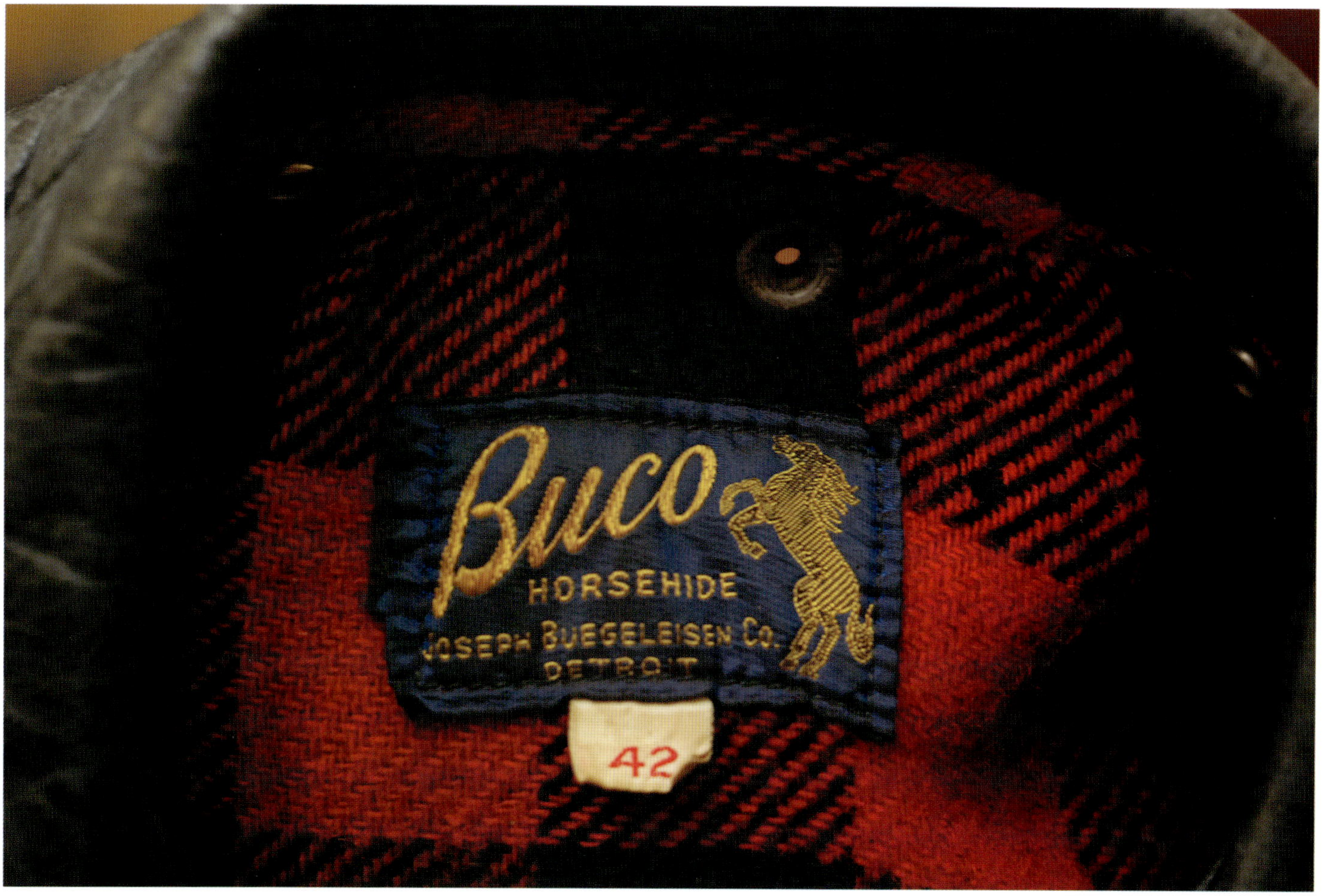

1950's
Buco J-27
rider jacket

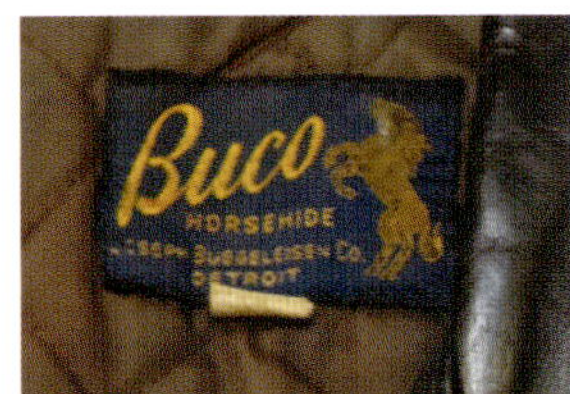

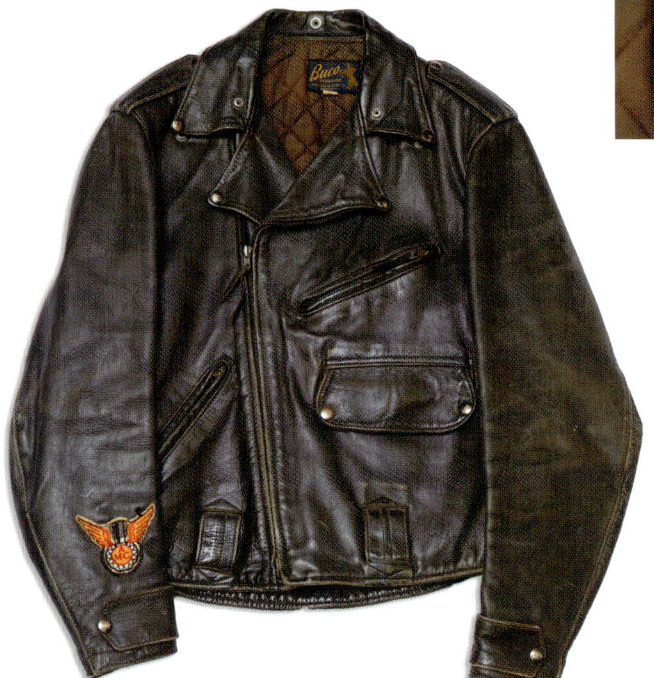

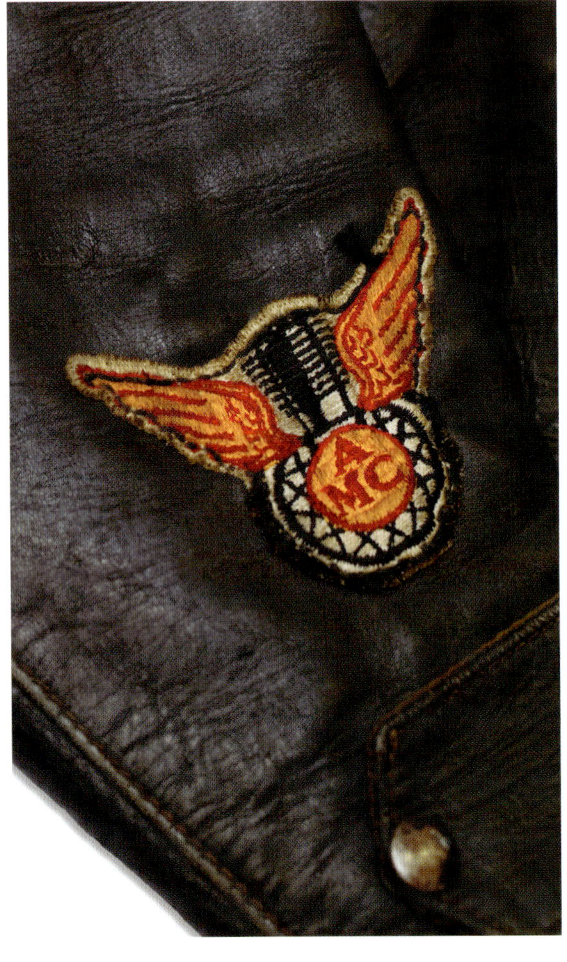

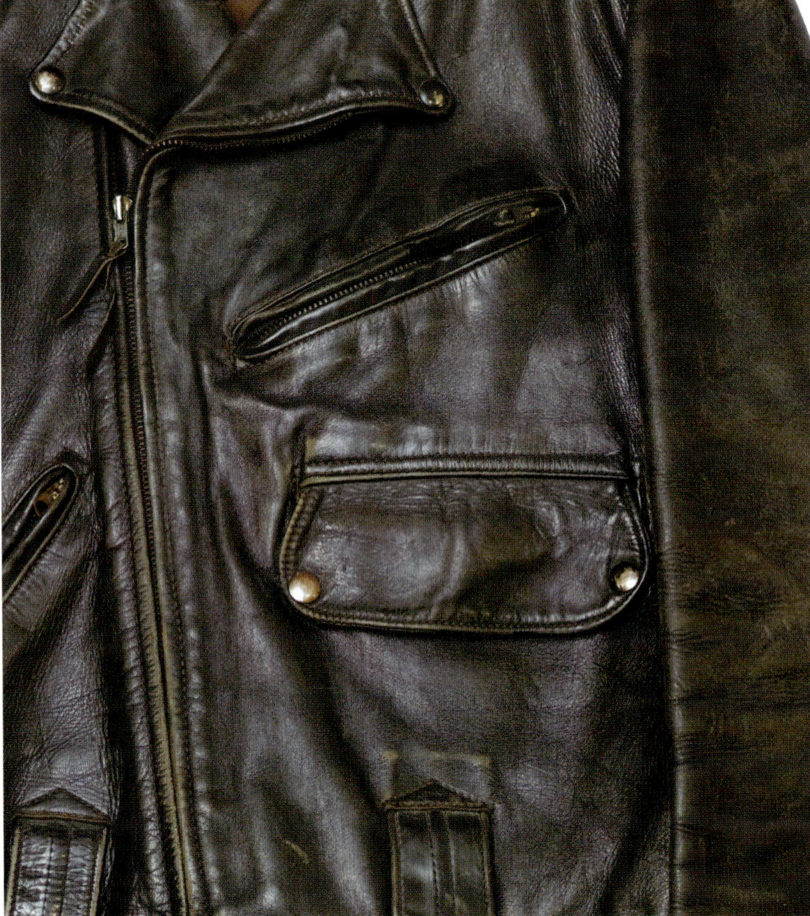

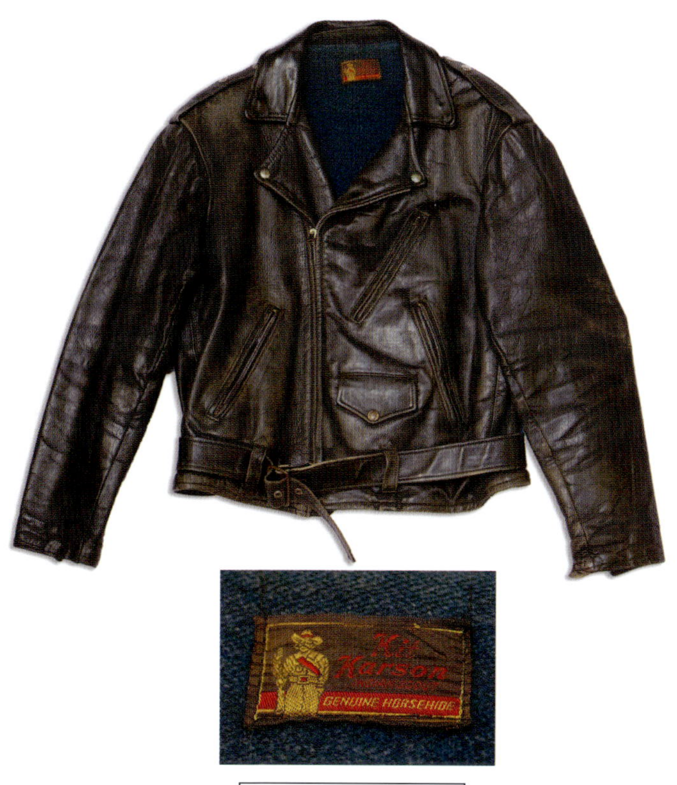

1950's
Kit Karson
rider jacket

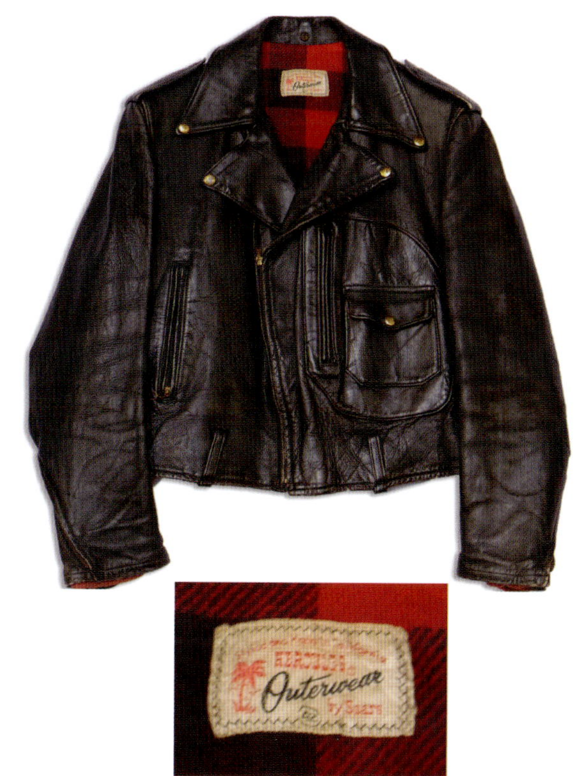

1950's
Hercules
rider jacket

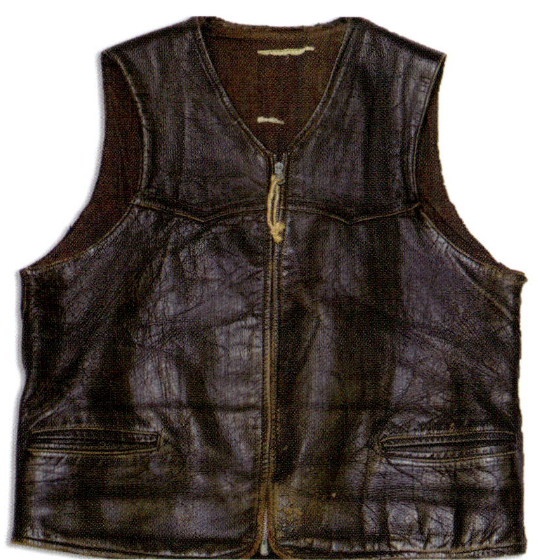

1950's
Unknown
Rider vest

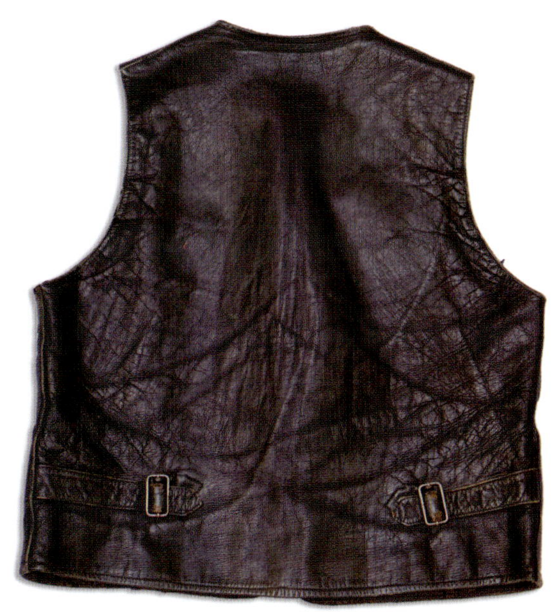

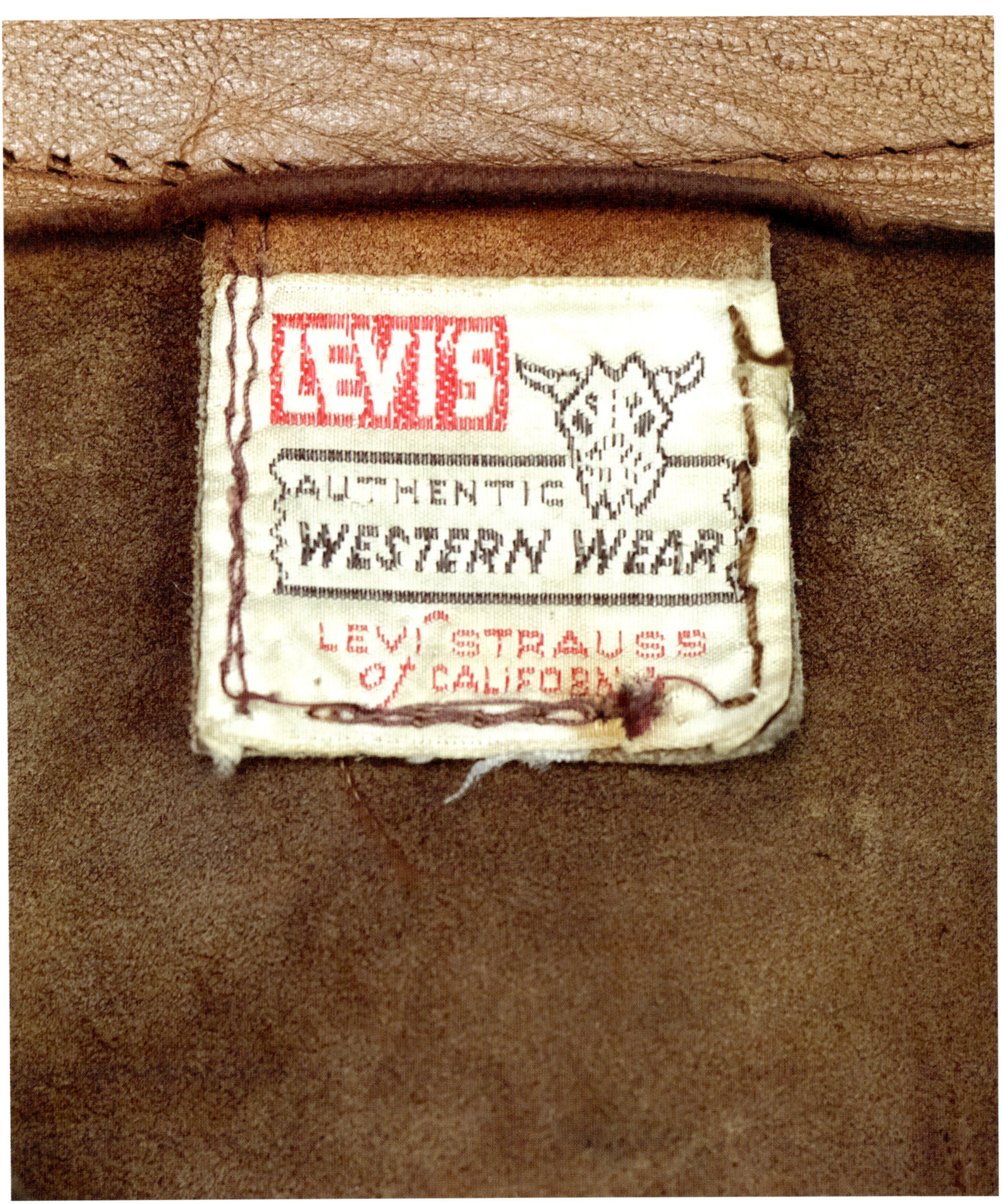
LEVI'S
AUTHENTIC
WESTERN WEAR
LEVI STRAUSS
OF CALIFORNIA

1950's
Levi's Type III jacket
"Short horn Big E"

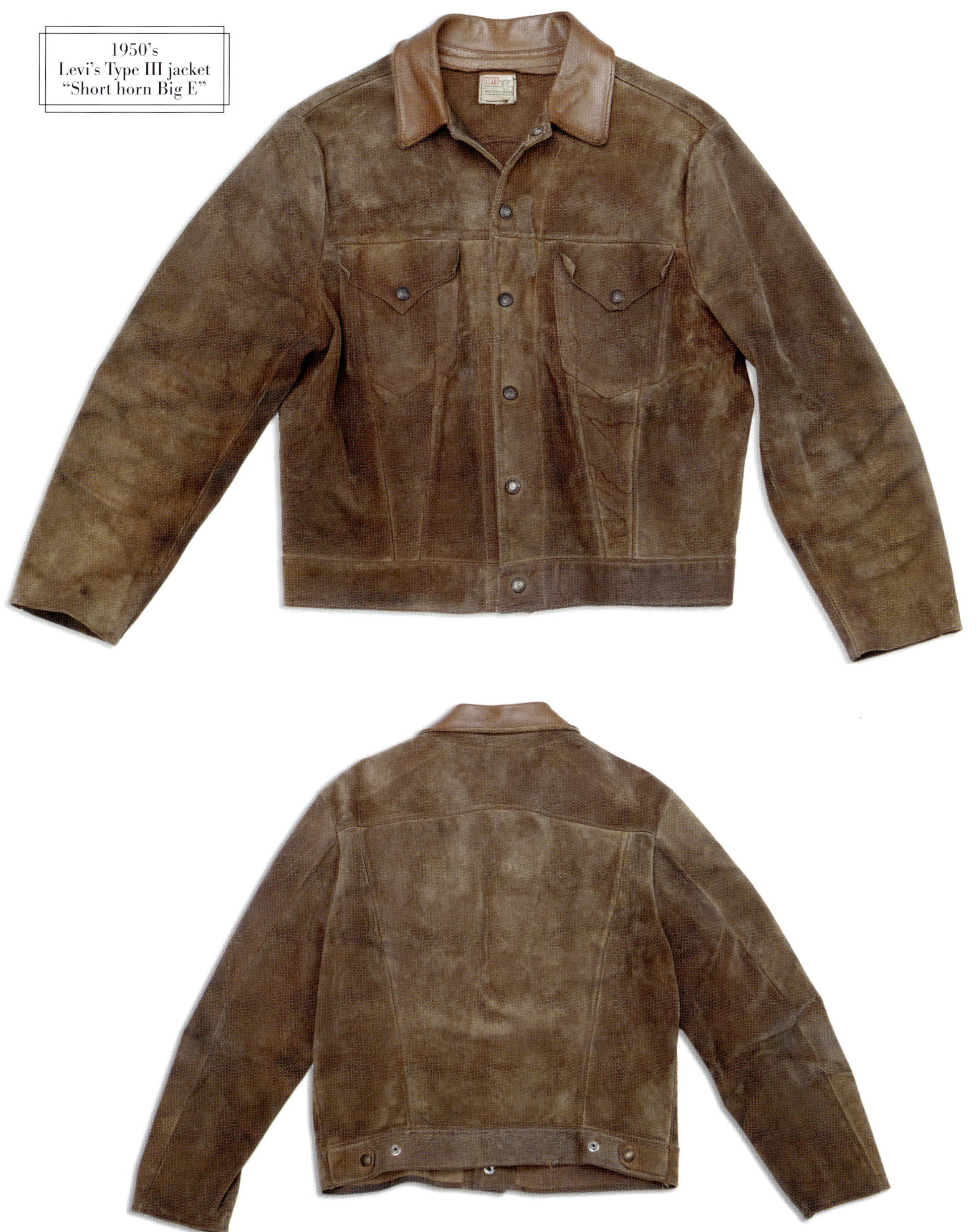

1960's
Levi's Type III jacket
"Big E"

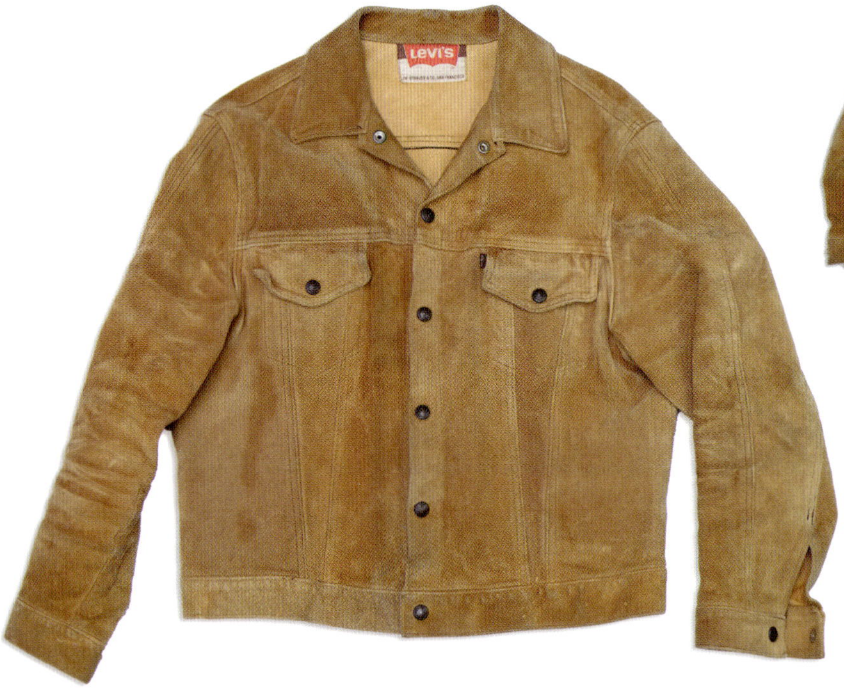

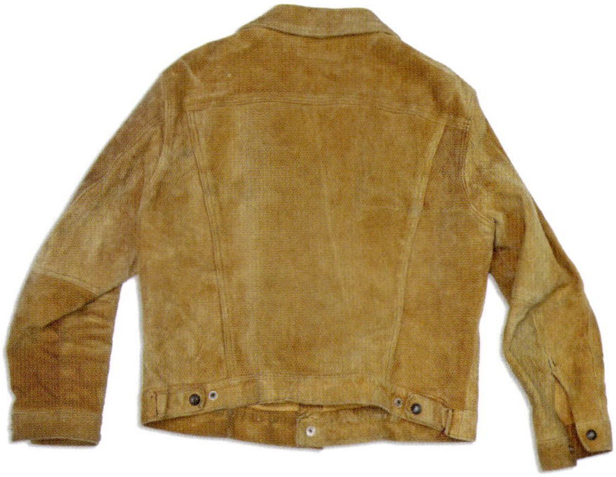

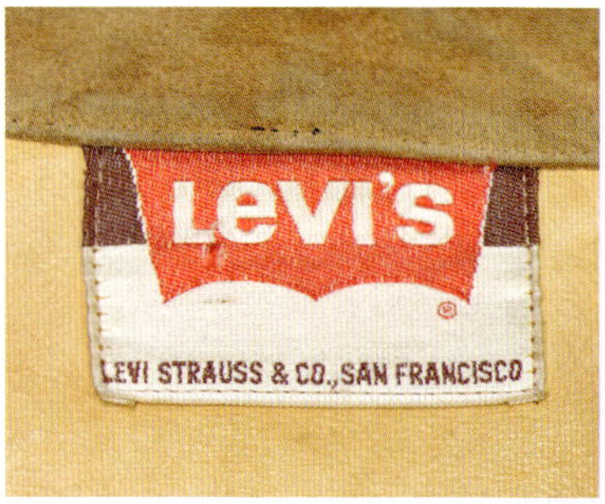

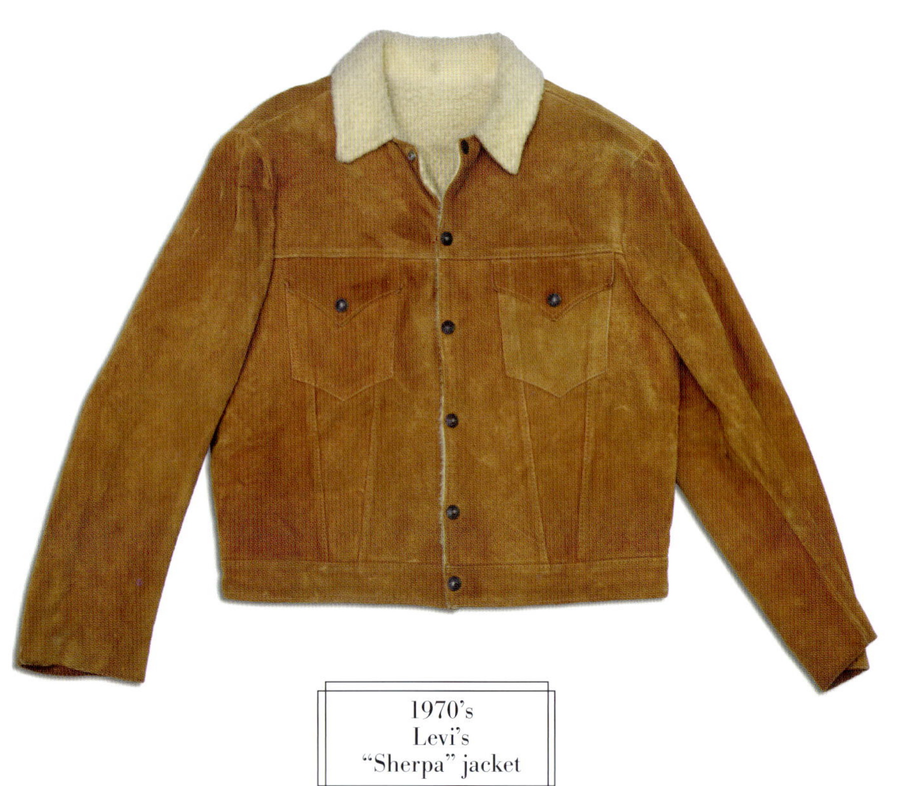

1970's
Levi's
"Sherpa" jacket

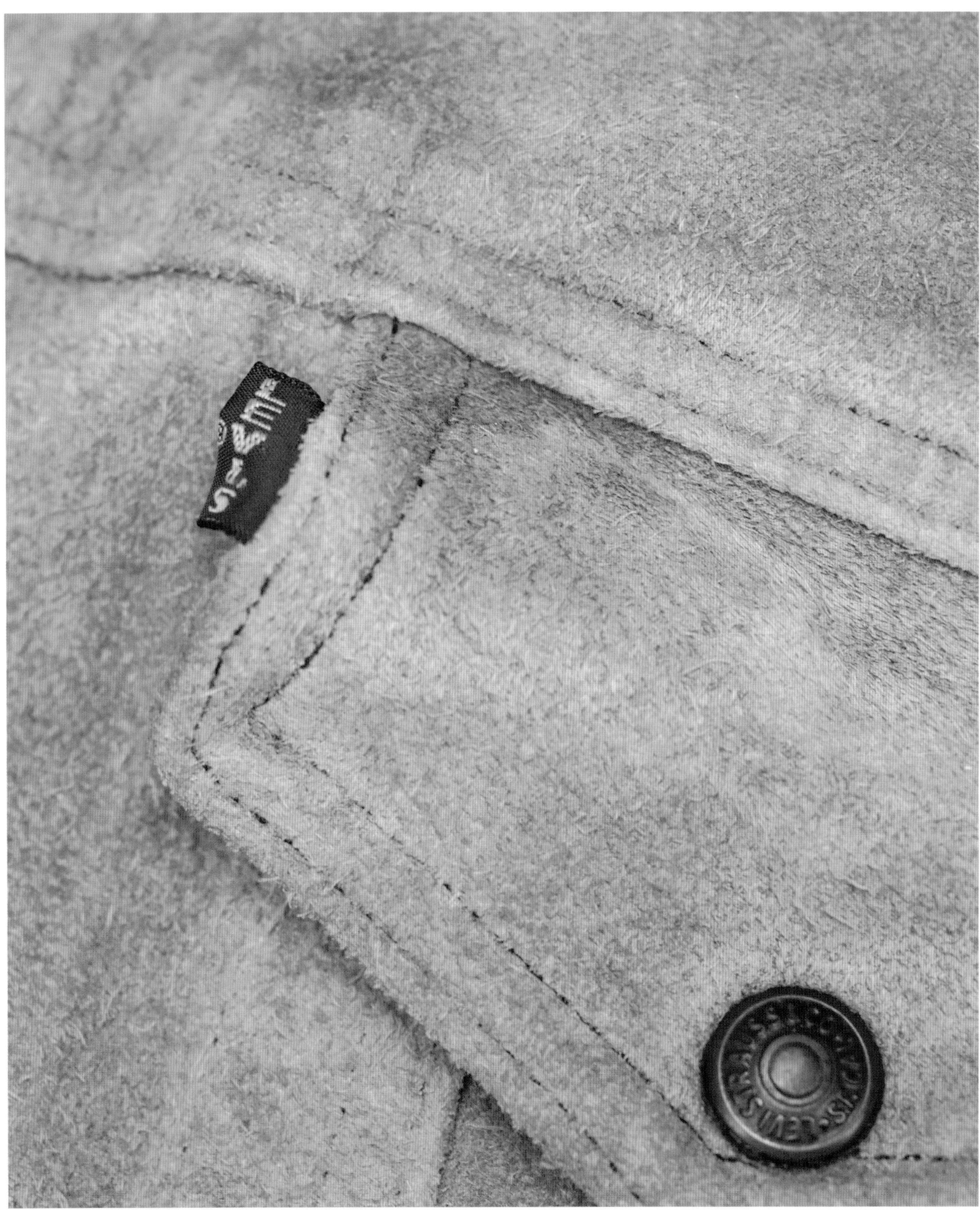

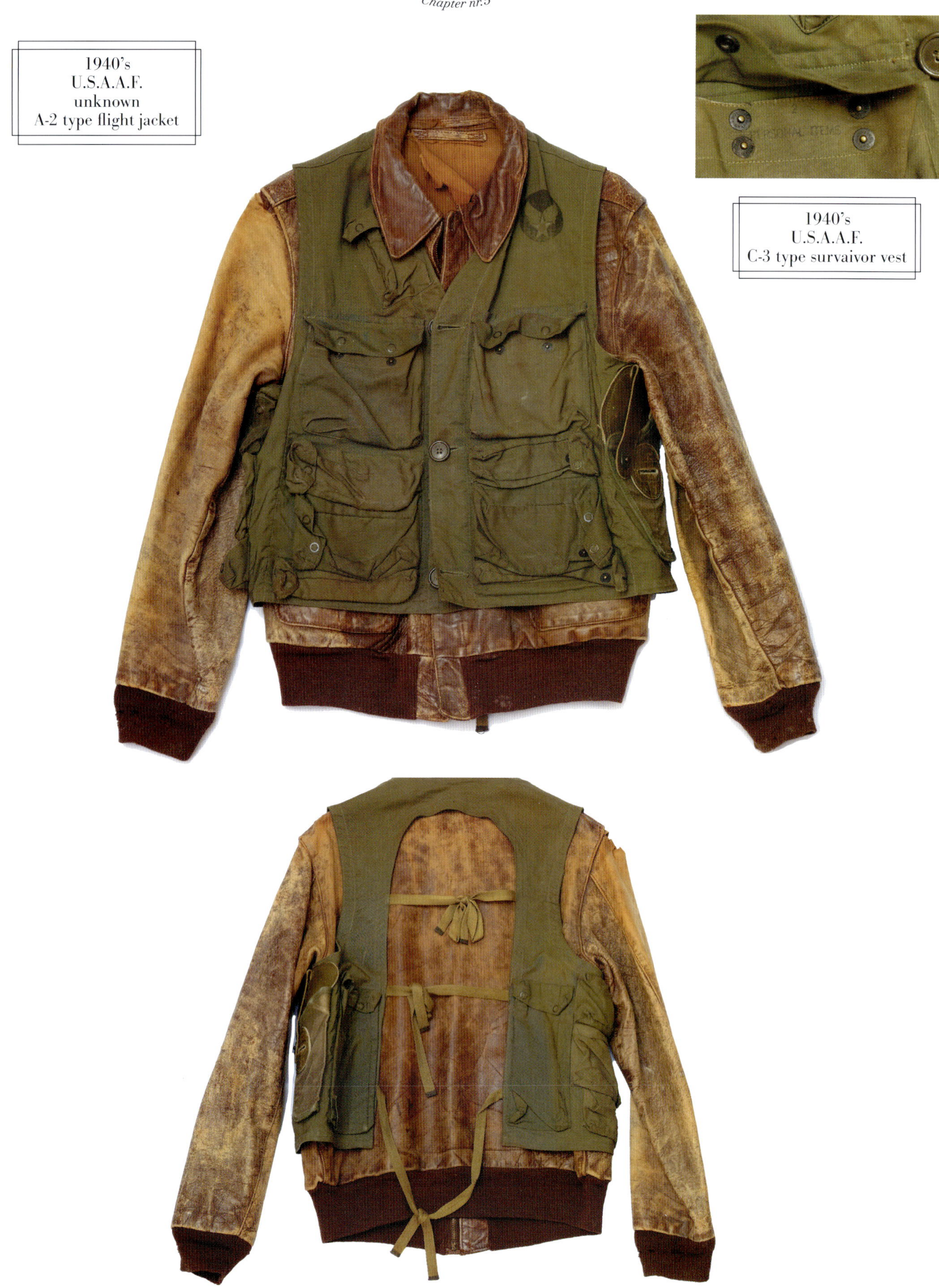

1940's
U.S.A.A.F.
unknown
A-2 type flight jacket

1940's
U.S.A.A.F.
C-3 type survaivor vest

1940's
U.S.A.A.F.
A-2 type flight jacket

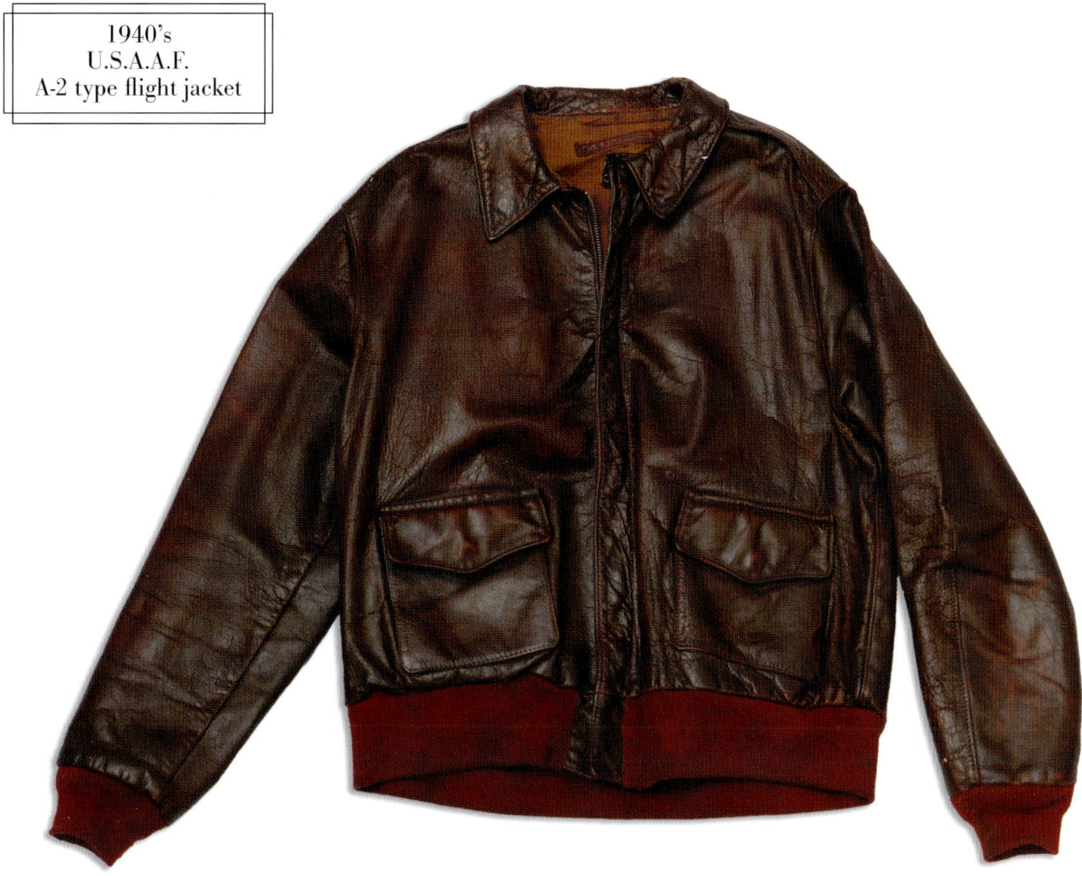

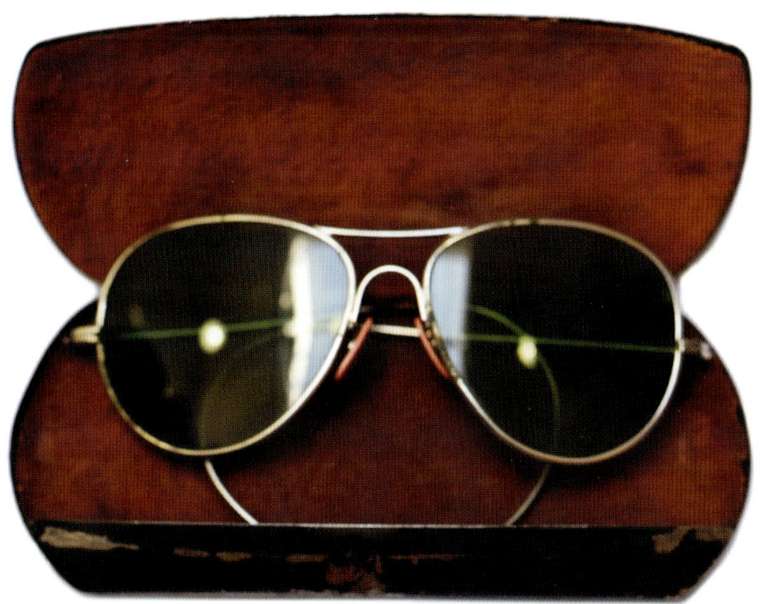

1940's
U.S.A.A.F.
aviator sunglasses

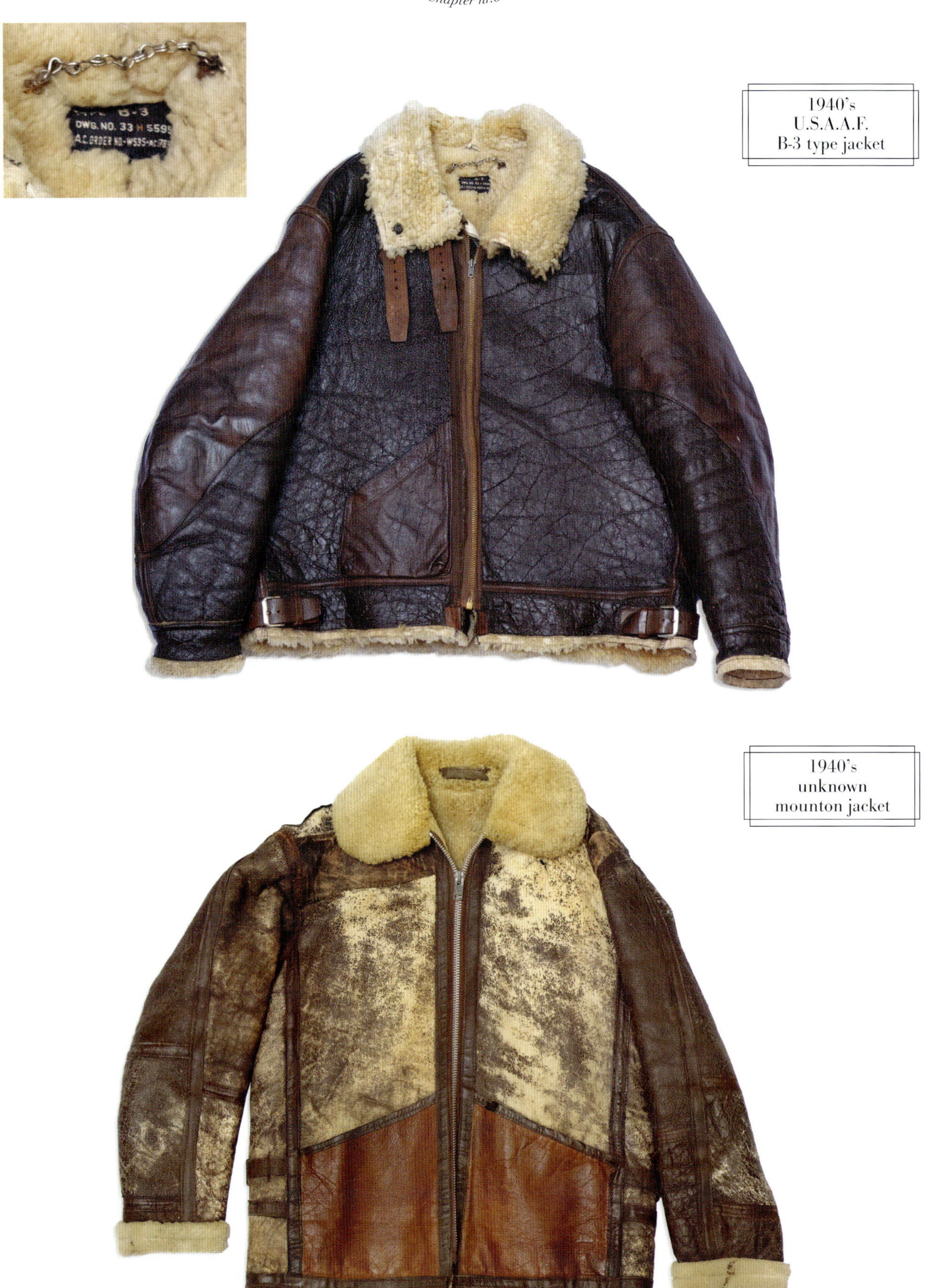

1940's
U.S.A.A.F.
B-3 type jacket

1940's
unknown
mounton jacket

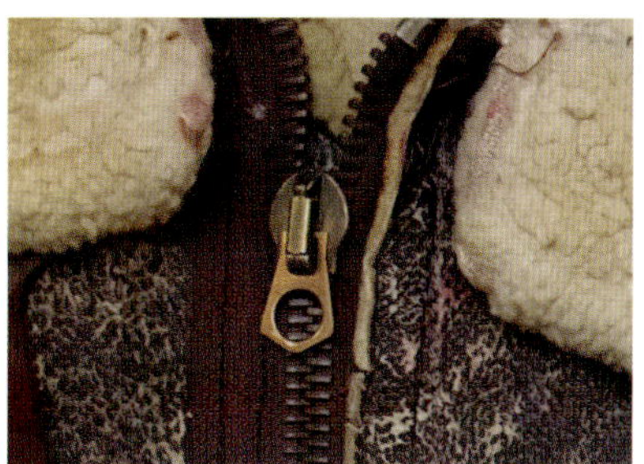

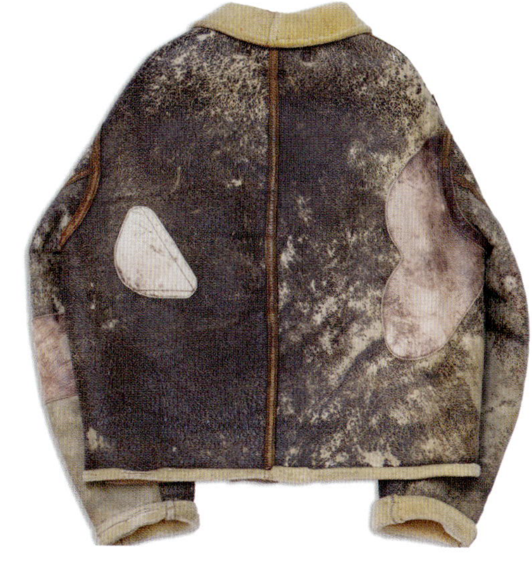

1940's
U.S.A.A.F.
D-1 1st type jacket

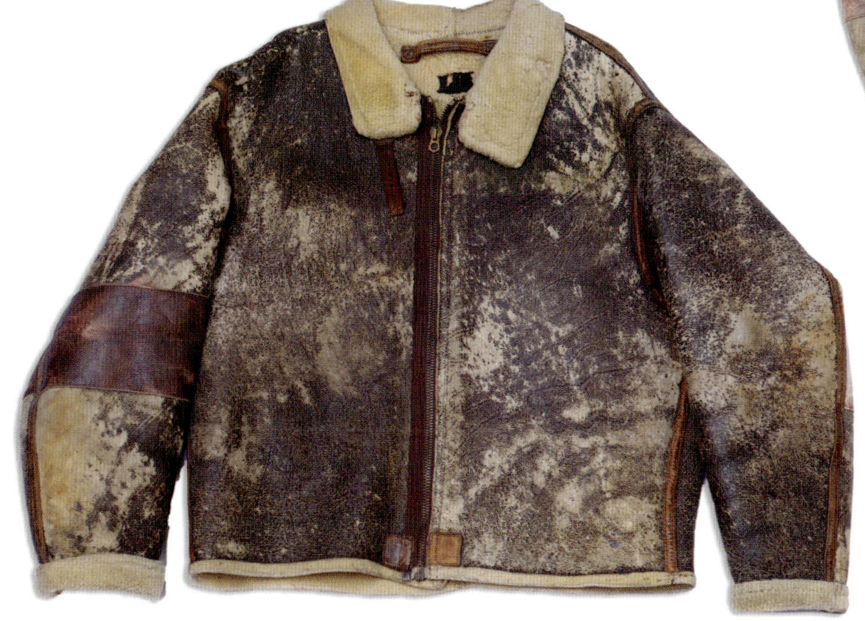

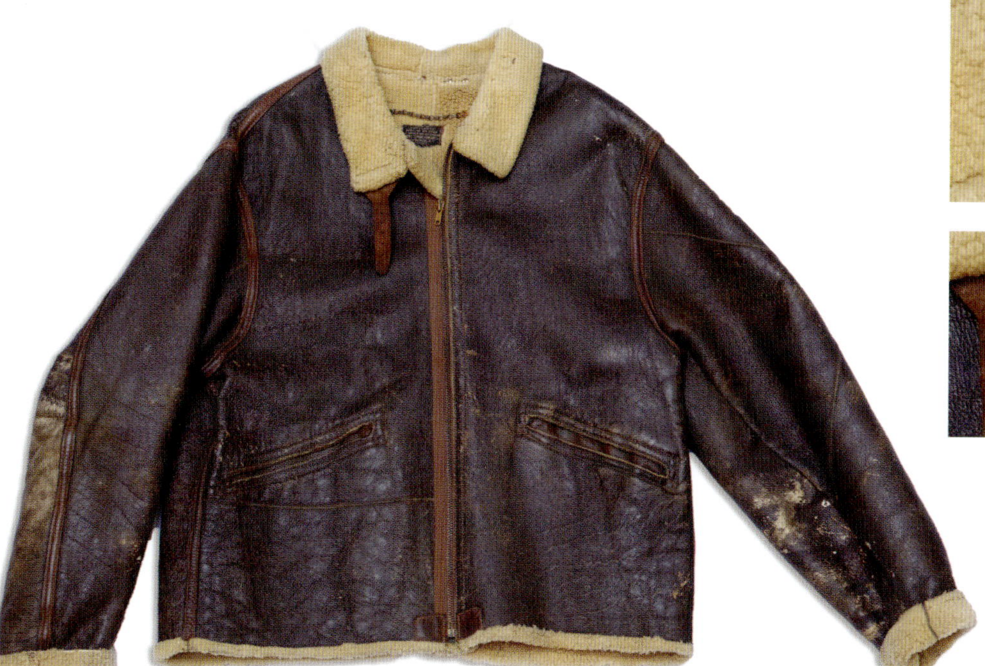

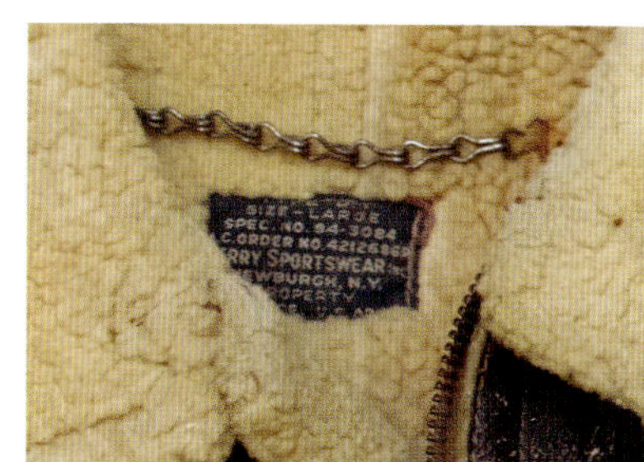

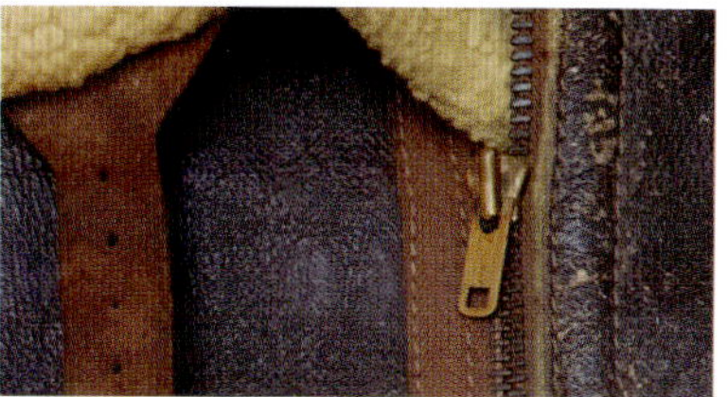

1940's
U.S.A.A.F.
D-1 2nd type jacket

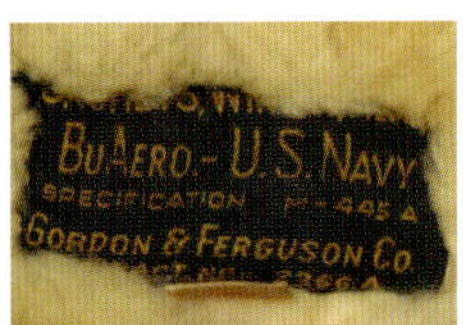

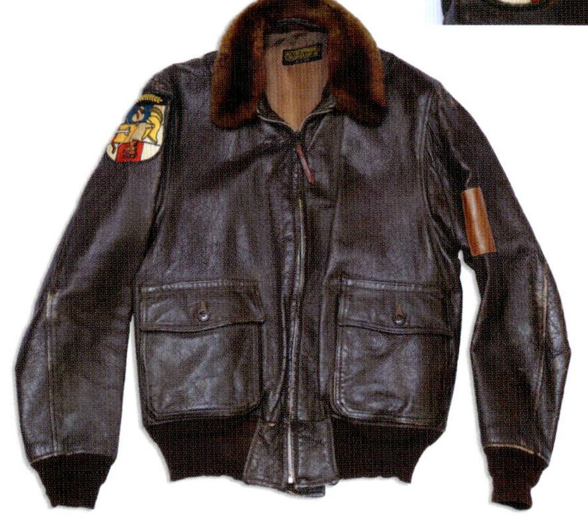

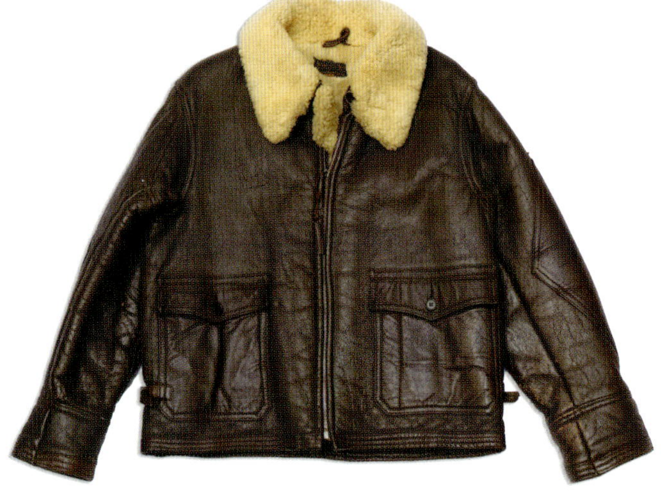

1940's
U.S.N.
M-445 type jacket

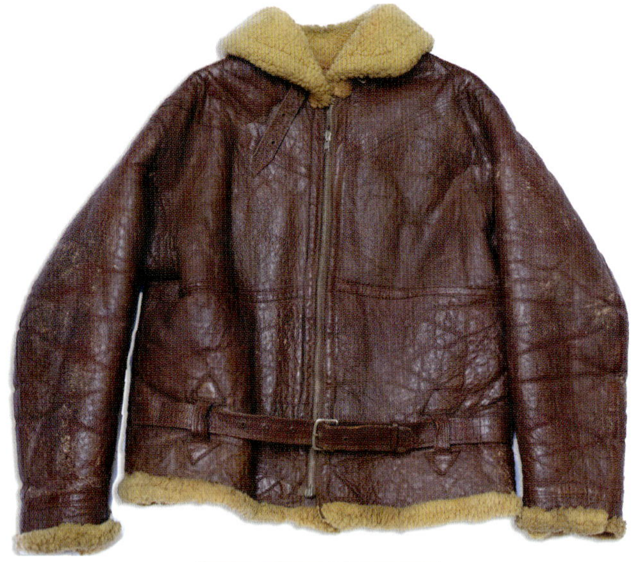

1950's
U.S.N.
G-1 type jacket J-7823 (AER)

1940's
RAF
Irvin Flying Jacket

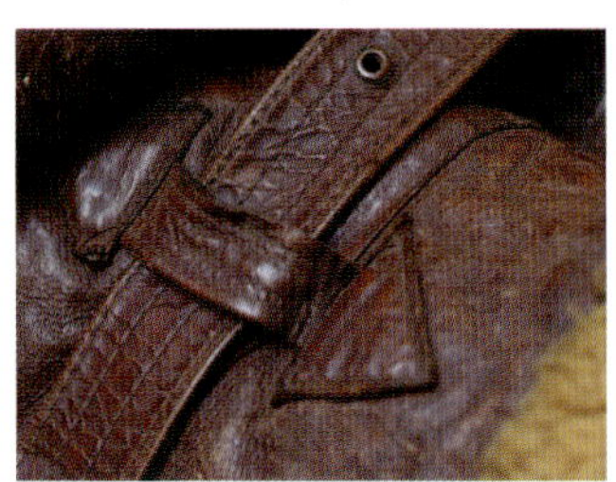

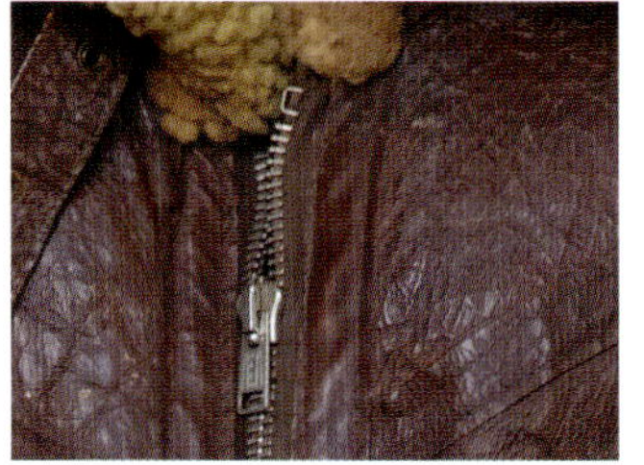

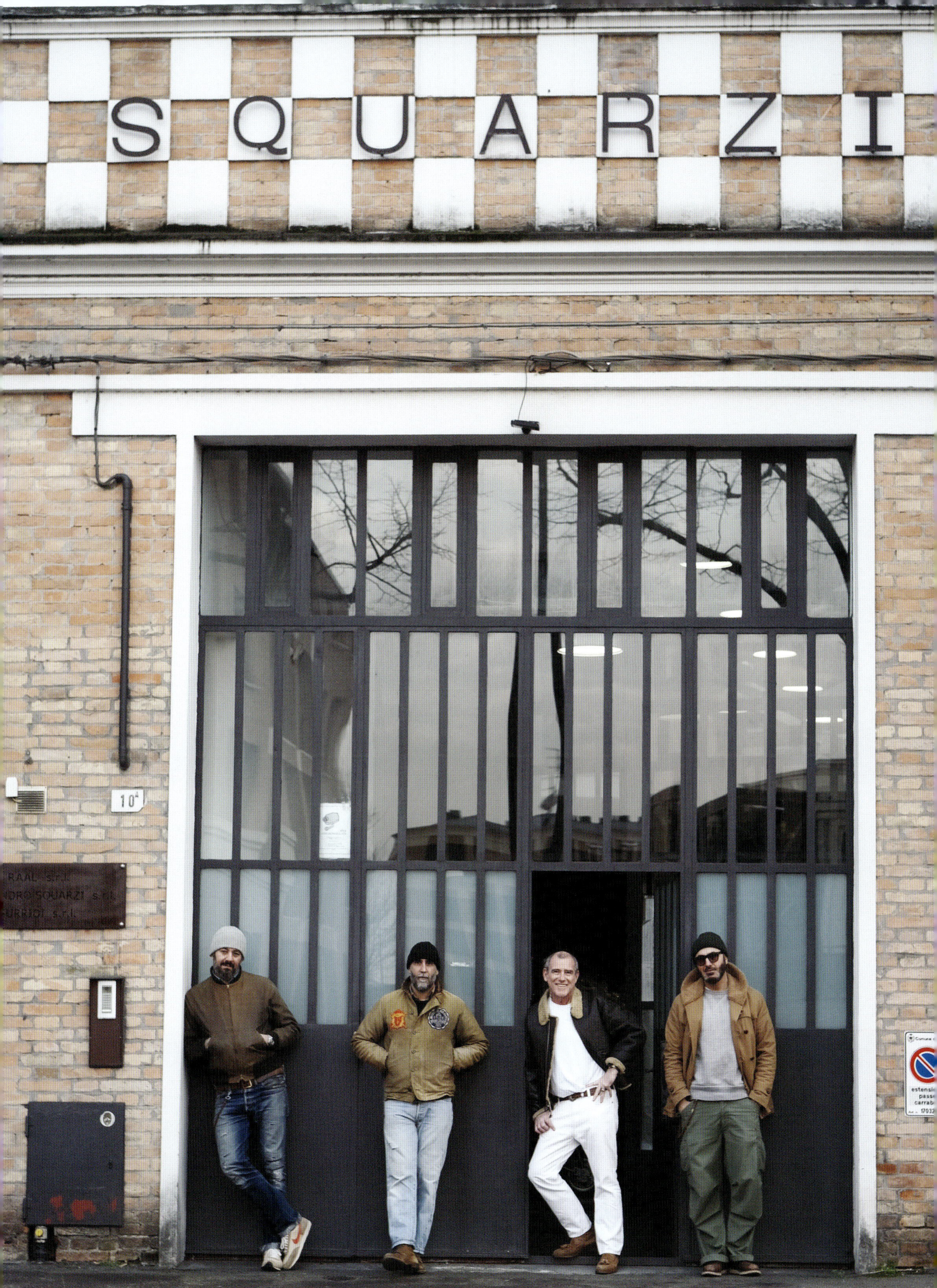

SQUARZI

"What will there be in vintage in 20 years?
Work clothes are made of fabrics destined to disappear, and new technologies
lead to modernity that ends up in nothing."

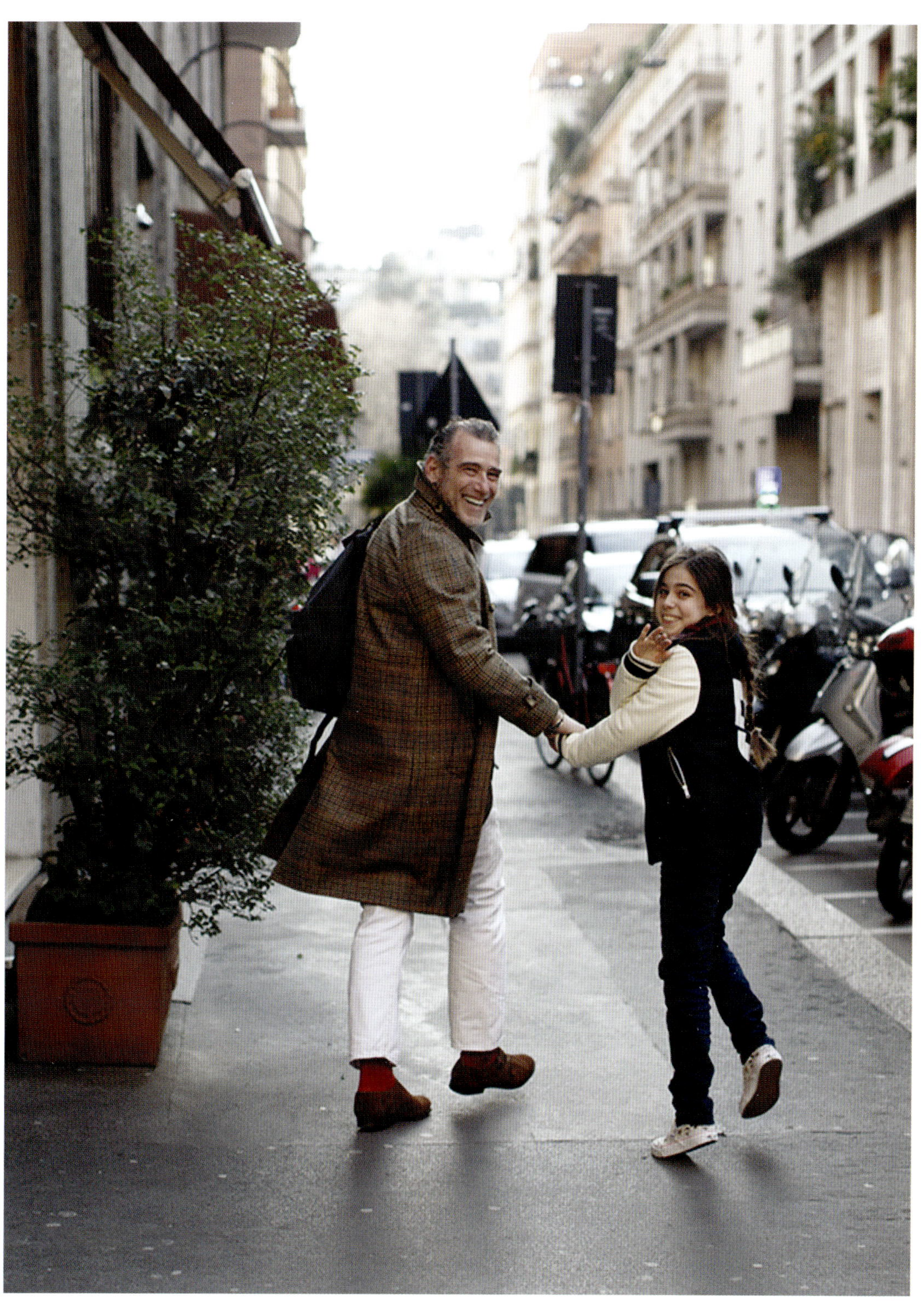

Alessandro and his daughter Allegra
Downtown, Milano
Photo courtesy of Scott Schuman

Other Schiffer Books on Related Subjects:

Rugged Style War–Rome by Mirko Di Giovanni and Andrea Ventura,
Photographs by David Petrini
ISBN: 978-0-7643-6130-2

Denim Branded by Nick Williams with Jenny Corpuz
ISBN: 978-0-7643-5577-6

Jeans of the Old West, 2nd Edition by Michael Harris
ISBN: 978-0-7643-5263-8

Text Copyright © 2024 by Mirko Di Giovanni and Andrea Ventura

Photographs Copyright © 2024 by David Petrini

Collection by Alessandro Squarzi

Graphic Design by Andrea Ventura and Mirko Di Giovanni

Library of Congress Control Number: 2024932175

Designed by Andrea Ventura, Mirko Di Giovanni
Photography by David Petrini
Collection: Alessandro Squarzi
Type set in Bodoni

ISBN: 978-0-7643-6846-2
Printed in China

Published by Schiffer Publishing, Ltd.
4880 Lower Valley Road
Atglen, PA 19310
Phone: (610) 593-1777; Fax: (610) 593-2002
Email: info@schifferbooks.com
Web: www.schifferbooks.com

For our complete selection of fine books on this and related subjects, please visit our website at www.schifferbooks.com. You may also write for a free catalog.

Schiffer Publishing's titles are available at special discounts for bulk purchases for sales promotions or premiums. Special editions, including personalized covers, corporate imprints, and excerpts, can be created in large quantities for special needs. For more information, contact the publisher.

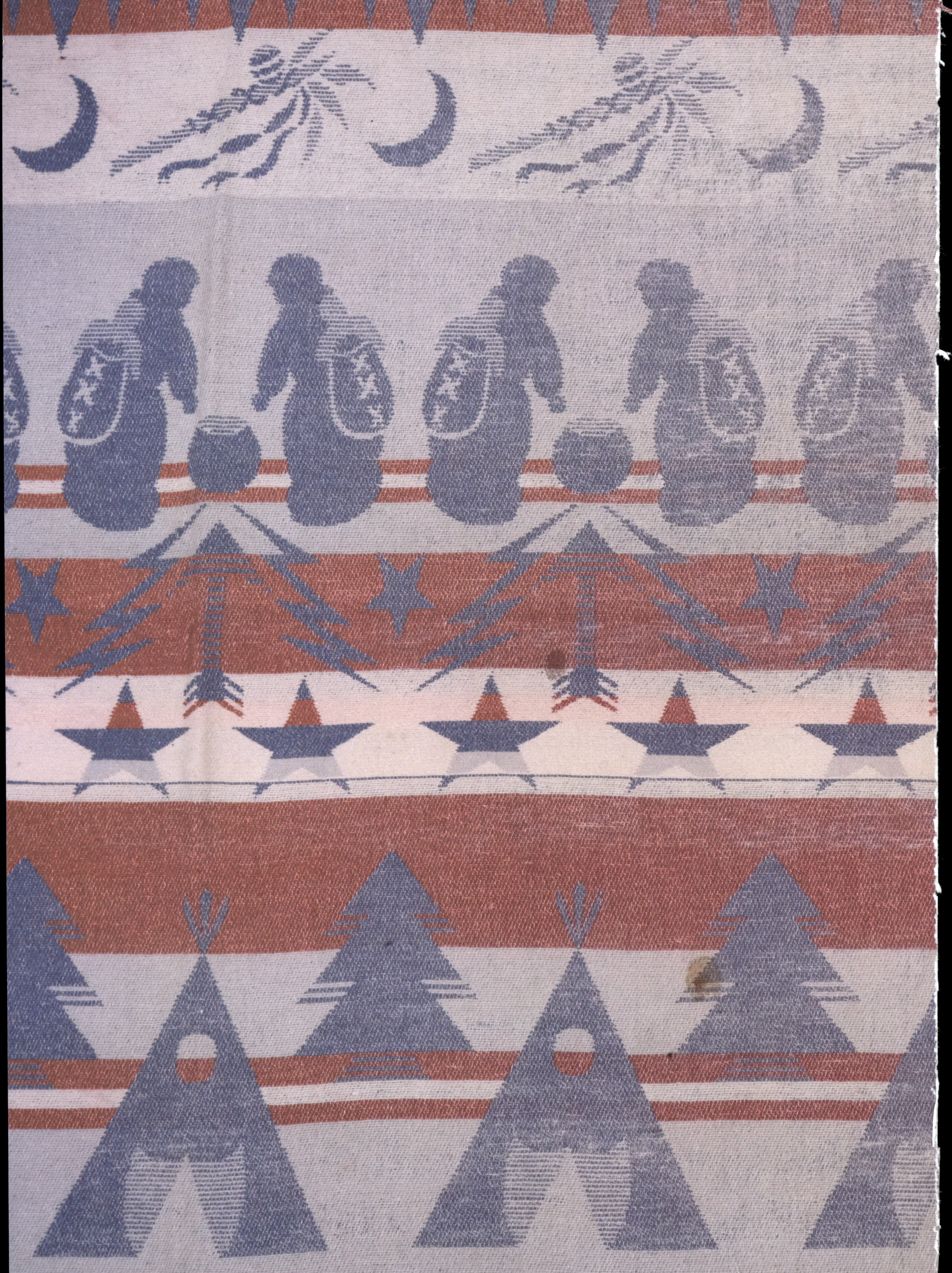